DATE DUE			

THE POLITICS OF AMERICAN SCIENCE
1939 to the Present

Revised Edition

Edited by

JAMES L. PENICK, JR.
CARROLL W. PURSELL, JR.
MORGAN B. SHERWOOD
DONALD C. SWAIN

THE MIT PRESS
CAMBRIDGE, MASSACHUSETTS,
AND LONDON, ENGLAND

Originally published in 1965.
Revised edition published by The MIT Press in 1972.

New material copyright © 1972 by
The Massachusetts Institute of Technology

Printed and bound by
The Colonial Press Inc.
in the United States of America.

Library of Congress Cataloging in Publication Data
Main entry under title:

The Politics of American science, 1939 to the present.

    1. Science and state — U. S. I. Penick, James L., ed.
Q127.U6P55 1972   353.008′55   70–170859
ISBN 0–262–16053–6
ISBN 0–262–66014–8 (pbk)

CONTENTS

PREFACE TO THE
REVISED EDITION

This is a collection of readings rather than a general history. The subject is science and the federal government. Our aim has been to illustrate by selected documents a changing relationship of great moment in the national life of Americans. We have been guided by two considerations in making the selections: to keep the book within reasonable bounds and to illuminate questions of policy and administration rather than the technical problems of science. The problems of science in this book are problems of politics. We hope it will be useful to readers seeking to understand the public role of science today.

More than just the publisher is new with the issue of this revised edition. Parts Two through Five of this volume comprised the original book. Part Two was the work of Carroll Pursell, Jr.; Donald Swain and Morgan Sherwood did Three and Four, respectively; and Part Five was my handiwork. Apart from minor editorial changes to make them consistent with the new additions, these sections have been left untouched. Parts One and Six are offered as fresh material. Part One was added to provide a historical survey for readers as a reference point for the documents that follow. We hope it will increase the value of the book as a classroom tool for students unacquainted with the subject. Finally, the selections and commentary of Part Six should serve to bring the book up to date.

We have sought to retain the original spirit of the work and to provide in this new edition the flavor of documentary history from sources not easily available to the general reader. With few exceptions the documents are from original sources. As to the division of labor in the new sections, the difficult portion, namely the scholarship, went to Carroll Pursell, Jr. He selected the documents and wrote the commentary. My task was to impose editorial uniformity on the whole and serve as factotum. To Morgan Sherwood goes the credit for prodding us to undertake this revision.

The editors acknowledge with gratitude the permission of the following individuals and publishers to reprint selections in this book: Joel Hildebrand, Clarence A. Mills, C. J. Van Slyke, Homer D. Babbidge, Jr., Arthur Flemming, the Harry S. Truman Library, the National Academy of Sciences, the Carnegie Institution of Washington, the *Washington Post,* the American Physical Society, the Federation of American Scientists, the *Proceedings of the New York University Third Biennial Conference on Charitable Foundations* (Matthew Bender and Company), the American Council on Education, the *Journal of Southern Research,* the Council on Foreign Relations, Inc., the *New Scientist, Physics Today, Science,* the *New York Times,* the American Academy of Political and Social Science, Conover-Mast Publications, and *The Graduate Journal.* Finally, we thank Hunter Dupree, who has been our teacher, friend, and demanding critic.

James. L. Penick, Jr.

Evanston, Illinois

PART ONE

INTRODUCTION

A Historical Overview

❡ A. *In this opening selection the universities are seen as part of an interrelated system. It is a perspective that enabled the authors to write a historical appraisal of the relations of science and the federal government that is much broader than the title suggests. National Academy of Sciences,* Federal Support of Basic Research in Institutions of Higher Learning *(Washington, D.C.: National Research Council, 1964), 16–56.*]

CONGRESS AND SCIENCE

The Congress has had continuous and fruitful relations with science ever since the early days of the republic. Long before the end of the nineteenth century, it had learned some obvious lessons about the administration of science. For instance, the attempt by the Joint Library Committee to arrange for the publication of the scientific results of the Wilkes Expedition (the first major national effort in the professional use of scientists in exploration, 1838–1842) had demonstrated the inappropriateness of any attempt by Congress to oversee directly a scientific enterprise in every technical detail. Congress had played its part in the creative resolution of the problem of overlapping scientific jurisdictions when the United States Geological Survey was established in 1879. If larger appropriations for the scientific work of the government were not always forthcoming, they were not withheld after 1865 because of any theoretical doubts about the propriety of federal support. The Allison Commission amply aired the whole subject between 1884 and 1886.

One characteristic of the governmental posture toward science in the nineteenth century is worthy of special note: the Congress at no time took a stand against the government's participation in basic research. Through the continuous spectrum of scientific activities, from the pursuit of knowledge for its own sake to the intensive application of the fruits of research, the government was naturally at all times concerned with the applications that would further its missions. Yet the rule to which nineteenth-century lawmakers gave allegiance was that the federal government should do "such work as is within neither the province nor the capacity of the individual or of the universities, or of associations and scientific societies." When the ability of private colleges to conduct research was low, the federal government considered it part of its responsibility to help science as such. As Thomas Jefferson said, "a public institution can alone supply those sciences which though rarely called for are yet necessary to complete the circle, all the parts of which contribute to the improvement of the country, and some of them to its preservation." The Smithsonian Institution is the major example of the federal government's commitment to basic research in the nineteenth century, but it is not the only one. In an age particularly conscious of the sphere of action of local institutions, both public and private, Congress saw the need for basic research and attempted to meet it.

THE FEDERAL SCIENTIFIC ESTABLISHMENT BEFORE 1939

Congress opened the twentieth century with an increasing awareness of the government's need for research institutions to carry out many of its functions. For instance, in 1901 it met the constitutional demand for standards of weights and measures by changing a modest and administratively orphaned program into the National Bureau of Standards. The charter was broad and flexible enough to give the new institution a place among the national physical laboratories of the world and to enable it to cope successfully with rapidly changing scientific and technological developments.

By 1916 an impressive federal scientific establishment with its own laboratories and highly educated personnel had taken clear shape. It was responsive to the government's need for research in its own operations, such as the Army and Navy, at the same time that it served some large interests of the country that could not provide their own research. American agriculture had at its disposal a unique and flexible research service that had few parallels and was already beginning to affect the welfare of the nation in a broad way. Even so recent a development as the airplane called forth a governmental response in the creation of the National Advisory Committee for Aeronautics in 1915.

THE CONSTITUTIONALITY OF FEDERAL ACTIVITY IN SCIENCE

Congressional enactment of legislation, creating the federal research establishment over a long period of time and in response

3

to many different needs, provides important background for the constitutional position of science within the government. Each piece of legislation stands the test of constitutionality in terms of solving a problem of the government, rather than in terms of specific authorization in the Constitution. Science is specifically mentioned in the Constitution only in connection with patents, but among the founding fathers the advancement of science was generally considered to be closely related to the advance of political freedom and representative government. Patents, weights and measures, and the census were all matters that suggested in 1787 the interest of the federal government in activities that were to grow in range and depth with the increasing development of science and technology. By the twentieth century the growth of the government's scientific establishment was clear evidence that the power to tax for the general welfare, to regulate commerce, to establish post offices and post roads, to raise and support armies, to provide and maintain a navy, involved the power to conduct research in furtherance of government missions.

Public health provides an example of the constitutional basis for government support of research. Not mentioned specifically in the Constitution at all, public health became an object of concern to the federal government as early as 1798, when it undertook the specific task of providing hospitals for merchant seamen. Yet health is a common concern that transcends community, state, and national boundaries. Federal responsibility for public health has followed disease and the conditions that produce disease into areas where no local authority is capable of acting effectively. The commerce clause, the taxing power, the appropriation power, the postal power, the treaty-making power, and the national war power have all contributed to the development of the public health function of the federal government. In 1912, the act creating the Public Health Service stated that the "Public Health Service may study and investigate the diseases of man and conditions influencing the propagation and spread thereof. . . ." This grant of power was recognized even in the 1930's as "broad enough to cover virtually any activity in the field of public health. . . ." Thus Congress has built up through its legislation a many-rooted statutory structure which upholds the government's research operations.

PROFESSIONAL SCIENTISTS AND THE NECESSARY CONDITIONS
FOR RESEARCH IN GOVERNMENT SERVICE

In a continuous conversation with Congress over a century and a half, the scientific community also has taken a solicitous interest in the building of the federal research establishment. Those scientists who have undertaken the responsibility of carrying out research for the government and of administering the scientific bureaus have not been backward in stating the special requirements that science demands of its partner – the government. Though varying in intensity as times and issues change, these requirements are so stable that Ferdinand Rudolph Hassler, the first director of the United States Coast Survey, formulated most of them before 1842 in almost their modern form. The major requirements that one generation of scientists after another has urged upon the government may be summarized in the following propositions.

(1) *The need for long-term support.* The scientist cannot fit his experiments or the staffing and equipping of a laboratory into short periods arbitrarily laid down by a budget tied to a calendar.

(2) *The need for flexibility in objectives.* Research, as an exploration of the unknown, by definition precludes rigid projection of the shape of scientific thought and experimentation very far into the future.

(3) *Freedom to publish.* The discovery of knowledge without its communication leaves the process of research incomplete. American scientists have insisted on this point early and late, and they have suffered when it has been breached, as when the brilliant explorations of Lewis and Clark failed to have their full effect because of the lack of machinery for publication of the results.

(4) *Access to the international scientific community.* Government research, like all other research in the United States, grew up under the shadow of European accomplishments. To break communication with Europe meant not only cutting off a source of knowledge of great value but also blocking the avenue for American science to add to its stature by making contributions of its own.

(5) *The need to improve the position of the professional scientist in American society.* The people who represented science in discussions with the government were aware that pay

and conditions of work were a reflection of the value that Americans placed on science, and they worked incessantly to raise that value because of their sense of what science could contribute to the national life.

CONGRESSIONAL FRIENDS OF SCIENCE

As the spokesmen for science urged these five themes before Congress through the years, they had to contend with many difficulties. Scientists could not attract attention by their numbers, and in the earlier periods they had trouble establishing an obvious connection between their research and the practical interests of the common man. The lament of Senator Simon Cameron, as he slashed at a $6,000 appropriation for the Smithsonian Institution in 1861, echoes down through the years. "I am tired of this thing called science here." Yet the Senate voted the $6,000 by twenty-eight to six. Joseph Henry, the secretary of the Smithsonian, had friends in Congress, and scientists have in every generation had effective help from members of both Houses. The two groups — scientists and politicians — built the research establishment together.

The friends of science in Congress may or may not have constituted a majority. They have usually not had a scientific education, and their interest in science has not stemmed from any professional connection with it. Sometimes their attention has been called to the subject by people and institutions within their home districts, but usually they have discovered science as an area of public policy through their specialized work on committees in Congress. The friends of science have usually joined the scientists who appear before them in considering science "nonpolitical" in any narrow sense of the term. As a corollary, they have come from all political parties and have often divided among themselves on other issues. It has been their constant work over the years to hold the hearings, to study the issues, to draft the organic acts, and to defend the appropriations that have made the federal scientific establishment possible.

THE STATUS OF THE VARIOUS SECTORS OF SCIENCE SUPPORT

Great as had been the accomplishments of the government in institution-building and precedent-building for science, the years between the onset of the Great Depression and the second World War brought into sharp relief the shortcomings of the American research structure and the need for more and better research. Each of the major sectors of science support had its own tradition and internal coherence, but their greatest limitation was a lack of clear relation, even in some cases a lack of communication, between them. The four major sectors of American society that provided the support of science were: the government, the universities, industry, and the private foundations.

(1) *The government.* The government's research establishment had lost some of the luster of its position relative to other sectors of science support by the 1930's. The depression had meant severely cut budgets that did not rebound quickly. The bureaus had trouble holding good scientists and in securing adequate laboratories and equipment. The Department of Agriculture, with its network of experiment stations and land-grant colleges, weathered the storm better than many other agencies. The military departments were able to carry on research only at a very modest level through most of the 1930's. In terms of financial support, national security ranked well below agriculture and only a little above natural resources in the functional categories of government research and development.

(2) *The universities.* In contrast, the American university had clearly emerged by the 1930's as the home of basic research. It had also, thanks to federal grant programs to the states beginning with the Morrill Land-Grant Act of 1862, developed a distinctive capability for conducting research in certain broad fields of applied science such as agriculture. Yet the American university was a strikingly recent phenomenon in the nation's experience. It had scarcely begun to take form in 1880, and much of the development of its strong and specialized departments, its laboratories, and its great research libraries came after 1900. The best creative brains of American science found a haven as professors at a small number of universities, where they taught graduate students and performed research supported in part by university funds derived from state or private sources. In part also, university research was supported by the professors themselves, in the sense that they did not render accounting to anyone for their time or for many minor expenditures. They simply did what research their other duties and their own pocketbooks allowed them to do.

(3) *Industry.* Industrial research as a distinct sector had crystallized even later than the universities. The spread of the industrial research laboratory among the corporations of the United States had been one of the most striking developments

of the years after World War I. And the laboratories had found for themselves an increasingly well-defined and effective place in corporate structure. More and more businesses were finding science not only a useful handmaiden in testing and production but also an organized source of innovation and diversification. In some industries, notably electrical manufacturing and chemicals, research had moved to the center of the stage. In these industries, increasing emphasis on creative thinking and basic research could be noted. By and large, industrial research was tied to corporate organization, and research as an independent business or as the function of industry associations was a minor theme. In only a few instances, where the number of economic units was large, as in the case of the Bureau of Mines, did the federal government play the direct role in industrial research to which it was quite accustomed in agriculture. The morale was high in the industrial sector in the late 1930's, and an air of confidence and self-sufficiency was evident.

(4) *Private foundations.* The remaining sector, which held a position almost as a peer of the three already described, was the private foundations. Since early in the twentieth century, when the fortunes of Rockefeller and Carnegie took form as foundations, private wealth in the hands of professional foundation executives had played an important role in science. The foundations pioneered in the art of supporting science both by institutional grants, such as those by the Rockefeller Foundation's General Education Board, and by grants to individual projects — for instance, those that became common with the Rockefeller Foundation after 1928. Some had developed research departments of their own — for instance, the Carnegie Institution of Washington.

So dramatic had been the arrival of the great foundations on the American scene that they were for a time accustomed to function in areas that, in other periods, might be the responsibility of some other sector. The worldwide medical programs against yellow fever and hookworm were on a scale suggestive of government rather than private action. And, between the wars, grants from the foundations had supported such efforts at coordination of the national research structure as were being made by the National Academy of Sciences and the National Research Council. The support of President Franklin Roosevelt's Science Advisory Board by the Rockefeller Foundation, between 1933 and 1935, gave evidence of activity in an area very close to the public purposes of the government itself. The very effective National Research Council fellowships, earmarked for science, came from the private foundations. Yet in the late 1930's the foundations, their own capital funds battered by depression, could see little prospect of rapid expansion of their resources.

Thus the sectors of science support existed alongside one another in the late 1930's, each with a tradition and a self-sufficiency of its own. Each one felt that it had a clear mission independent of the others. The universities did basic research; the government did applied research related to its own missions and served a few special groups such as the farmer; industry applied science in its own laboratories; the foundations alone kept up a slight interchange with the other sectors, but even they thought in terms of special missions peculiarly appropriate to themselves. The interrelated system — the totality of arrangements by which the sectors of science support work together — which has developed since the 1930's consists of a tight interweaving of all the sectors, and the government has taken its place at the center of the system. The key link that will concern us henceforth in this account is that between the government and the institutions of higher learning. It was a weak link in the late 1930's, so weak that many denied its existence at all, and its strengthening was a crucial factor in making the world a different place almost overnight.

SCATTERED INDICATIONS OF IMPENDING CHANGE

A few portents in the 1930's foreshadowed the interrelated system as the postwar world has come to know it. In hindsight, one can almost see it coming even before the crisis of World War II, which intervened and hastened it. The establishment of the National Cancer Institute in 1937, as a part of the Public Health Service, brought with it grants-in-aid to private institutions as well as advanced training programs. The National Advisory Committee for Aeronautics had close ties with aeronautical engineering departments in leading universities and made a number of contracts for special investigations. A few scattered advisory committees to government agencies kept open a channel to university scientists. An unsuccessful try at a comprehensive organization was made by Karl T. Compton as chairman of the Science Advisory Board between 1933 and 1935. A new self-consciousness concerning the role of research is reflected in the studies of the National Resources Planning Board, which attempted an analytical and statistical profile of the sectors of science support and their relations. Indeed, the title of those studies, *Research — A National Resource*, was to become the watchword of the new system.

Yet, as war clouds gathered around the world before and after Munich, the critical question for science in the United States stood out starkly clear: Could research affect military events quickly enough to determine the outcome of the war? The modest research programs of the armed services were entirely inadequate in the new situation. There was no time to build new laboratories and train new career scientists to enter government service. The only realistic hope for deploying science lay with the university scientists and laboratories, and the weakness of the existing link between the government and university science made formidable the task of bringing the two together.

THE WARTIME LEADERS OF SCIENCE

By creating the National Defense Research Committee (NDRC) in 1940, and by expanding it into the Office of Scientific Research and Development (OSRD) in 1941, President Franklin Roosevelt provided the new framework of government-university relations even before Pearl Harbor. The link between universities and government research for national security had been established in a remarkably complete form. One of the many contributions the scientific community made to the war effort was the leadership that proposed this channel and then made it work. Four men from among a great many deserving scientists may be mentioned as providing this crucial administrative leadership: Vannevar Bush, James B. Conant, Karl T. Compton, and Frank B. Jewett. Chance plays a part in the good fortune of the United States here. The group possessed just the right combination of youth and seasoned experience. Only Jewett had played a role at high levels in World War I, and yet the others had had major administrative experience in the 1930's to season them.

Bush, Conant, Compton, and Jewett had an importance beyond their own personal qualities, impressive as those were. They were, in an unofficial way, representatives of the various sectors of science support. Conant, of course, was a distinguished chemist and president of the oldest and most prestigious private university in the country. Compton had within a few years made the Massachusetts Institute of Technology into the nation's leading scientifically oriented technical institution. Jewett was both a senior leader of industrial research, as president of Bell Telephone Laboratories, and the recently elected president of the National Academy of Sciences. Bush had served as a professor of electrical engineering and as a vice-president of M.I.T., but he was now in the strategic position of president of the Carnegie Institution of Washington. He also was chairman of the National Advisory Committee on Aeronautics. Thus all the sectors of science were handsomely represented by men who commanded major respect, and Bush, an engineer at home in the universities, private foundations, and government research, was the natural spokesman of the movement. These men had an effective knowledge of the whole sweep of American research institutions and their scientists. Their job was to determine the military needs of the country and relate them to the research capability they knew to exist in the universities and industrial research laboratories. The need was so great that considerations of field of science and institutional affiliation made little difference. Nor could long-run effects on the science establishment, such as the supply of scientists for future years or the accumulation of basic knowledge, take precedence over the cardinal requirement of adequate weapons to win the impending war.

POLICIES OF THE OSRD

After a year's trial with the NDRC of 1940, an executive order of June 28, 1941, created the more comprehensive OSRD, of which Bush was director. This order set up the Committee on Medical Research as parallel to the weapons-oriented NDRC. Although many of the basic decisions were made between June 1940 and June 1941, we shall for convenience use the designation OSRD in describing the salient characteristics of the system. It operated no laboratories of its own. It did not supplant projects already under way under the Army and Navy. It made contracts with both universities and corporations. It early adopted the principle that the contracting institution should neither make a profit nor suffer a loss as a result of OSRD research. This led immediately to the allowing of a charge for overhead costs not easy to specify in the contracts. Since by definition these costs were hard to determine, the OSRD adopted for educational institutions the formula of 50 percent of the actual labor payroll involved in a project.

The urgency of war placed its stamp on every OSRD decision. No distinctions were made between private and public universities, or between land-grant and non-land-grant institutions. Where work could be broken down into small lots, investigators were left at their own institutions. When great concentration was necessary, as in the case of the Radiation Laboratory at M.I.T., the institution was chosen purely on the ground of its ability to perform the work. In this case Karl Compton avoided a conflict of interest simply by refraining from taking part in either the discussion or the decision.

The OSRD was early confronted with the problem of delimiting its mission. Because in the twentieth century all parts of the spectrum of activities from basic research to its applications are dependent on one another, the OSRD could have gone off in a number of directions. Most of the key men, both on the panels doing the selecting and among the investigators chosen, were university-connected and had worked on basic research before the war, so that the organization might have been expected to favor basic research at least covertly. Or it might have sought immediate applications from the introducers of new designs and mechanisms, the inventors. Or it might have used its contracts deliberately to change the pattern of research institutions in the country along some preconceived path. It could have taken up the responsibility of providing general research service to industry. . . . However, it early set its face against those who wanted any or all of these things. As time went on, the OSRD became less and less concerned with the basic research end of the spectrum and more and more concerned with development, but no diminution in the reliance on university scientists accompanied this shift.

THE OSRD CONTRACT

The OSRD contract for research and development deserves special mention. As Irvin Stewart wrote at the end of the war, the "heart of the contract problem was to reconcile the need of the scientist for complete freedom with assurances that government funds would not be improperly expended." The procurement contracts in use by the Army and Navy were not well adapted for research and development, so that the legal division of OSRD set out to provide an instrument of sufficient flexibility to accommodate both the government and the scientist.

The United States of America was one party to the contract, an institution the other. "Whereas, the Government desires that the Contractor conduct studies and experimental investigations as hereinunder specified requiring the services of qualified personnel, and whereas the Contractor is willing to conduct such studies and experimental investigations on an 'actual cost' basis . . ." described the essential transaction. By 1944, the OSRD made a distinction in function within its own staff by designating in the contract a "Contracting Officer," to be responsible for the business and fiscal aspects of the work, and a "Scientific Officer," usually a chief of division, to direct the scientific aspects. Not specifically mentioned but strongly implied, both by the phrase "qualified personnel" and by the fact that an object of research was specified, was the existence of a scientist or group of scientists to take over the responsibility for the work at the contracting institution. Indeed, the principal investigator was often already at work gathering a staff and beginning operations, on the basis of a letter of intent, before the contract was signed. Thus the OSRD by its contract assembled the entire cast of the new system of government support: the fiscal officer and the scientific officer on the government side, and the university administrative officer and the principal investigator on the university side.

The contract laid down the rules for cost determination (of salaries and overhead, for example), disposition of property, responsibility of the contractor, and patent and security provisions. In each of these matters the OSRD set important precedents and educated large numbers of people in the government and in the universities in the fundamentals of the new support system for research.

CONGRESS AND SCIENCE DURING WORLD WAR II —
THE KILGORE SUBCOMMITTEE

How did Congress and the American people get the opportunity to approve or disapprove the OSRD? Some had thought of asking for legislation in 1941, but the urgency of the times argued that it be done by executive order under temporary war powers. An announcement of the formation of the agency was published, but the need for security so sheltered it that Stewart, as executive secretary, could handle public information and Bush, as director, could handle congressional liaison all by themselves. A tacit agreement between Congress and OSRD tended to give force to Bush's insistence, which went all the way back to the beginnings of the organization, that it was a purely temporary agency. Once the emergency was over — once the narrow objective of weapons for this war had been accomplished – the OSRD had no thought but to place science and the agency before Congress for fundamental decisions about the shape of the future.

So great was the obvious relevance of science to the war effort, however, that not everyone was willing to wait until the shooting was over to find out whether the OSRD's strictly delimited program was adequate. Senator Harley Kilgore, Democrat of West Virginia, arranged major hearings before a subcommittee of the Senate Committee on Military Affairs in 1942, 1943, and 1944. Senator Kilgore and his staff came at the whole problem of science and government from the point of view of war industry. Hence they stressed patents, inventions, industrial research for small business, and the imperfect utilization of technical manpower. Since the OSRD started with a problem and tried to find the men best qualified to work on it, it took no responsibility for the scientists, often geologists or biologists whose specialties were not in great demand, who were left outside the war effort. And, since the OSRD has long insisted that it was not working on materials or methods of wide use in industry, it did not concern itself with supplying research support to war industry generally. Hence the Kilgore Subcommittee aimed at an organization to work in such an area. On July 8, 1943, a group of senators, headed by Kilgore and referring directly to his hearings asked James F. Byrnes, then Director of War Mobilization, to set up a central scientific and technical body. Among the 23 signers, both parties and all major geographical regions were well represented.

SCIENCE — THE ENDLESS FRONTIER

Bush, already on record as opposing Kilgore's big agency for scientific and technical mobilization, became increasingly aware, as the successful conclusion of the war in Europe loomed up, that a major reorientation of scientific support was on the way. His oft-reiterated intention of closing down the OSRD at the end of the war had the effect of forcing a full-dress examination of science's role in American life. And that examination would eventually have to be made in the public arena, with fundamental legislation the result. But first the scientific community, if it did not wish to be caught unawares, had to examine the postwar support of science and come forward with a program. Although the OSRD could not by itself take up the study of the shape of postwar science, it formed a natural framework. Therefore, President Roosevelt, in a letter dated November 17, 1944, asked Bush for his recommendations. The letter carefully referred to the OSRD as "a unique experiment of team-work and cooperation in coordinating scientific research and in applying existing scientific knowledge to the solution of technical problems paramount in war." The letter asked Bush to give his considered judgment personally, "afer such consultation as you may deem advisable with your associates and others." Roosevelt thus empowered Bush to convene an advisory committee-of-the-whole of the scientific community to answer four questions. They were:

First: What can be done, consistent with military security, and with the prior approval of the military authorities, to make known to the world as soon as possible the contributions which have been made during our war effort to scientific knowledge? . . .

Second: With particular reference to the war of science against disease, what can be done now to organize a program for continuing in the future the work which has been done in medicine and related sciences? . . .

Third: What can the Government do now and in the future to aid research activities by public and private organizations? The proper roles of public and of private research, and their interrelation, should be carefully considered.

Fourth: Can an effective program be proposed for discovering and developing scientific talent in American youth so that the continuing future of scientific research in this country may be assured on a level comparable to what has been done during the war?

Bush, having made his opportunity, took advantage to the fullest by appointing distinguished committees to study each of the four questions. The committees for questions three and four, headed by Isaiah Bowman and Henry Allen Moe, respectively, were the ones that considered in detail most of the features of the government-university link. A committee representing medical research in the universities had its say on question two. While university men, especially presidents, predominated on all the committees, the other sectors of science were also represented. The only major group not represented as such (although Bush, Conant, I. I. Rabi, and perhaps a few others bridged the gap) were the atomic scientists, still hidden even from the OSRD by compartmentation within the confines of the Manhattan project. As nearly as one could expect the scientific community to have a voice, it had one here.

Bush's report, *Science — the Endless Frontier*, attempted a profile of American science and a prescription for the future. The basic principle of the interrelated system appears in the body of the report.

The Government should accept new responsibilities for promoting the flow of new scientific knowledge and the development of scientific talent in our youth. These responsibilities are the proper concern of the Government, for they vitally affect our health, our jobs, and our national security. It is in keeping also with basic United States policy that the Government should foster the opening of new frontiers and this is the modern way to do it. For many years the Government has wisely supported research in the agricultural colleges and the benefits have been great. The time has come when such support should be extended to other fields.

The effective discharge of these new responsibilities will require the full attention of some over-all agency devoted to that purpose. There is not now in the permanent governmental structure receiving its funds from Congress an agency adapted to supplementing the support of basic research in the colleges, universities, and research institutes, both in medicine and the natural sciences, adapted to supporting research on new weapons for both Services, or adapted to administering a program of science scholarships and fellowships.

Therefore I recommend that a new agency for these purposes be established. Such an agency should be composed of persons of broad interest and experience, having an understanding of the peculiarities of scientific research and scientific education. It should have stability of funds so that long-range programs may be undertaken. It should be recognized that freedom of inquiry must be preserved and should leave internal control of policy, personnel, and the method and scope of research to the institutions in which it is carried on. It should be fully responsible to the President and through him to the Congress for its program.

The National Research Foundation envisaged in the Bush report had about it a comprehensive nature that matched the situation into which it would move. It would have a Division of Medical Research and a Division of National Defense parallel to its Division of Natural Sciences. The Foundation was to have the power to "make contracts or grants' for the conduct of research by negotiation without advertising for bids." Many characteristics of the OSRD were included, such as the principle that the research should be "conducted, in general, on an actual cost basis without profit to the institution receiving the research grant or contract." No geographical or other formula was proposed because the "Foundation must... be free to place its research contracts or grants not only with those institutions which have a demonstrated research capacity but also with other institutions whose latent talent or creative atmosphere affords promise of research success." In general it was envisaged that the National Research Foundation would adopt the historic goals of scientists in their relations with the government and extend them to the contract-grant system of tying the universities to public purposes. At the same time, the Bush report was explicit on the ultimate responsibility of the President and Congress. "Only through such responsibility can we maintain the proper relationship between science and other aspects of a democratic system. The usual controls of audits, reports, budgeting, and the like, should, of course apply to the administrative and fiscal operations of the Foundation, subject, however, to such adjustments in procedure as are necessary to meet tthe special requirements of research."

THE END OF THE WAR

Science — the Endless Frontier, which did not mention uranium or fission or nuclear energy, appeared the same month as the Alamagordo test — July 1945 — and only a month before the world learned of the atomic bomb with Hiroshima. Dramatic impact made atomic energy seem like a separate area of science policy to be dealt with as a thing apart. Indeed it proved to be, as the creation of the Atomic Energy Commission in 1946 showed. But meanwhile the problems attacked in *Science — the Endless Frontier* had their day in Congress. Senator Kilgore introduced a bill which represented his long-standing interests, while Senator Warren G. Magnuson introduced a bill embodying Bush's ideas.

On September 6, 1945, President Truman, in a special message to Congress on reconversion, set the keynote of the discussion when he said: "No Nation can maintain a position of leadership in the world of today unless it develops to the full its scientific and technological resources. No government adequately meets its responsibilities unless it generously and intelligently supports and encourages the work of science in university, industry, and in its own laboratories." In calling for a single federal research agency for science, Truman clearly confirmed the concept of an interrelated system of "universities, industry, and Government working together," and promised in unmistakable terms the freedom demanded by the nature of science. "Although science can be coordinated and encouraged, it cannot be dictated to or regimented. Science cannot progress unless founded on the free intelligence of the scientist. I stress the fact the Federal research agency here proposed should in no way impair that freedom."

THE KILGORE-MAGNUSON HEARINGS

Senators Kilgore and Magnuson arranged jointly for hearings on science legislation that lasted through most of the fall of 1945 and gave the wartime leaders of science and many others a chance to express themselves on the shape of the future for science in the United States. The striking thing about these hearings is that every one of the witnesses except one supported the principle of some sort of science foundation in the government. Senator Kilgore led off by saying: "As the war has so dramatically demonstrated, science is a national resource of the greatest importance for our whole national life. Scientific skills and scientific know-how have enabled us to win rapid and decisive victory on the war fronts. The same skills and know-how must now be converted and expanded to meet the needs of peace — the improvement of our national health, the security of our national defense, the promotion of our prosperity." As one eminent scientist put it, "we require the mass will of the people as expressed by the Government. Science and technology need the direct help of the Government. The Government needs ever more urgently the help of science and technology."

Yet below the level of this large fundamental agreement, tensions predictable in a democracy's first public airing of an unfamiliar concept promptly emerged. *Science — the Endless Frontier* had proposed a part-time board of people otherwise unconnected with the government, not merely as an advisory body but as a responsible head of the agency — appointing the director, formulating over-all policy, and making grants and contracts. Senator Kilgore's bill favored a straight-line organization, with the director appointed by the President. Harold Smith, then director of the Bureau of the Budget, was strongly of the same opinion, equating the responsibility of the director with the control of public funds. "I believe that the most important principle involved in these bills is that an agency which is to control the spending of government funds in a great national program must be a part of the regular machinery of government. If the government is to support scientific research, it should do so through its own responsible agency, not by delegating the control of the programs and turning over the funds to any nongovernmental organization."

President Edmund E. Day of Cornell University, representing the Association of Land-Grant Colleges and Universities, advocated a formula by which a percentage of the foundation's funds would be distributed to the land-grant institutions, making "as a counterweight an independent, Federally financed program administratively directed by the important public institutions in the several States. . . . "

On this issue, Harold Smith and the Bureau of the Budget were on the side of *Science — the Endless Frontier* and geographically unrestricted grants and contracts. The "proposed foundation should be free to support the advancement of knowledge in any institution which, in the judgment of the foundation, is able to do effective and competent research." He went on to link the freedom of the foundation to support excellence, in specific packages wherever found, to the ability of the government to safeguard the use of the taxpayers' money.

Only by specific contracts, rather than general purpose contracts, can it make sure that it is supporting in each institution only the type of research which that institution is qualified to perform. This is not to say that it will restrict the proper degree of freedom of research, or impose a narrow type of administrative supervision over the institutions with which it deals. But it would obviously be improper and ineffective to give funds to private institutions without some assurance of their ability to further the purpose of the program, and the foundation must have freedom to select the institutions that are able to do so.

The patent problem occupied more hearing time than any other. In general, Bush stood for the OSRD practice of leaving patents in the hands of contractors whenever possible, while Kilgore hoped for government ownership of patents produced in the course of government-supported research. As it became clearer in the course of the hearings that the foundation would support basic research rather than industrial applications, more and more witnesses expressed doubt that science legislation was the place to reform the patent system.

THE FAILURE TO MAKE THE NATIONAL SCIENCE FOUNDATION PARALLEL THE ATOMIC ENERGY COMMISSION

Despite the broad areas of consensus evident in the fall of 1945, legislation for a foundation did not clear both Houses of Congress until 1947. The seriousness of the organizational issue was demonstrated by the subsequent veto from President Truman.

Our national security and welfare require that we give direct support to basic scientific research and take steps to increase the number of trained scientists. . . . However, this bill contains provisions which represent such a marked departure from sound principles for the administration of public affairs that I cannot give it my approval. It would, in effect, vest the determination of vital national policies, the expenditure of large public funds, and the administration of important government functions in a group of individuals who would be essentially private citizens. The proposed National Science Foundation would be divorced from control by the people to an extent that implies a distinct lack of faith in democratic processes.

The failure of legislation to emerge in 1946, the last session of the Seventy-Ninth Congress, is partially explained by the bitter controversy over atomic-energy legislation. Two of the main issues dividing the May-Johnson bill from the McMahon bill — organization of the commission, and patents — were parallel to the issues dividing the opposing forces on the science legislation, which reflected the dissension more faithfully than it reflected the urgency of atomic energy as a policy area. The closest students of the legislative history of the Atomic Energy Act of 1946 have noted that "many thousands of Americans had expended millions of words in public debate. . . . The final bill was not what any single one of them would have written. Yet, it was probably better than any individual could have produced. In this fact, perhaps, lay the secret vitality of American democracy."

In the case of the science foundation, the congressional ability to be cautious in the face of conflicting philosophies dominated the result for the time being. But the vitality of American democracy had already been at work to create the interrelated system. The need for it had outrun the ability to create over-all institutions, and even before the war's end practical arrangements were being made by Congress and the Executive to insure the nation against the limitations in the organization of government-supported science that had prevailed in the 1930's. The OSRD would go out of existence, but the system it created had to live on.

POSTWAR RECONVERSION

The determination not to return to the 1930's, only dimly sensed by scientists who had served in the wartime projects, was explicit in the minds of those responsible for national science policy. Europe, for the first time in American history, could no longer be relied upon to send over a sufficient stream of basic research results relevant to the rapidly changing frontiers of science and technology. The need to revive a free flow of information was acute, but the need to begin new knowledge from the basic end of the scientific spectrum was the only hope for a healthy growth of technology. Because the universities had almost shut down graduate education during the war, a shortage of scientific manpower was also in everyone's mind; fellowships were needed to close the gap in the ranks created by the war's diversions.

Military and civilian leaders in all the services were especially insistent that the partnership with university scientists be continued. James V. Forrestal, Robert P. Patterson, and General H. H. Arnold emphasized it as a necessity when they appeared at the Kilgore-Magnuson hearings. General Eisenhower, as Army Chief of Staff in 1946, made a particular point of the Army's commitment to basic research. He advocated a separation of "responsibility for research and development from the functions of procurement, purchase, storage, and distribution." In short, the military itself did not wish to lose its new-found partnership with science. Without the OSRD, it had the choice either of building up its intramural laboratories or of maintaining by contract its liaison with the university scientists. And the choice was really not free, for few scientists in 1945 and 1946 were willing to accept civil service careers in the government laboratories. Therefore all the services had ultimately to think in terms not only of keeping as much classified and applied research as possible within their own laboratories, but also of making contracts with the men who, after having performed prodigies in the defense laboratories during the war, were now back on university faculties thirsting to work on basic research problems rather than hardware.

THE OFFICE OF NAVAL RESEARCH

The Navy, for various reasons, made the clearest and earliest response to the necessity for a contract program after the end of the war. Men at several levels in the Navy had been thinking about the future of science in the Department at least since 1942. As a result, the Office of Research and Inventions was, by September 1945, under way on reallocated funds and ready with proposed legislation that would give congressional approval to its operations. The Vinson Bill, which became law in August 1946, became the charter of the Office of Naval Research. The act's preamble indicates the comprehensive vision of the founders of ONR:

> . . . to plan, foster, and encourage scientific research in recognition of its paramount importance as related to the maintenance of future naval power, and the preservation of national security; to provide within the Department of the Navy a single office, which, by contract and otherwise, shall be able to obtain, coordinate, and make available to all bureaus . . . world-wide scientific information and the necessary services for conducting specialized and imaginative research. . . .

The ONR Act provided, in addition to ample authority to make research contracts, for a Naval Research Advisory Committee.

Thus, the ONR possessed all the elements of a model program for the interrelated system. It had a direct administration with a regular navy officer as director. In practice the chief scientist served as deputy director and headed a staff of program directors knowledgeable in particular fields. The advisory committee and a large number of subsidiary committees and panels brought eminent scientists in from the universities on a part-time basis to help the navy decide what projects to support. As soon as word got around, ONR did not have to solicit proposals from the scientists; they came in a flood. The ONR officials did, however, have to establish rapport with university administrations to convince them to make the contracts which would allow the scientists to go to work.

In their missionary work with university presidents, the ONR representatives had to convince administrators, already harried by the dislocations of war and the returning flood of G.I.'s, that they should take on navy contracts for research. The document they used was already far from the straight military procurement contract. "Contracts are not new to the Navy, but the idea of conducting contractual relationships in the field of basic research with independent agencies and institutions..., using tasks instead of specifications, is a new departure in Government contracting."

The men who made the ONR a success in the eyes of both the Navy and the universities had a driving belief in four major propositions:

(1) The primary aim of much of the Planning Division's scientific program is *free* rather than directed research. Instead of being pointed toward direct solution of some practical problem, its intention is to explore and understand the laws of nature, both animate and inanimate.

(2) Practically none of the basic research work conducted by the Navy is in a confidential or secret status.

(3) We want to have listening posts in various scientific fields and we want to maintain contact with the most imaginative people in science.

(4) To date, there has not been established a unit similar to the proposed National Science Foundation; nor has any agency, other than the Office of Naval Research, indicated its willingness to accept even *pro tempore* some of the associated responsibilities.

University officials suspicious of military domination eventually came to believe the ONR.

It might be asked how a military agency could achieve rapport with scientists, even while the National Science Foundation legislation was stalled because too many scientists feared a single director appointed by the President and insisted on a part-time board. The answer lies in the fact that the Navy recognized the level at which the independent advice of scientists was at that time most needed. No general board, or even the Naval Research Advisory Committee of fifteen members, could constitute an adequate representation of all the disciplines and subdisciplines of science. Therefore it set up an extensive network of advisory committees by fields of science to assist in the screening of research proposals. In 1948 the list of fields under consideration included: geophysics, astronomy, mathematics, chemistry, undersea warfare, fluid mechanics, psychophysiology, biochemistry, human ecology, physiology, microbiology, and psychology.

From the point of view of the government, re-establishing

scientific merit as the major criterion for spending money, and obtaining the most reliable and experienced university scientists to make the decisions, meant the best available insurance to the taxpayer that there would be no waste. Who, other than a microbiologist, could judge the scientific worth of a proposal in the field of microbiology? From the point of view of the investigator making the proposal, the advisory committee represented one of the most ancient and cherished rights of the Anglo-American legal tradition — the judgment of his peers. From the point of view of the university, even the largest of which did not have enough microbiologists to form a disinterested jury, the national committee relieved the local administration of the necessity of making substantive decisions on individual projects. For the advisory committee members, who were by definition the men with the best reputations for research, life began to include periodic trips to Washington.

Other networks of advisory committees spread over Washington in the postwar years. The four groups brought together by the OSRD contract for weapons research — the scientific program director with his advisory committee in the agency, the agency's contract administrator, the administrative officer in the university, and the principal investigator in the university — were brought together in a close partnership in the name of basic research by ONR. By 1949, the agency had expenditures of the order of $20,000,000 for 1,200 projects in 200 institutions, engaging nearly 3,000 scientists and 2,500 graduate students. It was to that time "the greatest peacetime cooperative undertaking in history between the academic world and the government." If a serious flaw existed in the effective Navy program between 1945 and 1950, it was that the American people did not know that they had a productive partnership between government and their universities.

THE NATIONAL INSTITUTES OF HEALTH

In the organization of the government-university partnership, medical research has always been a special problem area. The problems stemmed, on the negative side, from the increasingly heavy costs of both medical care and medical education. The medical schools in universities reflected these problems, and the OSRD was set up in part to give medicine special administrative handling in the Committee on Medical Research. On the positive side, no field offered more promise in the peacetime world envisaged in *Science — the Endless Frontier* than did medical research. A people who had entered the war without penicillin emerged from it with altered expectations. A reproach against the federal research establishment in the early 1900's had been "that more pains are now being taken to protect the health of farm animals than of human beings." Because of the strength of the Department of Agriculture, this taunt was still valid in 1945, though clearly neither the Congress nor the people accepted the situation as an expression of their will. The result was pressure to do something in medical research. The National Research Foundation of *Science — the Endless Frontier* was not ready. The OSRD was closing down. The Public Health Service seized the opportunity, not merely because its leaders were ambitious, but also because the Congress had already prepared them for the task by statute.

Much was made in the 1945 discussion of the inadvisability of a research agency with extramural contracts also operating in its own laboratories. *Science — the Endless Frontier* recommended against it, and the Atomic Energy Commission had only contract laboratories. Many old-line agencies that did not develop significant extramural programs — the National Bureau of Standards and the Geological Survey, for instance — have found the postwar decades a period of trial.

The Public Health Service was unimpressed by this seeming incompatibility. It had an impressive program of intramural research in its Hygienic Laboratory, which after 1930 was called the National Institutes of Health. It had begun making grants-in-aid to medical schools through the National Cancer Institute, established in 1937. Observation of the effectiveness of the Committee on Medical Research led the National Institutes of Health of the war period to become enthusiastic about research in universities as an adjunct to their intramural program. Therefore, in the Public Health Service Act of 1944, Congress conferred upon the Surgeon General of the Public Health Service the power to "make grants-in-aid to universities, hospitals, laboratories, and other public or private institutions, and to individuals for such research projects as are recommended by the National Advisory Health Council, or, with respect to cancer, recommended by the National Advisory Cancer Council." The next year, R. E. Dyer, director of the National Institutes of Health, testified at the Kilgore-Magnuson hearings that the Public Health Service already had "all of the authority in reference to health and medical research that is contemplated for the proposed foundation."

Since authority is one thing, and money is another, the Public Health Service Act of 1944 did not assure the future of the National Institutes of Health as a major source of support of medical research; nor did it assure the future of the grant instrument as the most important means of linking university research to the government. In 1944 and 1945 the Bureau of the Budget withheld permission from the Public Health Service to seek funds for a grant program in general medical research. Only when the OSRD Committee on Medical Research went out of existence, and its contracts were transferred to the National Institutes of Health, did the nucleus of an extramural grant program come into existence. Thus it was the National Institutes of Health that carried on beyond OSRD in medical research. By 1951, when a National Science Foundation came into existence, the National Institutes of Health expenditures for health research were of the order of $30,000,000, more than half of which was spent through extramural grants. The pattern of the congressional appropriation exceeding the budget proposal sent up by the President had already put in an appearance.

The National Institutes of Health system of research support bore striking resemblances to that of the Office of Naval Research. The grant, a simple letter from the agency to the institution stipulating in broad terms the purpose of the research and the financial aspects of the transaction, brought the responsible officer of the government and the responsible administrative officer of the university into essentially the same relationship as that created by the Office of Naval Research contract. The investigator presented his proposal describing his research in a similar way. The study sections of the National Institutes of Health, which corresponded to the advisory committees of the Office of Naval Research, were organized by fields of medical research to obtain the part-time advice of leading university research men. Thus the government again gained the assurance of quality and the investigator gained the judgment of his peers.

Some significant differences appear between the two operations, however. In the first place, while medicine depends on basic research in many sciences, it is itself an applied science with a highly specific object, the human being. The National Institutes of Health could argue for broad and fundamental studies, but it could also argue the practicality of its research in a way that the Office of Naval Research could not, at least if it were to maintain its flexibility. In the second place, also related to the nature of medicine, the National Institutes of Health could serve uniquely well in promoting certain lines of research. Diseases made such obvious targets that even the members of the appropriations subcommittees in the House and Senate could see areas such as cancer chemotherapy and virus study as worthy of special emphasis.

In the third place, the Office of Naval Research's Naval Research Advisory Committee, even though set up by law, had less specific authority than the Advisory Councils of the National Institutes of Health, which by statute had to recommend a grant before the Surgeon General could act. Thus the voice of the scientist was more authoritative in the National Institutes of Health than in the Office of Naval Research, however similar the practices of the two agencies. Finally, the grant-in-aid, as applied by the National Institutes of Health, was explicitly and unequivocally a support for research and not a purchase of research. In practice the Office of Naval Research contract also supported research rather than purchasing it, but the government's vast machinery for procurement contracts put the Office of Naval Research at a theoretical disadvantage.

OTHER NICHES OCCUPIED — AEC AND WEAPONS RESEARCH

The period 1945 to 1950 saw other agencies profit by the example of OSRD and fill niches left by its demise. The Atomic Energy Commission could and did contract with universities for much research on a project basis. But it also built upon the university-operated laboratories inherited from the Manhattan District to create a system of national laboratories. Oak Ridge provided the site for one, close to operating plants of the Commission. Others, notably Argonne National Laboratory at the University of Chicago and the Lawrence Radiation Laboratory at the University of California, had close physical and intellectual ties with their universities. In the case of Brookhaven National Laboratory on Long Island, the Atomic Energy Commission made its contract with Associated Universities, Incorporated, set up by several eastern universities for that purpose.

The national laboratories were technically institutions that conducted contract research, and much public commentary concerning the government-university interrelated system actually refers to incidents and arrangements at these famous institutions. Actually their work is not in the same category with project research performed by individual professors on campuses. A single contract may well cover an entire laboratory, with its large scientific and supporting staffs and its huge and costly machines. The laboratories have traditions of free research, and the red tape of administering such large organizations rests but lightly on the investigators. The laboratories play a significant role in graduate education, and they have carried the United States to pre-eminence in many fields of physics which, without large-scale government support for expensive and highly specialized equipment, could not have been entered at all.

The armed services, in the throes of unification and faced with the prospect of the Cold War, had to evolve a weapons-research establishment after the end of the war without benefit of OSRD. The Office of Naval Research and contract programs in the other services provided for a continuing link between the military and the universities; but, as the diplomatic stalemate with the Soviet Union set in, and as weapons became so unconventional that research, relative to production, became an ever greater percentage of military expenditures, two major trends became evident. One was the heightened emphasis on intramural research by the military departments. The other was the increasing use of the research contract to purchase development on weapons systems from both profit and non-profit corporations. While not directly related to the government-university thread of this account, the contracts in the weapons area have had the indirect but sometimes almost overpowering effect of adding to the over-all cost figures for research and of increasing the demands on the scarcest commodity of all, brainpower. Moreover, the research and development contracting officers, becoming accustomed to dealing with profit corporations, tended to apply the same procedures to research contracts with universities.

THE STEELMAN REPORT

In spite of the accomplishments at the working level that put the Office of Naval Research, the National Institutes of Health, and the Atomic Energy Commission laboratories and many university scientists to work, the failure of the immediate postwar reconversion to deal explicitly with the arrival of university science as a major national resource aroused concern. A feeling of unease led President Truman to appoint a President's Scientific Research Board under the chairmanship of John R. Steelman. Urgency and a sense of competition still radiate from the major recommendations of that committee, dated August 27, 1947:

(1) That, as a Nation, we increase our annual expenditures for research and development as rapidly as we can expand facilities and increase trained manpower. By 1957 we should be devoting at least one per cent of our national income to research and development in the universities, industry, and government.

(2) That heavier emphasis be placed on basic research and upon medical research in our national research and development budget. Expenditures for basic research should be quadrupled and those for health and medical research tripled in the next decade, while total research and development expenditures should be doubled.

(3) That the Federal Government support basic research in the universities and nonprofit research institutions at a progressively increasing rate, reaching an annual expenditure of at least $250 million by 1957.

(4) That a National Science Foundation be established to make grants in support of basic research, with a director appointed by and responsible to the President.

(5) That a Federal program of assistance to undergraduate and graduate students in the sciences be developed as an integral part of an overall national scholarship and fellowship program.

(6) That a program of Federal assistance to universities and colleges be developed in the matters of laboratory facilities and scientific equipment as an integral part of a general program of aid to education.

(7) That a Federal Committee be established, composed of the directors of the principal Federal research establishments, to assist in the coordination and development of the Government's own research and development programs.

(8) That every effort be made to assist in the reconstruction of European laboratories as a part of aid to peace-loving countries. Such aid should be given on terms which require the maximum contributions toward the restoration of conditions of free international exchange of scientific knowledge.

Any member of the public who wished to could read these recommendations, and, thus having before him the agenda for the next decade, should not have been overly surprised at the development of federal support for science in the decade 1947–1957. In fact, the Steelman Report's target figures were in every case far under the actual totals for fiscal 1957.

THE BELATED CREATION OF THE NATIONAL SCIENCE FOUNDATION

Since the interrelated system developed so vigorously in the late 1940's, the impulse for a National Science Foundation could have been sustained only by people who still felt that important values were involved. The friends of science in Congress never let the idea die even after the veto of 1947. The Senate passed a bill regularly, so that the main discussion shifted to the Interstate and Foreign Commerce Committee of the House, where the late Representative J. Percy Priest carried the main burden in behalf of the legislation.

On the scientists' side, an Inter-Society Committee for a National Science Foundation brought together a group through which the nation's scientific societies could scrutinize the complexities of the legislative process and keep in touch both with congressional staffs and with the Bureau of the Budget, who, of course, handled the examination of the drafts of legislation for the Administration. The patent issue was largely laid aside as the conviction grew that the Foundation would concentrate on basic research. The organization of the National Science Board and its relation to the Foundation gradually yielded to a compromise in which the President appointed the director as well as the board, to whom certain direct powers of approval for grants were reserved.

As applied research dropped out of the concept of the Foundation, the bill became easier to pass because of the disappearance of the patent issue, but harder to pass because basic research was not clearly and obviously related to the missions of government agencies. The major addition to the concept of the Foundation in these years was the coordinating role in the government research establishment. This feature brought in the support both of those who feared inefficiency in government spending and of those who thought of over-all planning as a necessity if science was to be directed to national goals. In 1950, after the sponsors of the bill had accepted a $15,000,000 ceiling on appropriations (less than the Office of Naval Research was using for contracts and the National Institutes of Health for grants), the National Science Foundation Act passed both Houses of Congress and was signed by President Truman.

By 1950, Congress had clearly adopted the attitude that research required broad and flexible legislation. Under the National Science Foundation Act of 1950, the new foundation was authorized and directed:

(1) to develop and encourage the pursuit of a national policy for the promotion of basic research and education in the sciences;

(2) to initiate and support basic scientific research and programs to strengthen scientific research potential in the mathematical, physical, medical, biological, engineering, and other sciences, by making contracts or other arrangements (including grants, loans, and other forms of assistance) to support such scientific activities and appraise the impact of research upon industrial development and upon the general welfare. . . .

In some respects the Act said even more about government science policy than its substantive provisions stated. Geographical distribution of research funds by formula — the formula of the land-grant college system or other — was rejected. And the National Science Board was not specifically made representative of particular fields of science. But the legal requirements for membership carried with them the implied policies. Members "(1) shall be eminent in the fields of the basic sciences, medical science, engineering, agriculture, education or public affairs; (2) shall be selected solely on the basis of established records of distinguished service; and (3) shall be so selected as to provide representation of the views of scientific leaders in all areas of the Nation." Implied here was a check on the power of the government and a safeguard to a free science. Indeed, a minority report by six senators on an earlier version of the bill had put this apprehension concerning too strong a director into words.

The Administrator . . . will plan and direct a science program with the full force of two hundred or three hundred million dollars per year. He can ignore the Board's advice in any field he chooses regardless of his competence in that field; he can ignore their advice in all fields and dictate his own ideas. . . .

Today our educational institutions are proud of their independence and freedom. If in a few years they become dependent upon funds from the Federal Government . . . they will not be able to resist the authority for dictation of this Czar of science — the administrator. Only those schools . . . satisfying one man will receive the Federal money.

If one proposition is fundamental to the whole postwar debate regarding the structure of science and its link to the government, it is that few — either in Congress or in the scientific community — wished a czar of science. The Act of 1950, by its construction of the National Science Board and the Division

31

Committees, expressed the judgment of Congress that the system of advisory scientific panels was a legal and necessary part of the government's machinery.

THE YOUNG NSF AND THE CHOICE OF THE GRANT INSTRUMENT

The first director of the National Science Foundation, Dr. Alan T. Waterman, moved not in the direction of becoming a czar, but to set up a system of support for basic research that would justify its stewardship of the taxpayers' money by careful scrutiny of each project by nongovernment scientists. As the former chief scientist of the Office of Naval Research, Waterman adopted many of its ground rules and practices.

At the same time, the young National Science Foundation was aware of the precedent in the National Institutes of Health for using grants in the support of research. Because of the breadth of the National Science Foundation Act, the Foundation was in a position to make a choice of the legal instrument best suited to the needs of supporting basic research in the universities. As a working paper used in the Foundation in July, 1951, put it, "recognizing the inherent heterogeneity of basic research and the difficulty of fostering its conduct through a single administrative mechanism, the Congress has provided the Foundation with a sufficiently liberal grant of authority to meet almost any conceivable admixture of need." According to the working paper analysis, "unquestionably the arrangement most widely used by governmental agencies for supporting research is the contract.... In theory, at least, there is a *quid pro quo* relationship between the parties to the contract; but in practice, through a gradual (evolution) of the contract form in recent years, this relationship tends to become less rigid and to take on some of the attributes of a cooperative or grant arrangement."

A grant, on the other hand, according to the working paper, "is, in a formal sense at least, a unilateral action by one party by which a sum of money, property, or other valuable consideration is given to another party for accomplishment of an agreed-upon purpose." After reviewing the "elaborate overload of financial and property accountability which has often proved excessively burdensome to both contracting parties" in the use of contracts, and pointing to the wide use of grants by private foundations as well as the Public Health Service, the working paper commended the grant to the Foundation's use. "Because of its flexibility, the grant is most appropriate to undertakings in which initiative and freedom of action play a decisive role and in which the production of *some* beneficial result is more to be sought than attainment of a set goal in a prescribed manner." When the National Science Foundation chose the grant, it added a new dimension to the interrelated system. The Office of Naval Research definition of basic research and its organization of advisory committees were wedded to the legal instrument of the National Institutes of Health, creating an organization highly satisfactory for the continued alliance between university scientists and the government. With little money and an excellent system of advice, the National Science Foundation quickly established a reputation for responsibility in the administration of its grants.

MISSION-RELATED BASIC RESEARCH

A major problem that faced the National Science Foundation in its early years was finding a rationale for basic research independent of any of the particular missions recognized by the government. An assumption that had some currency in the early years was that the National Science Foundation would "take over" in the form of transfers the basic research already being performed by the Atomic Energy Commission, the Department of Defense, and various other agencies of the government. If this happened, one could say that the mission of the National Science Foundation was basic research, especially in the universities, while the Navy would support applied research related to its mission. Although some people took some time to get over this simple notion, it soon became clear that major transfers were impractical and that the well-established agencies could make a strong case for continuing their university contracts. The fundamental reason for this was that basic research activities and applied research activities had become so intertwined that the various agencies of the government felt a need that was no less urgent because it did not fit accepted definitions — the need for "Mission-related basic research." If such a category were admitted, was there a real need for a National Science Foundation, after all?

The answer of the Eisenhower Administration to this question was "yes." In Executive Order number 10521, dated March 17, 1954, arrived at after extensive consultation, President Eisenhower said,

As now or hereafter authorized or permitted by law, the Foundation shall be increasingly responsible for providing support by the Federal Government for general-purpose basic research through contracts and grants. The conduct and support by other Federal agencies of basic research in areas which are closely related to their missions is recognized as important and desirable especially in response to current national needs, and shall continue.

While this did not say anything that the Congress had not already said in a number of organic acts, the reiteration confirmed the Foundation's mission as "general-purpose" basic research. At the same time it gave other agencies grounds to argue that they had full scope to conduct mission-related basic research. Such a plural system made possible the support of basic research in a variety of different ways and assured those concerned with missions in health and weaponry of vigorous scientific activity in their areas among university scientists. A National Science Foundation that consolidated everything called basic research might have become rich and powerful quickly, but the plural linkage added much to the strength and flexibility of the interrelated system.

The National Science Foundation took the attitude that fostering mission-related basic research in other agencies strengthened science as a whole. To make the plural system described in Executive Order 10521 even more effective, and to make rapport between other government agencies and university scientists easier, the National Science Foundation encouraged the passage of legislation in 1958 by which Congress authorized all federal agencies to use grants instead of contracts for the support of scientific research. The law, in effect, put both the National Science Foundation and Congress on record as favoring basic research in widely dispersed agencies of the government.

THE STRENGTHS AND LIMITATIONS OF A PLURAL SYSTEM

The virtues of the plural system of the mid-1950's were many. The investigator had several chances to seek support for his ideas. The steady flow of proposals, the periodic gathering of the panels and study sections, the judgment of peers, the grant letters and contracts which emerged, became a settled and familiar pattern in the government. The interplay of actions that determined the proportion of federal funds allocated to each field tended to produce a kind of balance in which rapid changes of priority assigned to different fields were hard to accomplish. Indeed, no clear mechanism existed for making priority decisions, either among fields or among agencies.

Occasionally a special circumstance could produce some change in priority. The International Geophysical Year, an event that required the contribution of many countries to a coordinated series of experiments probing the entire environment accessible to man or his instruments, was occasion for a deliberate change in priority. Congress fully supported the emphasis by appropriations. But the plural system allowed such a shift to occur only when the most careful, vigorous, and foresighted action joined an especially appealing opportunity. An external event which disturbed the even tenor of the plural system was sure to create a demand for a more vigorous coordination of the government's role in science.

In a system in which a plurality of executive agencies supported science in a plurality of universities, that Congress should make a plural response is not surprising. The Congress, almost by definition, is largely engaged in resolving conflicts among the plural interests of American life as a whole. In addition, the committee system of Congress makes a single response difficult and a plural response the expected thing. Senators and congressmen gain respect and power by concentrating on a few areas. which are the particular spheres of the committees on which they serve. In the early 1950's science policy as such did not have a high priority among the general issues on which all members of Congress have to be informed. Hence the number of full-dress debates on the floor concerning science were few, but there were always specialists who were following the development of parts of the interrelated system closely. Scientists were often confused by this combination of poor understanding of science in the Congress and intimate knowledge of the workings of the system on the part of a few congressmen.

Among the well-informed committees on science matters, the standing committees that had substantive cognizance over the great executive agencies naturally took first place, and of these the Joint Atomic Energy Committee is an outstanding example. It took a detailed interest in the affairs of the Atomic Energy Commission, and some of its members gained a high degree of expertise on the administrative side, and even, in a general way, on the scientific side, of the Commission. The committees of both Houses that had cognizance over the armed services became accustomed to the concepts that underlay the extensive research operations of the Department of Defense. And the committees on commerce and agriculture continued and deepened their historic interest in research.

One of the objectives of the scientific community in its dealings with the government had been, as we have already seen, to get away from short-term authorizations. Science sometimes requires abrupt and unforeseen changes in response to a changed research situation, but it equally requires the long-term support that makes sustained effort possible over periods of time up to several years before decisive results can be shown. Thus the provision of financial support for basic research on a year-by-year basis has often been the bane of science in government programs. In recognition of the need for greater stability, Congress has often appropriated funds for research programs on an open-ended basis — that is, to be available until obligated — so that commitments can be made for research extending over several years.

This practice, together with the practice of authorizing research programs with no definite dollar limitation, gives the appropriations committees a major role in the review of research programs. Some of the legislators most actively interested in scientific programs during the 1950's were members of the appropriations committees.

The mistrust that many rank-and-file members of the scientific community feel toward Congress reached a high pitch in the early 1950's because of the investigations by Senator Joseph R. McCarthy for the Senate Committee on Government Operations. The challenges of the loyalty of scientists, and of their ability to serve the government in sensitive areas, made them fear that the investigatory powers of Congress did not serve the government-science alliance well. Some other hearings of the period did nothing to allay the fears that had been aroused, or to make scientists feel that the investigatory powers of congressional committees were constructive forces.

Yet the pluralism of the government-science scene was so complete in the early 1950's that any channel of coordination might serve the potentially useful purpose of offsetting the sometimes conflicting interests and missions of the several science agencies. In the Congress, the impulse toward coordination would not likely come through the standing substantive committees, linked as they were to individual agencies. The investigatory power, then in the hands of members of Congress outside the senior leadership on the standing substantive committees, was the main hope for an over-all look at the interrelated system and for raising questions about the coordination of its components.

The Committees on Government Operations of the House and Senate might not appear to headline readers as likely instruments to create increased coherence in the interrelated system. Yet even while the Army-McCarthy hearings filled the newspapers, a subcommittee of the House Committee on Government Operations raised many fundamental questions about research and development in the Department of Defense that would never have seen the light of day if the hearings had not been held. Furthermore, most of the leaders of the scientific community gained a chance to put their views before the Congress and the public, which they would otherwise not have had.

The Committee asked fifty leading scientists a series of questions; among them were: "To what extent should the Department of Defense contract with non-governmental institutions to carry on military research and development programs? To what extent should private, nonprofit institutions participate? To what extent should private industry participate? How much in-house research is required for the military services to be capable of exercising qualitative control over research and development conducted by outside laboratories?" As research and development became an ever more prominent area of government activity, and its over-all organization became a cause for apprehension, the Committees on Government Operations became a natural focus for interest in science. If a major disturbing factor were to enter the picture, the Committees on Government Operations could be expected to step up their interest in the over-all organization of research and development.

· · ·

Competition with the Soviet Union was the disturbing factor that put a new series of stresses on the now well-established plural and interrelated system of government-supported university research. Sputnik symbolized the competition and the challenge of the Soviet Union to the whole American people. The National Science Foundation had already discovered that Nicholas DeWitt's book, *Soviet Professional Manpower*, published in 1955, had a marked effect in interesting Congress in support of its program for education in the sciences. But, with Sputnik, millions who had not previously thought about the government's science policy developed a strong feeling that some priorities should at least be re-examined.

CHANGES IN ORGANIZATION BY PRESIDENT AND CONGRESS

The Eisenhower Administration responded promptly with the appointment of Dr. James R. Killian, Jr., president of M.I.T., to the newly created post of Special Assistant to the President for Science and Technology. The President's Science Advisory Committee was reorganized to report directly to the President. Soon thereafter, as a result of the report of the President's Science Advisory Committee, *Strengthening American Science,* the President also set up the Federal Council for Science and Technology.

In the wake of Sputnik, the Congress took a lively and concerned interest in the plural interrelated system. It markedly strengthened the National Science Foundation and passed the National Defense Education Act. To a much greater extent than usual, congressional leaders took the lead in shaping the legislation which created the National Aeronautics and Space Administration and the National Aeronautics and Space Council. It also realigned its committee system by creating two new standing committees — Aeronautical and Space Sciences in the Senate, and Science and Astronautics in the House. The Democratic leadership of the Congress had thus worked with the Eisenhower Administration in creating a whole new set of institutions in both the executive and legislative branches. The senate committee limited itself to "Aeronautical and Space Sciences." But the house committee, by adopting the term "Science and Astronautics," projected a broader role than that of a standing committee for the National Aeronautics and Space Administration.

In the stresses of 1958, with Soviet competition foremost in everyone's mind, with searching questions being asked about the whole range of American education, with the Congress and the Executive controlled by different parties, it would have been surprising if members of Congress outside the regular committees had not given close attention to the workings of the interrelated system. It would also have been surprising if the Committees on Government Operations had not come strongly to the fore with questions about over-all coordination. A subcommittee of the Senate Committee on Government Operations held hearings on a whole series of bills to create a Department of Science and Technology and a cabinet post of Secretary of Science and Technology. At the same time, the subcommittee and its staff became particularly interested in the coordination of scientific information. Their efforts helped in the creation of the Office of Science Information Services in the National Science Foundation through a provision in the National Defense Education Act of 1958. But their interest did not stop there. A series of reports on science information has continued to emanate from the subcommittee, a clear example of how sustained congressional interest can provide long-term stimulation to a matter of science policy.

Congressional interest in a Department of Science and Technology was given a particularly sharp edge because the coordinating structure, erected by the Eisenhower Administration around the Special Assistant for Science and Technology, was located within the White House, and thus was not available for questioning by congressional committees. A senator complained that when

a legislative subcommittee has to dig around and do its own investigation and sleuthing, that is when the trouble starts. That is when the half-truths come out. That is when you get the misrepresentation that takes place. . . . It seems to me somewhere, somehow, there ought to be the openness, the frankness of contact and of communication that the present situation requires, because the scientific program of this Government is no better than the knowledge of Congress about it, because we can either make it or break it either through our lack of knowledge or of enlightenment on the problems involved.

Although a consensus for a Department of Science and Technology never developed, either within the Congress or within the scientific community, the interest stirred up by the subcommittee had the great merit of indicating the need for coordination both in the Executive and in Congress, and of pointing up the necessity for good communication between the two branches. The proposal for a commission to study the creation of a department of science stemmed from these hearings and has passed the Senate regularly since then.

Another subcommittee of the Senate Committee on Government Operations also entered the post-Sputnik arena of science policy coordination through an investigation of national security machinery. This subcommittee sought the opinions of many members of the scientific community and included a section on science policy in its final recommendations, which appeared in the first days of the Kennedy administration. The subcommittee saw the virtues of the science policy machinery set up within the White House, but urged the President to use his reorganization powers to move the structure out of the White House and into the Executive Office of the President, thereby allowing the Special Assistant for Science and Technology to appear before congressional committees. The step recommended by the subcommittee was taken by President Kennedy in Reorganization Plan No. 2 of June 1962. With this change, the movement for a separate department of science has lost momentum.

Thus the Congress gained a regular channel of communication to the fourfold structure within the Executive which was concerned with over-all science policy. The President's Special Assistant for Science and Technology now serves as an adviser to the Chief Executive. As chairman of the President's Science Advisory Committee, he presides over a group of scientists from private institutions who provide the Executive with advice from the scientific community. As chairman of the Federal Council for Science and Technology, he presides over a group of high-level representatives from government agencies with major research and development programs. And finally, as director of the Office of Science and Technology in the Executive Office of the President, the Special Assistant is available to give information to congressional committees that seek it. Staff work organized through the Office of Science and Technology helps the Special Assistant to coordinate his several roles in the service of the President.

On the House side, the Committee on Government Operations also responded to the post-Sputnik stimulus. As the Senate groups had done, it took a stance outside the regular committees that dealt routinely with the interrelated systems. The Subcommittee on Intergovernmental Relations took a rather different tack from that of its Senate counterpart, but at its base was the same concern for an over-all congressional view of research and development. The House subcommittee chose the rapidly expanding health research area for a detailed examination of granting procedures. In 1961, after two years of investigation, it issued a report dealing with the major features of the linkage between the government and universities supplied by the National Institutes of Health. It reviewed the administration of grants and training programs and the always thorny problem of indirect costs. . . .

In the post-Sputnik era, the alliance between the government and the universities had to acquire new dimensions, yet the basic relationship could not be forgotten in the urgent attempt to meet immediate national needs. Science was now a yardstick of Soviet-American competition, but the historic urge of the scientific community to preserve the conditions necessary for its creativity could not cease.

◄ *B.* Toward a Science Policy in the United States. *Report of the Subcommittee on Science, Research, and Development to the Committee on Science and Astronautics, U.S. House of Representatives, 91st Cong., 2 sess., October 15, 1970, pp. 90–91, 108–112.*]

POST-SPUTNIK TO THE PRESENT

The decade following Sputnik stands out in recent history as a "season of plenty" for existing, glamorous ventures in science and technology. Federal expenditures for research and development increased during most of this period at a rate of approximately 15 percent annually, and scientists expected this trend to continue indefinitely. There was little thought that in nature nothing can increase indefinitely without limit. Science took its place in the White House for the first time on a continuous and organized basis. Science too became a specific concern for the Congress. The existing array of subcommittees to the Appropriations Committees and existing substantive committees was augmented by special new, science-oriented committees. Federal aid to education, including education of future scientists, became an overt and accepted concept. Military and space activities claimed the largest part of the Federal funds for research and development, with health and atomic energy research also well provided for. Basic research spending, while it accounted for only about one-tenth of the total, became a vital form of Federal financial aid to academic institutions. So desirable was Federal support of scientific research in academe that Federal moneys went without public challenge to private institutions, including church-affiliated institutions.

Although science and technology received a great deal of Federal attention during this decade as it had also in the previous one, there was less urgency for a science and technology policy

41

which would fit the components into an established pattern. In fact, there was even support for continuation of an unstructured, even unwritten policy for science. Dr. DuBridge made this point at the science policy hearings:

When research and development were growing at such a rapid rate, and extending into so many fields of science and technology, and when there was strong public support for this rapid growth, the need for a Federal policy governing Federal research and development did not seem urgent. As a matter of fact, there was some fear that the adoption of a specific policy statement might be more restrictive than encouraging to federal R&D activities. Such policy as existed, mostly in unwritten form, encouraged each agency of the Government to pursue and support such R&D activities as it deemed necessary and desirable, applying such a fraction of its overall budgetary allocations to R&D as the agency deemed to be a good investment.

Federal funding for research and development peaked at a little over $17 billion in fiscal 1968 and has declined to an estimated $15.7 billion for fiscal 1971. Although combined Federal and private spending for R&D activity in the United States has continued to increase, since then, even this increase has not kept pace with the rate of inflation, and therefore in terms of level of effort supportable with depreciating dollars, the funding in essence has been reduced.

A final note: In the literature of public administration, it is common to observe the progressive change in a public policy as it proceeds "full circle" from an initial position through many changes until it returns to where it essentially stood at the outset. The period 1957–1967 represents exactly one-half such a circle. It began with an intensive inquiry in Congress as to why the Department of Defense was not doing more to support research and development, and ended with congressional inquiry into why the Department of Defense was spending so much for research and development. . . .

EMERGENCE OF NEW NATIONAL PROBLEMS

The momentum which rocketed Federal support for research and development activities to ever-increasing heights after the space race began in 1957 could not continue indefinitely. Nor could the national economy support a continued outlay for R&D at the 15 percent annual rate of increase, which characterized

Federal funding for science and technology for several years after 1957.

By the middle 1960's several new national problems had begun to compete for a larger share of the Government's attention and resources. Chief among these new factors were the emergence of major national problems with a strong social content relating to the environment and urban needs such as improved transportation, housing, and education, and also the military demands arising out of the U.S. involvement in Vietnam. In competition with these demands upon public resources, financial support of academic science and for the training of future scientific manpower became lower in priority.

The realization that the technological applications of science could have undesirable consequences was forcibly brought home to the Nation as Federal action became increasingly necessary to deal with the pollution of the air, water, and soil. During the 89th Congress alone — 1965 and 1966 — legislation was enacted to:

Increase research into the effects of pesticides; establish a national policy for the prevention, control, and abatement of water pollution; establish a Federal Water Pollution Control Administration; make grants to assist in waste treatment demonstration projects; amend the Clean Air Act of 1963 to accelerate research on techniques to reduce air pollution from motor vehicles, and provide for Federal grants to assist in control programs; and encourage the development and application of new methods of solid waste disposal.

During these two years the issues posed by the deteriorating environment were considered by many science advisory groups including the President's Science Advisory Committee, the National Commission on Technology, Automation, and Economic Progress, a Committee on Pollution of the National Academy of Sciences-National Research Council, and the Research Management Advisory Panel to the House Committee on Science and Astronautics.

The 1966 hearings and subsequent report of the Subcommittee on Science, Research, and Development on the adequacy of technology for pollution abatement performed a useful service in defining what could and could not be achieved by applying science and technology to the abatement of pollution.

Other aspects of the environment which received attention of scientific advisers were weather and climate modification,

43

handling of toxicological information, water pollution from boats and ships, and lake pollution.

In addition to problems of the environment, other problems relating to unanticipated side effects of drugs and food additives demanded Federal attention.

During the 1960's also, public pressure to resolve urban and social needs was accelerated, resulting in an increase of attention and funding for improved housing, transportation, and educational opportunities. The Office of Education programs for the disadvantaged expanded greatly. Two new executive departments were established: a Department of Housing and Urban Development in 1965 and a Department of Transportation in 1966.

The emergence of urban and social problems has given rise to a need for increased research in the social sciences. Because many of these modern problems have mixed social, life, and physical aspects, the late 1960's have seen special interest in combining inputs from these sciences and engineering in an interdisciplinary and multidisciplinary approach to research. The compartmentalization of science has to be overcome by the application of the integrated research in order to deal with these perplexing problems. While these new agencies clearly must depend upon continuing advancements in science and technology, their funding of research and development has not expanded rapidly. Consequently some may argue that the research focused on these problems has not been commensurate with the needs.

REASSESSMENT OF THE RESEARCH ROLE OF THE
DEPARTMENT OF DEFENSE

Even as domestic needs clamored for attention, the escalation of U.S. involvement in the Vietnam conflict began to involve large numbers of American men with the related costs of their military operations in addition to the large sums of military and foreign assistance that had already been committed. It became necessary to request ever-increasing funds for the Department of Defense, and with it increased funds for research and development. When it became necessary to seek additional revenues through higher income taxes, in part to finance these higher defense costs, a serious effort began to reduce the Defense budget, including its research and development. However, this cost-cutting effort must be regarded as only a final action in a series of instances in which the blank check that had been given to the military during the post-World War II period came under question.

One instance of an attempt to bring military spending under closer congressional control was the legislation enacted in 1962, which required that from calendar year 1963 onward the research, development, test, and evaluation portion of the Defense budget must be annually authorized. This provided an opportunity to Congress for a more extended examination of DOD planning for research and development than had been possible before.

In 1964, the Department of Defense at hearings concerning geographical distribution of R&D funds defended its practice of awarding grants and contracts for research according to the most competent investigators and proposals wherever it could expect the best results without considering geographical distribution of this work.

The Defense Department came under attack in 1965 because a social science research project it had been supporting abroad, designated Project Camelot, embarrassed U.S. relations with the host country, Chile, and conflicted with the State Department in its conduct of foreign relations. In consequence, President Johnson required State Department clearance of future projects when he requested the Secretary of State "to establish effective procedures which will enable you to assure the propriety of Government-sponsored social science research in the areas of foreign policy." Since that time there has been a concerted effort to reduce defense spending for international social science research, which is more properly regarded as a responsibility of the State Department.

Unpopularity of the U.S. commitment in Vietnam was reflected in an increase of unrest among students. This dissatisfaction was expressed in pressures on universities to discontinue classified defense research. As a result, many institutions decided not to perform this type of research. A further consequence was the legal separation from the universities proper of some Defense-financed laboratories where military research was being conducted.

Still another area of concern which came under attack was chemical and biological warfare research, which critics charged was endangering unnecessarily the health of our allies as well as the American people. This led to a requirement for an annual reporting on CBW operations.

The most recent attack upon the Department of Defense research has centered around the issue of "relevance" of the basic research it funds to DOD needs. The relevance concept was enunciated in President Eisenhower's Executive order of March 15, 1954, on the administration of research, which marked out an increasing role for NSF in the funding of research while sanctioning the continued support of basic research "in areas which are closely related to their missions" by other Federal agencies. Relevance was also mentioned in Public Law 85–934 of September 6, 1958, which conferred authority upon departments and agencies to make grants for basic research.

So the idea is not new. The difficulty of applying a test of relevance, of course, lies in the subjective nature of any attempt to define relevance of basic research that deals with the future to immediate problems.

The test of relevance was given new emphasis in 1969 by Senator Mike Mansfield in his initiative to realign the Federal support of basic scientific research and to reduce the dependence of such research upon military appropriations. In a statement submitted for the record of the science policy hearings, Senator Mansfield reviewed the rationale for his actions.

In essence, the basic question concerned the relationship of the Department of Defense and other mission agencies to the conduct of basic research. Since the end of World War II, the Department of Defense has funded well over half of the Federal research and development effort. During this time the Department has funded research "in almost every scientific discipline imaginable." It was able to do this because it was able to get the money and because security considerations and the threat of communism provided a convenient cloak that hampered close scrutiny. Part of the reason for expansion of defense interests so far afield, the Senator maintained, was due to the lack of adequate interagency information systems concerning ongoing or past research effort.

The Department of Defense's continued insistence that all fields of science and technology and all research projects it sponsored were somehow relevant to Defense needs was cited by Senator Mansfield as responsible for his introduction of a rider to the military authorization bill (Public Law 91–121) for fiscal year 1970 as follows: "None of the funds authorized to be appropriated by this Act may be used to carry out any research project or study unless such a project or study has a direct or apparent relationship to a specific military function or operation."

This provision caused the Department of Defense to review 6,600 research projects being funded and resulted in a determination that projects totaling about $8.8 million or 4 percent of the $223 million obligated by the Department during fiscal 1970 could not meet the relevancy test. At the same time, general tightening of the Defense research budget was responsible for an additional $64 million reduction, or almost eight times as much.

The passage of section 203 resulted in an increased competition for funds. To meet this need, the 1971 NSF budget contained an increase of $10 million for project funding, primarily to cover projects formerly funded by other agencies.

Opponents of the concept of section 203 point out that while it relates primarily to the Department of Defense, in times of tight budgets, it can be seized on by other agencies as a justification for cutting their own basic research effort. The continued role of mission agencies in the support of basic research in the light of section 203 was assessed by the Committee's Research Management Advisory Panel early in 1970. In its report to the subcommittee, the Panel recommended the reaffirmation by Congress of the "historic national policy that the mission agencies fund their proportionate share of basic research."

The text of section 203 did not appear in the military authorization bill for fiscal 1971 (H.R. 17123) as passed by the House. However, it was later incorporated into the bill as section 204 and unanimously approved by the Senate. In conference, the wording of the section was modified to read: "None of the funds authorized to be appropriated to the Department of Defense by this or any other act may be used to finance any research project or study unless such project or study has, in the opinion of the Secretary of Defense, a potential relationship to a military function or operation."

Also approved in conference was a new section 205 expressing the sense of Congress that "(1) an increase in Government support of basic scientific research is necessary to preserve and strengthen the sound technological base essential both to protection of the national security and the solution of unmet domestic needs; and (2) a larger share of such support should be provided hereafter through the National Science Foundation."

Both amendments were subsequently approved in both the

47

House and the Senate, and the legislation was signed on October 7, 1970 (PL 91-441).

OTHER RECENT DEVELOPMENTS

The reader's attention is called to certain recent developments that have not received adequate treatment in this historical presentation. Among these are the renewal of interest in greater centralization of Federal science activities, the increasing desire to assure the optimum utilization of Federal laboratories, and a growing awareness of the necessity for developing some way to assess in advance the probable consequences of major technological changes. All these problems have been the subjects of intensive investigation by the Subcommittee on Science, Research, and Development.

PART TWO

PREPAREDNESS AND WAR

From its very inception, the federal government had called upon science to aid in the discharge of its growing number of responsibilities. By the 1930s, scientists were serving in scores of executive bureaus representing a wide spectrum of disciplines from plant pathology to nuclear physics. When faced with its ultimate responsibility, however, that of defending its very existence, the government realized that its own scientific establishment was wholly inadequate to support a war effort of unprecedented dimensions.

Most of the nation's scientific research, of course, was being carried on outside of government laboratories: in educational institutions, private foundations, and industrial laboratories. The clear need was for some mechanism by which the government could coordinate and draw upon the total research capacity of the country, and bring it to bear upon the problems of defense.

The First World War had left a tripart legacy to those who saw and attempted to meet this need: a precedent for putting scientists into uniforms and bringing them to work in Washington; the existence of the National Research Council, created as an arm of the National Academy of Sciences in 1916; and a cadre of scientist-administrators who had come to the fore during the first war and had maintained leadership in the two decades since. For various reasons and to varying degrees, all three of these paths were bypassed in the drive for preparedness. To a remarkable extent, history was allowed to instruct rather than obstruct the future.

I. American Science in a World at War

❦ A. *At dawn on September 1, 1939, Nazi troops began their invasion of Poland, and two days later the United Kingdom and France declared war on Germany. After long winter months of "sitzkrieg" and "phoney war," Germany's dive bombers and Panzer divisions struck to the west in the spring of 1940. Nazi troops entered Paris on June 14, and in July the Battle of Britain began. It was a different kind of war than that of two decades before. Instead of a stable battlefield, marked by trenches and a narrow no man's land, tanks raced across whole countries in a matter of days and bombers brought carnage to the civilian populations of cities.*

Vannevar Bush watched the progress of war with growing apprehension. Late the Vice President of the Massachusetts Institute of Technology, he had moved to Washington in 1939 to become president of the Carnegie Institution of Washington. Both his institutional connection and his geographic location in the nation's capital gave him a vantage point from which to follow events and to gauge their impact on both international science and the safety of America. In his annual reports to the Institution, he grappled with the problems of science in a world at war, and those of the nation facing a war of science. "Report of the President," Carnegie Institution of Washington Year Book No. 38, July 1, 1938 – June 30, 1939 *(Washington: CIW, 1939), 5-7; also No. 39, July 1, 1939 – June 30, 1940, 4-5; and No. 40, July 1, 1940 – June 30, 1941, 3-5.]*

[1939] Much of the world is at war. We are fortunately able to stand aside, but no evaluation of the condition and program of an institution can be completely divorced from the stress of the times in which it operates. Even in these fortunate United States all plans are thus conditioned, and every individual is thus affected.

The scientist in particular is faced with a quandary. The same science which saves life and renders it rich and full, also destroys it and renders it horrible. Is it then possible to remain in a detached atmosphere, to cultivate the slowly growing body of pure scientific knowledge, and to labor apart from the intense struggle in which the direct application of science now implies so much for good or ill?. . .

The quandary may be immediate and direct. Science and its applications have produced the aircraft and the bomb. Entirely apart from all questions of national sympathies, from all opinion concerning political ideologies, we fear to witness the destruction of the treasures of civilization and the agony of peoples, by reason of this new weapon. As science has produced a weapon, so also can it produce in time a defense against it. Science is dedicated to the advance of knowledge for the benefit of man. Here is a sphere where the benefit might perhaps indeed be immediate, real and satisfying. Can a scientist, skilled in a field such that his efforts might readily be directed to the attainment of applications which would afford protection to his fellow men against such an overwhelming peril, now justify expending his effort for any other and more remote cause?

Every individual scientist must of course render his own answer. Only a very small percentage are in such fields that their efforts could in any case be suddenly altered so as to become immediately effective, and these only are directly faced with the problem. Even for most of these the opportunity will be rare. . . .

[1940] For the scientist whose talents apply directly to the means by which a nation defends itself, the way is glaringly clear. He needs to remember that there are many who labor on the unspectacular for every one who manipulates the vital controls, and that the inevitable confusion which accompanies a change in the whole mode of life of a nation necessarily wastes fine capabilities on minor things. He should realize that anonymity and isolation replace the public appreciation and the open scientific fellowship to which he is accustomed. He may well regret deeply that his efforts, so long devoted to an altruistic ideal embracing the whole of mankind, become limited for a time to a narrower national aim. But he shares in that primal joy that comes from intense group effort in defense of his home, sublimated it is true, but just as real as though he stood at the mouth of a cave with a few strong men of the clan armed with stone axes against a hostile world.

[1941]   Events of the past two years have profoundly altered the plans and outlook of every scientific institution in
the world, and of the great majority of individual scientists.
The Carnegie Institution of Washington is so constituted that
it is bound to be deeply involved in that aspect of the present
intense national effort which is concerned with the application
of the natural sciences to national defense, and it is necessary
and fitting that the Institution should respond fully to the call
of government in this regard. Inevitably, therefore, many of its
long-range programs of research in the field of pure science
have now been changed or held in abeyance. . . .

In previous reports, during this period of stress, it has
been emphasized that the Institution has a duty in addition to
that of participation in defense. Fundamental scientific research is almost completely stopped all over the world, except
in this hemisphere. The inspiration passed from master to
disciple, and the subtle evolution of great ideas when powerful minds collaborate, or compete, are part and parcel of the
rapid progress of modern science. This implies continuity of
effort. If the thread is broken it may be long before it can be
mended. With science and scientists in other lands completely
distracted by immediate requirements, an organization such
as ours has a responsibility for preserving some of the more
important threads intact. This duty has not been forgotten,
although its fulfillment becomes increasingly difficult. . . .

In accordance with authorization from the Trustees, the
services of staff members and the use of laboratory facilities of
the Institution have been made available to the government.
In some cases staff members have been given leave of absence
in order to enter the rolls of governmental organizations; in
others, their services have been made available while they
remained on salary with the Institution, working either in our
own or in governmental laboratories. . . .

This type of work is now being done in scientific laboratories all over the country; it was concentrated at first, of
necessity, in some of the larger institutions, but gradually it is
reaching out to others. The whole program is being enlarged
to meet increased needs, especially in the field of medical
research.

❡ B.   *Other scientists about the country were also concerned with the role of technical men in the nation's pre-*

paredness program. Those old enough to have been active during the First World War drew upon that experience for precedents to follow and pitfalls to be avoided. University scientists were the most insulated from governmental activities, and the nature and extent of their integration into the defense machinery was one of the knottiest problems facing those who were seeking to mobilize science. Joel H. Hildebrand, an outstanding chemist at the University of California, was one who thought early and deeply about this problem. Hildebrand to Vannevar Bush, July 25, 1940, Records of the Office of Scientific Research and Development, Office File of V. Bush, National Archives, Washington, D.C.]

My experiences during the World War in the Chemical Warfare Service, beginning in Washington and extending to directorship of the laboratory in France and later the command of the experimental field and A.E.F. [American Expeditionary Force] gas defense school, having given me some familiarity with the problem of coordinating scientific effort with military problems, I naturally feel more concerned over the present situation than a good many of my university colleagues. This led me to assemble an unofficial group recently, composed of men who have had some similar experiences or have been in touch with government activities. The group included such men as Alsberg, G. N. Lewis, B. M. Woods, and H. B. Walker. I would have had Ernest Lawrence if he had been in Berkeley at the time. I have since discussed these matters with him. We had a very interesting conference and reached agreement upon certain matters which I transmitted to President Sproul. I believe that some of these conclusions will be of interest to you in view of your present responsibilities:

(1) We should encourage members of the faculty in general to stay on the job rather than to rush impulsively into some governmental or other outside activity. We believe that in general the experts within the University can be more effective in the university environment with its extensive facilities for investigation. Several of us were in a position during the late war to see how slowly one can get started in the usually hectic atmosphere of an expanding government activity. We believe that the task ahead should be regarded not merely as a temporary emergency but one which will make

demands upon the university for years to come. It is essential, therefore, that the University should not be weakened. We are already feeling the pull particularly through the offering of higher salaries to junior engineering instructors.

(2) The University and its staff should not undertake work on a level below those of its normal activities that can be performed by other agencies. In this category would come the training of mechanics, accountants or other groups representing a vocational rather than a professional level. We may, however, supply the organizing ability or special knowledge necessary to assist in inaugurating such programs elsewhere. The Extension Division may continue to serve a useful purpose in organizing such activities as it has the program for training pilots.

(3) The University should endeavor to serve as an agency for the government in selecting experts. This institution, with the extensive knowledge it possesses of professional qualifications not only of its staff but of its graduates, will usually be in a far better position to discover experts for certain tasks than a government bureau. This we regard as most important and believe that it should become a national policy. The National Research Council is probably in the best position to secure the adoption of this policy on the part of both the government and other universities.

(4) It is important to maintain the efficiency of such portions of our plant as are likely to be called upon for special services. This applies particularly to the engineering and scientific laboratories.

(5) The University should anticipate the possible necessity of increasing the number of students being trained in certain fields important in national defense. This may apply to medicine, nursing, engineering, chemistry, to mention several.

(6) The University should be prepared to simplify and speed up the education process. There is no reason why able students should not be allowed to complete their education in less than four years.

I should like to add, further, my conviction that we should not depend solely upon officers in the regular army and navy to discover the problems. The education of these men has not served to develop in them much scientific imagination and the problems they discover are not always the most fruitful for investigation. They are too likely to think of the next war in terms of the last. I believe it to be highly important, therefore, that scientific men should be brought into direct contact with those likely to direct military and naval operations in order that they may be in a better position to suggest more radical changes than the military men themselves would be likely to think of. If scientific workers are too far removed from field operations there is a double disadvantage that the problems submitted to them will be comparatively trivial and that the solutions they present will be evolved in comparative ignorance of battle conditions.

As an example of the latter, the C.W.S. workers in Washington constructed a field gas testing laboratory put up like a suitcase. This would do the work all right but nobody would carry it into battle any more than he would carry a canary bird in a cage.

Again, an engineer constructed a flame thrower operated by steam pressure on the design of a giant blow torch. He and his equipment were sent to France at great expense and the work of my post was interrrupted for several days while we prepared to demonstrate it to General Pershing. The impracticality of the apparatus would have been apparent at a much earlier stage to one whose experience enabled him to imagine battle conditions.

We undoubtedly face the future much better off than we were in 1917 to coordinate scientific and military activities. I have no doubt that you are already aware of much of the foregoing. I take the liberty of writing only because some of these points may deserve more emphasis than they have yet received.

II. The New Agencies

⟨ A. *Already well-informed about the scientific activities of universities, industry, and the philanthropic foundations, Vannevar Bush, in 1938, was appointed to the National Advisory Committee for Aeronautics, and soon became chairman of that body. In this new position he was able to observe and evaluate the scientific preparations of the government for war. It soon became apparent to him that the military had little clear idea of what science could provide, and that scientists were equally ignorant of what the military needed. After discussions with friends highly placed in the various sectors of civilian and government science, the nature of the problem and possible solutions were thrashed out. By the late spring of 1940, a small group of the country's most influential scientists, including Bush, had decided what they wanted and how to get it. The following undated, unsigned memoranda are in the Records of the OSRD, Central Classified File (Organization), National Archives.]*

The creation and improvement of military devices involves three stages: fundamental research, engineering development, and production. This memorandum deals with the first stage.

The National Advisory Committee for Aeronautics carries on important fundamental research, and correlates military and civil research activites, on aeronautical devices. No similar agency exists for other important fields, notably antiaircraft devices. The NACA is composed largely of men of aeronautical background, and should not attempt to expand its field.

The National Academy of Sciences assembles groups of distinguished scientists and engineers to advise government on specific scientific problems. This valuable activity was greatly expanded during the last war, is now increasing, and can again be expanded to similar advantage.

There appears to be a distinct need for a body to correlate

governmental and civil fundamental research in fields of military importance outside of aeronautics. It should form a definite link between the military services and the National Academy. It should lean on the latter for broad scientific advice and guidance. It could supplement, and not replace, activities of the military services themselves, and it should exist primarily to aid these services and hence aid in national defense. In its organization it should closely parallel, the form which has been successfully employed in the National Advisory Committee for Aeronautics. It should perform a very valuable function indeed in stimulating, extending, and correlating fundamental research which is basic to modern warfare.

It should not be created unless it would be welcomed, and hence supported by the three bodies primarily concerned, the War and Navy Departments, and the National Academy of Sciences. If it has their support, it will also be able to enlist the support of scientific and educational institutions and organizations, and of individual scientists and engineers, throughout the country.

[*Draft of Executive Order appended to the above memorandum.*] A National Defense Research Committee is hereby established and the President is authorized to appoint not to exceed twelve members, to consist of two members from the War Department, two members from the Navy Department, two members from the National Academy of Sciences, one member from the National Bureau of Standards, and five additional persons who shall be men eminent in science or in its application: PROVIDED, That the members of the National Defense Research Committee shall serve as such without compensation: PROVIDED FURTHER, That it shall be the duty of the National Defense Research Committee to coordinate, supervise, and conduct scientific research on the problems underlying the development, production, and use of mechanisms and devices of warfare, except scientific research on the problems of flight. The Committee is authorized to construct and operate research laboratories, and to make contracts for research, studies, and reports with educational and scientific institutions, with individuals, and with industrial and other organizations for scientific studies and reports in its field, and is authorized to conduct research and experiment in such laboratories as may be placed under its direction: AND

PROVIDED FURTHER, That rules and regulations for the conduct of the work of the Committee shall be formulated by the Committee and approved by the President.

Appropriations of such sums as may be necessary are authorized: PROVIDED, That an annual report to the Congress shall be submitted through the President.

❡ *B. The NDRC, which was established by Executive Order on June 27, 1940, gave official recognition and power to the informal group which had grown up around Vannevar Bush. In essence, the scientific members of the Committee were ambassadors from the four estates of American science: industry, universities, foundations, and from the government. The backgrounds of these members were neither fortuitous nor unimportant, for the success of the NDRC was dependent upon the extent to which it could establish effective liaison between available men, existing institutions, and urgent problems.* Irvin Stewart, Organizing Scientific Research for War: The Administrative History of the Office of Scientific Research and Development *(Boston: Little, Brown and Co., 1948), 4-9, 16-17, 35, 49-51.*]

... It was apparent to a few key scientists in the spring of 1940 that the United States was in imminent danger of being forced into a war for which the country was pathetically unprepared from the standpoint of new weapons. While others may have had the same feeling, four in particular discussed the matter among themselves and took steps to enlist the support of President Roosevelt to improve the situation. They were Vannevar Bush, President of the Carnegie Institution of Washington; Karl T. Compton, President of the Massachusetts Institute of Technology; James B. Conant, President of Harvard University, and Frank B. Jewett, President of the National Academy of Sciences and of the Bell Telephone Laboratories. Of this group, Bush was the one who carried the major part of the responsibility of impressing the need for action upon President Roosevelt and his advisers and of persuading the heads of the military forces of the need for a more effective mobilization of science for a program of improvement of weapons of warfare. . . .

Useful though the Academy had been in the Civil War and the Research Council in World War I, the situation in the spring of 1940 appeared to demand a new approach. The number of men in the armed services capable of knowing what was needed was small. They, with all other officers, would obviously be swamped with the gigantic task of building an army and navy of the size which would be needed if the United States were to be adequately prepared....

...What was needed was an organization which could make its own assessment of what the armed services needed and which could then, preferably with the assistance of the Services but over their opposition if necessary, go about the business of getting the necessary weapons developed... It was this conception which Bush and his colleagues sold to President Roosevelt and to which General Marshall and Admiral Stark gave their blessing prior to the issuance of the order of the Council of National Defense, which on June 27, 1940, established the National Defense Research Committee of the Council of National Defense....

One of the most significant facts about this group was the sense of urgency with which it was imbued; the need for speed in developing new and improved weapons was the central core of all its operations. The fact that the civilian members were well known to each other, both personally and professionally, made it easy for them to work together effectively with a minimum loss of time.

The Committee was directed to correlate and support scientific research on the mechanisms and devices of warfare, except those relating to problems of flight included in the field of activities of the National Advisory Committee for Aeronautics. It was directed to aid and supplement the experimental and research activities of the War and Navy Departments; and it was authorized to "conduct research for the creation and improvement of instrumentalities, methods and materials of warfare." The Committee was authorized in carrying out its functions to utilize, to the extent that such facilities were available for the purpose, the laboratories, equipment and services of the National Bureau of Standards and other Government institutions. Within the limits of appropriations allocated to it, it was authorized to transfer funds to such institutions and to enter into contracts with individuals, educational or scientific institutions (including the National Academy of Sciences and the National Research Council), and industrial organizations for studies, experimental investigations, and reports...

One field later to attract a great deal of public interest was specifically mentioned in the President's letter [appointing Bush as Chairman of NDRC]. A committee headed by Dr. Lyman J. Briggs, Director of the National Bureau of Standards, which had earlier been appointed to "study into the possible relationship to national defense of recent discoveries in the field of atomistics, notably the fission of uranium" was instructed to report to Bush inasmuch as the NDRC might consider it advisable to support special studies on this subject. . . .

With the scope of the Committee's activities outlined in general terms in the order creating it, borderline situations were inevitable. One spectacular problem upon which national attention was being focussed was that of the shortage of natural rubber and the need for large-scale production of synthetic rubber. Should rubber be considered a material of war to which the Committee should give attention?

The NDRC decided to place a strict interpretation upon the scope of its authorized activities. This interpretation was formalized by a resolution adopted at the fifth meeting of the Committee on November 29, 1940. The resolution read as follows:

RESOLVED, that the National Defense Research Committee by reason of the order of the Council of National Defense which established it, is concerned with scientific research on and development of new instrumentalities or materials of war, or of new materials or methods to be used primarily in the manufacture of instruments of war; and of the improvement of existing instrumentalities or materials of war, or of existing material or methods to be used primarily in the manufacture of instruments of war. Where a material or method is widely used or useful in industry, in addition to its use in the manufacture of instruments of war, as for example in the case of substitute materials of wide utility, the research and development involved do not lie within the province of the National Defense Research Committee, but rather within the province of many existing industrial and scientific research agencies, and in particular, when appropriate requests for investigation or research in such fields are made by government agencies, within the province of the National Academy of Sciences and the National Research Council. . . .

The initial decision limiting the scope of NDRC activities is believed to have been sound. In a period of total war it becomes difficult to say what part of the economy is not related to national defense. It would have been easy for the NDRC to have construed its charter as opening a much wider field of activities. In view of the liberality with which funds were appropriated during the war years, it is quite probable that the Committee would have been able to obtain funds to support a broader program. In practice, the limiting factor upon the Committee was always that of manpower. Widening the scope of the Committee's activities would not have added to the number of men available to work on the program. It would have resulted in a dilution of effort which might have obtained significant results in other areas, but in all probability only at the expense of work bearing more immediately on weapons. By deliberately confining its efforts to a relatively narrow field, the Committee was able to concentrate manpower in those areas which seemed most likely to be productive of the best results. It may be charged that by refusing to enter certain lines of activity, the Committee was responsible for delay in obtaining answers to other important problems confronting the nation. The easy answer to such a charge would be to point to what the Committee did with the available manpower and inquire whether the diversion of that manpower to the other problems would have been in the over-all national interest. The members of the Committee never had any doubt as to the accuracy of the original decision to limit the scope of NDRC activities. . . .

While NDRC was doing an excellent job in its field, big gaps remained in the program of preparation for the scientific aspects of modern war. A step toward closing those gaps was taken with the issuance of Executive Order No. 8807 of June 28, 1941, which established the Office of Scientific Research and Development. Bush was a leader in urging the issuance of the order, the need for which had become apparent on at least three counts.

In the first place, the program of the National Defense Research Committee was one designed to stress research on instruments of warfare. Between the completion of research and the initiation of a procurement program there was a substantial gap which the armed services were slow to fill. It was becoming increasingly apparent that for the research sponsored by NDRC to become most effective, it was essential that the research group carry its projects through the intermediate phase represented by engineering development. It is significant that while the original NDRC carried only research in its title, the new office covered both research and development.

In the second place, there was but little machinery for the correlation of research carried on by NDRC with that carried directly by the Services or by the National Advisory Committee for Aeronautics. The Advisory Council provided for in the order creating the OSRD helped fill a need by providing a place where men conversant with the research programs of the Army, Navy, NDRC and NACA might discuss their various programs and their relation to each other.

In the third place, no satisfactory provision had been made for the stimulation of research in the field of military medicine. The need for such research had been apparent for some time but it had been impossible to get agreement on a program satisfactory to the various groups involved. The success of NDRC in the field of weapons suggested to President Roosevelt the desirability of a comparable committee in military medicine, and led to the creation of OSRD with parallel committees on weapons [NDRC] and medicine [Committee on Medical Research]. . . .

The effectiveness of the Office of Scientific Research and Development was materially strengthened by other activities of its Director [Bush]. In addition to a number of temporary assignments during the period of OSRD operations, he had four wartime assignments and one postwar one which bore directly upon the work of the OSRD. Prior to the creation of the National Defense Research Committee, Bush had been Chairman of the National Advisory Committee for Aeronautics, and he continued as a member of that body. In consequence he was well acquainted with its personnel, scope of activities and methods of procedure. The contacts which he had made with the military departments as a member of NACA for some years prior to the establishment of NDRC stood him in good stead in his new position. Furthermore, his knowledge of the NACA program and operations aided the NDRC in avoiding conflicts of jurisdiction with the NACA. . . .

Bush's chairmanship of [The Joint Committee on New Weapons and Equipment of the Joint Chiefs of Staff (JNW)]. . . meant that the scientific point of view could be introduced fairly close to the top levels of military strategy. JNW was an appropriate supplement to the activities of OSRD, making it possible during the war to get strategic consideration of OSRD-developed equipment in a way which otherwise might have been impossible.

The third principal assignment of the Director of OSRD during the war was that of scientific adviser to the Manhattan District. The uranium program was put under the NDRC at the time of the Committee's creation in June 1940. When OSRD was established, the subject was left with NDRC for a while and then transferred to a group outside NDRC reporting to the Director of OSRD. When the results of research under OSRD auspices had shown the possibility of the production of an atomic bomb and had indicated to some degree the magnitude of operations which would be necessary to produce the bomb, the project was transferred from OSRD to the newly created Manhattan District of the Corps of Engineers of the Army. Bush, Conant and Tolman were extremely active as advisers to the Manhattan District from the time of its origin. Bush served as a member of the Scientific Advisory Committee to Major General Leslie R. Groves, the Director of the Manhattan District, and also as a member of the Military Policy Committee of the Manhattan project.

The fourth of the principal assignments was a series of four questions asked Bush by President Roosevelt in a letter of November 17, 1944, with a view to securing for times of peace the benefit of the experience gained by OSRD in its operations for war. . . .

In addition to these specific assignments, Bush acted as an informal scientific adviser to President Roosevelt. He had access to the President and operated at all times with the assurance of the President's support. . . .

It was the genius of OSRD that Bush left it flexible, moulding the organization to meet the requirements of the situation and the personalities with whom he had to deal rather than attempting to shape the program to fit the organization. . . . The objective was to get the best results in the hands of the troops at the earliest possible moment. The means employed were those which in the light of the surrounding circumstances seemed best calculated to achieve this objective.

❧ *C. The OSRD was the most important, but not the only new agency created to handle wartime research and development. Bush's organization operated largely on the principle of each key man picking, often from among his acquaintances, those men who were to work immediately with or under him. A different approach, that of a detailed list of technical men with nationwide coverage, was institutionalized through the National Roster. The assumption upon which the OSRD operated, that the top men in any field were known to each other, worked well enough for some purposes but tended to break down if large numbers of less highly trained men were needed. It was this need that the Roster best filled.* Report of the National Academy of Sciences. Fiscal Year 1940-1941 *(Washington, D.C.: GPO, 1942), 37-38.*]

The need for systematized personnel data concerning all individuals with specialized competence has been keenly felt by many who are concerned with the organization of scientific effort at the present time. A number of scientific societies had already begun several years ago to collect such information from their membership and the division of chemistry of the National Research Council had also engaged in the compilation of certain lists of men and facilities in the field of chemistry. Discussion of this subject in relation to the whole field of science and technology began in the National Research Council over 2 years ago (summer of 1939) and the preparation of a scientific register, patterned on the one prepared in England by the Royal Society, was proposed by one of the Council's representatives, in the science committee of the National Resources Planning Board. A similar need was also felt in the social sciences, the humanities, and education; consequently in July 1940 the movement for the preparation of what is now known as the National Roster of Scientific and Specialized Personnel got under way under the auspices of the National Resources Planning Board and the United States Civil Service Commission. President Leonard Carmichael, of Tufts College, was appointed director, and Mr. James C. O'Brien, of the United States Civil Service Commission, executive officer. The Council was asked to participate in the project and to appoint a representative on the advisory committee. The function of the Council . . . has been to provide lists of societies whose combined membership lists constitute a great body of scientifically trained men, to assist in the preparation of questionnaires, and to set up evaluating committees in each of the fields represented by the Council, who are, when required, to pass on the qualifications of names selected mechanically from the roster cards. The data from the questionnaires have been coded on punch cards. The roster has now covered the fields represented by the National Research Council. It has already been put to much use and has proved to be of inestimable value in the selection of specialized personnel. The roster staff have cooperated effectively with the office of scientific personnel of the Council, which was set up at the request of the Government for the selection of workers in certain fields, where relatively large numbers are needed. It is particularly in physics and certain fields in engineering that the demand for research workers is greatest in proportion to the supply.

❧ *D. No trait of the American character is more widely believed in or respected than Yankee inventive genius. It was correctly assumed in Washington that the defense emergency would loose upon the government a flood of suggestions for new devices, ranging in form from vague intuitions to working models accompanied by detailed drawings. To cope with this situation, a National Inventors Council was organized as a focus for civilian inventive effort and a handy reference point for overworked agencies. National Inventors Council,* Administrative History of the National Inventors Council *(processed, National Inventors Council, Department of Commerce, n.d.), 1, 4-5, 9-11.*]

The National Inventors Council was created in August 1940, by the Secretary of Commerce with the concurrence of the President of the United States. The plan for the organization evolved from a series of informal discussions conducted by Secretary Harry Hopkins with Mr. Lawrence Langner, patent attorney, Mr. Thomas Midgley, Jr., research chemist, Dr. Vannevar Bush, newly appointed head of the National Defense Research Committee, and the Hon. Conway P. Coe, Commissioner of Patents.

The purpose of the Council was described by the Secretary in his letter of July 11, 1940, appointing as Chairman, Dr. Charles F. Kettering. Mr. Hopkins wrote:

With the object of stimulating inventions by members of our civilian population and subsequently to evaluate these in relation to national defense, I am about to create, with the full concurrence of the President, a National Inventors Council. Confidently counting on both your competence and your consent to serve as head of that Council, I appoint you as its chairman.

It is planned that the National Inventors Council shall function in close and constant collaboration with the military and naval branches of the Government, bringing to their attention all such discoveries and mechanisms as appear to have defensive value. You may be certain of my active cooperation with the Council. . . .

I feel that in the present exigency, as never before in the life of this country, we should muster American inventive genius in the cause of national welfare, defense and security. I am confident that our inventors, both recognized and unknown, will be eager to contribute to the mastery of the problems and difficulties confronting us. . . .

This letter and a subsequent letter of August 26, 1940, bearing the President's approval of the initial appointments to the Council, form the basis of authority for operation of the body. The organization meeting of the National Inventors Council was held at Washington, August 6, 1940.

At the first meeting of the . . . Council, the chairman indicated that the work of the organization would fall into two well-defined channels:

(a) The location and organization of inventors of the United States so that they would be available to work on specific inventive problems.

(b) The handling of unsolicited inventions submitted by the public. Procedures and facilities were required to receive such inventions, evaluate them, and distribute worthwhile suggestions to proper agencies.

In effect, the Council was supposed to function as liaison service between the public and the armed forces. The Services welcomed the idea, since it promised to relieve harassed research officers from a time-consuming burden of correspondence and interviews with inventors and their representatives.

No conflict developed between the functions of the Council and those of the National Defense Research Committee. The latter agency was organized to work out solutions to specific military and naval problems presented by the services. NDRC was interested in the ideas submitted by the public on these specific problems, which required close liaison relations between the agencies.

The National Inventors Council has also been compared to the Naval Consulting Board established during the First World War. Again there was a fundamental difference in purpose. The primary purpose of the NCB, like the NDRC, was to provide an opportunity for the different branches of the Navy to consult with and obtain the assistance of the best scientific and inventive resources of the country. . . .

The examining staff which reviewed the thousands of suggestions submitted by the public was composed of engineers, chemists, and physicists. The qualifications for a successful examiner are unusual. Not only must he have thorough scientific training, but he must have sufficient imagination and vision to recognize an idea of merit, regardless of how novel or unorthodox it may at first appear.

During the months after Pearl Harbor the number of personnel on the staff reached a maximum of 55, of which 9 were technical. The staff was gradually reduced as the work load declined to 28 (5 technical) on VJ-day. . . .

The psychology of invention, like the psychology of all creative thought, is but imperfectly understood. No one has explained the origin of a hypothesis—the shock of genius or insight required to transform a problem into a solution. This proved unfortunate, for the National Inventors Council was pledged to encourage invention and there was no guide book available showing how to go about it.

Shortly after the Council was organized an effort was made to solicit inventions from recognized inventors. A list of more than 700 outstanding inventors was obtained from the records of the Patent Office. This group was addressed by letter and the inventors invited to submit ideas having potential military merit.

The response was disappointing. Many inventors were already engaged in war activities either in industry or Government. Perhaps more important, however, was their reluctance to spend time and effort in a field about which they knew so little. Apparently an inventor must be thoroughly acquainted with the problem he hopes to solve. He needs to know the scientific principles involved, as well as the "state of the art" and the alternative solutions which have been tested and rejected.

Consequently, the next logical step was to acquaint inventors with the current problems of the armed services. But this involved the factor of national security, and during the early stages of the war, the Army and Navy were understandably reluctant to release information about their needs. Publication of such information might disclose vital weaknesses to the enemy or tip him off to our strengths.

On the other hand there was a great area of problems of a more general nature, many involving mechanical and design principles, which could not be thus tied to specific applications. As time went on several lists of these problems were obtained from the Army and Navy. These were given wide distribution to the inventing public through technical and professional societies and journals. They were also picked up by the daily press and the general magazines.

One surprising condition brought to light by the problem releases was the uncertain liaison between the various branches of the armed services. Often one agency was found to have a solution for a problem confronting another, and the Council was able to clear up the matter by telephone....

Not unnaturally problems of a relatively simple mechanical nature invoked the greatest response. Gadget-minded Americans in their basement workshops could develop an automatic release for cargo parachutes to operate when the cargo hit the ground preventing its being dragged. Over 200 suggestions were submitted to an appeal for a method of transmitting rotary motion through a watertight surface. But development of a rocket projectile or a nighttime binocular using infra-red rays was beyond the financial and technical resources of the ordinary gadgeteer....

The records of the National Inventors Council show that over the life of the agency 208,975 inventions and ideas were evaluated and 13,887 interviews were conducted with inventors or their representatives. Of this total, 8,615 ideas (4.1 percent) were considered of sufficient value to place in the classified files, while more than 5,000 were sent to the armed services or war agencies for review. Further sifting by technical experts in the services reduced the number to 757, which were considered worthy of further investigation, development, and testing. By June 30, 1946, a total of 106 items were actually known to have been put into production, while at least 105 additional items were still under investigation....

It is certainly true that ideas beget ideas. By opening up a free area for speculation and radical theorizing, the Council served to expose the research officials of the services to a series of undisciplined attacks on standard problems. . . .

Perhaps the most significant fact about the National Inventors Council is that it served as an inspiration and a clearing house for the independent inventor at a time when research was becoming more highly institutionalized than ever before. Almost all major research facilities in the country were mobilized for specific, pre-determined objectives. While such mobilization produced immense results, as exemplified by the Manhattan project and the Radiation Laboratory [at M.I.T.], it would be calamitous if such institutionalization resulted in the stifling exclusion and discouragement of the individual, free-lance inventor.

True enough, the individual inventor does not have the money, the staff, the laboratory facilities or the organized body of knowledge necessary to carry through successfully modern research undertakings, which necessarily bring to bear on a single problem the full resources of theoretical physics and chemistry and the technical potentialities of all branches of engineering.

Nevertheless, imagination, boldness, speculation, and inspiration are not institutional products. The individual might produce practical dreams which institutions could bring into reality. . . .

The outstanding weakness of the Council, both in organization and operation, was its informal, almost casual approach. Established as an advisory body to the Secretary of Commerce, the Council had no statutory authority. The members were always aware, perhaps too much so, that they served in an advisory capacity only.

❡ *E.   The OSRD, concentrating its efforts on weapons and medical research, resisted attempts to push it also into the problems of production engineering and shortages of strategic materials. It was finally decided that such research should be under the supervision of the War Production Board as the agency most actively concerned with shortages and production bottlenecks. U.S. Congress, Senate, Subcommittee on War Mobilization to the Committee on Military Affairs, Report, "The Government's Wartime Research and Development, 1940-44, Part I.—Survey of Government Agencies," 79 Cong., 1 sess. (Jan. 23, 1945), 227-228, 230.]*

The objective of the Office of Production Research and Development is to plan, direct, and coordinate the scientific and engineering evaluation, research, and development work within the War Production Board in order to insure rapid appraisal and maximum effective utilization of mechanisms, materials, processes, and inventions in war production; to this end to utilize, as far as possible, existing research personnel and facilities.

The invention and development of improved or even wholly new weapons and other instruments of war have been prosecuted with vigor, almost ever since the war began in Europe, by the Office of Scientific Research and Development, or by its predecessor, the National Defense Research Committee. In its special field the National Advisory Committee on [sic] Aeronautics has also done notable research work. In general, the work of both of these research groups has been directed toward helping to determine what should be produced, rather than how or from what it should be produced. These two questions belong in the field for which the War Production Board is responsible.

The question of from what the things that both the armed services and the civilian population need shall be produced — that is, the whole problem of raw materials and substitutes — is one that had long concerned the War Production Board. It is being attacked on the one hand by limitation orders, the controlled materials plan, and other methods intended to reduce the demand for critical materials by prohibiting their use for purposes not deemed essential to the war effort. It is also being attacked on the other side by a variety of efforts to increase the supply of critical raw materials in every feasible way.

The Office of Production Research and Development has five omnibus service contracts under which miscellaneous appraisal and advisory reports can be asked for as needed on a variety of subjects. The first is with the National Academy of Sciences and it is the medium by which the services of the War Metallurgy Committee are made available to the War Production Board. The second is with the American Society of Mechanical Engineers Manufacturing Engineering Committee which is rendering similar service in the field of production engineering. The third is with the University of Illinois and was written to cover a number of appraisals of patents in the chemical field on which the agency from time to time desires information. The fourth is with Armour Research Foundation to cover a miscellaneous group of exploratory experimental appraisals of ideas with which the agency is dealing. The fifth is with Research Corporation, a nonprofit organization in New York City, to cover a number of special developmental projects.

In all of these cases, work is undertaken by the cooperating agency only on specific request and is done at cost. . . .

The scope of the authority and duties of the Office of Production Research and Development was established by General Administrative Order 2-66 of the War Production Board, issued November 23, 1942. Work began the same day. . . .

Emphasis has been shifted from a search for new sources and processes for producing raw materials to a greatly intensified study of technical methods for getting improved quality or an increased quantity of finished products from existing facilities with the same or reduced manpower.

Ideas, projects, and problems reach the Office of Production Research and Development mainly from the industry divisions and other divisions of the War Production Board. However, a considerable number come from outside agencies such as those listed above, from war contractors, from the National Inventors Council, and from individual inventors. The Director of the Office passes upon the desirability of each project and, if financing is indicated, approves the contract or request for transfer of funds to another Government agency.

After a problem has been presented to the Office of Production Research and Development, every effort is made to determine whether a solution is available through research already accomplished. This is done through the knowledge of the technical staff and consultants, specialists in their fields, and by consultation with the various scientific committees. If experimental research proves to be desirable, contact is made with various industrial and educational institutions known to be capable of carrying on the required research with existing facilities. Availability of necessary manpower is also considered. Proposals submitted by the institutions are studied carefully to determine which can do the job most economically in the shortest time. After a prospective contractor has been selected, the contract is negotiated and processed.

III. The Old Agencies

◖ A. *The OSRD was undoubtedly the single most impor-*
tant scientific agency of the government during the war, and it
had the primary responsibility for coordinating the disparate
elements of American science. Nevertheless, the pre-existing
governmental and semi-governmental agencies of scientific
importance continued operations during the war. The OSRD
saw as its job the provision of services which were otherwise
neglected, rather than the taking over of going scientific
activities. Generally, the old-line agencies were reorganized
for defense, by executive action, in the immediate prewar
period. It was decided that they should remain separate from
the military establishment, but interagency liaison was
strengthened. Peacetime lines of research were subordinated
to others more directly connected with defense and war, but
were seldom completely abandoned.

At least on paper, the quasi-governmental National
Academy of Sciences was the most obvious organization to
provide scientific leadership for the war effort. The formation
of the NDRC was a tacit admission that, for many reasons, the
Academy could not act as the coordinator of wartime re-
search. Nevertheless, it too took steps to prepare itself for
whatever role it might be called upon to play. Frank B. Jewett,
President of the Academy during the war, explained his orga-
nization and its role to Congress in 1942. U.S. Congress, Sen-
ate, Subcommittee of the Committee on Military Affairs,
Hearings, "Technological Mobilization," 77 Cong., 2 sess.
(Nov. 20, 25, 27, and Dec. 4, 10, 11, 1942), II, 310-312.]

MR. JEWETT: When you are speaking of the academy, you
are really speaking of the academy per se, which is the control
body, and its permanent agency, which is very much bigger,
the Research Council. But both of them are still under the
obligations of the original charter of the academy, to serve
whenever requested, and to do it without remuneration. And

the reason that Congress did that thing is due to the fact that the most—and they have no authority or initiation, they can't tell the Government to do anything, nor can they tell the Government how to use the advice they give them—and the reason that Congress did that is the age-old thing, that the strongest authority that you can give to anybody is the authority of distinction without power, a thing that Mr. Root, who was very much interested in the academy, always harped on. If you want to get things done, don't give people police authority to do it, make them so distinguished that nobody dares run counter to their advice.

Now, when the storm clouds of this present situation began to develop over here, the question again took the form that it had at the beginning of the World War, and it was clear to a lot of people, not only in the academy and the Research Council, but a lot of people in this country, that it was a scientific war, and a lot of stuff had to be done. And there was a lot of talk and a good many movements started, to implement science for this war effort. Some of them got quite a lot of impetus behind them, but were obviously proposed by people who really didn't know what these things were, and some of the scientific people said, "Well, this thing ought to be again organized under the academy and the Research Council."

Then it appeared to some of us in the academy and the Research Council, notably Dr. Bush and Dr. Compton and Dr. Conant, and four or five of us who were responsible for these operations, as we took a look at the thing and came to the conclusion that you couldn't do in an organization like the academy and the Research Council, under its charter, that the things which had to be done and which involved the initiation of work and the spending of Government money, would require a change in the academy's charter. Further, that to change the academy's charter to make it an executive organization would be to destroy the very thing which Congress set it up to do, because it would then become just another agency of Government, and that the best thing to do was to set up—at that time the principal problem was instruments and instrumentalities of warfare—was to set up an ad hoc agency in the executive departments which could be given money—it had a Government status, not a quasi-government status but a real status—to do the work that could best be done by civilians in that sector.

The result of that discussion, all of which was taken part in by members of the academy—the group I have mentioned, . . . it ultimately resulted in the Executive order which created the National Defense Research Committee, the original one back in 1940, with Dr. Bush as its chairman, and all of the civilian members . . . with the exception of the three Government officers . . . were all members of the academy, and they are today.

Powers of initiation were given to that group. On matters of advice they turned to the academy and council, where it was an advisory type of stuff. Where it is the actual initiation of projects, spending Government money, they turn to other agencies, whether in the Government or outside . . . .

SENATOR KILGORE: Now, the National Academy, under the charter granted by Congress, has an obligation to render certain services, but by the same act those services were limited to, shall we say, the answering of inquiries, and any original ideas that might emanate from the scientific minds of the academy were precluded. In other words, the academy couldn't come out and advocate anything?

MR. JEWETT: Yes; the academy could come out and advocate it, but it had no authority to do anything about it, it was just like anybody else that could come out and advocate.

SENATOR KILGORE: Oh, yes; you could advocate—

MR. JEWETT: But we had no executive power to do anything, and many of the ideas—of course, this charter of the academy not only says "advise," but "experiment," so that a large part of the work which is being done by the academy and the Research Council now, for which the Government is paying the out-of-pocket expenses of between a million and a half and two million a year for traveling and living and clerical hire—a large part or a considerable part of it is experimental work, but experimental work initiated by Government itself. Indirectly much of it has been initiated by the ideas which have come from the academy and the Research Council, conveyed informally to departments of Government for their consideration, and where they think those things are worth while they would ask to have it done, and enter into a contract.

◀ B. *After the war, Jewett again took up the problem of the Academy's role. "Review of the Years 1939-47,"* Report of the National Academy of Sciences—National Research Council. Fiscal Year 1946-1947 *(Washington, D.C.: GPO, 1948), 1-3.*]

Practically the entire 8-year interval [1939-47] was covered by activities concerned with preparation for war; the war years; and the early postwar period. While many of the normal functions of both the Academy and Council continued, they were subordinate to the functions imposed by the Academy's Act of Incorporation which constitutes it as the official advisor to Government in matter of science and technology. During most of the time few papers of a scientific or technical character were available or, if available, could be presented.

To a large extent the Academy ceased to function as a learned society in the traditional sense. While the regular two meetings a year were held, they were devoted mainly to the dispatch of routine business. Such scientific sessions as were possible were closed to the public and were confined to the presentation of confidential reports to the members on war research. In part these were reports by members and in part by high-ranking officers of the military establishments. . . .

The impact of the war years has, however, left an indelible imprint on both the Academy and Council. Their activities in aid of so many departments of Government—both civil and military—have so firmly established the capacity of both organizations to give completely unbiased scientific advice at the highest level and to administer intricate research undertakings, that increased calls on them in the future are inevitable. These will be not only from departments of Government but from civilian organizations and foundations as well. . . .

The first impact of war preparedness on the Academy and Research Council came in the form of urgent requests from various branches of the Military Establishment—notably the offices of the Surgeons General—for aid in organizing civilian science for war research and development work in fields recognized as certain to be of major importance to the military. These requests were directly in line with what the Academy and Council were uniquely qualified and obligated to do under the Academy charter. Further, they were directly in conformity with the procedure of World War I when the Council was not only the Science Division of the Council of

National Defense, but also the civilian scientific operating agency of many of the departments of the Army and Navy.

For a time it appeared that the Academy, although willing and anxious to undertake the work, might not be able to comply with the requests.

The difficulty arose out of modifications in governmental structure and practice which had taken place in the interval subsequent to World War I.

In that period the Comptroller General's office had been established and had formulated rules which rigidly prohibited departments of Government from advancing money on work requested under contract prior to actual completion unless specific authorization for it was contained in the congressional acts of appropriation. This rule had of course to be revised drastically later under the stress of war when only government was in position to supply the vast amounts of money needed by contractors as working capital.

While, therefore, the Academy was willing to undertake the work and the requesting departments were willing to pay the cost of it, the Academy, under the ruling of the Comptroller General, was required to supply the working capital. As the Academy had no such funds at its disposal nor, because of its character, the ability to make commercial loans, it appeared for a time that it would have to default on its statutory obligation.

Fortunately a number of the foundations took the position that the Academy could not in the national interest be permitted to be placed in this position. As a result, during the years 1939-40-41 they made grants of many hundred thousand dollars to the Academy and so enabled it to comply with all requests.

When, therefore, the military and civilian departments of Government were finally implemented properly, much of the preliminary work was already done; further work adequately organized; and much valuable time saved. . . .

As was the case in the days before World War I, appreciation of the vital role of science in the impending conflict was sensed first by leading scientists in the days before World War II. Then, as in the earlier conflict, consideration of its effective organization headed up in the Academy.

Both because of the part played by the Academy and Research Council in the first war and because the permanent

Research Council was established at President Wilson's request, specifically among other things to provide a civilian agency for aid to the military, it was natural that the first approach should have been toward reactivation of the Council for war.

Two serious obstacles to this appeared almost immediately. One of these was the changed conditions as to funds referred to above. This could only be changed effectively by act of Congress or by amendment of the Academy charter. The other was the fact that in the preceding 25 years when the Council was little used by the military it had developed almost wholly along civilian lines. Its formal organization and the character of the personnel constituting it were those indicated for this work rather than those best qualified for the problems of war. To alter these conditions would have been a slow major operation which the urgency of the situation did not permit.

These obstacles made it clear that an effective temporary organization must be set up in the structure of the executive department with the Academy and Council acting in cooperation. So it came about that the National Defense Research Committee, whose civilian members were all members of the Academy, was created and later enlarged to be the Office of Scientific Research and Development.

◖ C. *One of the nation's oldest and most respected scientific organizations was the Smithsonian Institution. Over the years, however, its once dominant research activities had become overshadowed by curatorial duties, a fact which tended to reduce its relevance to the scientific war effort.* "A Brief Summary of the Smithsonian Institution's Part in World War II," *Annual Report of the Board of Regents of The Smithsonian Institution . . . 1945 (Washington, D.C.: GPO, 1946), 459-460, 472.*]

With the onset of World War II, so many new agencies were created to cope with problems facing the Government and the Army and Navy that for a time the chief concern of the Smithsonian was to find its place in the scheme of war activities, and how best to make its resources count in the Nation's total war effort. Many research organizations with physical and chemical laboratories were immediately called upon for aid in urgent wartime investigations, and their problem was mainly how to accomplish promptly all that they were asked to do. At the Smithsonian, where the sciences dealt in — chiefly anthropology, biology, geology, and astrophysics — were of less obvious war usefulness, and where the facilities consisted of museums, art galleries, and small laboratories, staffed by highly specialized scientists in the disciplines just mentioned, the problems were to find its field of war service and to make its resources known.

The Secretary of the Institution, sensing this situation shortly after Pearl Harbor, met it by appointing a War Committee to canvass the Institution's possibilities and to recommend specific lines of action. As a result, a large part of the effort of the staff was diverted to work connected directly or indirectly with the war, and the Smithsonian Institution was found to be an essential cog in the great war machine in Washington. Although its role was inconspicuous as compared with those of the large war agencies, nevertheless it was found to offer services not readily available elsewhere — services whose lack might well have led to costly mistakes and delays. The war was to an unprecedented degree a war of science, utilizing not only the physical sciences, but also anthropology, biology, and geology — branches of science with which the Institution is particularly concerned. Its staff of highly trained specialists in these and other fields, as well as its location near the nerve centers of the Army and Navy and the other war agencies, made the Institution a ready source of quickly needed technical information and hence a valuable arm of the war services in Washington. . . .

After the outbreak of war, as it became apparent that the Smithsonian Institution was not to be assigned definite war duties, the Secretary planned a deliberate effort to make its resources of the greatest possible usefulness in the prosecution of the war. He appointed a War Committee, which canvassed every facility of the Institution and recommended lines of action. A roster of the geographical and specialized knowledge of every member of the staff was compiled. Thousands of requests for technical information from Army and Navy were handled, both directly by the Institution's staff and through the Ethnogeographic Board, a clearinghouse set up jointly by the Smithsonian and three other agencies [National Research Council, American Council of Learned Societies, and Social Science Research Council]. Members of the scientific staff undertook a number of war research projects, and the engineering laboratory assisted the National Inventors Council in working out certain inventions. The Institution took an active part in the Government's program of improving cultural relations with the other American republics. A number of publications having a direct war bearing were issued, the most outstanding being the new series of War Background Studies, of which the Army and Navy used over 400,000 copies. Other wartime activities included special library service to war agencies, service on wartime committees, special war exhibits, and special features for members of the armed forces. No particular administrative problems were involved in the Smithsonian's war activities, as most of them were merely extensions of its normal peace-time work.

❧ *D. While concerned more with service functions than research, the Weather Bureau ranked as one of the most important scientific agencies of the government. The relevance of its activities to the needs of the military was obvious and immediate. U.S. Department of Commerce, The Weather Bureau Record of War Administration: Part 10, World War II History of the Department of Commerce (Washington, D.C., July, 1948), 6, 68, 70.]*

While the principal projects, programs and objectives of the Weather Bureau in wartime are not fundamentally different from those in peace, war naturally leads to a shift in emphasis with respect to details of meteorological activity, and the paramount interests of the military departments obviously obscure or considerably alter some of the peacetime principles of its organization. With this in mind, and to provide for the greatest possible utilization of the far-flung meteorological facilities of the National Meteorological Service by the military in the prosecution of the war, the President designated the Weather Bureau as a war agency. This was accomplished by the issuance of Executive Order 8991, dated December 26, 1941, under authority vested in the President by the Constitution and statutes of the United States. It designated the Secretary of Commerce as Coordinator, and the Chief of the Weather Bureau as Liaison Officer of civil meteorological facilities and services to meet the requirements of the Army and Navy and other vital defense activities for essential and effective weather information, and to protect the secrecy of such information as was considered by the Secretary of War and Secretary of Navy to be of value to the enemy....

In accord with the directive of the President, issued by the Director of the Bureau of the Budget under date of September 23, 1941, to Heads of Departments, the Weather Bureau put its house in order during the National Defense era by effecting as many readjustments of its functions as was possible within the limitations of appropriations in order to provide for anticipated defense operations. Therefore, when war was declared it had a readjusted organization on which to superimpose, by means of supplemental appropriations and transfer of funds from the military agencies, the special forecasting and other services designed to facilitate artillery and aircraft tests and to serve Army (and Navy) posts and bases, construction projects, munitions plants, and the Ferry Command; increase the number of upper-air observations to aid military aviation; extend communications networks to serve Army establishments whenever necessary; expand the Alaskan and Caribbean weather services to meet the special military needs of those areas; assemble and organize a staff of communication experts to provide means for the transmission of weather information to the fighting forces; and provide a staff of expert meteorological statisticians to produce significant analyses of the weather and climates of domestic and foreign areas of actual and potential military interest to the United Nations forces....

Perhaps the most important consideration in regard to the question of militarization of the Weather Bureau is the effect on conversion to war and reconversion to peace. If the national meteorological service were made a part of one of the military services, it is likely that the all-out war effort would result in a weakening of the weather service on the home front. This would be bad enough, but reconversion and demobilization might result in a reduction of the national weather service to a point far below prewar standards, making it ineffective in supporting the effort to win the peace, and bring conditions to normal.

In World War II, the Weather Bureau continued to operate as a civilian organization. If there is any serious criticism of the subdivision of meteorological activities into military and civilian in World War II, it is that the civilian organization, at least during the early stages of the war, was limited in its actual operations more than it should have been. This is true of other phases of the war effort as well as weather. . . .

No matter how carefully the military program is planned, in time of peace it is subject to legislative action. History shows that the longer we continue in a status of peace the smaller and more inefficient our military forces are likely to become. As an illustration of this point bearing directly on meteorology, in 1941 the Army Central Weather Office in Washington included one captain, one clerk and one stenographer. It is quite obvious that in the face of war the expansion of a unit of this size to meet the situation must depend on the national civilian meteorological service.

IV. Dissent

❡ A. *The mobilization of science during the Second World War was selective rather than general. Large contracts tended to go to those institutions which already had the greatest research capabilities; great responsibility tended to be put upon scientists of proven ability; and those scientific disciplines were in greatest demand which had the greatest immediate relevance to military problems. Administrators with important positions to fill turned to their colleagues rather than to the National Roster. Technical needs were turned over to large industrial laboratories rather than published for the benefit of individual inventors at work in their small shops. The pressures of time, the need for secrecy, and the great complexity and sophistication of modern warfare all conspired to make far-reaching distinctions within the scientific and technical communities.*

It was inevitable that such a situation should convince many that the mobilization of science was dangerously incomplete and inefficient. Many who wished desperately to make some unique contribution to the war effort felt shut out or overlooked. Although the executive branch of the government was not without critics of the scientific effort, the major thrust of dissent was from the Congress. In 1942 Senator Harley M. Kilgore, Democrat from West Virginia, introduced a bill to more fully mobilize science. Senate Hearings, "Technological Mobilization," I, 1-3.]

A BILL   To establish an Office of Technological Mobilization, and for other purposes [S. 2721, 77 Cong., 2 sess.].

Whereas the war in which this Nation and the other United Nations are engaged for the preservation of democracy and freedom and the liberation of the conquered peoples is a conflict in which victory highly depends upon the degree of mechanization of the armed forces; and

Whereas the full and immediate utilization of the most

effective scientific techniques for the improvement of production facilities and the maximization of military output is essential for the successful prosecution of the war to a sure and speedy victory: Therefore,

Be it enacted by the Senate and House of Representatives of the United States of America in Congress assembled, That this Act may be cited as The Technology Mobilization Act.

Sec. 2.   The purposes of this Act shall be —

(a)   To regain, maintain, and surpass our previous technical preeminence and attainments; and to make forever secure America's world leadership in the practical application of scientific discoveries, a leadership now gravely threatened by the arms and achievements of the Axis;

(b)   To mobilize for maximum war effort the full powers of our technically-trained manhood; and similarly to mobilize all technical facilities, equipment processes, inventions, and knowledge; and

(c)   To accomplish the above objectives —

(1) by breaking the bottlenecks that today choke up these technical forces and result in the diversion of vast amounts of material, time, and effort from war and essential civilian use to less essential and nonessential uses; by making fully available all patents and all applied technical knowledge for full war use;

(2) by fully utilizing the facilities of small business, technological laboratories, inventions and inventors, and maximizing the output of war goods and essential civilian supplies;

(3) by providing adequate supplies of substitutes for goods normally containing critical materials and by discovering and developing new sources of critical raw materials;

(4) by stimulating new discoveries and inventions, developing more efficient materials and products, and improving standards of production; and, in general,

(5) by promoting the use and development of those processes, products, and materials most efficient for the successful prosecution of the war to a speedy and secure victory.

Sec. 3.   (a) There is hereby created an independent agency to be known as the Office of Technological Mobilization under the direction of a Director to be appointed by the

President of the United States, by and with the advice and consent of the Senate. . . .

Sec. 4. (a) The Office of Technological Mobilization is authorized and directed to have full access to all governmental and private information and to collect such additional information as may be necessary. . . .

(b) The Office is authorized and directed to appraise the current use being made of scientific and technical personnel and facilities, both public and private and to draft all such personnel and facilities failing to submit or to accept plans for immediate conversion of their efforts to work deemed more essential by the Office of Technological Mobilization. Such personnel as may be drafted for Government assigned and financed work will be compensated at reasonable rates of compensation. . . .

Sec. 5. (a) The Office of Technological Mobilization is authorized and directed to collect or acquire, for reasonable compensation where it deems proper any and all scientific, technical, and other information which it deems may be useful in planning or carrying out the development of a new or improved technique, process, or product; and the Office shall have access to all such information held by public agencies or private persons including full information on current research programs and developments, together with details and characteristics of processes, materials, and products, both military and civilian. Reasonable compensation shall be determined by the Office, subject to review by the courts.

(b) The Office of Technological Mobilization is authorized and directed to review all projects for research and development, including practical development of inventions which may be brought to its attention; and it shall promote such projects as it deems appropriate that are consistent with the purposes of this Act; and it shall also initiate through a staff of its own such additional projects as it can. . . .

❡ *B. The Kilgore bill had little to recommend it to those scientists who were running their part of the war effort. The Director of the OSRD was the logical spokesman for those who were opposed to a more complete and rigid mobilization of science and technology. Vannevar Bush to Hon. Harley M. Kilgore, December 7, 1942, in U.S. Congress, Senate, Subcommittee of the Committee on Military Affairs,*

Hearings, "Scientific and Technological Mobilization," 78 Cong., 1 sess. (June 17, 1943), III, 259-260, 262-263.]

The whole problem of technological mobilization for modern war is one of extreme breadth and difficulty. For 2 1/2 years now I have been deeply immersed, not only in carrying on one aspect of this matter, but in a deep study of the appropriate organizational means by which it can be best furthered. The conduct of modern war depends in no small degree upon the skill and effectiveness with which science and technology are brought to bear. In fact, the entire course of events may be seriously affected by the question of whether our weapons are fully equal to those of the enemy, and this in turn depends upon a large number of steps. We need to utilize the inventiveness of our people, we need to bring to bear the best scientific and engineering skill, we need to manufacture effectively and promptly, and we need training programs that are adequate so that the resulting tools can be effectively and fully used. It is a fascinating and exceedingly important aspect of the entire war effort. I know of no aspect of our national effort that more clearly warrants all of the careful consideration that can be brought to bear upon it. Accordingly, I have followed your studies with the deepest interest.

Yet as I read the first draft of the bill which has been under discussion, S. 2721, I immediately feel that it is based upon inaccurate premises. The first two sections seem to me to be founded upon some feeling that we are far behind the enemy, that there are serious bottlenecks in our technical effort, and that in general we have a serious situation upon our hands which warrants radical changes. I cannot by any means, of course, urge that the present situation is not capable of being improved, but I am very far from subscribing to this preamble....

It may be well to summarize the course of an idea. Inventions, the first suggestions that lead to new military devices, arise in many places. Since a full grasp of actual needs and a keen realization of the practical conditions of combat is a prime criterion in any new device, the origin of an idea is most likely to arise in the mind of some individual in the armed services who is faced with the problem needing solution in a very forceful way. It may also arise in the mind of a scientific man closely associated with military activities. By comparison, the independent inventor is not nearly as likely to produce useful suggestions on strictly military matters, although it sometimes occurs. However, the individual inventor, in civil life, is much more likely to produce ideas which are applicable to industrial processes. When such an idea is received by the Inventors Council it is first reviewed by scientific groups. If it is in the field of aviation, it is then referred, if of apparent importance, to National Advisory Committee for Aeronautics. If it is of industrial nature, it will go to Dr. [Harvey N.] Davis' organization [Office of Production Research and Development, WPB]. If it applies to a new weapon, it becomes studied in the Army and Navy. It is usually a long way from the basic idea to its practical utilization. In all three instances above, however, there is provided means by which such an idea may be developed, along with the ideas that arise within the organization itself. . . .

I believe that this gives the present range of the technological effort in connection with the prosecution of the war. The principal question that immediately arises is whether a reorganization of this effort is necessary for its best functioning. My personal opinion is that no such reorganization is at present called for. There are undoubtedly many places where procedures and relationships can be improved in detail. However, a sweeping change that would place all technological effort under one head is not, in my opinion, desirable. Such a step is needed only where interests conflict and duplication occurs, where there is not proper liaison, and where there is overlapping of effort. None of this situation, in my opinion, obtains in regard to the technological effort at the present time. There is the closest of coordination, relationships are cordial throughout, and duplication is avoided. . . .

My summary of the situation, then, is as follows: I believe that the technological effort of this country is of exceedingly great importance, and I am glad to see it studied into thoroughly, and I hope that it will be studied into many times as our war effort proceeds, in order that it may be kept keenly alive to its opportunities and in order that any malfunctioning may be corrected. However, I do not believe that a bill that would join the various research and development agencies is now needed. On the contrary, I believe that the confusion which it would cause and the delays incident to the reorganization of effort which it would enforce would far offset any benefit which might come out of it.

❡ *C.   Those who favored some such plan as Senator Kilgore proposed had no single spokesman of the national stature of Vannevar Bush. Their dissent was in many voices and for many reasons. Otto Stuhlman, Prof. of Physics, University of North Carolina, to Sen. H.M. Kilgore, April 30, 1943, in Senate Hearings, "Scientific and Technological Mobilization," III, 237.*]

I agree with you that science should serve society in some constructive way after the present war effort, and that the future of science and its support must be faced by government as you have suggested in your science mobilization bill [S. 702, successor to S. 2721].

Evidence that "serious impediments" to the full application of science in our war effort do in fact exist, can be shown by the lack of such activity by as much as 50 percent of my colleagues in the southeastern part of our country.

There is no general clearing house for war problems that can be submitted to the various scientific organizations of our colleges. We are supposed to take the initiative. The initiative to do what? seems to be the cry. We don't know the Army's problems nor the Navy's desires for information, yet we are all anxious to help, especially those of us beyond military age.

I am convinced your bill is the solution. Some who attack this bill on the basis of "regimentation" of science and technology need only review the history of our Public Health Service, our civil aeronautics, and similar services performed by Government to prove how wrong they are.

❡ *D.   During the early Kilgore hearings, strong support for S. 2721 was given by Lyman Chalkley, then an economic analyst for the Industrial Engineering Division of the Board of Economic Warfare, and later on the staff of the OSRD. Senate Hearings, "Technological Mobilization," I, 8, 14-16.*]

MR. CHALKLEY: I became interested in it [technological mobilization] when I learned, in 1938, that the commanding general and the executive officer of the Chemical Warfare Service were neither of them chemists, hadn't had technical training; and then, that the National Academy of Sciences took very literally its charter, which suggests that they may give information when they are asked for it, but are not to volunteer any—and that they were making no preparations whatever for national defense at that time. . . .

SENATOR KILGORE: Now, is there any integration between . . . [scientific] agencies at all?

MR. CHALKLEY: No—well, through the President. . . .

There are still a lot of things to be done that are not even covered in these agencies. . . First we need a source of technical information for the nontechnical agencies of the Government. This is a highly technical war and there is no economic problem or administrative problem that doesn't somewhere run down to a technological factor. I don't mean to say that the technological factor is deciding—in some instances it is —but there is always one there. And there is no way that the nontechnical agency of the Government can get technical information readily. . . . There are various sections of the Government that have technical experts, such as the Bureau of Standards, the Department of Agriculture, and so on. Yet there are very few of the people in other agencies who know how to get in touch with the right person, and even though some Government agencies have good technical staffs they certainly are only a very small fraction of our scientific and technical resources of the country. Well, we are just not tapping those other resources at all at present for the information of the Government.

We need a reduction-to-practice agency, something that will take an idea or a scientific fact and reduce it to actual production of material, something we can use in the war, something tangible.

We have two agencies that are empowered to do that today in restricted fields, the Office of Scientific Research and Development does it on weapons of war; and the National Advisory Committee for Aeronautics can do it on airplanes, and they have some funds.

But the [OSRD] . . . has construed its directive quite conservatively. You will notice that in each of the statements as to what it can do, everything must be related to the national defense. Apparently from their actions they have felt that that limits them to actual warfare to weapons of war and things of that sort, and does not include production methods, or the development of processes for mining in a better way to get more strategic materials, or for the development of substitutes and things of that sort which are quite pressing now....

The third thing we need is the coordination of work in the Government laboratories themselves. We have extensive laboratories in the Government ... but they are entirely independent of each other, there is no coordination of their work, nothing that will prevent duplication or will make possible the efficient use of the whole research and scientific facilities of the Government.

Then we need some means for mobilizing our civilian technological resources. The civilian scientists and technologists who are not either employed by the Government or on contract with the Government have today no contact with the Government, no channel through which they can get to the Government or the Government can call on them for casual things, at least. If it is something very important, and a man is found, he is put under contract to do a job for some agency that wants it done. But there are great numbers of scientists and technologists that we have today who are not integrated into the war effort at all. The Government hasn't made a contact with them, and the honorary nature of membership in the National Academy, while it maintains a high standard of membership, acts in a sense as a barrier to all other scientists so that they don't have that channel through the Academy to the Government which I think President Lincoln must have had in mind when he originally set it up....

We need one other thing, I think, and I don't know whether an agency as such can do it—but a source of technological policy in the Government. There is no place where technological knowledge can be injected at the policy level in the conduct of the war today.

◖ E. *Waldemar Kaempffert, science editor of the* New York Times, *advocated greater mobilization of science and cast doubt upon the role of the individual inventor. Senate Hearings, "Technological Mobilization," I, 67-69, 71-72.*]

MR. KAEMPFFERT . . . I have been going around laboratories here and abroad for about 30 years, and it is only recently that there are any signs of coordination, either in the Government laboratories or industrial laboratories.

We have followed in scientific and industrial research what the economists call the laissez faire policy which is now outmoded in economics but which still prevails in research.

Industrial progress has been made in a haphazard way and in all countries, with the exception of Soviet Russia, research has grown up like Topsy; there has been no concentrated social purpose in planning, no direction, no organization, except since this war....

We have made enormous progress in physics and chemistry, because the profits lie there and the military advantage lies there, but after all, science must serve much larger—a much larger purpose than that, and the only government in the world, I regret to state, that has used science, or intended to use science to secure social security, social happiness and contentment, is Russia.

Now, I strongly disapprove of anything like the imposition of a state philosophy or ideology upon every shade of human thinking of the kind that you have in Russia.

On the other hand, I have nothing but admiration for the organization of science such as constituted in Russia. There you find that science is propagated on all fronts.

SENATOR KILGORE: Whether it is profitable or not?

MR. KAEMPFFERT: Irrespective of whether there is any profit in it. The Soviet Academy of Sciences, which is the equivalent of our National Academy of Sciences, is an integral part of the Government, and as much so as our Department of Agriculture or Department of Commerce. It plans the research activities of the entire country, and those plans extend right down into every shop. The result was that Russia found it least difficult of all the nations to turn over from peace to war.

They were already mobilized scientifically, whereas we were not, and not even the Germans as completely as they became in about 1936 or so.

So that we have at least an example there of what can be done for a purely social purpose.

What I like about your bill [S. 2721] is that it is the first attempt made in this country, to my knowledge, to look at technology and science in this broad way, and I hope if it is approved by Congress and by the President, I hope that it will not be just a wartime institution, but that it will become a permanent institution, because, why should we destroy this elaborate apparatus which is bound to produce much good, and then let ourselves drift along aimlessly as we have in the past? There is no earthly reason for that.

SENATOR KILGORE: I want to ask you a question at that point. Don't you think it would be good governmental economy to set aside each year a reasonable amount of money commensurate with the national income for that purpose, in peace as well as war?

MR. KAEMPFFERT: Yes, sir.

SENATOR KILGORE: Would it not save money in wartime from what was spent in peacetime?

MR. KAEMPFFERT: It would. The record speaks for itself. . . .

Now, this matter of competent men. . . .

We had, in the last war, considerable experience in tapping the country's inventive ingenuity. You will remember, we had the Naval Consulting Board, of which Thomas A. Edison was the head. That organization was primarily concerned with dealing with the submarine menace, and it welcomed ideas from anyone. We cherished the illusion that a nation which had produced Morse, McCormick, Bell, and others — hundreds of other important inventors — could surely solve this problem. . . .

Now, we come to our Inventors' Council. There is no question but that the public demands the Inventors' Council and there is no question but that we need it. We should tap inventive ingenuity wherever it is to be found, yet I have no great faith in it, simply because of the character of modern technology.

The time has gone, I think, when we can rely on the heroic inventor of the Morse or the Bell or the Edison type. The problems are too vast and intricate.

I think we shall always have the lone garret inventor with us, but I think he is going to give us fountain pens, vacuum cleaners, and contrivances of that kind. When it comes to problems like those involved in metallurgy or illumination or synthetic rubber, your lone garret inventor is simply hopelessly lost.

The example that has been set by Russia and by our own industrial laboratories indicates plainly enough that technological progress can be made only by competent planning, direction and organization, all of which you provide for, I am glad to see, in your bill. I do not mean to say that we must dictate what we want, and then get it. We should also receive projects from inventors and fit them into the plan where they can be fitted, and encourage them. But, there must be continuity of work; it must follow some plan. . . .

I should like to see scientific research and technology organized in this country largely for social purposes. Now, we are starting in on that already. We are making what is to my mind an extremely important experiment in the Tennessee Valley Authority. We should broaden that out, much as you have broadened it out in your bill, and make it a permanent institution which shall give industrial and scientific research a social purpose and direction under competent men, and which shall also get rid of the enormous amounts of duplicated effort in our governmental scientific bureaus here, and which shall encourage invention in a new way by guiding it or telling it what it should do. . . .

The time has come, probably, to revise the patent laws. Patents are granted much too easily in this country. The standards of invention are very high. Inventions that would have taken our breath away 50 or 60 years ago are now accepted as a matter of course. We consider them almost straight engineering designs. . . .

There is one point about your bill, I think I have had some discussion about with . . . others who do not agree with me, but I feel that the [OSRD] . . . , as far as I can judge, is the one war agency which is really properly planned, properly organized and properly directed. It has its own funds and it has the authority to spend those funds. It states the problems that it wants solved, it makes contracts with university professors of physics and industrial engineering, as well as industrial laboratories, to see to it that those problems are solved. . . .

It is to me inconceivable that this Office is not already approaching industrial problems, and that the men who have solved these problems are the very men who are probably most competent to tackle the industrial side, the purely industrial side of it, as well.

So I would like to see your proposed Office of Technological Mobilization either absorb the Office of Scientific Research and Development or form a branch of that, but there is no question that we need the organization of our scientific and industrial ingenuity, and that is one way of achieving it. Unless that amalgamation takes place, I foresee some duplication of effort, conflict even, of authority. I do not think that your bill gives your office enough authority to act. It can build pilot plants, to be sure; it can encourage invention; it can spend money; but can it also make the General Electric Co. or the Western Electric Co. use the invention except on Government order, for example, in wartime? That I wonder. Perhaps I misread the bill. But I do not think it gives sufficient authority in that respect. . . .

My plea for the continuation of scientific research as well as industrial research along the lines that you have indicated in your own bill is a permanent thing. . . . We cannot afford to ignore long-time research just because we are at war.

Nothing is so impractical as your practical man. If you want a flounderer, an inefficient and inept person, give me your practical inventor every time. A good theory that works means far more to an inventor than empirical tinkering. We got the airplane from the Wright brothers not because they were tinkerers but because they conducted theoretical experiments in wind tunnels. We got the modern electric lamp which Edison left in a very crude state because of the theoretical work done by men like Coolidge and Langmuir of the General Electric Co. We got nylon not through tinkering but through developing a theory of polymerization. . . .

◀ *F. Engineering schools had been seeking increased federal support throughout the 1930s. Although federal funds were now available in large amounts, many of the schools felt that they were not sharing in the new prosperity. Willis R. Woolrich, Dean of Engineering at the University of Texas, explained the problems faced by the members of the Engineering Colleges Research Association. Senate Hearings, "Technological Mobilization," II, 505-507.]*

MR. WOOLRICH: The objectives of the association, [are] to cooperate with the war agencies of the Government in the prosecution of experimental research needed for the war effort and to assist in organizing the research facilities of the engineering colleges to this end, also to assist in organizing the research facilities of engineering colleges, undertaking research design, and promoting post-war reconstruction, economic adjustments, new and improved processes affecting industry, public works and conservation and development of natural resources, public health, and similar activities; also to serve as a continuing agency for developing and coordinating industry and scientific research and for furthering advanced studies in the colleges of engineering of the United States, and also to collaborate with other associations and with governmental agencies concerned with research, in the interest of maximum utilization and development and engineering and scientific research facilities of the Nation and achieving coordination and preventing duplication of effort. . . .

THE CHAIRMAN: Do you feel from the information you get, and from your own experience with your own college which you represent, that the research staff and laboratory facilities of the engineering colleges of the country on the whole, are being used as effectively as they should be by Government agencies or by industry in connection with the war effort?

MR. WOOLRICH: In reviewing the work of the several engineering colleges of the United States, I would estimate that we are not using more than 10 to 15 percent of their capacity in engineering research. . . .

There are approximately $75,000,000 worth of investment in such facilities and plants that can be made available for extending research of an engineering and industrial nature, and connected with this investment, probably 5,000 engineering men of authority engaged in research or available for research on the faculties of these different engineering colleges that could carry on through the period or at least in part throughout the period of the war, and many of them could extend their activities even after the war . . . .

The principal factors that have contributed to our failure to be able to utilize all of this capacity toward the war effort has been the lack of a centralized contact here in the center of official Washington. We need to have more connections by which we can explore and utilize these facilities and tie them into the Government activities, especially as related to the productive industry of the United States . . . .

The research facilities of the engineering colleges are capable of being greatly expanded and much more productive use made in connection with the war effort, and it would be of great value to us if we had a Federal agency in which all research functions were administered and which could also

assist at the present moment in deferring the essential research personnel to be assigned directly on research and the
war effort, and which could provide a moderate financial
assistance for materially increasing the research output of
engineering colleges research laboratories, and when we have
this large investment and the personnel available to go ahead.

While we have research agencies in Washington that are
available, there is a need for a complete coordination, and
correlation and stimulation of their activities. . . .

MR. SCHIMMEL: Now, I want to take the case of State
colleges. Is it difficult for a State college to turn to the State to
secure problems of importance in the war at this time?

MR. WOOLRICH: It is not difficult to turn to the State to get
problems; it is somewhat difficult for the State to understand
why it should finance problems that are of national importance, or are principally for the war effort.

MR. SCHIMMEL: So that for problems which are primarily
of national importance, as so many problems are today, these
State colleges must turn to the Federal Government for funds
for a national research program.

MR. WOOLRICH: Yes; to really expand it in the way they
should be expanded.

V. Challenge and Opportunity

⁋ A. *During the 1930s, the social structure of American science had been shaken by depression and weakened by dissent. Its problems had been variously diagnosed and a wide range of cures had been proposed. Most solutions for the further appreciation and support of science involved some new and closer relationship with the federal government. Although many of these proposals found their way into the Congress, in 1940 change was more imminent than actual.*

The war, of course, brought changes aplenty although they were easier to sense than to understand, and no one could be sure which were irreversible. Assessment of the new situation started early in the war. The following summary of findings was made in Richard H. Heindel, The Integration of Federal and Non-Federal Research as a War Problem, *prepared for the Science Committee of the National Resources Planning Board, Technical Paper No. 9 (processed, Washington, D.C., July 1, 1942), ii-iv.*]

1. The integration of Federal and non-Federal research facilities has become a war problem of the highest importance, especially in view of the limited number of scientific specialists and the protection of the nation's research structure, now and in postwar reconstruction.

2. There has been an extensive development of decentralized research, especially in science, to implement the Government's war research program.

3. The Federal Government has been developing rich and valuable patterns of procedure and cooperation with all kinds of responsible research agencies which have proved useful during the war and which can be further extended. The types of research suitable for farming out are almost unlimited.

4. Federal agencies have farmed out research primarily because of economy and the advisability of using existing facilities and personnel not otherwise available. As shown in the report, the procedure has broad implications and by-pro-

ducts for planning, training, national prestige, the protection of American Scholarship, etc.

5. Contracting and cooperative research programs are affected by the existing expert personnel, the fields of study, the nature of the problems, by the structure of Federal and non-Federal agencies, and by the community of interest—or lack of it—of agencies willing to serve the nation as a whole.

6. The scheduling of research, always a difficult task, is more difficult under war conditions. Not all Federal bureaus or private agencies have wanted or achieved a balanced program for themselves. Contracting cannot be an easy remedy under such circumstances.

7. The achievement of a desired balance in the Government's fundamental and applied research program, as well as the nation's, raises difficult problems of coordination in the solution of which scientists and scholars must share. Cooperative research programs and contracting will be but one important device to achieve symmetry.

8. Where the Federal Government seriously needs more facts and knowledge for the best conduct of its affairs, cooperative procedures may be indicated.

9. Nearly all organized research groups have been affected by the war effort without sufficient attention being paid to the net national research gain or loss in the process of building up the Federal services. However, there remain, in spite of continuing dislocation, available private facilities that might be tapped by contracting or by cooperative research.

10. Enough is known about the procedures for using non-Federal research agencies to undertake and extend practical operations. This might be done piece-meal, or in trouble-shooting fashion, problem by problem or field by field, as the circumstances dictated.

11. Generally, the procedures developed have sucessfully freed research activity from subordination to policy-making and policy enforcing.

12. Significant farming out depends on more coherence and direction in the formulated needs of the Government, possibly through conferences, inter-departmental, inter-bureau committees, and a flexible intermediary agency.

13. Blending the use of the long-range type of private research with Federal needs subject to a rigid time limit is a major problem.

14. Quick adjustments to changing needs have been possible in cooperative research enterprises.

15. The obstacle of the confidential nature of certain official data has been greatly exaggerated and can often be overcome by several devices.

16. The collection of research data, which can usually be well-defined, also warrants more extensive cooperative arrangements.

17. The advance review and approval of research projects, which make possible a timely cooperation in technical advice, have been useful.

18. Many of the reasons for and against contracting with non-Federal facilities would apply almost as strongly to Federal inter-agency, inter-departmental cooperation.

19. New programs and major changes in Federal policy often should indicate to private research agencies the desirability of special research activities.

20. The demands for certain types of research may encourage within the university and elsewhere, a greater use of inter-departmental, inter-disciplinary approaches to research tasks.

21. The use of outside agencies has been facilitated by the existence of organized councils and associations of scientific specialists.

22. Post-war studies have been considered by several agencies a suitable opportunity to develop cooperative research in industry, universities, and elsewhere.

23. Cooperative research has been decided upon in some instances as one practicable way of attempting a fruitful synthesis of the conclusions of research specialists, administrators, and laymen throughout the country.

24. It is possible that more adequate provisions could be made for projecting research as between our Government and private research agencies and those of our Allies.

25. The problem of larger and more permanent Federal support in the direction of a high standard of research has a direct bearing on contracting viewed as a supplementary device, and because the issue will undoubtedly be revived after the war, and in different form, partly because of the wartime experience with farming out.

❡ B. *No one not immediately involved in wartime scientific research was closer to developments in that field*

*than Senator Kilgore and his staff. After the war in Europe
was over, but before the Japanese had yet surrendered, the
Subcommittee on War Mobilization tried to assess the impact
of the war on the government's scientific activities. U.S.
Congress, Senate, Subcommittee on War Mobilization, Report, "The Government's Wartime Research and Development, 1940-44; Part II. — Findings and Recommendations," 79
Cong., 1 sess. (1945), 20-22.]*

There is no single measure of the scientific and technological resources of the Nation. The best index of its magnitude and growth is perhaps the dollar investment in it. This
investment in the prewar years was in four main types of
facilities: (1) Industrial research establishments, (2) educational institutions, (3) private research foundations, and
(4) Government laboratories. . . .

The total national expenditure for research, by industrial
laboratories, by private foundations, by university laboratories, and by the Government, was in 1938 between
$300,000,000 and $350,000,000. The trend was upward. Even
without the hammer blows of war, the national investment in
research was steadily increasing.

World War II has been a war of resources. The national
resource of technology and science has given us much of the
strength necessary to win victory over the Fascist nations. But
the accumulated resource we had, great though it was, was not
enough for all-out war. The Nation had to step up its research
and development as never before. . . .

With the advent of war, all of our research facilities were
mobilized. There was a vast increase in the total expenditures
for research. Most of this increase came from accelerated
Government expenditures.

By 1944, the Government was spending more than
$700,000,000 a year on research — 10 times more than in 1938.

Much of this Federal expenditure has been through non-
Federal facilities. The mobilization of the Bell Laboratories
for war is illustrative. In 1939, Bell had contracts for Government research to the extent of $200,000, or about 1 percent of
Bell's total research expenditure. By 1941, this had increased
to $5,700,000, or about 22 percent of Bell's total research. By
1943, Bell was working on Government research contracts to
the extent of $41,800,000, or 82.5 percent of its total. By 1944,
Bell's work for the Government was still 81.5 percent of its

total, and Government contracts had risen to $56,000,000.

In the mobilization of science for war, the pattern of Government research expenditures was entirely altered. In 1940, 70 percent of Government research was being done in Government laboratories. Twenty percent was being done in non-Government laboratories. The remaining 10 percent was work of the Department of Agriculture in cooperation with State experiment stations and land-grant colleges.

By the middle of 1944, 70 percent of the greatly increased Government program was being done in non-Government laboratories. Fifty percent of Government research was being done in industrial laboratories and 20 percent in educational institutions and private research foundations.

The placing of Government contracts has intensified the prewar concentration of research in a relatively few laboratories. Preference has necessarily been given to well-established laboratories with the greatest experience and existing facilities. General Motors, for example, was awarded research contracts between 1940 and 1944 totaling nearly $39,000,000. The Massachusetts Institute of Technology received contracts in the same period totaling nearly $56,000,000. California Institute of Technology received more than $40,000,000, Columbia University, $19,000,000, Harvard, $15,000,000.

Of about 200 educational institutions receiving a total of $235,000,000 in research contracts from the Government, 19 universities and institutes accounted for three-fourths of the total. Of nearly 2,000 industrial organizations receiving a total of almost $1,000,000,000 in research contracts from the Government, less than 100 firms accounted for more than half of the total.

This great store of research presents the Nation with its greatest technological potential in its history. It presents, also, important questions as to the role of smaller businesses and of educational institutions in the maintenance of a high level of research and development in the postwar years.

PART THREE

POST-WAR PLANNING
FOR SCIENCE 1945-1950

Among the domestic problems facing the United States as the post-war period began, none was more important or more thoroughly debated in Congress than the question of science policy. The mushroom cloud over Hiroshima, signaling the advent of the atomic age, raised profound political and scientific issues. The dramatic medical advances of the war years produced expectations that new progress in medical research would be forthcoming. The increasing importance of research and development in the national defense program seemed to dictate the continuation of federal support for science. How, then, and to what extent should science be supported? What new government agencies would be necessary? How should atomic energy be developed? Should the government attempt to coordinate scientific research? In the five years from 1945 to 1950, politicians, government officials, and members of the scientific community grappled with these questions and sought, sometimes unsuccessfully, to find solutions.

I. The Planning Debate

⟨ A. *Senator Harley M. Kilgore, of West Virginia, was well informed about the nation's scientific organization, for he had spent more than three years studying the problems of scientific and technological mobilization. In 1945, as the war was coming to an end, he issued a report recommending that a National Science Foundation be established to support peacetime scientific research. Attractive to New Deal reformers and to anti-Bush scientists, his proposals touched off a long debate about post-war science policy. The following excerpt is from that Kilgore report. While reading it, keep in mind that the first atomic bomb had not yet been exploded; hence the complete lack of reference to atomic energy. U.S. Congress, Senate, Subcommittee on War Mobilization, Report, "The Government's Wartime Research and Development, 1940-44, Part II, Findings and Recommendations," 79 Cong., 1 sess. (1945), 26-29.*]

As a working basis for further discussion and study of the problems raised by the wartime growth of scientific research, a tentative draft of a bill has been prepared by several members of the subcommittee. The main features and principles of this bill are summarized below.

Any legislation of this sort should be designed to meet the problems of readjustment from war to peace. There is a definite need for a central scientific agency of the Government which will—

1. Provide for an increase, above the prewar level, in the Government's support of research and development activities in fields that are predominantly in the public interests, notably national defense, health and medical care, and the basic sciences.

2. Provide for an efficient formulation and coordination of all such federally supported research and development work, utilizing so far as possible the existing resources of public and

private research organizations, particularly nonprofit educational institutions and research foundations.

3. Stimulate a general expansion in research and development by private organizations and institutions.

4. Promote a wide flow of scientific and technical information to industry and agriculture and business, particularly small enterprises.

5. Encourage the rapid introduction and full use of scientific discoveries and the most advanced techniques and inventions.

A National Science Foundation should be established as an independent agency of the Federal Government. At its head should be a Director, chosen by the President with the advice and consent of the Senate and receiving a salary of $15,000 a year.

In exercising his authority and duties, the Director should consult with a National Science Board on all matters of major policy or program. This Board should consist of the Director, acting as Chairman, the Secretaries of War, Navy, Interior, Agriculture, Commerce, and Labor, the Attorney General, and the head of the Federal Security Agency, or their representatives, and eight members at large appointed by the President.

In general the administrative powers should be vested in the Director, but the allocation of funds to specific fields of research and development, the appointment of members to special advisory research committees, and similar duties or authority of primary importance should depend upon the approval of the Board. Thus, by providing guidance and acting as a check, the Board would share responsibility with the Director for the efficient operation of the Foundation.

The Foundation should not itself, as a general rule, perform any research or development work. Instead, it should make funds for this purpose available to other organizations, public or private, who are already staffed or equipped to do so. Wherever possible, these other organizations, including private individuals, should be encouraged to participate jointly in formulating, promoting, and carrying through the programs and projects which are deemed desirable in the public interest.

The National Science Board should be responsible for determining the allocation of research and development funds within the limits appropriated annually by Congress. As a guide, the proposed bill requires particular attention to be given to these categories of research and development: National defense; health and medical care; basic sciences; natural resources; methods, products, and processes which may be valuable for small business enterprises; and peacetime uses for wartime research and for wartime facilities.

The Board should be free to make such allocations of funds to these various categories as it sees fit, except in the case of research and development activities directed specifically toward the advancement of national defense or the advancement of health and medical care or the advancement of the basic sciences. For each of these three categories at least 20 percent of the annual research appropriations should be reserved. As a further guaranty of proper balance in the allocation of funds, at least 50 percent should be earmarked for nonprofit educational institutions and research foundations.

Three special research committees — one for national defense, one for health and medical care, and one for the basic sciences — should be set up within the Foundation to advise on the formulation of research programs and to assist in the selection of facilities and the determination of specific projects. Each of these research committees should be made up of representatives of other Government agencies, and members at large selected mainly from panels drawn up by the National Academy of Sciences, the American Association for the Advancement of Science, and other scientific groups. Members at large for each committee should be appointed by the Director and the National Science Board.

Funds allocated for research in fields which do not come within the direct purview of the three special research committees should be spent under the direct supervision of the Director and the National Science Board.

Organizations receiving funds should be free to conduct their research and development work in a manner which they think most productive subject only to routine supervision and review by the foundation. It is believed fundamental to the Foundation's own success in promoting cooperative research and development that individual scientists and technologists should be encouraged to exercise their creative talents and to develop promising new ideas, and, moreover, that they should not be prevented in any way from expressing their personal opinions and beliefs on scientific and technical matters (except when in violation of national security). The proposed bill offers such provisions.

Besides contracting for research in the national interest, the Foundation should be directed to discover and develop scientific talent, particularly in American youth. To this end it should be empowered to grant fellowships and scholarships in various fields of science.

The Foundation clearly should make a continuing survey of all research and development activities financed or conducted by the Government. Survey data could then be studied to determine what changes in administration or procedure might be desirable. Recommendations would be submitted to the agencies concerned for such action as they might wish to take.

The Foundation should also undertake to compile and maintain a comprehensive inventory of the findings and other pertinent data resulting from publicly financed research and development activities. It should be charged with making such information available in the form of reports or publications which could be distributed widely to persons and groups engaged in scientific or technical work. Information concerning inventions and discoveries which have resulted from wartime research and development would be included provided that military security did not demand continued secrecy.

In every way feasible the Foundation should promote a wide distribution of scientific and technical information. Specifically suggested in the proposed bill are abstracts and microfilm reproductions of materials assembled in the Foundation's library, and periodic reports reviewing scientific and technical advances and calling the attention of scientists and technologists to new problems that should be solved in the national interest.

To protect the taxpayer's interest, all research and development projects financed in whole or in part by the Federal Government should be undertaken only upon the condition that any invention or discovery resulting therefrom would become the property of the United States.

The Foundation should also be empowered to grant nonexclusive licenses to persons or organizations wishing to use any such invention, discovery, patent, or patent right. No charge should be made for such licenses.

The proposed bill does not specify any fixed amount as the sum which Congress should appropriate annually to the Foundation. It merely authorizes such sums as may be needed to carry out the provisions of the bill. Such sums would, of course, be supplementary to the regular appropriations received by departments and agencies of the Federal Government for research and development, and should be determined accordingly.

❡ B. *In November 1944 President Roosevelt asked Vannevar Bush to initiate a study of science policy and to recommend a post-war scientific program. As Director of OSRD, Bush was well qualified to undertake the assignment, for he commanded the cooperation and endorsement of the major spokesmen of American science. His report, submitted in July 1945, was entitled* Science the Endless Frontier, *from which the following passage is taken. Bush called for the creation of a National Research Foundation controlled by scientists, not by politicians. Notice that his suggestions on organization and patent policy differed with Kilgore's earlier proposals. The Bush report was widely quoted and quickly overshadowed the Kilgore report. The atomic explosion over Hiroshima had still not taken place when this was written.* Vannevar Bush, Science the Endless Frontier, A Report to the President on a Program for Postwar Scientific Research *(Washington: GPO, 1945), 11-12, 32-40.*]

It has been basic United States policy that Government should foster the opening of new frontiers. It opened the seas to clipper ships and furnished land for pioneers. Although these frontiers have more or less disappeared, the frontier of science remains. It is in keeping with the American tradition —one which has made the United States great—that new frontiers shall be made accessible for development by all American citizens.

Moreover, since health, well-being, and security are proper concerns of Government, scientific progress is, and must be, of vital interest to Government. Without scientific progress the national health would deteriorate; without scientific progress we could not hope for improvement in our standard of living or for an increased number of jobs for our citizens; and without scientific progress we could not have maintained our liberties against tyranny. . . .

[Yet] we have no national policy for science. The Government has only begun to utilize science in the Nation's welfare. There is no body within the Government charged with formulating or executing a national science policy. There are no standing committees of the Congress devoted to this important subject. Science has been in the wings. It should be brought to the center of the stage—for in it lies much of our hope for the future.

There are areas of science in which the public interest is acute but which are likely to be cultivated inadequately if left without more support than will come from private sources. These areas—such as research on military problems, agriculture, housing, public health, certain medical research, and research involving expensive capital facilities beyond the capacity of private institutions—should be advanced by active Government support. To date, with the exception of the intensive war research conducted by the Office of Scientific Research and Development, such support has been meager and intermittent.

For reasons presented in this report we are entering a period when science needs and deserves increased support from public funds. . . .

There are certain basic principles which must underlie the program of Government support for scientific research and education if such support is to be effective and if it is to avoid impairing the very things we seek to foster. These principles are as follows:

(1) Whatever the extent of support may be, there must be stability of funds over a period of years so that long-range programs may be undertaken.

(2) The agency to administer such funds should be composed of citizens selected only on the basis of their interest in and capacity to promote the work of the agency. They should be persons of broad interest in and understanding of the peculiarities of scientific research and education.

(3) The agency should promote research through contracts or grants to organizations outside the Federal Government. It should not operate any laboratories of its own.

(4) Support of basic research in the public and private colleges, universities, and research institutes must leave the

internal control of policy, personnel, and the method and scope of the research to the institutions themselves. This is of the utmost importance.

(5) While assuring complete independence and freedom for the nature, scope, and methodology of research carried on in the institutions receiving public funds, and while retaining discretion in the allocation of funds among such institutions, the Foundation proposed herein must be responsible to the President and the Congress. Only through such responsibility can we maintain the proper relationship between science and other aspects of a democratic system. The usual controls of audits, reports, budgeting, and the like, should, of course, apply to the administrative and fiscal operations of the Foundation, subject, however, to such adjustments in procedure as are necessary to meet the special requirements of research.

Basic research is a long-term process — it ceases to be basic if immediate results are expected on short-term support. Methods should therefore be found which will permit the agency to make commitments of funds from current appropriations for programs of five years duration or longer. Continuity and stability of the program and its support may be expected (a) from the growing realization by the Congress of the benefits to the public from scientific research, and (b) from the conviction which will grow among those who conduct research under the auspices of the agency that good quality work will be followed by continuing support. . . .

It is my judgment that the national interest in scientific research and scientific education can best be promoted by the creation of a National Research Foundation.

I. PURPOSES

The National Research Foundation should develop and promote a national policy for scientific research and scientific education, should support basic research in nonprofit organizations, should develop scientific talent in American youth by means of scholarships and fellowships, and should by contract and otherwise support long-range research on military matters.

II. MEMBERS

1. Responsibility to the people, through the President and Congress, should be placed in the hands of, say nine

Members, who should be persons not otherwise connected with the Government and not representative of any special interest, who should be known as National Research Foundation Members, selected by the President on the basis of their interest in and capacity to promote the purposes of the Foundation. . . .

3. The Members should serve without compensation but should be entitled to their expenses incurred in the performance of their duties. . . .

5. The chief executive officer of the Foundation should be a director appointed by the Members. Subject to the direction and supervision of the Foundation Members (acting as a board), the director should discharge all the fiscal, legal, and administrative functions of the Foundation. The director should receive a salary that is fully adequate to attract an outstanding man to the post. . . .

III. ORGANIZATION

1. In order to accomplish the purposes of the Foundation, the Members should establish several professional Divisions to be responsible to the Members. At the outset these Divisions should be:

A. Division of Medical Research. — The function of this Division should be to support medical research.

B. Division of Natural Sciences. — The function of this Division should be to support research in the physical and natural sciences.

C. Division of National Defense. — It should be the function of this Division to support long-range scientific research on military matters.

D. Division of Scientific Personnel and Education. — It should be the function of this Division to support and to supervise the grant of scholarships and fellowships in science.

E. Division of Publications and Scientific Collaboration. — This Division should be charged with encouraging the publication of scientific knowledge and promoting international exchange of scientific information.

2. Each Division of the Foundation should be made up of at least five members, appointed by the Members of the

Foundation. In making such appointments the Members should request and consider recommendations from the National Academy of Sciences....

V. PATENT POLICY

The success of the National Research Foundation in promoting scientific research in this country will depend to a very large degree upon the cooperation of organizations outside the Government. In making contracts with or grants to such organizations the Foundation should protect the public interest adequately and at the same time leave the cooperating organizations with adequate freedom and incentive to conduct scientific research. The public interest will normally be adequately protected if the Government receives a royalty-free license for governmental purposes under any patents resulting from work financed by the Foundation. There should be no obligation on the research institution to patent discoveries made as a result of support from the Foundation. There should certainly not be any absolute requirement that all rights in such discoveries be assigned to the Government, but it should be left to the discretion of the Director and the interested Division whether in special cases the public interest requires such an assignment. Legislation on this point should leave to the Members of the Foundation discretion as to its patent policy in order that patent arrangements may be adjusted as circumstances and the public interest require.

VI. SPECIAL AUTHORITY

In order to insure that men of great competence and experience may be designated as Members of the Foundation and as Members of the several professional Divisions, the legislation creating the Foundation should contain specific authorization so that the Members of the Foundation and the Members of the Divisions may also engage in private and gainful employment, notwithstanding the provisions of any other laws; provided, however, that no compensation for such employment is received in any form from any profit-making institution which receives funds under contract, or otherwise, from the Division or Divisions of the Foundation with which the individual is concerned. In normal times, in view of the restrictive statutory prohibitions against dual interests on the part of Government officials, it would be virtually impossible to persuade persons having private employment of any kind to serve the Government in an official capacity....

Since research is unlike the procurement of standardized items, which are susceptible to competitive bidding on fixed specifications, the legislation creating the National Research Foundation should free the Foundation from the obligation to place its contracts for research through advertising for bids. This is particularly so since the measure of a successful research contract lies not in the dollar cost but in the qualitative and quantitative contribution which is made to our knowledge. The extent of this contribution in turn depends on the creative spirit and talent which can be brought to bear within a research laboratory. The National Research Foundation must, therefore, be free to place its research contracts or grants not only with those institutions which have a demonstrated research capacity but also with other institutions whose latent talent or creative atmosphere affords promise of research success.

As in the case of the research sponsored during the war by the Office of Scientific Research and Development, the research sponsored by the National Research Foundation should be conducted, in general, on an actual cost basis without profit to the institution receiving the research contract or grant.

There is one other matter which requires special mention. Since research does not fall within the category of normal commercial or procurement operations which are easily covered by the usual contractual relations, it is essential that certain statutory and regulatory fiscal requirements be waived in the case of research contractors.... Adherence to the usual procedures in the case of research contracts will impair the efficiency of research operations and will needlessly increase the cost of the work to the Government....Colleges and universities in which research will be conducted principally under contract with the Foundation are, unlike commercial institutions, not equipped to handle the detailed vouchering procedures and auditing technicalities which are required of the usual Government contractors.

VII. BUDGET

Studies by the several committees provide a partial basis for making an estimate of the order of magnitude of the funds

111

required to implement the proposed program. Clearly the program should grow in a healthy manner from modest beginnings. The following very rough estimates are given for the first year of operation after the Foundation is organized and operating, and for the fifth year of operation when it is expected that the operations would have reached a fairly stable level:

Activity	Millions of dollars	
	First year	Fifth year
Division of Medical Research	$ 5.0	$20.0
Division of Natural Sciences	10.0	50.0
Division of National Defense	10.0	20.0
Division of Scientific Personnel and Education	7.0	29.0
Division of Publications and Scientific Collaboration	.5	1.0
Administration	1.0	2.5
	33.5	122.5

The National Research Foundation herein proposed meets the urgent need of the days ahead. The form of the organization suggested is the result of considerable deliberation. The form is important. The very successful pattern of organization of the National Advisory Committee for Aeronautics, which has promoted basic research on problems of flight during the past thirty years, has been carefully considered in proposing the method of appointment of Members of the Foundation and in defining their responsibilities. Moreover, whatever program is established it is vitally important that it satisfy the Five Fundamentals....

Legislation is necessary. It should be drafted with great care. Early action is imperative, however, if this Nation is to meet the challenge of science and fully utilize the potentialities of science. On the wisdom with which we bring science to bear against the problems of the coming years depends in large measure our future as a Nation.

¶ *C. President Harry S. Truman, although personally untutored in science, recognized the need for scientific research. He marveled at the advent of the atomic age and was persuaded that the federal support of scientific research should be continued in peacetime. The following excerpt illustrates his position. Notice that he too suggested the creation of a federal research agency and that he stressed the need for continued progress in science. Harry S. Truman, "Special Message to Congress Presenting a 21-Point Program for the Reconversion Period," Sept. 6, 1945, Public Papers of the Presidents of the United States, Harry S. Truman, 1946 (Washington: GPO, 1962), 292-294.]*

Progress in scientific research and development is an indispensable condition to the future welfare and security of the Nation. The events of the past few years are both proof and prophecy of what science can do.

Science in this war has worked through thousands of men and women who labored selflessly and, for the most part, anonymously in the laboratories, pilot plants, and proving grounds of the Nation.

Through them, science, always pushing forward the frontiers of knowledge, forged the new weapons that shortened the war.

Progress in science cannot depend alone upon brilliant inspiration or sudden flights of genius. We have recently had a dramatic demonstration of this truth. In peace and in war, progress comes slowly in small new bits, from the unremitting day-by-day labors of thousands of men and women.

No nation can maintain a position of leadership in the world of today unless it develops to the full its scientific and technological resources. No government adequately meets its responsibilities unless it generously and intelligently supports and encourages the work of science in university, industry, and in its own laboratories.

During the war we have learned much about the methods of organizing science, and about the ways of encouraging and supporting its activities.

The development of atomic energy is a clear-cut indication of what can be accomplished by our universities, industry, and Government working together. Vast scientific fields remain to be conquered in the same way.

In order to derive the full profit in the future from what we have learned, I urge upon the Congress the early adoption of legislation for the establishment of a single Federal research agency which would discharge the following functions:

1. Promote and support fundamental research and development projects in all matters pertaining to the defense and security of the Nation.

2. Promote and support research in the basic sciences and in the social sciences.

3. Promote and support research in medicine, public health, and allied fields.

4. Provide financial assistance in the form of scholarships and grants for young men and women of proved scientific ability.

5. Coordinate and control diverse scientific activities now conducted by the several departments and agencies of the Federal Government.

6. Make fully, freely, and publicly available to commerce, industry, agriculture, and academic institutions, the fruits of research financed by Federal funds.

Scientific knowledge and scientific research are a complex and interrelated structure. Technological advances in one field may have great significance for another apparently unrelated. Accordingly, I urge upon the Congress the desirability of centralizing these functions in a single agency.

Although science can be coordinated and encouraged, it cannot be dictated to or regimented. Science cannot progress unless founded on the free intelligence of the scientist. I stress the fact that the Federal research agency here proposed should in no way impair that freedom.

Even if the Congress promptly adopts the legislation I have recommended, some months must elapse before the newly established agency could commence its operations. To fill what I hope will be only a temporary gap, I have asked the Office of Scientific Research and Development and the Research Board for National Security to continue their work.

Our economic and industrial strength, the physical well-being of our people, the achievement of full employment and full production, the future of our security, and the preservation of our principles will be determined by the extent to which we give full and sincere support to the works of science.

It is with these works that we can build the highroads to the future.

❡ *D. Shortly after the publication of* Science the Endless Frontier, *a small group of men in the office of the Chief Executive determined that still another study of postwar science would be necessary. These men strongly objected to certain aspects of the Bush Report. First, they detected an underlying anti-democratic sentiment which they believed should be countered. Second, they thought that Bush had dealt unfairly with government science and that he had magnified the importance of university science. With the cooperation of John R. Steelman, one of Truman's assistants, they put together a report which placed questions of science policy squarely in a political context. Incidentally, they reinforced the Kilgore position. Notice particularly the suggestion that various science coordinating agencies should be established within the executive branch. John R. Steelman,* Science and Public Policy, *Vol. I,* A Program for the Nation *(Washington: GPO, 1947), 3-7, 61, 65.]*

The security and prosperity of the United States depend today, as never before, upon the rapid extension of scientific knowledge. So important, in fact, has this extension become to our country that it may reasonably be said to be a major factor in national survival. This fact lends an urgency to the studies of the President's Scientific Research Board.

A generation which has witnessed the awful destructiveness of the atom bomb or which has read newspaper accounts of developments in biological warfare needs no special demonstration of the relation of science to military preparedness. In the war, the laboratory became the first line of defense and the scientist, the indispensable warrior. There is no likelihood that this would be changed in event of another conflict. . . .

It is unfortunate that any part of the case for Federal support of science should rest upon its military importance. But no responsible person can fail to recognize the uneasy character of the present peace. The scientific isolationism which inevitably results increases the urgency of Federal support for science and influences the balance in any recommended program.

Scientific discovery is equally the basis for our progress against poverty and disease. This, alone, would provide adequate justification for public interest and support.

If we are to remain a bulwark of democracy in the world, we must continually strengthen and expand our domestic economy and our foreign trade. A principal means to this end is through the constant advancement of scientific knowledge and the consequent steady improvement of our technology....

The technology in which we excel and which has transformed us in some 80 years from a backward agricultural nation to a world power rests upon progress in the basic sciences. Only through research and more research can we provide the basis for an expanding economy, and continued high levels of employment.

Moreover, the future is certain to confront us with competition from other national economies of a sort we have not hitherto had to meet. Many of these will be state-directed in the interest of national policies. Many will be supported by new, highly efficient industrial plant and equipment—by the most modern technology. The destructiveness of the recent war makes it inevitable that much of Europe, in rebuilding its factories, will soon possess an industrial plant more modern than ours of today....

Our technology is sufficiently advanced and our resources sufficiently adequate so that there is no immediate prospect that we shall fall technologically behind. We shall in the future, however, have to rely largely upon our own efforts in the basic sciences to provide the basis for that improvement. The danger lies in the future.

As a people, our strength has lain in practical application of scientific principles, rather than in original discoveries. In the past, our country has made less than its proportionate contribution to the progress of basic science. Instead, we have imported our theory from abroad and concentrated on its application to concrete and immediate problems. This was true even in the case of the atomic bomb. The basic discovery of nuclear fission was made by Otto Hahn and F. Strassman in Germany, founded on preliminary research in Italy, and published in a German periodical in January, 1939, just before the laboratories of Europe went dark.

That free exchange of ideas which formerly permitted us to import to meet our needs no longer prevails. Europe's laboratories are still blacked out and are likely to remain so as long as the unsettled state of the world continues. . . . The unity of western civilization has been shattered, and for the first time in our history, we are on our own so far as the extension of knowledge is concerned.

It is to our national interest to make a maximum effort to restore the conditions of free international cooperation among scientists which existed before parts of the world came under totalitarian domination. It is equally important to our interest, as part of the plans for reconstruction of the devestated countries of Europe and Asia, for us to lend every possible aid to the re-establishment of productive conditions of scientific research and development in all those countries willing to enter whole-heartedly into cooperation with us.

There was little fundamental research during the war, but there was enormous progress in the application of existing theories and principles. In some areas, we have already reached a point where further development must wait on the discovery of new bodies of general principles. . . .

Most major nations of the world recognize the essential importance of science to them and are expanding their research and development budgets. The Soviet Union's 1947 budget, for example, is reported to provide $1.2 billion as compared with outlays of $900 million in 1946. In addition, the Russians have embarked upon a five-year program of stepped-up scientific training, under which they are reported to be producing 140,000 engineers and scientists each year. In Britain, the Barlow Committee recently recommended a program to double the annual production of scientists. Even a small country like Belgium, whose economy was seriously disrupted by the war, has recently doubled its research and development expenditures.

The drying up of European scientific sources, the disruption of normal international exchange of scientific knowledge, and the virtual exhaustion of our stockpile of basic knowledge in important areas alter every premise upon which our thinking about scientific research and development has been based.

It is against this broad background of world tendencies and developments that the investigations of the President's Scientific Research Board have been undertaken and recommendations worked out. Public policy cannot be shaped in a vacuum and recommendations for a national policy on science must necessarily reflect many considerations but remotely connected with the laboratory.

In the light of the world situation and of the position of science in this country, this report will urge:

1. That, as a Nation, we increase our annual expenditures for research and development as rapidly as we can expand facilities and increase trained manpower. By 1957 we should be devoting at least one percent of our national income to research and development in the universities, industry, and the Government.

2. That heavier emphasis be placed upon basic research and upon medical research in our national research and development budget. Expenditures for basic research should be quadrupled and those for health and medical research tripled in the next decade, while total research and development expenditures should be doubled.

3. That the Federal Government support basic research in the universities and nonprofit research institutions at a progressively increasing rate, reaching an annual expenditure of at least $250 million by 1957.

4. That a National Science Foundation be established to make grants in support of basic research, with a Director appointed by and responsible to the President. The Director should be advised by a part-time board of eminent scientists and educators, half to be drawn from outside the Federal Government and half from within it.

5. That a Federal program of assistance to undergraduate and graduate students in the sciences be developed as an integral part of an over-all national scholarship and fellowship program.

6. That a program of Federal assistance to universities and colleges be developed in the matters of laboratory facilities and scientific equipment as an integral part of a general program of aid to education.

7. That a Federal Committee be established, composed of the directors of the principal Federal research establishments, to assist in the coordination and development of the Government's own research and development programs.

8. That every effort be made to assist in the reconstruction of European laboratories as a part of our program of aid to peace-loving countries. Such aid should be given on terms which require the maximum contributions toward the restora-

tion of conditions of free international exchange of scientific knowledge. . . .

The task of policy formulation for the Federal research and development program requires establishment of a number of coordinating centers within the executive branch of the Government. These would be called upon to make determinations upon a number of interrelated problems, of which the most important are:

1. An over-all picture of the allocations of research and development functions among the Federal agencies, and the relative emphasis placed upon fields of research and development within the Federal Government must be available.

2. A central point of liaison among the major research agencies to secure the maximum interchange of information with respect to the content of research and development programs and with respect to administrative techniques must be provided.

3. There must be a single point close to the President at which the most significant problems created in the research and development program of the Nation as a whole can be brought into top policy discussions.

Setting up an organization to handle these diverse functions is not a simple task that can be solved, for example, by establishment of a Department of Science. Such an approach was considered in the course of these studies and, after consultation with scientists and administrators, was rejected. . . .

The three existing mechanisms in the Executive Branch for policy formulation with respect to research and development are inadequate when measured against the policy problems that must be more effectively dealt with.

The following steps should be taken:

1. An Interdepartmental Committee for Scientific Research should be created.

2. The Bureau of the Budget should set up a unit for reviewing Federal scientific research and development programs.

3. The President should designate a member of the White House staff for scientific liaison.

II. THE NATIONAL SCIENCE FOUNDATION CONTROVERSY

❡ A. *By mid-1945 both Senator Kilgore and Vannevar Bush had suggested the creation of a National Science Foundation, but no specific legislation had been placed in the Congressional hopper. At Bush's request, Senator Warren G. Magnuson introduced the first National Science Foundation bill in July 1945. Kilgore, who had expected to collaborate with Bush on this legislation, hastened to introduce his own bill. A series of joint hearings with both Magnuson and Kilgore participating then took place in the fall of 1945. These hearings were the most extensive and the most revealing of all the hearings held on the proposed NSF. The following memorandum, written several months after the hearings by a member of Steelman's staff, contains a summary of the issues over which controversy arose. J. Donald Kingsley to John R. Steelman, December 31, 1946, Official File 192-E, Papers of Harry S. Truman, Harry S. Truman Library, Independence, Missouri.]*

... One large group of scientists, rallying under the flag of Dr. Vannevar Bush originally supported S. 1285—the Magnuson Bill—to establish a National Science Foundation. Many other scientists, best identified as the Urey-Shapley-Condon group, supported S. 1297—the Kilgore (and Administration) bill. . . .

The differences between the two groups of scientists and the legislation they espouse are basic. The major ones may be summarized under three headings:

First: Organization. The Bush group favors a strong National Science Board which would control the Director of the Foundation and the Foundation's work. The director would be appointed by the President "upon the recommendation of the Board."

The Urey-Shapley-Condon group prefers an "inline" organization with a strong Director appointed by and responsible to the President. The National Science Board would be advisory but would not control.

Second: The Social Sciences. The Bush group opposes the inclusion of the Social Sciences among the Divisions of the Foundation. The Urey-Shapley group favors including the social sciences.

Third: Patent Policy. The Bush group (and the Magnuson and Mills Bills) would retain the traditional patent policy, followed by the Office of Scientific Research and Development during the war. Under this policy private interests could patent results of work supported wholly or partially by Federal funds unless this right was specifically restricted in the terms of the contract under which it was done.

The Urey-Shapley group (and the Kilgore Bill) favors a clearly outlined patent policy designed to insure that the results of government supported research are made available to all and are not patented by individuals or corporations.

The differences between the Bush group and the Urey-Shapley-Condon group are, very broadly speaking, the differences between a small "inner" group closely allied with a few powerful institutions and large corporations (where most wartime research was conducted), and on the other hand, a larger group of scientists with interests widely spread throughout the nation and with a desire to avoid—insofar as possible—the concentration of research and the power to control it. Very reputable and honest men can be found on both sides. While the Urey-Shapley group is much larger it has no monopoly on sincere and worthy scientists. The Bush group is probably more "conservative" as a whole; this partially explains their stand on the Social Sciences.

The Administration is committed to the Kilgore Bill (or the compromise bill S. 1850). This is made plain in the President's message of September 6, 1946 [*sic*,1945] and in Mr. John Snyder's letter of October 25 [1945] to Senators Magnuson and Kilgore, in which he speaks specifically for the President. Correspondence between the Director of the Bureau of the Budget, the Director of OWMR and Mr. Vannevar Bush also makes the Administration position abundantly clear. Notwithstanding the President's position, Mr. Bush, and to a lesser but still noticeable degree, the Secretaries of War and Navy, supported the anti-administration Magnuson Bill, then "reneged" on the compromise bill S. 1850.

The position of the armed forces against the Administration position centers largely around patent policy; that of Dr. Bush around all three of the issues outlined in this memorandum.

¶ *B. The question of organization — whether a board or a single director should run the National Science Foundation — caused heated debate. This selection from the testimony of Harold D. Smith, Director of the Bureau of the Budget, illustrates the anti-Bush point of view. Smith, as one of the President's closest advisers, was speaking for the Truman administration and, at the same time, defending the Kilgore position on organization. U.S. Congress, Senate, Subcommittee of the Committee on Military Affairs, Hearings, "Hearings on Science Legislation," 79 Cong., 1 sess. (Oct. and Nov., 1945), 103-105.*]

If there is one thing that we have learned in Government administration over the years, it is that we should get away from boards. We have had ample recent and other experience in the Federal Government that I think demonstrates that very clearly, and I feel quite keenly that it would be a great mistake to establish a board for this purpose.... I think the most successful formula we have been able to devise and which experience supports is the single administrator with an advisory board. That would be the result of our Federal experience, and it would be the result of our State experience....

I would not give advice on the theory and application of the atomic bomb. I have no hesitancy, on the other hand, in giving advice in the field of public administration. I think that we have learned something about that, and that it also has some of the attributes of science. I feel it is my duty to keep the scientists from making a mistake in the field of public administration....

As a matter of fact, I would say that the discussions in the hearings ... have made far too much of the problem of an administrative organization. My feeling is that there is a natural, perhaps justifiable attitude on the part of scientists to be a bit afraid of this new instrument. I know some of them personally, and I know some of their views and their fears. I think most of those fears are unjustified....

I think that we must enter this new program because of its

vast importance with an element of good faith on all sides, and I think that we should not, may I say, prostitute what experience has shown to be good administrative organization because of the fears on the part of those, many of whom have not entered the Government service and who know little about governmental work. I think the pattern of OSRD has been a good pattern, and that in itself is recent and very excellent experience that points to the single administrator with an advisory board, with many cooperating committees. . . . I see no reason for denying that experience, plus all of the other experience that I could indicate at length if I chose to do so.

❧ C. *The Bush point of view on organization had many champions. Perhaps the most articulate was James B. Conant, chemist and President of Harvard University. Senate Hearings, "Science Legislation," 982.*]

I have followed with interest the discussion which has been going on in these hearings about the relative merits of a single administrator directly responsible to the President, or an independent board. It seems to me that to some extent the proponents of the two schemes have had different ends in view. If this bill is for the establishment of another governmental agency which is going to operate in the usual way, then there is much to be said for a single responsible head to provide efficient administration. But if, on the other hand, we are here embarking on something new, which is the way I read the proposals, then the argument by analogy breaks down. As I see it, we are proposing to have the Federal Government undertake functions hitherto carried on largely by private foundations, namely, the support of fundamental research and the allocation of scholarship funds. We may as well admit that there will be difficulty in providing for the wise expenditure of this money. Human nature being what it is, in government, in education, in industry, anywhere, there will be pressure for money to flow here and to flow there for reasons that are not valid in terms of the objectives of the bill.

Now, I am not one of those who feel the Government cannot do this job, that anything that the Federal Government touches is bound to be so political as to be ineffective and inefficient. Quite the contrary, I believe if properly organized the Federal Government can do as effective a job as a private foundation. But I underline the phrase "if properly organized"....

It seems to me obvious a board will be more likely to take an impartial view than a single administrator, less likely to be subject to the harassing pressure of constituents who quite properly turn to their elected representatives every day in Washington. I am very much afraid that the scheme will be a failure if a single administrator is provided; with a board we stand a much better chance. University presidents are not unaware of politics and pressures. I feel it most fortunate that in my university I have little or no power to act alone. Only a board has the authority to act and a board, unlike an individual, is hard to get at and harder still to push around. That applies to a government, I take it, quite as much as to education.

I have heard it said that the proposal for a board is wrong because it introduces a novel procedure into government. I submit the whole idea of having the Federal Government make grants in aid to promote fundamental research is novel, and therefore justifies a special type of organization. A board rather than a single administrator has been found the best procedure by foundations with long experience with just such tasks; therefore, whether or not the procedure is novel in government, it is one that has been tested by experience.

◄ *D. Kilgore and Bush differed most vigorously over patent policy. The following excerpt, part of a face to face exchange between these two strong-minded men, is illustrative of their respective positions. Senate Hearings, "Science Legislation," 225-227.*]

THE CHAIRMAN: Doctor, my idea on this patent matter is somewhat different from yours.

DR. BUSH: Yes, I know that.

THE CHAIRMAN: The bill has never been intended by me as a patent reform. It has been intended, shall I say, as a governmental reform which I think must be effectuated if we are going to turn loose any great sums of money on research in this foundation.

For instance, looking at those patent clauses, they require the company to take a patent and give us a license. I think one of the things that we failed to think of, Doctor, is the fact that while the Government [gets] the shop rights on the patent...that is still not getting any good for the people of the United States. . . . We are still giving away something of vital importance to the people of the United States, who are the Government, really, if we are to believe the Constitution and the Declaration of Independence and a few other documents that we so carefully treasure.

DR. BUSH: You know, Senator, I would be much more enthusiastic about securing patent rights for government if I felt that the United States Government utilized its patent rights well after it obtained them. One of the things that we need to approach in any general discussion of patent matters is that problem. True, I have during the course of the war been instrumental in placing in the hands of government more patent rights and patents probably than were ever received before from any source, but it does trouble me exceedingly that after those rights are turned over to government, there is not, in my opinion, an adequate means for handling the patent rights that are owned by government.

There is a fallacy abroad that is a strange one, to the effect that if you destroy a patent you do something for the public. That, of course is a fallacy. If it were correct, there would be no sense in our having a large Patent Office down here, at great expense, to produce patents, and at equally great expense at some other point to destroy them... Yet when government receives a patent today in its hands, what does it do? It effectively destroys that patent. It licenses, ordinarily, all comers at no royalty, so that the effect is exactly the same as though no patent had been issued.

THE CHAIRMAN: Except for one thing. It does preclude anybody from having an exclusive use of patents... In the past, Doctor... the Government has never been able to get a patent itself. They got it by assignment by the individual patentee or the corporate assignee under the patent, and practically all the patents that we have acquired have been in the nature of national defense and matters pertaining thereto and have not had general application.

DR. BUSH: Yes; but it disturbs me here—

THE CHAIRMAN: So we had no experience in that?

DR. BUSH: Here in the field of electronics during this war, I have been instrumental in putting into the hands of the Government, the complete ownership in a thousand or more patents. Is that or is that not a good thing to do? For some parts of the industry, it may be a good thing, but for others, it may be very bad indeed. For example, suppose one of those patents covers fully some device that has commercial application that would be of benefit to the public, and that it would develop, but suppose in order to develop that device it is going to require the investment of a half million dollars to do the industrial designing, the engineering, the introduction of that into industry. We may have completely destroyed that particular thing. We may have made it impossible for anybody to produce that for the public use and benefit. We have put it in the hands of Government, and Government has no mechanism for doing that very thing. So I am not sure in my own mind, that we have done a good thing in every case when we have a complete assignment.

THE CHAIRMAN: Yes; but you must realize that these things you are talking about have all operated under secrecy. We don't know how business will react if they have free access to the information. Companies that can make it applicable may immediately come in and want to go into production on it, adding certain features of their own to it, and getting it into production. Isn't that a fact also?

DR. BUSH: But, I don't think that—

THE CHAIRMAN: (interposing) You think our industry is so monopolistically minded that they will not invest in anything unless they have a monopoly on it?

DR. BUSH: No; I am thinking of the little industry. All of my industrial experience has been with little organizations, small ones, some of which were utterly dependent upon the patent system for their continued existence. I am thinking about whether some little organization formed by some men who have returned from overseas, and who set up a little outfit and want to make an electronic device, can make that device, if there is a Government patent on it under which everyone is going to be licensed. If they get started and establish a market, anyone can enter.

THE CHAIRMAN: All right, but suppose, on the other hand, that that same patent you are talking about should be vested in some one of the big companies with monopolistic tendencies, who don't want competition, don't you also preclude that little group from getting any opportunity to take a crack on it unless they want to pay a high royalty, and also probably go into competition, plus the royalty, with the patent owner?

DR. BUSH: I haven't stated that the particular step that I might advocate would cure all of the difficulties of the patent system. I have simply said that it seems to me that it is a very large question, indeed, with many facets and I prefer to tackle it somewhere where it is being tackled on its generalities rather than as part of this bill.

THE CHAIRMAN: Doctor, I agree with you that the patent laws need some revision, they need a lot of revision, but that is a general patent law applying to everything. My thoughts on patents simply attempt to adapt the present situation to existing patent laws subject to such revision as may occur afterwards, and not leave it to future developments to protect the taxpayer in the money he spends in this.

❡ E. *Maury Maverick, one of the most colorful politicians of the New Deal era, held few men in awe, and certainly not men of science. During the Kilgore-Magnuson hearings, he listened to a parade of scientists point out the virtues of science and the vices of politics; he was tired. In his own testimony, as Director of the Smaller War Plants Corporation, he chose to reply to Isaiah Bowman, well-known scientist and President of Johns Hopkins University. The following passage, taken from that testimony, reveals not only an irritated politician but a certain anti-science sentiment. Senate Hearings, "Science Legislation," 368-369.*]

Without any tinge of sarcasm, it must be said that the doctor is a gentleman and a scholar of the first class, and a patriotic American.

But he need not be so smug.

I get a little tired of these hired hands of the monopolies and some of the professors, some of these bulldozing scientists, piously abrogating [sic] to themselves all the patriotism; I get tired of that. I get tired of their superior attitude. . . .

Permit me to reassure the worthy doctors who piously lecture the politicians—and lecture them a little.

Why should they cast suspicion of their fellow Americans who have been shown public confidence by having been elected in a free democratic election? Are these scientists jealous of the politicians?

Who was it who enacted the original National Academy of Sciences?

The Congress, and Abraham Lincoln. . . .

Let us speak of politicians. Who, for instance, was smart enough, and honest enough, to appoint Dr. Bowman to numerous scientific missions? A politician—and I might add, a statesman—named Franklin D. Roosevelt. Who appointed the great scientist, Dr. Vannevar Bush, to the Office of Scientific Research and Development? A duly elected public official, one Franklin D. Roosevelt.

Who, indeed, had the thinking to offer the legislation before you for the creation of this scientific body? Politicians —like the gentlemen of this committee. . . .

The moral character of politicians is just as high as the moral character of the American scientist. I say that deliberately—and I hope it will be heard by scientists everywhere. And I'm not sure but that the office holder has been, and is, more conscious of the public welfare than many scientists are. . . . The Congressional Record is public. Let the scientists make certain that the scientific record can be the same.

I do not wish to impugn even remotely the patriotism of the great scientists who have already appeared before you. Most of their testimony has been enlightening. But I suggest that all scientists remember there are other patriots in the world besides themselves and it would be a good idea to develop some social consciousness.

Let us all bear in mind that we have a political Government and that our Constitution is a political instrument. The political character of our Government guarantees democracy and freedom, in which the people, through their Government, decide what they want. A scientist, because he receives $50,000 a year working for a monopoly, or a big business, must remember that this does not necessarily make him pure except that he may be a pure scientist.

◖ *F.   Many scientists believed that to include the social sciences within the scope of the National Science Foundation would be a serious mistake. The next reading, taken from the testimony of Roger Adams, a prominent chemist, exemplifies the anti-social-science viewpoint and illustrates another area of controversy during the NSF hearings. Senate Hearings, "Science Legislation," 826-827.*]

The American Chemical Society is opposed to the inclusion of "Social science" mentioned in Committee Print S.

1285 of October 12 as one of the research and educational areas to be supported. Social science, which is primarily sociology and history, includes as well certain phases of psychology, political science, economics, and geography. It comprises all the phenomena of society, its origin and history, the progress of civilization, and the laws controlling human relations. But the methods of approach to the study of its problems, the complete lack of any fundamental laws, the necessity of analyzing vast bodies of facts, often unrelated, place this subject in the field of the humanities. It is not a science in the sense that the term "science" is to be interpreted in this bill. The importance of sociological studies cannot be questioned and the Government should support them, but its support should be in an independent bill and the control of the funds appropriated should be by individuals familiar with this field.

⟨ G. *Still another issue, that of geographical distribution of federal research funds, caused a flurry of debate. Kilgore and others wanted to insure the widest possible distribution of research support, claiming that without a formula for state by state distribution, most of the money would go to schools in the East. The Bush faction held that excellence should be supported regardless of other considerations. The issue was debated throughout the period 1945 to 1950. This selection, part of an article written in 1948, is by a Westerner who is convinced of the need for more equitable distribuiton of research funds. Clarence A. Mills, "Distribution of American Research Funds," Science, CVII (Feb. 6, 1948), 127-130.]*

Equity and wisdom in the distribution of Federal research funds seem of paramount importance in the years ahead. That such funds should and will be made available in large amounts seems now to be widely accepted. The drying up of private bequests has left no alternative. If our universities and research institutions are to continue fostering the American investigative spirit which has been so largely responsible for our past achievements, new sources of financial support must be found. Since the welfare of the whole country is directly concerned, it seems most appropriate that such aid be derived from Federal funds.

There exists no evidence that native intelligence is better in one part of the United States than in another. Opportunities for the blossoming of exceptional ability do vary sharply from region to region, however—a variation which is correlated closely with the availability of institutions of higher learning. This is particularly true of the development of young scientists; there is no way in which promising individuals can be discovered except by bringing them into close contact with science subjects. Encouragement of research in America must thus mean the greatest possible broadening of the base of student exposure, as well as the broadest possible support of promising individuals once they have been found. . . .

The obvious weakness of present distributional methods is that individual investigators are often the most biased in their appraisal of research proposals. Surely the projects they are working on seem most important to them; if not, they would not be so engaged. This weakness is of such basic significance today that it would almost seem imperative for disbursing committees to be prohibited from recommending grants to the institutions with committee representation. It seems clear that our top scientists are no more able to provide equitable distribution of funds at their disposal than are the politicians they have so castigated.

The author is well aware of the justification usually given for present distributional inequality—the larger research institutions receiving the lion's share of funds are best equipped for the prosecution of research. Such justification was very appropriate with the emergency needs for quick results during the war years. In peacetime, however, the basic need is not for quick results but rather for the broadest possible distribution of research opportunity to the country's whole population, especially where governmental funds or those collected from the whole country by popular subscription are concerned. . . .

Most large funds have been contributed, directly or indirectly, by the country at large, even though their distribution as grants from New York City assumes a distinct appearance of largess when minor sums go west of the Alleghenies. For Washington, D.C., to follow a similar course with purely public funds—in amounts which will soon dwarf into insignificance previous distributions for research—would mean a tragedy of major proportions to the scientific development of the country as a whole. Until the proper technique for assuring unbiased distribution of such funds has been devised, the President seems justified in withholding his approval of any science-support program. . . .

The time has arrived when the West should shake off the stunting dominance of the northeastern seaboard in scientific matters, insisting on autonomy and a just share of public funds for its scientific development. So long as the rich eastern institutions secure the major part of funds disbursed, western institutions will perforce remain relatively pauperized and their most promising young scientists drift eastward, where working facilities are more propitious.

Corrective measures, however, must go beyond restoring a proper balance between East and West. The present tendency to benefit representation on disbursing committees must be broken. Scientists themselves have demonstrated a most unfortunate inability to act without bias in overseeing the distribution of funds in their own fields. No one believes that the politicians would themselves do any better, but theirs is the duty of so legislating that the proper end will be accomplished where public funds are concerned.

In the long run, the greatest good to the greatest number would probably be served by securing the distribution of Federal research funds — or those collected by public subscription — on a state-population basis. Perhaps the less wealthy states should even receive an added bonus to stimulate development, instead of being almost completely cut off as at present. . . .

⬧ *H. Although Chauncey D. Leake, Vice President of the University of Texas, did not testify in 1945, he wrote to Senator Kilgore to point out the dangers of scientific orthodoxy. He was speaking for the scientists of the hinterland who were not well represented on the controlling boards of the scientific societies and who were fearful that a small number of men might take control of science. Senate Hearings, "Science Legislation," 967-968.*]

Proposed legislation before Congress for Federal support of scientific endeavor, and the report by Dr. Vannevar Bush to the President of the United States, entitled "Science, the Endless Frontier" (Washington, 1945), omit consideration of an important factor in scientific work. This is assurance of maintaining under any form of Government subsidy for scientific work that freedom for scientists which is requisite for the success of any scientific venture....

Science like democracy implies freedom. The ideals of scientific enterprise imply the utmost freedom in undertaking and conducting research, in publishing significant data, and in expressing opinions for which there is reasonable evidence....

It should become the clear responsibility of those placed in authority over a Federal program of scientific work, and who may exercise control over the federally supported scientific program, to prevent the development of any semblance of scientific orthodoxy in this country.

It is recommended, therefore, that the top control, as well as the various echelons of control of the proposed federally supported scientific program, be placed in professionally chosen groups which would have the widest possible geographical representation, and in which membership would be staggered so that representation would be regularly changed. It is recommended that under peacetime conditions no censorship whatsoever be permitted regarding the publication of scientific results obtained under Federal support. It is further recommended that no one should be selected to serve on any of the control committees or boards of the proposed federally supported scientific program who might at the same time hold office in a national scientific society, or be on the editorial board of a national scientific journal, or be on a national scientific committee of non-Federal character.

It is my considered judgment that these recommendations would materially aid in preventing the development of scientific orthodoxy in this country under Federal support, and that they would also prevent any interference with that freedom of research and reporting which is essential to the successful progress of scientific endeavor.

❡ I. *Frank B. Jewett was president of the National Academy of Sciences and Director of Bell Telephone Laboratories. He was nearing the end of a distinguished career. Despite his close collaboration with Bush during the war, he could not bring himself to embrace Bush's post-war program. He was, in fact, the only person to testify against the proposed*

National Science Foundation. He suggested that the tax laws should be changed to encourage individuals to support science voluntarily and in the traditional manner. U. S. Congress, House, Committee on Interstate and Foreign Commerce, Hearings, "National Science Foundation," 80 Cong., 1 sess. (March, 1947), 73-76.]

I think I would like to start by saying that my approach to this question of a Federal organization to dispense money in this field is the approach from a background of nearly 50 years of experience in the fields of science, both fundamental and applied, and engineering; and, of course, almost that amount of time in the observation of the way in which we here in America have, in the past, conducted our various institutions. . . .

The reason that has been given for the diminution of the amount of money which would be available for science and other things is the operation of the tax laws. Those are man-created things. If then, that being the case, Congress should decide that science should get more money than it is likely to get under the existing tax laws and should decide that it is more profitable to have that money flow in the traditional way, the process of directing a flow of money by voluntary giving is quite simple, viz, by changing the tax laws to stimulate increased voluntary giving. . . .

Now, over the years, if one looks at the history of giving in this country, one finds that at one period of time men and women were particularly interested in religion and churches, and the major part of the giving was in support of these, and at other times it was education, or medicine, or hospitals. More currently it has been in the fields of science. Always the pattern has been a gradually changing pattern, as men's interest changed. It has always been voluntary, however; and, in the main, it has resulted, I think, in a reasonable distribution of the best brains of the country into the several fields in which a complex civilization like ours has to be fructified with able people if the thing is going to function. It would be a calamity, in my judgment, to have one sector, whether it be law, or medicine, or engineering, or science, or what have you, elevated by law way above all the rest. Our economy simply would not work efficiently. . . .

So on two scores I am skeptical: First, as to the premise on

133

which the necessity for this foundation scheme is based, and, in the second place, I am very doubtful as to whether the people of the United States, for the money which is spent in this particular sector, will get as much value out of their dollars as they would get were they in a position to make the expenditures directly in the traditional way.

Further than that, it seems to me that if you set up a Federal corporation and furnish it with funds to spend in a particular sector of our economy, you are not only running the danger of overstimulating but you are certainly inviting the formation of pressure groups in the other sectors — the social sciences or a thousand and one other things — who feel that they have a valid claim of special treatment, and you are going to be confronted, in my judgment, in the not very distant future, with urgent claims to set up corresponding corporations to fructify other fields.

So from my own personal experience, and believing as I do that if you are sincerely interested and feel that science should be pushed forward faster than it is likely to go under present conditions and you want to get the most that you can out of it, I am quite certain that if you are willing to change the tax laws so as to put a slight premium on eleemosynary giving to those who give to science rather than to churches or hospitals or what not you will have more money through private channels than you can possibly justify through a channel of this kind. If you do it that way, you do not disturb any of the existing experiences — any of the existing channels of giving which have made this country great. At the same time Congress would not be subjecting itself to the political pressure which I think would be inevitable if a national science foundation is created. It will still have its hand on the throttle and it can regulate the flow of money in any way it sees fit by way of the tax laws.

◖ J. In 1947, after two years of compromise and political maneuvering, a National Science Foundation bill was passed by Congress. The Bush faction seemed to have won a great victory, but President Truman vetoed the measure. Although Truman favored the enactment of NSF legislation, he held that this particular bill was undesirable in many details. While reading his veto message, keep in mind that Congress passed another NSF bill in 1950 which received Truman's *approval.* Congressional Record, *Appendix (Aug. 15, 1947),* *A4442-A4443.*]

I am withholding my approval of S. 526, the National Science Foundation bill.

I take this action with deep regret. On several occasions I have urged the Congress to enact legislation to establish a National Science Foundation. Our national security and welfare require that we give direct support to basic scientific research and take steps to increase the number of trained scientists. I had hoped earnestly that the Congress would enact a bill to establish a suitable agency to stimulate and correlate the activities of the Government directed toward these ends.

However, this bill contains provisions which represent such a marked departure from sound principles for the administration of public affairs that I cannot give it my approval. It would, in effect vest the determination of vital national policies, the expenditure of large public funds, and the administration of important governmental functions in a group of individuals who would be essentially private citizens. The proposed National Science Foundation would be divorced from control by the people to an extent that implies a distinct lack of faith in democratic processes.

Moreover, the organization prescribed in the bill is so complex and unwieldy that there is grave danger that it would impede rather than promote the Government's effort to encourage scientific research. The Government's expenditures for scientific research and development activities currently amount to hundreds of millions of dollars a year. Under present world conditions this work is vital to our national welfare and security. We cannot afford to jeopardize it by imposing upon it an organization so likely to prove unworkable. . . .

The Constitution places upon the President the responsibility for seeing that the laws are faithfully executed. In the administration of this law, however, he would be deprived of effective means for discharging his constitutional responsibility.

Full governmental authority and responsibility would be placed in 24 part-time officers whom the President could not effectively hold responsible for proper administration. Neither could the Director be held responsible by the President for he would be the appointee of the Foundation and would be insulated from the President by two layers of part-time boards. In the case of the divisions and special commissions, the lack of accountability would be even more aggravated.

The members of the Foundation would also be authorized to appoint the full-time administrative head of an important agency in the executive branch of the Government as well as more than 70 additional part-time officials in whom important governmental powers would be vested. This represents a substantial denial of the President's appointing power, as well as an impairment of his ability to see that the laws are faithfully executed.

The ability of the President to meet his constitutional responsibility would be further impaired by the provisions of the bill which would establish an Interdepartmental Committee on Science. The members of this committee would be representatives of departments and agencies who are responsible to the President, but its chairman would be the Director of the Foundation. . . . Thus an officer who is not appointed by the President, and not responsible to him would be the man primarily charged with the performance of functions which are peculiarly within the scope of the President's duties; that is, the coordination of the work of executive agencies. . . .

There are other compelling reasons why control over the administration of this law should not be vested in the part-time members of the Foundation. The Foundation would make grants of Federal funds to support scientific research. The recipients of these grants would be determined in the discretion of the Foundation. The qualifications prescribed in the bill for members of the Foundation would insure that most of them would be individuals employed by institutions or organizations eligible for the grants. Thus, there is created a conflict of interests which would inevitably give rise to suspicions of favoritism, regardless of the complete integrity of the members of the Foundation. . . .

Adherence to the principle that responsibility for the administration of the law should be vested in full-time officers who can be held accountable will not prevent the Government from utilizing with great advantage the services of eminent scientists who are available only for part-time duty. We have ample evidence of the patriotic and unselfish contributions which such citizens can make to the success of governmental programs. The role to be played by such part-time participation, however, is more appropriately one of an advisory nature rather than of full responsibility. In other governmental programs of vast national importance this method is used to obtain advice and recommendations from impartial experts as well as from parties in interest. There is no reason why such a system cannot be incorporated in legislation establishing a National Science Foundation.

For the reasons I have indicated I believe that this bill raises basic issues of public policy.... If the principles of this bill were extended throughout the Government, the result would be utter chaos. There is no justification in this case for not using sound principles for normal governmental operations. I cannot agree that our traditional democratic form of government is incapable of properly administering a program for encouraging scientific research and education.

It is unfortunate that this legislation cannot be approved in its present form. The withholding of my signature at this time, however, will not prevent the Government from engaging in the support of scientific research....

I am convinced that the long-range interests of scientific research and education will be best served by continuing our efforts to obtain a Science Foundation free from the vital defects of this bill. These defects in the structure of the proposed Foundation are so fundamental that it would not be practicable to permit its establishment in this form with the hope that the defects might be corrected at a later date. We must start with a law which is basically sound.

I hope that the Congress will reconsider this question and enact such a law early in its next session.

III. The Quest for Control of
Atomic Energy

◀ A.   *When the first A-bomb was dropped in August 1945,
atomic energy became a great political and scientific issue.
Pending NSF bills were shoved aside and congressional interest was diverted to atomic energy legislation. With public
interest running high, the Truman administration raced to
prepare a program. The following is from Truman's message to
Congress requesting legislation to fix a policy for the use and
development of atomic energy.* U.S. Department of State,
International Control of Atomic Energy: Growth of a Policy
(*Washington: GPO, 1946*), *109-112*.]

Almost 2 months have passed since the atomic bomb was
used against Japan. That bomb did not win the war, but it
certainly shortened the war. We know that it saved the lives of
untold thousands of American and Allied soldiers who would
otherwise have been killed in battle.

The discovery of the means of releasing atomic energy
began a new era in the history of civilization. The scientific
and industrial knowledge on which this discovery rests does
not relate merely to another weapon. It may some day prove to
be more revolutionary in the development of human society
then the invention of the wheel, the use of metals, or the
steam or internal combustion engine.

Never in history has society been confronted with a power
so full of potential danger and at the same time so full of
promise for the future of man and for the peace of the world. I
think I express the faith of the American people when I say
that we can use the knowledge we have won, not for the
devastation of war, but for the future welfare of humanity.

To accomplish that objective we must proceed along two
fronts — the domestic and the international.

The first and most urgent step is the determination of our
domestic policy for the control, use, and development of
atomic energy within the United States.

We cannot postpone decisions in this field. The enormous investment which we made to produce the bomb has given us the two vast industrial plants in Washington and Tennessee, and the many associated works throughout the country. It has brought together a vast organization of scientists, executives, industrial engineers, and skilled workers—a national asset of inestimable value.

. . . Now that our enemies have surrendered, we should take immediate action to provide for the future use of this huge investment in brains and plant. I am informed that many of the people on whom depend the continued successful operation of the plants and the further development of atomic knowledge, are getting ready to return to their normal pursuits. In many cases these people are considering leaving the project largely because of uncertainty concerning future national policy in this field. Prompt action to establish national policy will go a long way toward keeping a strong organization intact.

It is equally necessary to direct future research and to establish control of the basic raw materials essential to the development of this power whether it is to be used for purposes of peace or war. . . .

I therefore urge, as a first measure in a program of utilizing our knowledge for the benefit of society, that the Congress enact legislation to fix a policy with respect to our existing plants, and to control all sources of atomic energy and all activities connected with its development and use in the United States.

The legislation should give jurisdiction for these purposes to an Atomic Energy Commission with members appointed by the President, with the advice and consent of the Senate.

The Congress should lay down the basic principles for all the activities of the Commission, the objectives of which should be the promotion of the national welfare, securing the national defense, safeguarding world peace, and the acquisition of further knowledge concerning atomic energy. . . .

The other phase of the problem is the question of the international control and development of this newly discovered energy.

In international relations, as in domestic affairs, the release of atomic energy constitutes a new force too revolutionary to consider in the framework of old ideas. We can no longer rely on the slow progress of time to develop a program of control among nations. Civilization demands that we shall reach at the earliest possible date a satisfactory arrangement for the control of this discovery in order that it may become a powerful and forceful influence toward the maintenance of world peace instead of an instrument of destruction.

Scientific opinion appears to be practically unanimous that the essential theoretical knowledge upon which the discovery is based is already widely known. There is also substantial agreement that foreign research can come abreast of our present theoretical knowledge in time.

The hope of civilization lies in international arrangements looking, if possible, to the renunciation of the use and development of the atomic bomb, and directing and encouraging the use of atomic energy and all future scientific information toward peaceful and humanitarian ends. . . .

I, therefore, propose to initiate discussions first with our associates in this discovery, Great Britain and Canada, and then with other nations, in an effort to effect agreement on the conditions under which cooperation might replace rivalry in the field of atomic power.

I desire to emphasize that these discussions will not be concerned with disclosures relating to the manufacturing processes leading to the production of the atomic bomb itself. . . .

But regardless of the course of discussions in the international field, I believe it is essential that legislation along the lines I have indicated be adopted as promptly as possible to insure the necessary research in, and development and control of, the production and use of atomic energy.

❡ B. *The Army had developed the atomic bomb; now it took the lead in suggesting legislation for the peacetime control of atomic energy. A committee of top-flight civilian scientists, working at the request of the Secretary of the Army, drafted proposals which were later introduced as the May-Johnson bill. In the next reading, General Leslie R. Groves, Director of the Manhattan Project, outlines some of the provisions of that bill. U.S. Congress, House, Committee on Military Affairs, Hearings, "Atomic Energy," 79 Cong., 1 sess. (Oct., 1945), 9-10.*]

In coming before your committee today we [the Army] are appealing for an opportunity to give you our existing powers. In the interest of the war effort, there was delivered into our care the responsibility for directing all activities relating to the release and use of atomic energy.

We have discharged that responsibility to the best of our ability. Thanks to the brilliant and selfless efforts of the thousands of scientists, engineers, industrialists, workers and Army and Navy officers associated with the project, and to the wise counsel of secretary Stimson and his advisers and the members of the Military Policy Committee, our work achieved its purpose....

But the individual responsibility that was desirable in wartime should not be continued today. The hopes and fears of all mankind are so inextricably bound up with the future development of atomic energy, and the problems requiring immediate solution are so fundamental that control should be vested in the most representative and able body our democratic society is capable or organizing.

The Bill you are considering today is intended to create such a body.

It would establish a commission of nine distinguished citizens, with a revolving membership to guard against political domination or the development within the commission of frozen attitudes that would act as a brake on experimentation and new ideas.

Within the limits of general policy, as defined by Congress, and of appropriations, as authorized by Congress, the commission would have broad power to conduct or supervise all research and manufacturing activities relating to the use of atomic energy for military or civilian purposes; to control the raw materials from which atomic energy may be derived and to provide for the security of information and property connected with the release of atomic energy. It is also the aim of this legislation that the commission capitalize on the initiative and ingenuity of American science and American industry by giving as much freedom and encouragement to private research and private enterprise in this field as it is possible to give consistent with the requirement of American security.

... At the root of this legislation lies a recognition of the importance of maintaining continued leadership by the United States in scientific progress, utilizing existing private and public facilities to the broadest extent.

The bill specifically provides for the most wide-spread practical distribution of licenses for atomic research and development within the United States and enjoins the Commission to discourage the growth of monopoly in trades and industries affected by these activities.

In order that the membership of the Commission may include outstanding leaders in American life, its members are not expected to devote their full time to the work of the Commission but are left free to engage in other activities.

The day-by-day work under the law would be carried out under the direction of an administrator and a deputy administrator, who will, of course, devote their entire time to their duties. These, too, should be men of the highest caliber who are willing to make the financial sacrifice necessary to accept such posts in the face of industry's ability to make more tempting salary offers . . . .

It is hoped that this work will attract young and highly talented scientists who will stay with the commission 5 or 6 years, after which they would leave to take better-paying jobs outside. I will say quite frankly that they should not be men who look forward to lifetime jobs on the project. The key staff of the project, both scientific and administrative, should be a rotating one so that the commission will not degenerate into a static organization with an inflexible approach to the problems involved in this vast and complicated field.

I should like before I close to emphasize . . . the desirability of speedy action on this measure. The decisions we now have to make will affect the welfare of the United States and of the world for many years to come. . . .

Here, more than ever before in our history, it is a case in which man is the keeper of his own destiny. In irresponsible hands, the power of the atom might destroy the world. Properly developed and properly administered, this same force can help light the way to a future of lasting peace and prosperity for all the people of the world. This bill is an important step in that direction.

❡ C. *Among the scientists who supported the May-Johnson bill was J. Robert Oppenheimer. This excerpt is from his testimony before the House Committee on Military Affairs.*

Notice the emphasis he places on the fact that Bush and Conant helped to draft the bill. House Hearings, "Atomic Energy," 127-128.]

. . . I would say a word or two about the bill. I did not have anything to do with the drafting of the bill, and I am not competent to judge of its adequacy.

It is certainly a bill which does not establish policy; it establishes a framework within which the policy agreed on by the Congress, by the American people, and expressed by the President, may be executed.

I share the confidence that the chairman has expressed in the ability of this Nation, in a matter of such great importance, to find nine reasonably intelligent and conscientious men to carry out whatever policy the country decides is right. I share his confidence that an administrator can be found who will carry out these policies in practice. No one that I have talked to would claim that the May bill makes it impossible to operate properly the many complicated and potentially dangerous elements in this project. The most that people claim is that it is not written into the bill just how these policies are to be formulated and how they are to be carried out.

In that connection I have one thing to add. The bill was drafted with the detailed supervision of Dr. Bush and Dr. Conant, with the knowledge and the agreement of the former Secretary of War, Mr. Stimson. I think that no one in the country carried a greater weight of responsibility for this project than Mr. Stimson. I think no men in positions of responsibility, who were scientists, took more responsibility or were more courageous or better informed in the general sense than Dr. Bush and Dr. Conant. I think if they liked the philosophy of this bill and urged this bill it is a very strong argument. I know that many scientists do not agree with me on this, but I am nevertheless convinced myself.

I would go one step further. It would in some ways be desirable to have a bill in which the powers of the Commission were much more carefully defined than they are in the May bill. I think that has not been done, for a good reason. It has not been done, because the subject is not only very important; it is very new. . . . Even if we forget the matters of policy connected with industrial exploitation, the matters

of policy connected with international relations, the dangers
of war and the possibilities of further war, we would still
have the fact that even the science in which this is working
is changing from day to day; and I hope it will change very
much in the next 10 years, because it is in these changes
that our real progress lies. . . . Dr. Bush and Dr. Conant, were
very much impressed by the rapidity with which they had
seen ideas change, by the rapidity with which they had seen
new possibilities brought in. They would have found it
unwise to write specific directives. . . . I think, therefore, it
is fair to say that the May bill has been written largely from
the point of view that we must have confidence in the Commission; we must have confidence in the Government of this
country. We are not in position to write detailed directives
that will be binding for any reasonable period in the future.
With the understanding that as the issues become clear it is
appropriate to reconsider the legislation, that it is appropriate not to regard it as a scheme for all eternity, but as a
measure which for the moment is the best that we could do.
In that sense I think it should be supported.

I want to say one thing purely as a representative of
scientists.

Scientists are not used to being controlled; they are not
used to regimentation, and there are good reasons why they
should be averse to it, because it is in the nature of science
that the individual is to be given a certain amount of freedom
to invent, to think, and to carry on the best he knows how.
Most of the scientists with whom I have talked would like
the assurances which are now in the bill, somewhat reinforced, about the intention of the Congress to direct the
Comission not to interfere with scientific work except when
there is a national hazard involved.

◀ *D. Opposition to the May-Johnson bill was slow in
developing, but a mass of negative opinion began to build
late in 1945. The Federation of Atomic Scientists, an organization hastily set up by the scientists who had built the bomb,
took the lead in the campaign against the bill. The following
is from the congressional testimony of Harrison Davies, who
was representing the Federation. U.S. Congress, Senate, Special Committee on Atomic Energy, Hearings, "Atomic Energy
Act of 1946," 79 Cong., 2 sess. (Jan.-Apr., 1946), 154-157.]*

I am here this morning to present the views of the Federation of Atomic Scientists, composed of scientists and engineers who have worked on the Manhattan project. For several months we have studied the various proposals for domestic legislation on atomic energy. As scientists, we desire legislation which will foster research and development in the field of atomic energy and will preserve the freedom necessary for the further advance of science. As citizens, we fear unwise laws on atomic energy for the same reason other citizens fear them: We, too, value our lives.

Long before the atomic bomb fell on Hiroshima we realized that it would affect political and economic ideas all over the world. While the rest of the world was preoccupied with war, we came to the view that our work might well have more far-reaching results than the winning of the war itself.

While we debated the issues and strove for a plan which might secure safety for the world and yet realize the full benefits of atomic energy, we lacked advice from other quarters. With the release of the bomb and the introduction of atomic energy legislation into the Congress, it became possible to form organizations, seek expert opinion in other fields, and publicize our views. We have done our best to add to our technical knowledge of atomic energy some understanding of the complex political, legal, and economic features of the problem.

The Federation of Atomic Scientists has developed a set of policies which our members believe should be embodied in atomic energy legislation. We now have the opportunity to compare our aims with the provisions of a specific bill. The McMahon bill satisfies these aims in great detail. . . .

I appear here today empowered by the groups which make up the Federation of Atomic Scientists to tell you why we like he McMahon bill; why we think that, with a few minor changes designed to strengthen the obvious intent of the bill, it will be the best practical solution of the problems of domestic legislation. . . .

There can be no real national security in a world in which many nations possess atomic weapons. There can be no solution of the problem of security short of an effective international control of atomic and other weapons of offense and of the elimination of war as a method of settling international disputes. Any domestic legislation must therefore encourage the international control of atomic energy. We believe that S. 1717 fulfills this requirement. The problem of the production of atomic bombs is treated specifically; responsibility is so fixed that international regulation must take precedence....

Vigorous research and development in nuclear science must be maintained. The use of the fission phenomenon and its byproducts in physical, chemical, biological, medical, and industrial research, as well as in power development, should greatly enrich our country and indeed all mankind.

Bill S. 1717 will foster such research and development through equitable distribution of fissionable material and of byproduct materials to all research workers, by granting funds to independent research organizations, such as universities, private and industrial laboratories, through the widest possible dissemination of information, and by creating a division of governmental research to insure a complete program....

Independent research is encouraged by the bill. Government research is not preferred above private research in the allocation of funds. We regard this as a highly desirable feature of legislation in the atomic energy field or for that matter in any other scientific field. The full development of science rests upon independent research by many individuals in many laboratories throughout the world.... All competent scientists should be allowed to study the problems of atomic energy and to obtain the materials and such funds as are necessary for their work....

The composition of the Commission has been discussed by the committee. Two hostile viewpoints have been presented. The Commission should be small for the sake of efficiency. On the other hand, the Commission, it is said, should be large in order to permit representation of the many groups whose affairs touch upon the Commission's activities. It occurs to us that a third and more desirable choice exists. We believe the Commission should be large enough to permit physically the discharge of its duties, but no larger. It should include among its members persons with pertinent specialized information. The Commission should include men with training and experience in, say, pure science and industry, not that the special interests of scientists and industrialists shall have voice but rather that the indicated experience shall be available. Commission members should have but one interest, the public welfare.... It is essential that their appointment be full time.

We wish to go on record most strongly as favoring complete exclusion of the military from any policy-making function on the Commission. By this we do not mean to exclude efficient liaison between the Commission and the armed forces... However, it is in best tradition of American Government that policy be made by civilians. A subject fraught with such tremendous significance to our foreign policy as the development of atomic energy in this country must certainly be freed from every vestige of military control.

◀ E. *As the campaign against the May-Johnson bill gathered momentum, the issue of civilian versus military control of atomic energy became paramount. Senator Brien McMahon and the science lobby claimed that Army officials were attempting to insure continued military control of atomic energy. They pleaded that is was essential for civilians to assume that control. The next reading is a newspaper column, part of a series written during the heat of the civilian control controversy. Alfred Friendly, "Debate Over Atom Confused by Clamor for Civil Control," Washington Post, March 21, 1946.*]

The most confusing aspect of the controversy now raging over civilian versus military control of atomic energy is the fact that all of the disputants say they favor civilian control.

For example, there is the case of Senator Vandenberg (R., Mich.).

The most important bill now pending in the Senate is that proposed by Senator McMahon (D., Conn.). It would establish an exclusively civilian commission to direct atomic research, development and applications. Senator Vandenberg proposed an amendment, which was adopted 10-1 (Senator McMahon dissenting), in the Senate Special Committee considering the legislation. The amendment provides for a military liaison board to work with the civilian commission.

The vocal opponents of the Vandenberg Amendment do not take the position that the armed services should be frozen out of the atomic picture.... They admit that... at present the dominant aspect of atomic energy is its use as a weapon. Therefore the Army and Navy should be guaranteed direct participation and full flow of information on all military phases of the problem.

But they insist the Vandenberg Amendment is wrong in

method. They contend that its broad wording gives the armed services domination over every aspect of atomic energy. More important, they claim that the proposed military board would have what amounts to veto powers over the civilian commission. . . .

But Senator Vandenberg does not see it this way. He says his amendment is strictly in line with President Truman's policy of civilian control — that, in fact, it merely translates that policy into legislation.

Another example: The Army has generally been credited with leading a fight for military command over atomic matters. But Secretary of War Patterson, citing a long and imposing record of statements and reports, asserts that the Army took the lead in urging civilian direction.

Even before the atomic bomb was tested, he reports, the Army advocated divesting itself of control. That was its policy, still is its policy, always will be its policy, he says. He, too, insists that the War Department stands four square with Mr. Truman's ideas on the subject.

And even Major General Groves, head of the Army's atom bomb project, and the man generally considered to be the No. 1 advocate of military domination, declares he favors civilian control. Even in urging that military officers be appointed to the control commission, he has plumped for having civilian members in the majority.

But despite the statements of Patterson, Groves, Vandenberg and the 10 members of the Senate Special Atomic Energy Committee, who supported his amendment, an opposition group contends that there is a concerted and determined drive to vest control in the military. . . .

This is the record they cite:

After V-J Day, the first legislation on the subject of atomic energy control was drafted in the War Department. It was introduced in the house by Representative May (D., Ky.) chairman of the Military Affairs Committee. In the Senate it was offered by Senator Johnson (D., Colo.).

It provided, among other things, for a part-time commission of nine men and a full-time administrator and deputy administrator. The bill contained explicit exemptions from the laws passed since 1870 barring military officers from civilian jobs. Thus, in appointing the commissioners and administrators under the proposed act, the President would be permitted, though not compelled, to name Army and Navy officers.

There is a unique provision in the bill. It declares in effect that the administrator is obliged to keep the deputy administrator informed at all times of what he is doing.

One explanation given for this apparently superfluous provision is that there was a "deal" between the Army and Navy to obtain the latter's support to the Army bill. An Army officer, presumably Groves, would be urged on the President as Administrator, and a Navy officer would be recommended as his deputy. But the Navy, frozen out more often than not in cooperation with the Army, apparently was writing its insurance in the bill itself. . . .

The man who stopped the May-Johnson bill, it is known, is one Harry S. Truman. Taking cognizance of the national storm of protest and the vigorous work in opposition to the bill by the young Federation of Atomic Scientists, the President convened a series of White House conferences on the subject.

He made his decision in flat opposition to the bill and to the principle of military control. It seems clear that he made his point of view known to congressional leaders, including Representative May. There are indications that he told the Army, in sharp words, to cease support of the bill and conform to his decision. He made his opinion public on February 1 [1946] in a letter to Senator McMahon. . . .

Despite the public and private statements of the Commander in Chief . . . there has been the unprecedented circumstance of a high Army officer, General Groves, publicly speechifying for military participation on the commission. He also testified to this effect as a "private citizen" before the Senate Special Committee. How a Regular Army Officer can become a private citizen for two hours, on demand, has not been explained.

◖ F. *Secretary of War Robert Patterson was much distressed by the charges leveled against the Army. Nevertheless, he decided to stop pressing for the May-Johnson bill and to support the McMahon bill, which now seemed to have the best chance of passing. He believed that some kind of legislation was urgently needed. In his final testimony before the House Committee on Military Affairs, he announced that he would bow in favor of McMahon; but at the same time he presented a spirited defense of the Army's position. Shortly after this testimony, the McMahon bill was passed and became the basis for the establishment of the Atomic Energy Commission. U.S. Congress, House, Committee on Military Affairs, Hearings, "Atomic Energy," 79 Cong., 2 sess. (June, 1946), 18-20.]*

... The War Department caused the bill later known as the May-Johnson bill to be introduced....

The House Military Affairs Committee held prompt hearings. This was last October. Some witnesses criticized the bill as not containing sufficient safeguards for independent research. The War Department recalled the scientific panel and requested the members of it to consider these objections. The scientific panel suggested certain clarifying language to reinforce the provisions relative to research. The War Department tendered these provisions as amendments. This committee, after giving effect to these amendments and other amendments, reported the bill favorably last November.

... The bill then reported out marked the first legislative effort to chart a national policy on control of this new force that inevitably will bring about profound changes in the future of all peoples... There was and still is need for avoiding undue delay. The project was in charge of the War Department as a war measure. The War Department was not charged with responsibility for long-range development of atomic energy for peacetime uses. Continued uncertainties as to future policy were bound to be damaging to current operations of the enterprise. And with international arrangements on atomic energy clearly called for, it was vital that something be done to put our own house in order.

The May-Johnson bill came in later for heavy criticism. It was said that the bill was drafted by the military. This was conclusively disproved by the fact that the bill represented the conclusions of the special committee named by Secretary Stimson, with all members civilians; and a very distinguished and eminent committee it was....

It was also said that the bill was to perpetuate military control of atomic energy. A reading of the bill rebutted that charge, since complete control was to pass to the proposed civilian agency. No vestige of authority was left in the War Department. But the critics would not read the bill. Then the charge was made that at any rate the bill permitted the President to appoint military personnel as members of the new Commission, and likewise permitted the Commission to employ military personnel. That charge was true, but the provision was merely permissive. Unless the President or the Commission saw fit to appoint them, no one in the Army or Navy would have a place in the enterprise.

I am not saying for a moment it would have been a bad feature to have had them in it, but nevertheless the bill did not do it.

These matters were all set forth, but the censure continued nonetheless. There was never any substantial basis for these complaints. The issues raised were utterly unreal.

The Senate last fall created a special committee on atomic energy. That committee devoted a large amount of time to a study of the subject and to the taking of testimony. Senator McMahon introduced S. 1717, and that bill after many amendments was reported favorably by the committee. It was passed by the Senate last week. That is the bill before you now.

S. 1717, in the content passed by the Senate, does not depart in objectives or in principal provisions from the program suggested last summer by the Stimson committee. There are many differences in detail, and a number of new features have been added in response to later developments. But in the main the treatment is the same—a new civilian agency composed of members appointed by the President—nine in the former bill and five in this bill; part time in the other bill and full time in this one.... The bill calls for civilian control, and the War Department at all times has supported civilian control, notwithstanding statements to the contrary....

In the view of the War Department this bill is in the national interest. The field of atomic energy has limitless possibilities.... Any bill that is passed now is bound to require later amendments as the situation unfolds and as new applications are realized.

S. 1717 answers the needs as we can appraise them today. It gives adequate attention to the aspects of atomic energy that relate to national defense. I believe that it is sound legislation.

There are urgent considerations in favor of prompt action. We asked for prompt action last year, because of the unfortunate effects of uncertainty on the operations of the project and because of the need of deciding domestic policy on atomic energy before taking action on international arrangements.

These factors are even more pressing now, with the United Nations Commission on Atomic Energy due to meet in a few days. In view of the recent passage of S. 1717 by the Senate, it offers much better prospects for expeditious action than the May-Johnson bill or any other bill on the subject of atomic energy. And on those grounds I urge a favorable report.

❡ G. *While the debate over domestic atomic policy was raging, the United States government was preparing an extraordinary plea for international control of atomic energy. Scientists and politicians agreed that the international control of atomic development was the only sure way to avoid the horrors of atomic warfare. Bernard M. Baruch, as requested by President Truman, prepared a program of international control to be administered by the United Nations. It was an unusual plan, for the United States volunteered to give away its atomic advantage. The next passage is from Baruch's speech to the U.N. Atomic Energy Commission on June 14, 1946. U.S. Department of State, the International Control of Atomic Energy, 138-139, 144-147.*]

My Fellow Citizens Of The World:

We are here to make a choice between the quick and the dead.

That is our business.

Behind the black portent of the new atomic age lies a hope which, seized upon with faith, can work our salvation. If we fail, then we have damned every man to be the slave of Fear. Let us not deceive ourselves: We must elect World Peace or World Destruction.

Science has torn from nature a secret so vast in its potentialities that our minds cower from the terror it creates. Yet terror is not enough to inhibit the use of the atomic bomb. The terror created by weapons has never stopped man from employing them. For each new weapon a defense has been produced, in time. But now we face a condition in which adequate defense does not exist.

Science, which gave us this dread power, shows that it can be made a giant help to humanity, but science does not show us how to prevent its baleful use. So we have been appointed to obviate that peril by finding a meeting of the minds and the hearts of our peoples. Only in the will of mankind lies the answer....

In this crisis, we represent not only our governments but, in a larger way, we represent the peoples of the world. We must remember that the peoples do not belong to the governments but that the governments belong to the peoples. We must answer their demands; we must answer the world's longing for peace and security.

In that desire the United States shares ardently and hopefully. The search of science for the absolute weapon has reached fruition in this country. But she stands ready to proscribe and destroy this instrument—to lift its use from death to life—if the world will join in a pact to that end.

In our success lies the promise of a new life, freed from the heartstopping fears that now beset the world. The beginning of victory for the great ideals for which millions have bled and died lies in building a workable plan....

Science has taught us how to put the atom to work. But to make it work for good instead of for evil lies in the domain dealing with the principles of human duty. We are now facing a problem more of ethics than of physics.

The solution will require apparent sacrifice in pride and in position, but better pain as the price of peace than death as the price of war.

I now submit the following measures as representing the fundamental features of a plan which would give effect to certain of the conclusions which I have epitomized.

1. General. The Authority should set up a thorough plan for control of the field of atomic energy, through various forms of ownership, dominion, licenses, operation, inspection, research and management by competent personnel. After this is provided for, there should be as little interference as may be with the economic plans and the present private, corporate and state relationships in the several countries involved.

2. Raw Materials. The Authority should have as one of its earliest purposes to obtain and maintain complete and accurate information on world supplies of uranium and thorium and to bring them under its dominion. The precise pattern of control for various types of deposits of such materials will have to depend upon the geological, mining, refining, and economic facts involved in different situations....

3. Primary Production Plants. The Authority should exercise complete managerial control of the production of fissionable materials. This means that it should control and operate all

plants producing fissionable materials in dangerous quantities and must own and control the product of these plants.

4. Atomic Explosives. The Authority should be given sole and exclusive right to conduct research in the field of atomic explosives. Research activities in the field of atomic explosives are essential in order that the Authority may keep in the forefront of knowledge in the field of atomic energy and fulfill the objective of preventing illicit manufacture of bombs. Only by maintaining its position as the best-informed agency will the Authority be able to determine the line between intrinsically dangerous and non-dangerous activities.

5. Strategic Distribution of Activities and Materials. The activities entrusted exclusively to the Authority because they are intrinsically dangerous to security should be distributed throughout the world. Similarly, stockpiles of raw materials and fissionable materials should not be centralized.

6. Non-Dangerous Activities. A function of the Authority should be promotion of the peacetime benefits of atomic energy.

Atomic research (except in explosives), the use of research reactors, the production of radioactive tracers by means of non-dangerous reactors, the use of such tracers, and to some extent the production of power should be open to nations and their citizens under reasonable licensing arrangements from the Authority....

7. Definition of Dangerous and Non-Dangerous Activities. Although a reasonable dividing line can be drawn between dangerous and non-dangerous activities, it is not hard and fast. Provision should, therefore, be made to assure constant reexamination of the questions and to permit revision of the dividing line as changing conditions and new discoveries may require.

8. Operations of Dangerous Activities. Any plant dealing with uranium or thorium after it once reaches the potential of dangerous use must be not only subject to the most rigorous and competent inspection by the Authority, but its actual operation shall be under the management, supervision, and control of the Authority.

9. Inspection. By assigning intrinsically dangerous activities exclusively to the Authority, the difficulties of inspection are reduced. If the Authority is the only agency which

may lawfully conduct dangerous activities, then visible operation by others than the Authority will constitute an unambiguous danger signal. Inspection will also occur in connection with the licensing functions of the Authority.

10. Freedom of Access. Adequate ingress and egress for
all qualified representatives of the Authority must be assured.
Many of the inspection activities of the Authority should
grow out of, and be incidental to, its other functions. Important measures of inspection will be associated with the tight
control of raw materials, for this is a keystone of the plan. . . .

11. Personnel. The personnel of the Authority should be
recruited on a basis of proven competence but also so far as
possible on an international basis.

12. Progress by Stages. A primary step in the creation of
the system of control is the setting forth, in comprehensive
terms, of the functions, responsibilities, powers and limitations of the Authority. Once a Charter for the Authority has
been adopted, the Authority and the system of control for
which it will be responsible will require time to become fully
organized and effective. The plan of control will, therefore,
have to come into effect in successive stages. These should be
specifically fixed in the Charter or means should be otherwise
set forth in the Charter for transitions from one stage to
another, as contemplated in the resolution of the United
Nations Assembly which created this Commission.

13. Disclosures. In the deliberations of the United Nations Commission on Atomic Energy, the United States is
prepared to make available the information essential to a
reasonable understanding of the proposals which it advocates.
Further disclosures must be dependent, in the interests of all,
upon the effective ratification of the treaty. When the Authority is actually created, the United States will join the other
nations in making available the further information essential
to that organization for the performance of its functions. As the
successive stages of international control are reached, the
United States will be prepared to yield, to the extent required
by each stage, national control of activities in this field to the
Authority.

14. International Control. There will be questions about
the extent of control to be allowed to national bodies, when
the Authority is established. Purely national authorities for

control and development of atomic energy should to the extent necessary for the effective operation of the Authority be subordinate to it. . . .

And now I end. I have submitted an outline for present discussion. Our consideration will be broadened by the criticism of the United States proposals and by the plans of the other nations, which, it is to be hoped, will be submitted at their early convenience. . . .

All of us are consecrated to making an end of gloom and hopelessness. It will not be an easy job. The way is long and thorny, but supremely worth traveling. All of us want to stand erect, with our faces to the sun, instead of being forced to burrow into the earth, like rats.

IV. THE RISE OF MEDICAL RESEARCH

❧ A. *The war had a revolutionary effect on medical research. A far-flung extramural research program was established and dramatic medical advances were achieved. For the first time, the federal government poured huge sums of money into medical investigations. These and other factors materially changed the pattern of medical research and established essentially a new research system, the key to which was increased federal support. The next reading explains the changes that occurred as a result of the war and summarizes the problems facing medical research in the postwar period. Steelman,* Science and Public Policy, *vol. V,* The Nation's Medical Research, *4-9.*]

Medical research has been a function of the Federal Government for more than half a century; but not until the war brought fresh and substantial sums of money to bear upon the Nation's total scientific effort in this field, did the Government occupy a prominent position as an entrepreneur of medical science. In the Public Health Service, formal research began in 1887. Although activities increased progressively thereafter, rapid expansion did not begin until 1935 when provisions of the Social Security Act more than doubled authorized expenditures for disease and sanitation investigations. Prior to the war, neither the Army nor the Navy formally recognized research as a distinct function of their medical departments. Research in the Food and Drug Administration grew slowly after that agency was created in 1905. The Veterans' Administration conducted no research in its between-war medical program.

The war had a revolutionary effect upon medical research as a whole. Medicine and medical research received a tremendous impetus, under which scientists produced phenomenal discoveries and advances. Scientists in colleges, universities, and hospitals accepted a controlled, directed medical research program, and they vigorously cooperated with the Government in it, under a special agency created to coordinate scientific effort. The Federal Government became the leading supporter of medical research.

But, at the same time, fundamental research practically ceased in favor of applied research and development; investigation was concentrated exclusively upon diseases and conditions of military importance.

The war defined the problems in military medicine which demanded study and prompt solution. Many of these problems were already of serious concern to civilian medicine; for example, the problems of shock and infection in injuries, burns, and traumatic surgery; malaria, veneral infections, and other parasitic diseases; aviation medicine; and nutrition. Military operations greatly intensified some of these problems.

What is more important, the war changed the whole direction of civilian research in medical and allied fields, focusing all scientific resources upon these problems. Moreover, it gave an urgency to finding solutions such as medical scientists and institutions probably had never felt before. The leisurely, independent pursuit of knowledge had to give way to an organized hot pursuit of specific objectives: chemicals to combat disease-bearing insects and animals; drugs to control traumatic and surgical infection; a quicker, safer cure for syphilis; more and better blood substitutes.

The task of meeting medical research and development objectives during the war was given to the Committee on Medical Research, a major administrative unit of the Office of Scientific Research and Development. The Committee followed the standard method of its parent body by drawing upon leading civilian scientists for advice and direction. Its extraordinary accomplishments need not be recounted here, but a few facts are especially pertinent to this report.

The Committee on Medical Research organized 12 major working committees, in aviation medicine, chemotherapeutic and other agents, convalescence and rehabilitation, industrial medicine, information, medicine, neuropsychiatry, pathology, sanitary engineering, shock and transfusions, surgery, and treatment of gas casualties. Because of the varying magnitudes of these problems, some of the committees were, naturally, more active than others. Thirty-four subcommittees with 315 members were organized for technical advice.

Nearly $25 million was expended on their projects in 4 years. This sum, huge in contrast with the totals spent by the Government for medical research in any previous 4 years, was only 5 percent of total expenditure by the Office of Scientific Research and Development. . . .

When the Office of Scientific Research and Development ceased to operate as a contracting agency in December 1945, all outstanding medical contracts were transferred for completion and termination to the War and Navy Departments and the Public Health Service.

During the war, the medical departments of the Army and Navy established several new research facilities. Research in the medical and allied sciences became an established function in several major administrative units of the War and Navy Departments. The research program of the Public Health Service also was substantially expanded for war purposes.

Thus, through the contract program and expansion of activities in its own agencies, the Federal Government moved during the war into a leading position: It supplanted foundations and university endowments as the primary sponsor and supporter of medical research.

There has been no indication since 1945 that the wartime increase of Federal activities in medical research will be reversed. With Congressional approval, the Army and Navy have continued their warborn activities. The research programs of the National Institute of Health, the National Cancer Institute, and the operating divisions of the Public Health Service have been substantially expanded. A new institute — the National Mental Health Institute — has been authorized, and additional funds have been appropriated for research grants to outside investigators and for research fellowships. The reorganized Veterans' Administration has established research as essential to better care for its patients. The Civil Aeronautics Administration has initiated a small program, insisting that research in aviation medicine and psychological testing is indispensable to the effective promotion and regulation of private and commercial flying.

As a whole, the potential gains in medical science are greater than the losses. Nevertheless, barriers have arisen which we must remove if we are to take fullest advantage of the advances, and the promise of wartime progress.

The war made tremendous inroads upon the supply of medical investigators, not only in the medical schools and affiliated hospitals but also in the basic science departments of universities. These institutions have always been the principal sources of medical discoveries, and they bore the brunt of the Government's war program at a time when they were particularly short-handed. What is more important, the war disrupted the training of research scientists and depleted the faculties of medical schools to a critical extent. Shortages which had existed before the war were intensified, and new problems incident to the production of scientific personnel were created.

The serious shortage of investigators in nearly all categories and disciplines constitutes a major barrier to progress in medical science. Moreover, lack of operating funds soon may force some medical training centers to curtail both training and research at a time when expansion of both is vitally needed. An even more acute financial need exists in the graduate schools for basic sciences. Thus, the training grounds for medical investigators—the very roots of medical research—are threatened.

The medical schools and the basic science departments of universities have been at once the producers of new knowledge and the training grounds for investigators. Before the war, 90 percent of medical research was conducted in universities and hospitals; and the bulk of investigations is still in the Nation's medical training centers. Both laboratory and clinical research have been almost exclusively the province of professors. At first, research was carried on independently and solely as an expression of the teacher's intellectual curiosity and creative thinking. But early in the twentieth century, the medical schools recognized that research was an essential part of the training program; since that time, increasing proportions of medical faculties have been engaged in research and larger amounts of the individual teacher's time have been absorbed in investigations.

Thus, if research suffers, the standard of training physicians for clinical practice will be lowered. Reduction in quality is inevitable unless operating funds, as well as research money can be provided.

A far larger proportion of the total expenditure for medical research during the war was devoted to applied research and development than to basic research. Both industry and the armed forces have been interested primarily in the development of end-items, products, or methods, such as new drugs, drug usages, medical and sanitary supplies and equipment. Basic research undertaken in their programs has been incidental to developmental investigations, although some recent projects of the armed services have no objective other than the finding of new knowledge. Support for basic research and the training of investigators has come principally from the foundations, the universities, private philanthropy, and the National Institute of Health.

Basic research is perhaps the most difficult type of scientific endeavor. The quest for new fundamental knowledge has no end. Basic problems require original thought of a high order by trained, creative minds. The ultimate solution of fundamental problems, or even the keys to their solution, may not be found for many years. The best scientists may follow a number of fruitless leads before the key piece of information finally is discovered. Even this discovery may not attract public attention, it may have no immediate application, but it may be the basis of full discovery, application, and development. The scientific world is of one mind that fundamental research in medicine must be continued and augmented, as in all other sciences. Only institutions with substantial resources can afford to support it comprehensively.

❡ *B.   Vannevar Bush conceived of medical research as an integral part of the American scientific establishment. In his report to the President in 1945 he strongly recommended increased federal support for medical studies. In the next reading, taken from that report, notice that the necessity for supporting research in the nation's medical schools is emphasized, while nothing is said about increasing the scope of the government's own medical research work. Bush,* Science the Endless Frontier, *15-16.*]

The primary place for medical research is in the medical schools and universities. In some cases coordinated direct attack on special problems may be made by teams of investigators, supplementing similar attacks carried on by the Army, Navy, Public Health Service, and other organizations. Apart from teaching, however, the primary obligation of the medical schools and universities is to continue the traditional function of such institutions, namely, to provide the individual worker with an opportunity for free, untrammeled study of nature, in the directions and by the methods suggested by his interests, curiosity, and imagination. The history of medical science teaches clearly the supreme importance of affording the pre-pared mind complete freedom for the exercise of initiative. It is the special province of the medical schools and universities to foster medical research in this way—a duty which cannot be shifted to Government agencies, industrial organizations, or to any other institutions. . . .

Between World War I and World War II the United States overtook all other nations in medical research and assumed a position of world leadership. To a considerable extent this progress reflected the liberal financial support from university endowment income, gifts from individuals, and foundation grants in the 20's. The growth of research departments in medical schools has been very uneven, however, and in consequence most of the important work has been done in a few large schools. This should be corrected by building up the weaker institutions, especially in regions which now have no strong medical research activities.

The traditional sources of support for medical research, largely endowment income, foundation grants, and private donations, are diminishing, and there is no immediate pros-pect of a change in this trend. Meanwhile, research costs have steadily risen. More elaborate and expensive equipment is required, supplies are more costly, and the wages of assistants are higher. Industry is only to a limited extent a source of funds for basic medical research.

It is clear that if we are to maintain the progress in medicine which has marked the last 25 years, the Government should extend financial support to basic medical research in the medical schools and in the universities, through grants both for research and for fellowships. The amount which can be effectively spent in the first year should not exceed 5 million dollars. After a program is under way perhaps 20 million dollars a year can be spent effectively.

❡ C. *The Steelman report also emphasized the necessity for the broad support of medical research. It pointed out that in addition to the medical schools certain medical research*

agencies of the federal government deserved increased finan-
cial support. Steelman, Science and Public Policy, *Vol. V,* The
Nation's Medical Research, *113-117.*]

More than $110 million is spent annually for research in
medical and allied sciences in the United States. Industry
spends a minimum of $50 million annually, primarily for
developmental work in drugs, pharmaceuticals, medicinal
chemicals, foods, and medical and surgical supplies. Private
foundations and voluntary health associations spend approximately $25 million in support of medical research.

The Federal Government expended an estimated $28
million for medical research in the fiscal year 1947. Nearly half
of this sum was spent by the Public Health Service, and one-
fifth each by the War and Navy Departments. . . .

As quickly as possible, national expenditures for medical
research should reach $300 million annually—nearly three
times the present rate. Most of this expansion must come from
public funds. Industrial research can and probably will expand, but it cannot and should not be counted upon to provide
the needed impetus for basic research. . . .

In the past, 90 percent of all medical research work was
done in medical schools and affiliated hospitals. The graduate
schools in the physical and biological sciences, however, have
become increasingly important sources of medical research
and of training. Their importance in all likelihood will continue to increase.

The precarious financial situation of many medical
schools and graduate science schools is a threat to research
also, since research is inseparable from the training of scientists.

The stimulation of fundamental discoveries must be a
keystone in the over-all expansion of medical research. The
Federal Government must take the lead in this field by increasing promptly its support of basic research.

There is a critical shortage of investigators in all categories of medical and allied research. This shortage was precipitated by huge expansion of all research, and by the curtailment
of training of research scientists during the war. It is intensified in the postwar period by the financial crisis in medical schools and other training centres, and by the attraction to
new graduates of private practice and employment in the

expanding research programs of industry and the Government. The quality, as well as the quantity, of medical and scientific personnel are threatened by the situation in the schools.

The National Institute of Health junior and senior fellowship program should be expanded substantailly within the next few years. Senior fellowships should be lengthened from 1 year to at least 2 years and an option provided for additional years in special cases....

While there is no coordinating mechanism for medical research in the Government, there is also very little duplication of effort. The greatest need for coordination lies in the necessity to utilize all facilities most effectively and fully in the public interest.

A system has been adopted voluntarily by the agencies administering medical research grants and contracts under which notifications are exchanged, summarizing applications received and the disposition thereof. This system promises well but incomplete or delayed reporting has been preventing maximum efficiency....

All Federal agencies rely heavily on outside scientific advisers. The scope and purposes of such advice vary considerably among the agencies. The Veterans' Administration has relied on the National Academy of Sciences for the development and operation of virtually all of its medical research work. The office of Naval Research submits periodic summaries of its medical research contracts and plans for future contract research to advisory groups. The Surgeon General of the Army asks advice on methodology and on suitable contractors for Army-defined projects. The Air Surgeon of the Army Air Forces asks civilian advisers to guide research in aviation medicine. The National Institute of Health uses advisory committees to sift applications for research grants.

The reliance of Federal agencies upon outside scientific advisory groups has brought to Government medical research indispensable counsel of a quality not otherwise obtainable. At the same time, the system sometimes encourages the concentration of medical research funds in the larger institutions, primarily those in the northern and eastern sections of the country.

The Federal Government should continue its sound policy of utilizing outside scientific advisers. It must, however, resist any tendency to create medical research monopolies. . . .

Several agencies of the Federal Government have official responsibilities which require continual experimentation with new methods and techniques. These are the Food and Drug Administration, the Quartermaster Corps, the Chemical Corps, and the Medical Corps of the War Department, and the Bureau of State Services of the Public Health Service. None of these agencies can afford to be satisfied with their present standards or methods, whether it be clothing for soldiers, analysis of new drugs, or organization of health services. Experimentation is the very satisfactory basis for improvement and it should be continued.

❬ *D. In* Science the Endless Frontier, *Bush suggested that the National Science Foundation should undertake the support of medical research. The U.S. Public Health Service had other ideas and determined to make its own research branch, the National Institutes of Health (NIH), the hub of the nation's medical research program. Public health officials arranged for the continuation under NIH of many of the valuable medical investigations sponsored by OSRD. A program of research grants and fellowships was initiated, which proved both popular and successful. The following is from an article by a Public Health Service official explaining the NIH grants program. C. J. Van Slyke, "New Horizons in Medical Research,"* Science, *CIV (Dec. 13, 1946),559-564.*❭

A large-scale, nationwide, peacetime program of support for scientific research in medical and related fields, guided by more than 250 leading scientists in 21 principal areas of medical research, is now a functioning reality. The program, based on U.S. Public Health Service Research Grants financed by public funds, supports research—conducted without governmental control—by independent scientists. The purpose of these grants is to stimulate research in medical and allied fields by making available funds for such research and by actively encouraging scientific investigation of specific problems on which scientists agree that urgently needed information is lacking. Accompanying this purpose is complete acceptance of a basic tenet of the philosophy upon which the scientific method rests: The integrity and independence of the research worker and his freedom from control, direction, regimentation, and outside interference.

The U.S. Public Health Service Research Grants, in operation as a medical research program of scientists and by scientists, may have early and profound effects upon the course of medical history and the national health.

The program, both in principle and as administered, has been welcomed and approved wholeheartedly by leaders in medical research. A total of 264 research projects, supported by $3,900,000 granted from the inception of the program late in 1945 up to 15 October 1946, already have been undertaken in 77 universities, hospitals, and other public and private institutions in 26 states. Although the program is less than a year old and has been little publicized, interest is rapidly widening, and new applications already are being received at a rate greater than 800 per year.

It is obvious that enormous savings of public and private money would result from research leading to wholesale prevention or cure of cancer, tuberculosis, diabetes, chronic nephritis, pernicious anemia, mental disorders, the common cold, heart diseases, and other widespread ailments.

Medical research costs money, however, and in the past a large amount of potentially very important research has not been conducted because funds have not been available to pay for it. Many universities and other nonprofit institutions have extremely limited funds for research, even though their teaching staffs, graduate students, and other personnel have the talent, training, and interest necessary for scientific investigation. Although research conducted by industrial organizations does add considerably to the total fund of medical knowledge, such research quite often must be directed toward specific goals. . . .

During the war it frequently was necessary to sacrifice fundamental, not immediately applicable research in order to arrive at specific objectives promptly; promising bypaths often had to be by-passed. In the normal course of scientific investigation, however, the bypaths quite often lead to more important findings than do the roads from which they branch. Much of the most important research may not appear immediately to lend itself to clinical application, but it builds a large body of information, assembled parts from which may later have wide clinical applicability. The necessity for immediately restocking and enlarging the storehouse of fundamental data which forms the basis on which further advances in the medical sciences can be made is widely recognized, and the opportunity to do this, curtailed during the war, is now greatly broadened. . . .

Three Advisory Councils have been designated by the Congress to make recommendations to the Surgeon General of the U. S. Public Health Service regarding means necessary or appropriate to carry out his responsibilities with respect to research and investigations.

One of the important functions of the Councils is to act upon applications for Research Grants, with the advice and recommendation of special Study Sections composed of groups of scientists in the major categories of medical research.

The National Advisory Health Council consists of 14 members, 10 of whom are outstanding civilian scientists. The other experts are the director of the National Institute of Health and one representative each from the Army, the Navy, and the Bureau of Animal Industry as ex-officio members of the Council. This Council makes recommendations regarding all Research Grants except those relating specifically to research in the fields of cancer and mental health. Membership on this Council is for a period of five years; two new members are appointed each year to replace two retiring members.

The National Advisory Cancer Council which, in addition to the Surgeon General, who serves as chairman, ex-officio, consists of 6 members selected from among leading medical and scientific authorities who are outstanding in the study, diagnosis, and treatment of cancer, reviews applications for Grants for research projects which show promise of making valuable contributions to the cause, prevention, or methods of diagnosis or treatment of cancer. Membership is for a period of three years; two new members are appointed each year to replace retiring members.

The National Mental Health Council consists of 7 members, including the Surgeon General, who is ex-officio chairman, and 6 members appointed from among leading medical or scientific authorities outstanding in the study, diagnosis, and treatment of psychiatric disorders. This Council reviews all applications for Research Grants for studies relating to the cause, prevention, and treatment of mental diseases. Membership is for three years, and two new members appointed each year replace retiring members.

At the request of the three Advisory Councils the fields of medical research were classified into major categories by the Research Grants Division of the National Institute of Health. Special Study Sections made up of consultant experts in more than 20 major categories have been set up to provide the Advisory Councils with the benefit of their advice and judgment in passing upon applications for Research Grants. Members of the Study Sections include many of the Nation's outstanding research workers in medical and related sciences.

The special Study Sections have two major responsibilities: (1) to review applications for Research Grants in their respective fields, approving them, suggesting changes or further study, or disapproving them, and forwarding their recommendations to the appropriate National Advisory Councils; and (2) as scientific leaders, to survey the status of research in their fields in order to discern neglected areas in which research is particularly wanting, and to stimulate the interest of workers competent to undertake needed research. . . .

Research "relating to the causes, diagnosis, treatment, control, and prevention of physical and mental diseases and impairments of man" falls within the scope of the Research Grants. Included is research in the fields of medicine, surgery, dentistry, antibiotics, bacteriology, biochemistry and nutrition, biophysics, cardiovascular diseases, endocrinology, gerontology, hematology, industrial diseases, malaria, pathology, pharmacology, physiology, public health methods, neurology, psychiatry, psychology, cancer, sanitation, venereal diseases, tropical diseases, virus and rickettsial diseases, and others.

In general, clinical work of a nonresearch character and nonmedical investigations in such fields as mathematics, physics, and chemistry are beyond the purposes of the program, although research projects in these fields may be conducted if they are considered likely to provide data applicable to medical science.

Whether a particular research proposal lies within these limits is determined by the appropriate special Study Section and National Advisory Council appraising the proposal. . . .

Research under the Research Grants program is conducted with full independence and autonomy of the research investigator. Support of research through the use of Research Grants funds does not imply in any way any degree of Federal control, supervision, or direction of the research project. . . .

In order not to divert the time of the researcher unnecessarily from the actual conduct of the research investigation, only annual scientific progress reports are requested. . . .

In order to avoid the possibility of restricting the autonomy of the research worker in any way, the Research Grants Division, the special Study Sections, and the National Advisory Councils will not review any papers proposed for publication, and therefore they are not in a position to indicate either approval or disapproval of such papers published solely at the election of, and under the complete control of, the research workers. This does not indicate any lack of interest in the results of research projects, but is aimed entirely at avoiding any degree of governmental restriction. . . .

Twice each year grantees submit simple financial reports to show current status of funds. The purpose of these reports is to facilitate routine auditing of Federal funds expended and to permit prompt regranting of any funds which may remain unused at the expiration of yearly grants. . . .

From the above it is seen that the U. S. Public Health Service Research Grants program represents a sincere and continuing effort to supply Federal funds for the support of necessary additional research in the fields of medical and related sciences without interposing any degree of government restriction, control, supervision, or regimentation. The program is a scientific one, scientific guidance of which lies wholly in the hands of scientists.

❮ *E. NIH grew very rapidly after 1946, with Congress appropriating more money each year for medical research. When the National Science Foundation was finally established in 1951, there was no need for it to support disease-oriented investigations. For NIH had become the giant of the medical research field. The last reading in this section, an excerpt from congressional testimony by Surgeon General Thomas Parran, reveals both the increasing confidence of the Public Health Service and its growing research interest in the so-called chronic diseases. U. S. Congress, House, Subcommittee of the Committee on Appropriations, Hearings,*

*"Department of Labor-Federal Security Agency Appropria-
tions Bill for 1948," 80 Cong., 1 sess. (Feb., 1947), 275-277.]*

Research in the health and medical sciences has been a
function of the Public Health Service since 1887. The gradual
accumulation of medical knowledge, and of experience in
research techniques and scientific teamwork has built the National Institute of Health into a potent weapon against disease.

I am happy to report that our programs of fellowships and
grants-in-aid for general medical research in universities,
hospitals, and other public and private institutions are being
received with singular favor.

These programs make it possible to enlist the services of
many more scientists in a broad-scale, coordinated attack on
important problems of health and disease. To wipe out our
wartime deficit of trained young research scientists these
programs must be steadily strengthened during the next few
years. . . .

With the advance in life expectancy, ours has become an
aging population. The relative importance of the chronic
diseases and the disabling conditions of later life has increased correspondingly. Today, for example, heart disease
and cancer are the leading causes of death.

Research in the cardiovascular disease, number one
among the leading causes of death, is of great importance.
With the appropriation available this year we have been able
to increase our work in this field. Some 55 research grants
have been approved. Our research, of course, is being supple-
mented by and affiliated with that of other institutions
throughout the country.

One goal is the development and improvement of methods for early diagnosis of cardiovascular disease; another is
the identification of persons who are especially susceptible, so
that proper care can be taken in time to avoid more serious
developments. . . .

The rise of cancer within 30 years from seventh to second
place among the chief causes of death is a dramatic example of
the shift which has taken place in our major health problems.
Cancer, primarily a disease of later life, will increase with the
increasing proportion of older people in our population unless
more effective means are found to check it.

Skilled men and additional research facilities are urgently

needed. The problems are of infinite complexity; their investigation is difficult and costly. Indeed, the National Cancer Institute, which in other respects is the outstanding cancer research center in the world, has been severely handicapped by not having clinical facilities immediately available....

The cancer program of the Public Health Service is planned to make the most efficient use of present resources. Additional research fellows have been appointed, to give as many scientists as possible an opportunity to work for a period at the Cancer Institute; this program should be further expanded. The small sum for research grants during the current year is almost exhausted, but the institute and the National Advisory Cancer Council have continued to review applications....

The National Mental Health Act defines [another] new area of health activity recently assigned to the Public Health Service. In attacking the problem of mental illness, we face a monumental task—first, because of the millions of our people affected or threatened by mental illness; second, because of the lack of sufficient scientific knowledge about its nature and treatment; third, because of the critical need for trained personnel....

The need for research in mental health is basic. Historically, our present knowledge is comparable with our knowledge of infectious disease before the time of Pasteur.

V. NEW CONCEPTS IN MILITARY RESEARCH

◀ A. *During World War II the military establishment utilized science as never before. The atomic bomb, the proximity fuse, and many types of improved military equipment testified to the efficacy of the research and development program. With the cessation of hostilities, military officials and scientists agreed that a civilian scientific board should be established to advise and coordinate defense research. Congress undertook a study of the subject and in the familiar pattern initiated hearings. One of the first men called to testify was Vannevar Bush. U.S. Congress, House, Committee on Military Affairs, Hearings, "Research and Development," 79 Cong., 1 sess. (May, 1945), 3-5.]*

In keeping this Nation vigorously able to defend itself, there is no more important factor than that of scientific research enthusiastically and energetically pursued. Both the nature of war and the strategy of war have been changed by science and research. Even more radical changes in the tactics of war are in prospect when the developments of our laboratories become known to all armies. It is exceedingly important that we keep fully abreast of these developments in the future. Continuing scientific research is, therefore, essential if we are not to be hopelessly outclassed in technology, weapons, and equipment. This continuing scientific research, however, need not be, and in fact, must not be confined to research on military problems alone. The primary objective should be a fully developed, well-rounded, and healthy science under a democratic regime. It is the continuing contributions to fundamental knowledge by healthy basic research which furnishes the best scientific preparation for peace, as well as for war.

I welcome, therefore, H. R. 2946, which is before this committee today. It is evident that this Congress is aware of the enormously responsible role which continuing scientific research must play both in the development of a strong industrial society and in securing our national existence against the sudden onslaught of war. . . .

I put down . . . two basic principles for successful Government participation in scientific research. First, the research organization must have direct access to Congress for its funds; second, the work of the research organization must not be subject to control or direction from any operating organization whose responsibilities are not exclusively those of research.

Industry learned a long time ago that it was fatal to place a research organization under a production department. Research and an operating responsibility, such as production or sales, are incompatible. An operating group is under the constant urge to produce in a tangible way, to meet existing standards, and existing schedules. An operating group has neither the time nor the inclination for research. An operating group is judged by production standards. Research, however, cannot be judged by production standards. Research is the exploration of the unknown. It is speculative and uncertain. It cannot be standardized. It succeeds, moreover, in virtually direct proportion to its freedom from performance controls, production pressures, and traditional approaches.

It is fundamental, accordingly, that research on military problems should be conducted, in time of peace, as well as in war, in part by civilians independently of the Military Establishment. The armed services exist to fight. It is their primary responsibility to train the men, make available the weapons, and employ the strategy that will bring victory in combat. The armed services cannot be expected to be experts in all of the complicated fields which make it possible for a great nation to fight successfully in total war. There are certain kinds of research — such as research on the improvement of existing weapons — which, of course, can be done best by military men within the Military Establishment. The job, however, of fundamental scientific research should be entrusted to the civilian scientists who are best trained to discharge it thoroughly and successfully. It is essential that both kinds of research go forward. We have just learned, for example, that one of the primary reasons why German science failed to maintain its superiority over the Allies is because in the early stages of the war German scientists were diverted from fundamental research for concentrated effort toward the improvement of existing weapons.

An able research scientist is the product of the intensive and specialized training of many years. The military man, who must acquire many other skills, cannot acquire that degree of specialization and training in science which is essential if broad and important scientific advances are to be made on military matters. Nor is the military tradition or the position of the military man within the services conducive to fundamental scientific research. The scientist must be free from restrictive controls. He must not be under the compulsion to produce immediate results in order to obtain advancement. Moreover, there must be parallel research attacks on a great problem by several groups approaching from different points of view. This has been demonstrated times without number in industry and in our own war experience....

Lest there be some misunderstanding, I should make it completely clear that the participation of civilian scientists in research on military problems neither should, nor can, supersede research by the armed services themselves. The civilian scientists are simply partners in the research effort. They should supplement the research done within the armed services.... However, numerous changes in the organization of the Army and Navy are necessary if research within the services is to be effectively organized.

The bill which this committee is now considering, H. R. 2946, presupposes the establishment within the National Academy of Sciences of a Research Board for National Security, composed of outstanding civilian scientists, together with representatives of the Army and Navy. Such a board was originally recommended last fall by an impartial group of civilians, Army officers, and Navy officers, headed by Charles E. Wilson, then Executive Vice Chairman of the War Production Board. In this regard also H. R. 2946 follows the recommendation of the House of Representatives Select Committee on Post War Military Policy, under the chairmanship of Representative Woodrum. It is generally agreed that through the medium of such a board the armed services will be able successfully to enlist the aid of civilian scientists in active partnership in research on military problems....

I have consistently favored the establishment of a Research Board for National Security. I have favored it, however, as an interim measure designed to bridge the gap between the termination of the OSRD, an emergency war agency, and the eventual creation of an independent research agency under mandate from the Congress. I believe that the Research Board for National Security must be an interim measure since the shape of the over-all postwar organization of Government both in its civilian aspects and particularly in its military aspects, is far from clear.

The problem is one of timing. If we now knew with any certainty what the postwar military structure of the United States would be, if we now knew whether the two services are to be linked with each other into one over-all organization, if we knew whether the Air Forces were to fit in, and whether the Joint Chiefs of Staff were to continue, if we knew these things and more, it might be possible to eliminate the interim step and move directly to the establishment of an independent and permanent research agency. . . .

Similarly, we would be able to construct a more permanent organization for scientific research on military problems if we now knew what the over-all agency for research on nonmilitary matters within the Government was going to be. Some such nonmilitary research organization is clearly desirable. It is particularly important that we do not allow problems of military research to occupy a disproportionate number of our best scientists. A balance between purely military research and fundamental scientific research of general utility must be struck. A proper balance would place far the greater emphasis on the basic research which is primarily of peacetime importance to the health of our citizens, to industry, and to our national well-being. The balance must be set and maintained by the Congress.

The Government in previous peacetime years has not made the maximum use of science and scientific research. Greater use of our scientific resources must be made, not only to achieve military security but also to insure national progress.

◖ B.   Frank B. Jewett was also called to testify. The organization of which he was president, the National Academy of Sciences, had been asked to set up the Research Board for National Security, which was to be a temporary agency to coordinate military research until the defense establishment had been reorganized. Jewett believed that the National Academy of Sciences was the logical place for such an *advisory board, whether temporary or permanent. Although the OSRD had directed the wartime scientific effort rather than the ineffectual National Academy, Jewett held out hope that his venerable organization could be strengthened and made vital enough to do this peacetime job. Notice his emphasis on the historic role of the National Academy of Sciences-National Research Council. This proposal for a Research Board for National Security came to nothing, but the Defense department later established a coordinating agency for military research. House Hearings, "Research and Development," 42-51.]*

In order fully to understand what is contemplated in the Research Board for National Security which the National Academy of Sciences has established at the request of the Secretaries of War and Navy; the field of activity in which it is designated to work; the limitations placed on its operations in the letter of request and the methods to be employed in those operations, it is essential to keep clearly in mind certain things about the Academy.

It is also desirable to keep clearly in mind the experiences of the present war and the considerations of those experiences which led the Secretaries to request the formation of the RBNS as a mechanism for preserving in the postwar years such measure of those experiences as will be helpful to the military in enhancing national security.

The National Academy of Sciences is not an agency of Government in the sense that it is part of the executive department.

It is a private corporation created by the Congress in the furtherance of a far-sighted State policy. It was created by an act of incorporation approved March 3, 1863. . . .

Congress in the wording of the act imposed on the Academy and its members the highest of all human obligations, namely, the obligation to serve the State to the best of the uninfluenced ability of the members and to do this without expectation of compensation. This obligation has been scrupulously observed for over 83 years. It has also determined the character and qualifications of the men and women elected to be members of the Academy. . . .

The National Research Council mentioned by Dr. Bush yesterday is a permanent committee or agency of the Academy which, as he explained, is designed to tie together all the national scientific and technical societies of the United States to the end that the Academy can at all times fully discharge its obligations of service to the Government.

It is this combination, in the corporation created by Congress, of an Academy composed from among the most distinguished men in every sector of physical science and a council which brings to their aid all the organized power of the national scientific and technical societies of the Nation, which makes the Academy unique and the most powerful agency in the world for the mobilization of science in aid of government whenever that aid is needed or requested.

The Research Council was established as a permanent part of the machinery of the Academy in response to a request of President Wilson.... The request was made in order to perpetuate the temporary National Research Council established in 1916 as a war measure. This earlier National Research Council was in effect the Office of Scientific Research and Development of World War I.

Dr. Bush has testified that the OSRD is purely a temporary war agency and will cease to exist when the war emergency is over. This is true not only because it derives from the war power acts which will terminate but more it is true because it is in fact something which simply cannot exist and function efficiently in peacetime. It has been a marvelous tool in aid of a nation at war and has done great things in aid of the military. It has been able to do this because for the time being, the best scientific and technical men of the Nation have been willing to abandon their normal ways of life and devote themselves unstintedly to war work to the exclusion of all else. Practically every condition under which they have worked is repugnant to the normal procedures of science and technology. Almost without exception, every man in the great organization is anxious to return to his creative peacetime work....

When, almost exactly a year ago, it began to be clear that the war would terminate successfully and that OSRD would begin to liquidate and finally to terminate, the Secretaries of War and Navy, and we of OSRD became concerned with the problems of future security, of how best to salvage in the post-war years such of the long-range pioneering research as was likely to lead to radically new and unthought of instrumentalities of warfare as were essential to an adequate national defense; likewise, to maintain in some measure the close association between top civil science and top military thinking, which had proved so fruitful during the war.

The result of these first considerations was the appointment by the Secretaries of War and Navy of the Committee on Postwar Research, to which Dr. Bush referred yesterday. It consisted of eight high-ranking Army and Navy officers and four civilian scientists with a civilian chairman, Mr. Charles E. Wilson. I was one of four civilian members.

The Committee labored through the summer of 1944....

When the Committee made its report to the Secretaries it was unanimous on two points, namely, (1) on the make-up of an initial RBNS under any auspices and, (2) on the desirability of asking the Academy under its congressional charter immediately to set up a RBNS to function until the whole question of postwar military organization could be finally determined by Congress....

On November 9, 1944, the Secretaries of War and Navy addressed a letter to me as President of the Academy ... asking the Academy "... to establish promptly within the Academy a Research Board for National Security" to operate until Congress made that determination.

This letter was specific in its prohibition on two points, namely (a):

(5) The Board shall, in no way, relieve the Army and Navy or other governmental agencies of their responsibility for, or authority over, research and development work conducted under their legal cognizance.

and (b):

(7) The Board shall make use of existing laboratories and facilities, where practicable. The Board shall not operate laboratories under its own auspices.

Paragraph 11 of the letter provides for funds for the Board in separate items in the War and Navy Department appropriation bills. It is this paragraph that H. R. 2946, if approved, would amend by having Congress make direct appropriations to the Academy of the funds needed for the actual expenses of the Board as it deems proper to allocate to this type of work in any fiscal year. If it fails to make any appropriation the Board would automatically cease to exist without further action by Congress.

That, we consider, is the fundamental basis of the organization which this bill seeks to implement with funds....

The ideas back of [RBNS] are threefold. One is to continue, in peacetime, when men of science are going to be concerned primarily, not with military things, but with other things, to maintain as far as possible a continued amount of interest in national security matters.

Second, to maintain the close cooperation, which has proved so very fruitful between top science (and I am not talking about the vast amount of underlying secondary talent) and top military thinking. That will be a very difficult problem in peacetime.

And, third, to seek to shorten the period between the emergence of an idea which is the embryo of an entirely new military tool and the time when the military can pick the idea up and develop it into a victory weapon.

The whole past history of mechanized warfare, without a single exception so far as I know, shows that the course that things have taken is about as follows: An idea emerges from the work of fundamental scientists, which has in it the elements of a military method, weapon, or tool. Likewise the elements of a civil development generally, if not always, the civil use of the idea develops first. It is only after the civilian possibilities have been pretty clearly proven that the military values begin to appear, and the military then adapts the civilian usage to the particular requirements of warfare.

It is hoped that with this new type of arrangement— whether Congress ultimately determines that this RBNS set-up is a good permanent one, or whether they want to handle it in some other way—we can maintain over the years a close cooperation of the top groups and can shorten the period between the emergence of a new idea in science and its realization by the military and its adaptation by them....

I am opposed to setting up more agencies, on general principles. I am particularly skeptical about the desirability of setting up a new agency now in connection with this very intricate problem which confronts the Congress.

The reason why I am skeptical, or averse to the thing at this time, is the fact that we just do not know how we will operate or what the conditions confronting us will be in the future. We do not know what pattern Congress will finally set up. We do not know how far we can enlist the active interest of top science in this thing in peacetime. We do not know what kind of a board our experience will show is the best type of board to do the job in a way that Congress and the military want it done.

It seems to me if we can get some experience in an organization which is flexible, where we can change it readily without legislative action and deal with conditions as we find them, we will put both the military and the Congress in a far better position to make their final determination with a degree of certainty which they do not now possess.

This National Academy is not a new agency. It is a corporation which Congress set up. It is an existing agency and it operates under a very simple mandate from Congress, which is meticulously observed. Its normal operations are handled on the request of Government, on an annual basis. Those requests can be modified or discarded at any time. It has no vested interests except that of uncompensated service.

To change its operations Congress does not have to destroy an existing agency. It seems to me and, particularly considering this type of organization, which can well be employed in this interim period, when we are seeking information as to how to set up a final organization — it seems to me this type of organization can be employed to great advantage during that period.

❡ *C. One of the more significant post-war developments in American science was the establishment of the Office of Naval Research (ONR). The Navy had maintained a vigorous scientific program during the war, although somewhat overshadowed by the Army's program. Long before the fighting stopped, a small group of naval officers, mostly young reservists, began to think about the Navy's post-war scientific needs. They also began to maneuver to obtain the political and scientific support they thought the Navy needed. Called "The Bird Dogs," these young officers did not stand alone; they received influential help from many sources. It is clear, however, that they were in the center of the drive which culminated in ONR. The following is their account of the origins of ONR. The Bird Dogs, "The Evolution of the Office of Naval Research,"* Physics Today, *XIV (Aug., 1961), 30-35.*]

The campaign to sell the concept of establishing a central office to foster basic research and research coordination within the Navy Department was a lengthy, and sometimes bloody, struggle. The story of the evolution of ONR is really the tale of an educational process carried on over a five-year span (providing we are permitted to ignore pre-World-War-II struggles). This educational process required the concerted efforts of many people to create an atmosphere in the Navy Department, in the Executive Branch, and in Congress, which was favorable toward long-range research. Key people had to be convinced that future military strength depends to an increasing degree on the rapid and effective development of new weapons and weapons systems through a strong, balanced research effort.

It is recognized that history must be recorded from several points of view before all the facts are exposed. The story here presented was that as seen by a small group of Naval Reserve officers who were fortunate enough to have had a five-year worm's-eye view of the entire evolution of ONR from a vantage point within the Office of the Secretary of Navy. We were, in the parlance of the day, lowly skippers of LSD's (Large Steel Desks). . . .

[The establishment of OSRD] led Secretary of Navy Frank Knox to study what steps the Navy might take to increase its effectiveness in the prosecution and utilization of research and development.

There existed some controversy on this point. Rear Adm. H. G. Bowen, Director of the Naval Research Laboratory, had recommended on January 29, 1941, the centering of all research for the Navy in that Laboratory, giving it Bureau status; whereas the General Board in a rebuttal on March 22, 1941 had recommended that no change in Bureau cognizance for research be made and that the Chief of Naval Operations be made responsible for all research policies, including the operation of the Naval Research Laboratory.

Secretary Knox, at the suggestion of Rear Adm. J. H. Towers, therefore enlisted Prof. J. C. Hunsaker, the Chairman of the NACA as well as a member of the OSRD, and a graduate of the Naval Academy, to advise him. Out of this advice arose the first step in the long road to ONR. At the suggestion of Hunsaker, Knox issued General Order 150, July 12, 1941, which established to Office of the Coordinator of Research and Development in the Office of the Secretary of the Navy. This order provided that the Coordinator advise the

Secretary broadly on matters of Naval research, and placed the Naval Research Laboratory under the cognizance of the Bureau of Ships.

At the urgent request of Secretary Knox, Dr. Hunsaker agreed to serve as the first Coordinator of Research and Development on an interim basis in order to get the Office organized and functioning. He was named Coordinatior on July 15, 1941, and immediately selected a small staff consisting of two highly capable regular officers, Capt. Lybrand P. Smith and Comdr. E. W. Sylvester, and four young Naval Reserve officers having technical backgrounds. Hunsaker then proceeded to inspire these young men, whom he called "bird dogs," and train us in his effective manner in the basic elements of sound research program planning, administration, evaluation, and coordination. Another important facet of this training concerned the ways and means of getting things accomplished in wartime Washington in the face of odds, or even open opposition. . . .

In order to carry out more efficiently his prior commitments to the NACA and OSRD, Hunsaker resigned the position of coordinator and turned it over to his carefully selected choice, Rear Adm. J. A. Furer, USN, on December 15, 1941. However, Hunsaker's superb advise and counsel always were, and at this writing still are, available to and continually utilized by the Navy Department. Other changes included the naming of Furer to the OSRD, Smith to the NDRC, the acquisition of Comdr. R. D. Conrad, USN, a truly brilliant technical man, as a replacement for Sylvester, and the addition of two more technical Naval Reserve officers.

During the first three years of World War II the work of this Office was aimed almost entirely at liaison between the NDRC and the Navy, assisting in the planning and establishment of research projects, following the progress thereof, and aiding in bringing about the utilization of the results by the Navy. . . .

However, from the very outset another important subject occupied the thoughts of the personnel of the Office of the Coordinator of Research and Development. All of us knew that the excellent OSRD—NDRC civilian research groups would probably evaporate as soon as the war ended. Therefore, at each step of the way, a gnawing thought occupied the minds of all: how could the Navy better organize and administer its own research? . . .

In a remarkably short time it was possible to categorize those persons who would do everything possible to stimulate better research programs, organization, and utilization of results, and those who stood firm upon the twin, and usually backward, defenses of cognizance and entangling red tape.

Fortunately within the Navy there arose almost immediately a solid core of highly intelligent people who welcomed and assisted the drive to push research on all frontiers. This was in part a tribute to the well-established Navy system of postgraduate study in various universities which had developed in many officers an understanding and appreciation of science....

We continually sought out and nurtured the progressive, intelligent core group. One of the first persons to be uncovered who showed vital interest in the postwar reorganization of research in the Navy was George B. Karelitz of Columbia University, a former Russian who was working with the Bureau of Ships.

Two of the "bird dogs" began in 1942 to meet bimonthly at home in the evening with Karelitz. Tragically, Prof. Karelitz died in 1943, but fortunately not before he contributed immensely to the shape of things to come. Out of these sessions the initial pattern of ONR was almost completely conceived — the essential elements consisting of establishing a central research office in the Office of Secretary of the Navy, headed by an admiral, receiving funds from Congress for research projects, and having a powerful research advisory committee made up of top scientists, were actually all drawn up and recorded as early as November 1, 1943 by two "bird dogs." Of course much ground work involving numerous persons both within and outside of the Navy remained to be accomplished before any such plan could become a reality....

In the summer of 1944 the "bird dogs," stimulated by the work of the Committee on Post-War Research, further developed their plan for a Navy office to key in with whatever outside agency Congress might establish. It was on September 6, 1944, that two of the "bird dogs" first set down a new organization chart for an Office of Naval Research which entailed the naming of an Assistant Secretary of the Navy for Research with broad powers, an Advisory Committee, a Rear Adm. Chief of Naval Research, program emphasis on basic research work, and the transfer of the Naval Research Laboratory to the Office. This was a vitally important improvement over their earlier plan which had called for a rear admiral as head of the Office. This plan for an Assistant Secretary of the Navy for Research was discussed with Dr. Hunsaker and Dr. Bush who enthusiastically supported the idea. . . . Adm. Furer, Capt. Smith and Capt. Conrad all quickly endorsed the thought. . . .

By September 1945 the "bird dogs" had a Congressional bill all drafted for the establishment of an Office of Naval Research to be headed, in deference to Mr. Forrestal, by a Rear Admiral. This draft, which included the establishment of a Naval Research Advisory Committee composed of eminent scientists, was to become known as the Vinson Bill.

There remained one serious hurdle, outside of Congressional action, before the establishment of ONR could become meaningful. This was to get the Universities, where the majority of basic research is performed, to be willing to accept Navy contracts. In this struggle Capt. Conrad became the recognized leader. Accompanied by Various "bird dogs" Conrad visited many top universities in the winter of 1945. There was a definite feeling on the part of the scientists after four years of war to wish to forget the Navy and return to former pursuits. But Conrad was able to crumble all opposition by making superb speeches around the country, and by working with legal and·contract people to pioneer an acceptable contract system. This would permit one over-all contract with a university with new task orders to be attached as agreed upon, permit basic research to be contracted for, and permit the work to be unclassified and publishable. Once the legal eagles got this worked out, there was no holding the persuasive Conrad, and he was quickly able to get such institutions as Harvard, Chicago, University of California, California Institute of Technology, and MIT to agree to accept Navy work. Tragically, he contracted a lingering but fatal case of leukemia at his moment of triumph.

With Adm. Bowen and his influential partners and Capt. Conrad maneuvering effectively, the Vinson Bill passed with flying colors and became Public Law 588 on August 1, 1946. It turned out to agree almost verbatim with the 1945 draft by the "bird dogs." This was indeed a day of rejoicing, culminating some four years of effort entailing long hours of teaching, lots of perseverance, and even a little intrigue. As stated at the outset, the victory belonged not to a few, but to many scientists, naval officers, and political figures, some of whom are still unrecognized.

❧ D. With the well-manned Navy lobby working in its behalf, ONR grew rapidly. It supported basic research because, in the long run, the Navy would benefit. Accordingly, a large amount of scientific work in the universities received financial support. Because Congress was still deliberating over the National Science Foundation, ONR came to perform many of the functions envisioned for the NSF. The following passage, taken from an ONR report, explains both the Navy's motivation in supporting science and the scope of its work. U. S. Navy, Annual Report of the Office of Naval Research, 1949, pp. 1-3.]

The huge university research program of the Navy Department is the greatest peace time cooperative undertaking in history between the academic world and the government. This significant educational and scientific experiment now embraces approximately 1,200 projects in about 200 institutions with a total expenditure of approximately $20,000,000 a year. Nearly 3,000 scientists and 2,500 college and university graduate students are actively engaged in basic research projects in the many fields of vital interest to the Navy. These projects were neither requested nor assigned by the Navy. The original proposals were initiated by the investigators. Contracts made by the Navy with their universities made the actual research possible. In many cases, the financial contribution of the university equals or exceeds that of the Navy.

Four facts of great importance have molded the program since it began in 1946. First, the security and prosperity of this country depend upon its scientific strength, and this is sustained by the unpredictable but inevitable results of basic research. Second, basic research is essentially a long-term, peace-time activity which cannot be conducted effectively in a war-time rush development atmosphere. Third, during the past war, America's store of basic knowledge was exploited to the point of diminishing returns; it needed badly to be replenished. Finally, the Navy does not have basic knowledge essential to develop the weapons, counter-weapons, improved materials, equipment and processes urgently needed.

The shortage of scientific and technical personnel has been acute. In many scientific fields the principal basic research had traditionally been carried out in Europe, but until recently scientific activities on the continent have been almost completely dislocated. Thus, the Office of Naval Research had to encourage creative work in fields which prior to the war received little or no attention in this country — for example, the science of low temperatures, cryogenics.

Participants in the research program have attempted to use the vast experience gained during the war in various techniques of accelerating investigations. These include group attacks on one problem by scientists of different traditions and backgrounds, new approaches as a means of opening fresh fields of research. An example of the last of these is the use of microwaves to study molecular and atomic structure. Experience has shown repeatedly that in time of stress, scientists can bring their talents to bear in many fields outside of their specialties. Many of the great advances in microwave radar were made by nuclear physicists, and remarkable improvements in rockets and propulsion were the result of the joint efforts of astronomers, nuclear physicists, and aerodynamicists.

Since the technical strength of the Navy is dependent upon the nation's scientific well being, research receives support on the basis mainly of the specific needs of the Navy which also contributes to the broad scientific needs of the nation. In addition to providing financial support, ONR makes arrangements to use Naval facilities and personnel in carrying out projects. Naval ships, submarines, and aircraft are transporting scientists and instruments to regions where significant data can be obtained. Rockets and balloons carry instruments to unprecedented heights.

The various branches of the research divisions indicate the breadth and scope of the program. The Physical Sciences Division is made up of branches in chemistry, electronics, fluid mechanics, geophysics and geography, mathematics, mechanics and materials, nuclear physics, physics, and astronomy and astrophysics. Close relationships between the branches of this division and others have facilitated cross-fertilization in various scientific fields. An obvious case is the use of radioactive elements in tracer techniques. The Mechanics and Materials Branch which uses the findings of surface and solid state physics and chemistry in its daily work automatically stimulates this cross-fertilization.

This division guides broad programs in oceanography, meteorology, and earth physics. Before World War II, applied mathematics was not fashionable in this country; the activities of the Mathematics Branch have done much to raise the scientific level of this country in mathematical statistics, numerical analysis and computing devices. The work will contribute greatly to aerodynamics, hydrodynamics, problems in rockets and guided missile development, problems in logistics and many other fields.

Branches in biophysics, microbiology, psychophysiology, physiology, human ecology, dental science, psychology, biochemistry, and manpower, constitute the Medical Sciences Division. . . .

The university program is by no means exclusively under the Navy. It has many joint projects with the Army and the Air Force. In some cases, contracts are with the Army, with ONR transferring funds to the Army, and in others, the reverse is true. For example, one of the strongest electronics research centers in this country is supported equally by the Navy, Army and Air Forces. This is the type of positive coordination which produces positive results.

One problem is how to maintain the present vigor and strength of the university program. An essential is a bilateral flow of scientific personnel between the universities and ONR, and between ONR and the research institutions. An appreciable fraction of the staff in Washington is on leave of absence from universities.

Similarly some ONR personnel are on leave from Washington to universities, or are spending part of their time in creative research.

The basic research program has made available to the Navy the advice and counsel of many of the outstanding scientists in the country. They have provided their knowledge either through individual consultation, or through membership on advisory panels and participation in symposia.

. . . The long war years drained not only the reservoir of basic scientific knowledge, but stopped the flow through graduate schools of those young scientists whose research in years ahead must replenish the supply. An indirect but nevertheless highly important phase of the program has been the impetus given to the training of these essential future scientists. The contracts with universities have in many instances required the services of laboratory assistants for research on the projects. Thus, in the course of performing research tasks, they have obtained both training and remuneration with which these students might perhaps help meet the costs of graduate study.

Should a National Science Foundation be established, there is general agreement that the National Military Establishment, and the Navy in particular, should be allowed and encouraged to continue the support of basic research at approximately present rates. There will of course be changes in the program. Obviously certain parts can and will be transferred to the Foundation, but any transfer must be accomplished through mutual agreement with the Foundation, ONR, the university and the investigator. The Navy will continue to have a vital interest in certain areas of the frontiers of science....

The fundamental philosophy of the Navy is that basic research will inevitably from time to time uncover new discoveries of overwhelming benefit not only to the military services, but also to the entire industrial and national economy. This is the reason for the existence of the sound scientific program which the Navy is supporting in the traditional sources of fundamental knowledge—the universities and other institutions of this country.

PART FOUR

THE MIDDLE YEARS 1950–1957

A Cold War, intensified by shooting in Korea, made science and technology valued resources in the American arsenal during the years 1950–1957. Federal funds for research and development increased astronomically, while the search continued for efficient techniques of science administration within the institutional framework born of World War II and postwar planning. The system was tested in an atmosphere of Cold War. Although the middle years lack any sharp historical focus, a variety of problems arose and begged for solution. Few of the solutions were permanent; most were ad hoc, *and as varied in character as the issues. It was a period of experimentation in the management of Federal science.*

I. A Problem of Definition

❡ A.   The efficient administration and organization of federal science, especially the allocation of public funds for research, required a more precise definition of science and the varieties of science than was current when scientific research was mainly a private pursuit. Terms like "basic research," "pure science," "applied research," and "engineering" meant different things to technical and non-technical persons. The specialists disagreed among themselves on definition as often as they disagreed with interested public officials. Science administrators tried throughout the period, usually after the fact, to justify their demands on the public treasury by defining their activities on various scales of worth to the whole society. "Basic research," generally accepted by scientists as the most prestigious of their pursuits, was the most difficult to explain to the public accountant. Toward the end of the Fifties, C. V. Kidd, an expert in the new field of science and government, concluded that basic research might be defined adequately to convey its general nature to the non-scientist, but the term might never be defined well enough "to permit an unambiguous, objective measurement of the dollars spent." ("Basic Research—Description versus Definition," Science, Vol. 129 [Feb. 13, 1959] 368.) In the meantime, attempts to evaluate the need and place of basic research in the agencies often took a facetious turn. A Department of Defense panel set up to study the subject speculated on what others implied that basic research was: it was unrelated to an end product; it was decidedly of no use to anyone; it sought knowledge not already available; it was undertaken only because the researcher wanted to do it; it carried no security classification; it was done by an investigator who could not explain exactly what he was doing; it was novel and in an area not likely to be considered practical. Solid working definitions for basic research, where they existed, came to emphasize the honesty and reputation of the researcher, and the likelihood *that if trusted, he would come up with something worthwhile to science if not always clearly applicable to practical affairs.*

The problem was not original with post-World War II American science. In 1880, Thomas Henry Huxley, Darwin's great defender in England, objected to the calcification of the definition of pure science. "Science and Culture," Science and Culture and Other Essays *(New York, 1882), 26.]*

I often wish that this phrase, "applied science," had never been invented. For it suggests that there is a sort of scientific knowledge of direct practical use, which can be studied apart from another sort of scientific knowledge, which is of no practical utility, and which is termed "pure science." But there is no more complete fallacy than this. What people call applied science is nothing but the application of pure science to particular classes of problems. It consists of deductions from those general principles, established by reasoning and observation, which constitute pure science. No one can safely make these deductions until he has a firm grasp of the principles. . . .

◖ *B. Vannevar Bush's report to the President,* Science the Endless Frontier *(called by one congressman, "Science the Endless Expenditure"), won wide and sometimes uncritical acceptance by American scientists. The report identified three categories, and announced a "perverse law" governing research: "applied research invariably drives out pure." How much if any "law," scientific or historical, is there in the statement? (Washington, 1960; originally published July 1945), 81-83.]*

Scientific research may be divided into the following broad categories: (1) pure research, (2) background research, and (3) applied research and development. The boundaries between them are by no means clear-cut and it is frequently difficult to assign a given investigation to any single category. On the other hand, typical instances are easily recognized, and study of them reveals that each category requires different institutional arrangements for maximum development.

Pure research is research without specific practical ends. It results in general knowledge and understanding of nature and its laws. This general knowledge provides the means of answering a large number of important practical problems, though it may not give a specific solution to any one of them. The pure scientist may not be at all interested in the practical applications of his work; yet the development of important new industries depends primarily on a continuing vigorous progress of pure science.

One of the peculiarities of pure science is the variety of paths which lead to productive advance. Many of the most important discoveries have come as a result of experiments undertaken with quite different purposes in mind. Statistically it is certain that important and highly useful discoveries will result from some fraction of the work undertaken; but the results of any one particular investigation cannot be predicted with accuracy.

The unpredictable nature of pure science makes desirable the provision of rather special circumstances for its pursuit. Pure research demands from its followers the freedom of mind to look at familiar facts from unfamiliar points of view. It does not always lend itself to organized efforts and is refractory to direction from above. In fact, nowhere else is the principle of freedom more important for significant achievement. It should be pointed out, however, that many branches of pure science increasingly involve the cooperative efforts of numerous individuals, and expensive capital equipment shared by many workers.

By general consent the discoveries of pure science have for centuries been immediately consigned to the public domain and no valid precedent exists for restricting the advantages of knowledge of this sort to any individual, corporation, State, or Nation. All the people are the beneficiaries. Governments dedicated to the public welfare, therefore, have a responsibility for encouraging and supporting the production of new knowledge on the broadest possible basis. In the United States this responsibility has long been recognized.

The preparation of accurate topographic and geologic maps, the collection of meteorological data, the determination of physical and chemical constants, the description of species of animals, plants, and minerals, the establishment of standards for hormones, drugs, and X-ray therapy; these and similar types of scientific work are here grouped together under the term background research. Such background knowledge provides essential data for advances in both pure and applied science. It is also widely used by the engineer, the physician and the public at large. In contrast to pure science, the objectives of this type of research and the methods to be used are reasonably clear before an investigation is undertaken. Thus, comprehensive programs may be mapped out and the work carried on by relatively large numbers of trained personnel as a coordinated effort. . . .

Applied research and development differs in several important respects from pure science. Since the objective can often be definitely mapped out beforehand, the work lends itself to organized effort. If successful, the results of applied research are of a definitely practical or commercial value. The very heavy expenses of such work are, therefore, undertaken by private organizations only [sic] in the hope of ultimately recovering the funds invested. . . .

The distinction between applied and pure research is not a hard and fast one, and industrial scientists may tackle specific problems from broad fundamental viewpoints. But it is important to emphasize that there is a perverse law governing research: Under the pressure for immediate results, and unless deliberate policies are set up to guard against this, *applied research invariably drives out pure*.

The moral is clear: It is pure research which deserves and requires special protection and specially assured support.

◖ *C. In 1956 the Bureau of the Budget adopted the following broad definitions for its special analysis of research and development to appear in the 1958 budget document. Bureau of the Budget Bulletin No. 57-6, November 19, 1956.*]

"Scientific research" is systematic, intensive study directed toward a fuller knowledge of the subject studied.

"Development" is the systematic use of scientific knowledge directed toward the production of useful materials, devices, systems, methods, or processes, exclusive of design and production engineering.

◖ *D. Although one important job of the new National Science Foundation was to clarify the term "basic research" in order to procure for it a fair share of federal funds for science, one study sponsored and published by the Foundation expressed a serious doubt that any clear definition was possible. Maxwell Research Center, Syracuse University,*

Research and Development by Nonprofit Research Institutes and Commercial Laboratories, 1953 *(Washington, 1956), 3.]*

A major difficulty in both the interviews and question-naire responses from all research concerns arose from lack of a common clear definition of basic research. If all research is viewed as plotted on a continuum, with one end representing research which has a known immediate practical application and the other end representing research which is completely unconcerned with application, then the inability to agree on what is basic research indicated a difference of opinion as to where the mark should be drawn on the continuum to separate the applied from the basic segment. Respondents varied in their comments on the distinction between basic and applied research, commonly interpreting these terms as synonymous with purposive or less purposive, sponsored or unsponsored, or general as contrasted with useful research; but none of these provides a usable distinction between pure and applied research.

... The doing of pure research is clearly a prideful matter among all research personnel even though there is neither general nor internal agreement as to what comprises such research.

◀ E. *In 1957, NSF published a sixty-four page booklet designed mainly to explain the meaning and value of basic research. The report was welcomed by some, criticized by others; in the last category was a former member of the National Science Board. For all its lack of specificity and questionable history, the report remained one expression of Foundation philosophy. The author, among other things, attempted to define basic research by example, and by describing some of its components. National Science Foundation,* Basic Research: A National Resource *(Washington, 1957), 1, 2.]*

... [the booklet's] major emphasis is on basic research — an expression of man's desire, his need to learn and explore — and, quite incidentally from one standpoint, the source of all technological progress. *As a continuing search for new knowledge, basic research has certain characteristics which help us distinguish it from other forms of scientific acitvity. The search is systematic, but without direction save that which the investigator himself gives it to meet the challenge of the unknown. He is strictly on his own, guided primarily by his interest in learning more about the workings of nature.*

His work may be contrasted with that of scientists and engineers conducting applied research (laboratory studies concerning the practical use of newly found knowledge) or development, which takes applied research out of the laboratory and translates it into production. In applied research and development an unexpected problem is essentially a negative thing. It represents a source of delays, an obstacle to be overcome, preferably in the not-too-distant future. Work proceeds under pressure to solve or circumvent the problem as quickly as possible because it interferes with the attainment of practical goals. Knowledge of the most fundamental sort may be needed and sought, but, as one engineer has put it, "not too much knowledge." Ideally, one would acquire only sufficient knowledge to solve the problem at hand, although the stopping point may not be easy to determine. But the practical goal and the time element are always there.

For the scientist specializing in basic research an unexpected problem is also an obstacle to be overcome. But it is a good deal more than that. In a fundamental sense it is the reason for his existence. Perhaps he will solve the problem. But the effort may take years or his entire career, and he knows he may never find a solution. If he does, he will soon seek new problems worthy of his mettle. The unexpected is what he thrives on. The odds are that work which proceeds too long without involving the unexpected, the element of surprise, is not fruitful work.

❡ *F. On the distinction between basic and applied research, the President's Science Advisory Committee, in 1960, took a position similar to T. H. Huxley's opinion of 1880.* Scientific Progress, Universities, and the Federal Government *(Washington, Nov. 15, 1960), 4.]*

Basic and applied science today are distinguished less by method and content than by motivation. . . . We do not believe in any artificial separation between basic and applied research or between science and engineering. The fact that a scientific advance is useful does not make it unscientific.

II. A Problem of Politics: The Battery Additive Controversy

❡ A. The first major domestic political controversy of the Eisenhower administration involved one of the country's most venerable scientific institutions, the National Bureau of Standards, and its director in March 1953, Allen V. Astin. Astin was asked to resign after he upheld the results of Bureau tests showing that a battery additive, AD-X2 (composed of sodium sulphate and magnesium sulphate—both effective cathartics), had no beneficial results on the life of lead storage batteries. The reaction of scientists, bench and administrative, was immediately sympathetic, loud and, in the end, decisive. Before the storm passed, several important issues were raised: 1) political control of scientific agencies—a Democratic senator wanted to know whether science was now to be the subject of the spoils system, the Republican administration was accused of Lysenkoism, and the Federation of American Scientists talked about political "additives"; 2) small business and science—to some onlookers the issue was small business versus big government and its regulatory agencies (NBS did the tests for the Federal Trade Commission and the Post Office); 3) conflict of interest—some Bureau scientists were accused of associating too closely with battery manufacturers. In exchange for cooperation by the National Academy of Sciences in two investigations—of the NBS setup generally and the battery additive matter specifically—Secretary of Commerce Sinclair Weeks agreed to retain Astin until the Academy reports were in. The second committee supported the Bureau tests, and Astin remained director.

Secretary Weeks, accompanied by Assistant Secretary Craig R. Sheaffer, appeared before the Senate Small Business Committee on March 31, 1953, and exposed the additive controversy to full view. U.S. Congress, Senate, Select Committee on Small Business, "Investigation of Battery Additive AD-X2," 83 Cong., 1 sess. (1953), 1-6.]

SECRETARY WEEKS: Mr. Chairman, I have a statement which I should like to read concerning the so-called battery additive AD-X2, which has been under discussion in the Commerce Department.

Even before I came to Washington my mail in Boston was heavy with letters from people telling me that an outfit in Oakland, Calif., making a product called AD-X2 to prolong battery life through reducing sulfation, was having tough sledding in Washington. Your committee, in fact, issued a report on the subject last December. One of the first things I did was to ask Mr. Sheaffer . . . to make a full and impartial investigation. He and his men have gone through file after file extending over the past 5 years.

Exhaustive examination of the files shows:

1. When this manufacturer put his product on the market in 1948 he was confronted with a pamphlet prepared by the National Bureau of Standards – No. 302 – condemning all battery additives. This pamphlet was obtainable from the Bureau of Standards for the asking by anyone interested in combating the sale of the new product.

2. When he asked for tests to prove the merit of his product the National Bureau of Standards resisted making further tests, stating that basically the product was the same as others previously tested. The manufacturer, under these circumstances, could only tell his customers that his product had not been tested by the National Bureau of Standards and, therefore, Pamphlet 302 did not apply to it.

3. The files show that scientists in the National Bureau of Standards were in touch with and worked closely with individuals and organizations who might have had an interest in the final outcome, submitting their work to them previous to publication and seeking their advice and guidance. . . .

4. While the manufacturer was having no luck getting the National Bureau of Standards to run tests which would show that his product was different from previous additives tested and had merit, I find the National Bureau of Standards suggesting to the National Better Business Bureau that tests would be made if requested by the Federal Trade Commission. The Federal Trade Commission very promptly docketed the case – and the Post Office followed through later – although in all this period I can find no evidence of one single complaint by a user of the product. On the contrary, there are a

great many testimonials from users stating that the product was saving them money by prolonging the life of their batteries. Many of these statements were made by reputable firms operating trucks, buses, and tractors, as well as industrial equipment depending on batteries. I further find that the Oakland Better Business Bureau circulated their findings of no complaints as to product, personnel, or methods of doing business.

5. The manufacturer claims that, to this date, he has not been able to get the National Bureau of Standards to run a test that would show the merit of his product. A test was agreed upon, but 10 modifications in the procedure were made by the National Bureau of Standards.

6. The manufacturer had independent tests made by the United States Testing Co. of Hoboken, N.J. — controlled field tests extending over a period of 362 days. These tests rendered credible the experience reported by consumers.

7. Your committee enlisted the aid of the Massachusetts Institute of Technology whose findings differed in some respects from the National Bureau of Standards' findings, even if, as some claim — including MIT — they cannot be interpreted as being so broadly favorable to AD-X2 as was done in the report of your committee dated December 18, 1952. However, Dr. Weber of MIT states that extensive tests might show the value of the product. Presumably, this statement put believability into the United States Testing Co.'s report.

8. The present status of the matter is that there is a suspended fraud order against Pioneers, Inc., Mr. Ritchie, his wife, and Mr. Hager, vice president of the firm, in the Post Office Department. After issuance on February 24, 1953, it was suspended by Postmaster General Summerfield at my request in order that I might investigate further. There is also an open docket in the Federal Trade Commission.

Throughtout this whole matter runs the fact that the National Bureau of Standards is the keystone on which other agencies of the Government depend. The Post Office calls it their supreme court on questions of fraud in a case like this. The Federal Trade Commission relies on its tests in a similar manner.

The Bureau, which is supposed neither to approve nor condemn a product, has, by its very setup, the power to make the introduction of a new product on the market very difficult, to prevent a product's being advertised by the Federal Trade Commission action, and to have people labeled "fraud" and denied the use of the mails. If this power is objectively and correctly used, it has great value to all the people of this Nation. However, if the Bureau's foot slips, a business starting in against all the normal competitive hazards, finds itself up against something with which it cannot cope, the vast power of the United States Government. Unless the small-business man knows a very great deal about Government, or has the finances to employ experts, he is obliged to quit.

I cannot bring myself to believe that the people making AD-X2 have the intent to defraud—and without intent, I do not see how there can be fraud.

I know that this business has suffered severely at the hands of certain bureaucrats. In fact, it is a wonder they are in existence at all after 5 years of struggle. Your committee might want to reexamine the legislation giving the Federal Trade Commission very broad powers in matters like this.

I am not a man of science, and I do not wish to enter into a technical discussion or be accused of overruling the findings of any laboratory. But as a practical man, I think that the National Bureau of Standards has not been sufficiently objective, because they discount entirely the play of the market place and have placed themselves in a vulnerable position by discussing the nature and scope of their prospective reports with the very people who might not want to see the additive remain on the market, and when their reports and results of tests were questioned, discussed the matter with other scientists, engaged by your committee to make separate, objective findings.

I cannot help but wonder how many similar cases have never been heard about—how many entrepreneurs who were convinced they have a good thing for the people, were licked before they started, whether they knew it or not and by their very own Government to whom they paid high taxes.

It can generally be said that there are no complaints but, on the contrary, many testimonials to the fact that the product is good and has saved the users money. As a practical man, I do not see why a product should be denied an opportunity in the market place. I believe that the purpose of the Congress in establishing the Bureau of Standards and in giving powers to such agencies as the Federal Trade Commission and the Post

Office Department to act to prevent unfair practices and the perpetration of frauds, was that they should be operated or their powers should be exercised in the interest of the general public and that such interest should be substantial and specifically and positively shown to be adversely affected before the power is used.

At this point, Pioneers, Inc., has a long way to go. It has to make its peace with the Post Office Department. It has to get off the hook with the Federal Trade Commission. It has to fight its way back in to customers it has lost, including the Government. It probably has to get financing to replace the funds lost through fighting the Government so far. . . .

Finally, a personal word which may be to the point: This particular battery additive, I found after I got into this thing—I had never known about it before, but the company with which I was formerly associated had a battery for which they had paid approximately $1,300. The battery was about licked. It was not functioning properly. . . .

We had gone out and bought a new battery for $1,300 when these battery AD-X2 people came along. We took it on a when-as-and-if issue basis, tried it out. It worked. The last report I had after at least 13 months, I believe, was that the new battery is still standing in the corner and has never been used. That is a modest personal experience that we had with this very thing we are discussing. . . .

SENATOR SALTONSTALL: . . . you felt strongly enough to ask a member of the Bureau of Standards to resign, to retire. In other words, was there any wrongdoing in this, or just poor judgment?

SECRETARY WEEKS: We have felt rather strongly about this particular situation. It is one of many phases of that particular picture that caused us to decide that it would be well to have a change in the administration of the department. . . .

SENATOR HUNT: You gentlemen both know, I am sure, that down through the years the Bureau of Standards has been looked upon by the people of the United States as the last word in accuracy and honesty and things of that type. You are aware of that, I am sure.

MR. SHEAFFER: Certainly I am aware of that. We hope it maintains that reputation.

SENATOR HUNT: Don't you think it is going a little far to

discharge a man like Dr. Condon over an incident of this type?

MR. SHEAFFER: It is Dr. Astin. . . .

SENATOR HUNT: Regardless of who the personality may be, I think that it is getting a little tough to ask the man to get out because of one mistake. He may have done a million things that were right.

MR. SHEAFFER: This is not the only reason that Dr. Astin is resigning. This is one factor in a number of reasons.

SENATOR HUNT: I think you should give the committee the rest of the reasons.

MR. SHEAFFER: We are not prepared to do so right now, sir.

◀ B.   *The prize-winning political cartoonist, Herblock, exhibited one popular reaction to the AD-X2 affair in the* Washington Post, *April 16, 1953.*]

◀ C.   *With few dissents, the nation's scientists rallied to the Bureau and Astin. Individuals and professional societies displayed openly their disagreement with Secretary Weeks' action. Highly placed science administrators like Hugh Dryden for the Interdepartmental Committee on Scientific Research and Development, Detlev Bronk of the National Academy of Sciences, Alan Waterman of the National Science Foundation, and Lee DuBridge of the Science Advisory Committee of the Office of Defense Mobilization, communicated directly with the White House and with the Secretary of Commerce on Astin's behalf. The distinguished physicist Enrico Fermi read the following statement of the American Physical Society before its annual banquet in 1953.* Physics Today *(June 1953), 20.*]

At a meeting of the Council of the American Physical Society held at Washington on May first, 1953, the following statement was approved unanimously:

The Council of the American Physical Society has been deeply concerned with the impact of the Astin dismissal on the morale and effectiveness of physicists in Government laboratories. The Council's apprehension has been partly relieved by the temporary reinstatement of Dr. Astin, and by the accompanying declaration of Secretary Weeks that his previous action did not imply any reflection on the scientific integrity of either Dr. Astin or the Bureau of Standards. However, more is needed to undo the harm that has been done; and a fundamental principle should be made very clear.

It is the duty of a scientist to investigate scientific and technical problems by openly-stated objective methods without shading his conclusions under political or other pressures. On this principle the progress of science depends. We never doubted that the work of the Bureau of Standards has been conducted in this spirit.

The Council urges that an authoritative statement be made that this principle forms the rule of ethics for scientists in Government service and that no scientist will be penalized for adhering to them. We believe that such a statement would do much to relieve the uneasiness caused by the Astin incident.

The Council commends the intervention in this matter of the National Academy of Sciences, which was motivated by the same beliefs as ours.

◀ *D. In the Astin affair, the Federation of American Scientists found an issue to enliven its open meeting in Washington, and ran its mimeographing machines overtime. David Hill, Chairman of the Federation's Council, wrote to President Eisenhower on May 18, F.A.S. Records, Washington, D.C.]*

The Council of the Federation of American Scientists has asked that I communicate to you our respectful request for clarification of the policy of your administration with respect to the scientific activities of the government. Recent events have raised grave questions, which have been most sharply framed by the abrupt dismissal (subsequently delayed) of the Director of the Bureau of Standards and by the testimony offered March 31st to the Senate Small Business Committee by the Secretary of Commerce in explanation of that action. Commonly accepted principles for relations between science and government appear to have been thrown into jeopardy;

Heretofore it has been generally accepted, at least in the Free World, that a research scientist should follow with scrupulous honesty the objective procedures of his science without the bias of personal preference, popular demand, or economic incentive. Secretary Weeks in his prepared testimony, however, has taken a position epitomized by his remarks, "... the National Bureau of Standards has not been sufficiently objective, because they discount entirely the play of the market place. ..." Scientists both in and out of government have received with mingled dismay and unbelief the suggestion by a cabinet officer that the rigorously defined procedures of scientific investigation are to be subordinated to the variable and inconclusive test of the market place. We oppose this suggestion just as we condemn the practice in Soviet Russia of requiring scientists to announce conclusions consistent with the State approved version of dialectical materialism. Nothing in the statements of the Secretary of Commerce subsequent to his appearance before the Senate committee has reversed this position. We know that you will agree, Mr. President, that much of the strength of our nation and much of the prosperity of the business community rests upon the honesty and independence of American science. It is therefore our hope that you will see fit to use the authority of your Office to issue a statement dispelling the widespread apprehension and confusion growing out of the unfortunate declarations of the Secretary of Commerce. ...

◀ *E. In June 1953, Astin, who had been silent or noncommittal at the peak of the controversy, appeared as a witness before the Small Business Committee. He traced quietly the history of the Bureau's association with AD-X2, lectured the congressmen on scientific method, and also mentioned in passing one feature of the affair not then explored fully by the press: the Bureau's testing procedure employed statistical analysis, a method of modern science not well understood and less well appreciated by the public. The committee hearing was chaired by Senator Thye. "Investigation of Battery Additive AD-X2," 218-224.]*

DR. ASTIN: The Bureau's work with battery additives, materials intended to improve the performance of lead-acid type storage batteries, goes back to the early 1920's. ... From 1931 to the start of World War II nine other battery additive materials were investigated either for the Federal Trade Commission, the Post Office Department or Members of the Congress. Most of these consisted primarily of combinations of sodium and magnesium sulfates, commonly known, respectively, as glauber salt and epsom salt. During World War II and since, 15 new additives were tested by the Bureau (some for a second time) for other Government agencies. Again most of these consisted of mixtures of sodium and magnesium sulfates. The Bureau also investigated a large number of materials considered as possible corrosion inhibitors to see if any of them would curtail the sulfation of lead-acid storage batteries that occurs on storage. This latter study was undertaken to determine the best means to recondition or store lead-acid batteries that were in surplus at the termination of World War II. Included in this latter test were again sodium and magnesium sulfate mixtures; they were found not to be beneficial. In response to the continuing demand for information from the public about battery additives, Letter Circular 302 was reissued in 1949 with only minor variations from its original form.

The first recorded contact at the Bureau with the Battery Additive AD-X2 occurred in April 1948. . . .

About the 1st of January 1949 the Bureau had started a series of tests on another battery additive for the Federal Trade Commission and it was decided that it might be of interest to run along with these tests an evaluation of AD-X2. Samples which had been transmitted by the Oakland Better Business Bureau were used for this purpose. . . .

In March of 1950, the Federal Trade Commission requested the Bureau to make tests on AD-X2. A report was sent them on May 11, 1950, incorporating the results of the tests which had been initiated in January 1949. Late in 1951, many members of the Bureau staff gave testimony at the Federal Trade Commission hearing on still another additive and, at that time, members of the Commission stated that they wanted further tests made from samples submitted by the Oakland Better Business Bureau and not by FTC. The Commission formally requested the additional tests in February 1952, and a report based on this new series of tests was submitted in July 1952.

In September 1951, the Post Office Department requested tests on AD-X2. The Bureau submitted a report in December 1951 again based on results of tests obtained on the sample submitted by the Oakland Better Business Bureau. Following receipt of this report, the Post Office Department also requested additional tests on samples submitted by them. Accordingly, the National Bureau of Standards initiated still another series of tests of AD-X2.

The results of the tests made for these two agencies disclosed no beneficial effect of the additive on the operational characteristics of lead-acid storage batteries....

As a result of interest of the Members of the Congress and also as a result of communications I had been having with Mr. Ritchie since December 1951, I agreed in May 1952 to run a new series of tests on Battery AD-X2, using a test procedure which Mr. Ritchie guaranteed would demonstrate the merits of his product. One of the major claims made by the distributors of AD-X2 in their letter-writing campaign to the Congress was that the testing procedure which had been used by the Bureau was not suitable to disclose the merits of the battery additive. Although I had no reason for questioning the adequacy of the test procedures the Bureau had used previously, I had hoped that by using a procedure described by him, the matter could be settled decisively for all concerned. A report describing the testing procedure and the results obtained therefrom had been furnished to members of your committee....

After all the observations were taken both on the group of batteries for electrical tests and the group for visual inspection of the plates, the information was turned over to the Bureau's statistical engineering group, previously mentioned. These analysts were first directed, also without knowledge as to which batteries were treated, to look for evidence of two groups of batteries with distinct performance characteristics. Had the additive produced a real effect on battery performance, this would have been possible. When no pattern of this sort developed, the analysts were next provided with the information as to which batteries were in each two groups, but not told which group was treated. After analysis showed no significant difference between the two groups they were told which group had been treated and they proceeded with the preparation of the report....

Now, this type of thing of a controlled experiment is very difficult for nontechnical people to appreciate. I think one of the best examples I can give to you is Sinclair Lewis' Pulitzer prize novel, Arrowsmith.

THE CHAIRMAN: Sinclair Lewis was a Minnesota man, and I knew him personally. I have been in his home. I have dined with him. He was a great writer. I would like to have him present right now, sir.

DR. ASTIN: Well, if you recall that story, it is about a scientist who develops a cure for some disease—I forget now what it is—and he thinks it is working, but he is not sure, but enough other people believe that the cure is working so that they want him to give the treatment to all sick individuals, but the scientist is more concerned with establishing his point, and he gives a treatment to only half of them. You see, that is the only way that you can prove something of this sort. You have to keep a control.

THE CHAIRMAN: Dr. Astin, since this question came up, and for the sake of a sort of amusing scientific argument, I saw a paper where two scientists had debated at great length on the question of whether boiled water would freeze quicker than unboiled water, and it was amusing to me to read the scientific language used in the debate on the simple question of whether water boiled would freeze more rapidly than water not boiled.

If the two scientists could use up more than a large printed page in a debate on that question, I can readily see when we get down to the question of a compound in a battery where I would be trying to argue with a scientist. I would be defeated before I uttered the first word.

But the simple truth of the question is that if a good, hard-fisted businessman has used the product in a fleet of motors and in the batteries serving those motors over a number of years and is fool enough to come up and place orders month after month, what is the matter with him? Or otherwise, what is the matter with the Bureau of Standards' test?

Now, that is the question, sir.

DR. ASTIN: The man with his fleet of cars might have some real data to debate on if over a rather long period of time he put the material in half the batteries of his fleet and took pains to make sure that each half of the fleet had roughly the same use conditions, and then checked them monthly. On that basis, it would mean something.

◖ F. *Unlike the problems of J. Robert Oppenheimer, the Astin case had a happy ending for its principal actor. The National Academy of Sciences committee on additives supported the Bureau's testing procedures and results. Astin remained Director of NBS and, toward the end of 1953, Eisenhower appointed him chairman of the Interdepartmental Committee; he now lives in Bethesda, Md., a surburb of Washington, on Battery Lane. There follow two brief excerpts from the Academy committee's report. National Academy of Sciences, Committee on Battery Additives, Report (Washington, October 30, 1953), 1, 33.]*

Conclusions:

1. From the study and investigations, the Committee concluded that the quality of the work of the National Bureau of Standards in the field of lead acid storage battery testing is excellent, and
2. that while Pioneers, Inc. claim that AD-X2 has substantial merit, the relevant data now available to the Committee on the effects of AD-X2 are adequate to support the position of the Bureau of Standards that the material is without merit. . . .

Complaint 7:

Certain of the personnel of the National Bureau of Standards were not objective and approached the AD-X2 tests with biased minds.

Answer:

We found no evidence of this but ample evidence of healthy objectivity. Insofar as the contact between the Bureau personnel and "outsiders" in the field of lead acid batteries is concerned, we found the relationships to be essentially those which could be expected among people having confidence in one another, with the common objective of arriving more nearly at the truth.

III. SELECTED DOMESTIC PROBLEMS OF THE MIDDLE YEARS

❧ A. The shooting war in Korea and the Cold War that followed were the central facts of American life between 1950 and 1957. The hot war and the warm peace triggered a giant barrage of federal funds toward science and technology. Pure as well as applied research was justified on the basis of its contribution to national strength. The support of many esoteric fields of natural science was recognized publicly to be in the national interest. Democratic ideals and institutions connected with the scientific sector were strained and sometimes altered in response to the threat to American security.

Some of the problems were old, others very new. An attempt to transfer water resource functions from the Army's Corps of Engineers to a civilian bureau aborted; it had been tried during the twentieth century by presidents before Eisenhower. Small business too often found itself unable to compete with large industry in obtaining government contracts for research and development, and in utilizing the results of research; Section 9 of Public Law 536, 85th Congress, 2d Session, was one attempt to alleviate the problem. The Atomic Energy Commission and the International Cooperation Administration fought for control of Eisenhower's Atoms for Peace Program. Behind all these activities and those which follow were the pressures which came with large-scale government spending for science.

Few problems captured as much space and time in the news media or irritated the scientific community more than issues of loyalty and security raised during the early Fifties. The case of J. Robert Oppenheimer was a cause célèbre, as much because Oppenheimer was well known and widely respected by his colleagues, as because the case raised certain fundamental questions of political philosophy. (Oppenheimer's troubles are described in a collection of documents edited by Cushing Strout, Conscience, Science, and Security:

The Case of Dr. J. Robert Oppenheimer [*Chicago: Rand McNally, 1963*]. *Many scientists felt that excessive security classification defeated the main reason for its existence: to insure the strength of American science. The point was made by Wallace R. Brode when he was President of the American Association for the Advancement of Science. While examining the selection, two questions may occur to the reader: (1) Is the scientist really more objective in his profession than anybody else? (2) Is the free exchange of information any less important to other professions or to other occupations or to the smooth working of American society as a whole? U.S. Congress, House, Subcommittee on Government Information of the Government Operations Committee, "Availability of Information for Federal Departments and Agencies, Part 15, Restrictions on the Flow of Scientific and Technological Information," 85 Cong., 2 sess. (January 20-22, 1958), 3488, 3489.*]

DR. BRODE: ... Today I am concerned ... with the general problems of science in the Nation.

Before I comment on the major problem before the committee, that is, the flow of scientific information, I feel it would be well to reaffirm what I believe are the basic concepts of a scientific method.

Scientists are not socially or intellectually a separate class of individuals, but rather they have a somewhat different approach to the advance of their knowledge and profession, which is necessitated by the nature of the subject matter concerned.

The scientist by nature maintains a critical attitude toward all unsubstantiated statements; his published papers are full of literature references to support those points upon which he does not present experimental evidence and his claims to new advances or discoveries are not accepted by others unless accompanied by sufficient reasoning or experimental details to permit those who doubt or do not comprehend to verify the conclusion experimentally.

Another characteristic of the scientific method is the recognition that progress in science is a cooperative and pyramiding affair in which each worker draws from the work of others to provide the base for his advances and in turn publishes the advances he has made so that others may profit.

This concept of publication and exchange of scientific

information is not one of egotistical bragging, but rather the very fundamental basis of our great scientific advances in this century.

Individual isolation of either scientist, laboratory, agency, or Government from the rest of the scientific community will not only slow down the world advance but produce even greater retardation in the isolated area.

Kettering aptly stated this concept some years ago when he said that if he locked the doors of his laboratory to others, he would lock out much more than he would lock in.

No group or nation has a monopoly on scientific discoveries and thought, and hence security islands may create a retarded advance if there is no exchange and only a one-way filter.

Scientists are not inclined to pass out to others their concepts and ideas prior to formulation and proof in the form for publication, unless they feel that some exchange is possible so as to help them over an impediment in their own approach.

Now, concerning security clearance, I believe that multiple security clearances are not only a nuisance but by mere duplication have been known to result in conflicting determinations.

If a great many investigators make separate calls to ask about an individual, people become suspicious and skeptical.

Not all of this duplication is the result of stubbornness on the part of the separate agencies in declining to take anyone else's word, but some is due to the laws establishing funds or programs requiring specific and separate clearances.

There does not seem to be reciprocity with regard to clearances or even ability to retain a clearance status when one changes a position. This may result in long delays and the deprivation of scientists from reference to their own experimental work.

Nondefense agencies who do no classified work except for defense agencies sometimes require separate security investigations, from the defense agency as well as their own.

Visiting foreign scientists who come to do unclassified work must have a full field classified investigation in some nondefense agencies. This clearance requires about a 6-month wait, and in authorizing the agency to receive the worker the security clearance is for "unclassified information only."

I feel that in some cases the security clearance procedure

and security classification is a deterrent to basic research and should be confined more generally to strategic information and hardware development.

Much has been said about the problem of over-classification and the need for declassification. I might cite only one case which indicates the principle and is perhaps a bit humorous.

One of the Nation's outstanding physicists has a hobby of archery, and is a pretty good archer. He has written books and articles, and has given technical and popular lectures on the physics of archery and the design of bows and arrows.

In the last world war he was one of the leaders in our advanced-science program, but at the same time managed to direct some experimental work on some new ideas on more efficient and effective bows and arrows.

This work was, of course, classified, and after the war he tried to get it declassified but without success. So far as I know it is still classified, although his motive in seeking de-classification was merely to include in a popular lecture and a published article the general information that modern science might provide interesting improvement in this ancient field.

❡ *B. The forms of federal support became a subject of debate among the research people themselves and between them and the administrators. How were grants to be administered? Who decided what project or which scientist received how much money? Should the government sponsor research within its own agencies, establish new laboratories, or contract outside government? If contracted out, should the universities, industry or nonprofit laboratories be used? For these and other issues, there were as many solutions as questions.*

John T. Wilson explained the relative merit of supporting research by project or supporting it with block grants to institutions. "Institutional Versus Individual Grantees," reprinted by permission from the Proceedings of the New York University Third Biennial Conference on Charitable Foundations *(Albany, N.Y.: Matthew Bender & Company, 1957), 91, 92.*]

The arguments in favor of the project system are:

(a) It has worked. When properly administered, it has made possible much fundamental, unrestricted research. . . .

(b) The projects selected by a group of scientific peers are more likely to be of higher quality than when an institutional committee makes the selection.

(c) The effects of institutional politics, dominant personalities, and other deterrents to objective evaluation can be minimized.

(d) The likely demands by members of the Congress for support of institutions in their state or district are avoided when it can be said that no projects deemed worthy by a panel of scientists have been submitted by the staff of the school in question. . . .

Among the reasons given for a curtailment of the project system, are the following:

(a) It is more appropriate for applied fields, with limited objectives, than for fundamental research. . . .

(b) Projects are selected by central staff, advisory panels, or referees. These individuals are likely to play it safe — to select proposals that have a definite and realizable objective.

(c) The younger and less well-known scientists and the support of research ventures requiring only a small amount of funds are in less favorable positions than they would be under an institutional grant.

❡ *C. The number and type of research facilities supported by the government proliferated after World War II. In 1957 the National Science Foundation, in a report to the Bureau of the Budget, published an "illustrative" list, not a census, of twenty-two types of research facilities, sponsored by over seven federal agencies.* Federal Financial Support of Physical Facilities and Major Equipment for the Conduct of Scientific Research *(Washington, 1957), 8, 9.*]

The financial arrangements under which financial support is given to the facility and equipment items . . . varies widely from agency to agency and among programs within agencies. These arrangements include the following: (a) construction grants on a matching basis, with recipient organization responsible for all operating costs; (b) construction at Federal expense and lease to institution; (c) construction at institution expense, with Government then paying a "user charge" under annual research and development contracts with the institution; (d) construction at Federal expense and operation through a "management contract" with institution or other organization; (e) direct Federal support of operation and maintenance through grants or contracts specifically designed to cover operating costs; (f) indirect Federal support of operation and maintenance through grants or contracts covering research projects at the facility and against which facility overhead and maintenance costs are prorated; and (g) various combinations or variations of the foregoing.

The research center as an institutional form emerged during the course of World War II. Faced with the need for research and development on new weapons and materiel involving an extremely wide range of research problems, the Government contracted with educational institutions and other groups to undertake work which under pre-war conditions might have been carried on in Federal laboratories. In some cases the size of the particular undertaking, its specialized nature, the requirements for unusual facilities and personnel, or the demands of military security dictated the creation of completely separate organizations to carry out the work. Many of these research centers were disestablished at the end of World War II; some became part of the Federal research establishment; a few were absorbed into the organizational fabric of the institutions; others like the Los Alamos Scientific Laboratory administered by the University of California, the Applied Physics Laboratory at Johns Hopkins University, and the Jet Propulsion Laboratory at the California Institute of Technology were continued into the postwar period; and a number of new ones have been formed during the postwar years.

◀ D. *The most spectacular project of them all was the International Geophysical Year, July 1, 1957 — December 31, 1958, a massive research effort to increase man's understanding of the earth on which he lives. U.S. Congress, House, Committee on Interstate and Foreign Commerce, House Report No. 1348, "International Geophysical Year, the Arctic, Antarctica," 85 Cong., 2 sess. (February 17, 1958), 9-11.*]

Geophysics is the application of the tools of physics to the earth; a study of the behavior of the earth.

Of fundamental and continuing interest to us all is the problem of our physical environment. The factors which make up this environment control many aspects of our physical life such as our food, our clothing, our domiciles, our travels, our communications systems, and, in some cases, our very lives.

To cope with these perplexing and often violent factors we must know more about them, their basic nature, how they operate, how they affect each other, and, perhaps more importantly, how we can circumvent the unfavorable results and amplify the beneficial ones.

The field of knowledge most directly concerned with these conditions is known as geophysics. As the name implies, it deals with the physics of the earth and its atmosphere and the space in the immediate vicinity of this atmosphere. A very important aspect of the problem is the sun itself. The sun is the principal source of all energy that reaches the earth and, therefore, is an important factor in most, if not all, of the physical phenomena which are included under the broad head of geophysics.

Over 70 years ago a young German lieutenant, named Karl Weyprecht, in considering problems on weather and the earth's magnetic field in the Arctic, recognized the importance of obtaining observations of these physical factors over as large a portion of the Arctic area as possible and within a relatively short time interval. His proposal that a concerted effort be made to measure certain geophysical phenomena was the basis for a period of special observations which has since been referred to as the first polar year. Some 10 nations, including the United States, participated in this undertaking during the period 1882-83. The gains in knowledge in the fields of meterology and geomagnetism fully justified Lieutenant Weyprecht's judgment.

Fifty years later, 1932-33, a second polar year was instigated and this time the United States and some thirty-odd other countries took part in the program. Again the Arctic regions received the principal effort, although there were some stations established in the Southern Hemisphere. Out of this period came a better understanding of the ionosphere and its effect on radio communications, a recognition of the importance of aerometeorological observations in weather-prediction processes, and an increased knowledge of characteristics and variations of such things as the earth's magnetic field, cosmic rays, and aurora.

In 1950, a group of American scientists met informally at

the home of one of them in Silver Spring, Md., to greet Prof. Sydney Chapman, of England, one of the world's leading geophysicists. Out of this very informal evening discussion came a suggestion from Dr. L. V. Berkner that a third polar year be organized during the 1957-58 period in order to take full advantage of the tremendous advances that had been made in scientific instrumentation during the preceding decade. A second impelling reason for such an interval was the realization that further progress in a number of fields of geophysics was becoming more and more dependent on the availability of synoptic data which could only be gotten through such a concerted effort. . . .

Sixty-seven countries now are participating cooperatively in what has evolved as man's greatest unified attack on the mysteries of the planet on which we live. During the International Geophysical Year (IGY), . . . studies are being conducted at over 2,500 stations girdling the globe manned by more than 10,000 scientists and technicians. The aurora is being investigated in both polar regions; the ionosphere is under intense study from hundreds of stations, including the south pole, as well as at several stations on the Arctic icepack; meteorological stations have been reinforced around the world, and a special pole-to-pole chain of stations has been established along the 70° to 80° west meridian through the Americas.

Corollary investigations of the earth's magnetism, the intensity and distribution of cosmic rays, and solar activity are also being conducted. Oceanographers are undertaking many special voyages, investigating currents, depths, obtaining and examining bottom cores, and attempting to gain a better understanding of the interaction of the ocean surface and the air above it. Glaciologists are encamped on scores of glaciers in the Arctic, temperate and equatorial, and Antarctic regions. Further investigations are being made of the high atmosphere with the use of newly developed rockets and satellites.

The earth satellite program is the most dramatic and publicized aspect of IGY. The satellite program, in effect, represents an extension of the rocket program, and is a tool which can provide data over a long period of time, over considerable heights above the earth, and over large expanses of the atmosphere about the earth. . . .

A concerted attempt is being made to make observations simultaneously from as many stations as possible during certain special events such as solar flares, eclipses, and other intervals of interest. A special worldwide warning system has been organized, which in a matter of minutes can flash a signal to hundreds of stations to intensify their operations for a special "solar" or other event. In many disciplines synoptic observations are of great importance, and special emphasis is made on maintaining continuity of work....

The United States National Academy of Sciences . . . accepted the invitation to join in the IGY and selected a United States National Committee for the IGY (USNC-IGY) during 1952. The committee with special regional subcommittees and technical panels gathered the Nation's leading geophysicists to develop the United States program, and an appropriate executive staff was organized. The USNC is under the competent and effective direction of Dr. Joseph Kaplan, Chairman; Dr. Alan H. Shapley, Vice Chairman; and Dr. Hugh Odishaw, Executive Director....

The National Science Foundation participated and cooperated in the planning of the United States IGY program and obtained special funds from the Congress for this purpose. In early 1954 a budget for $13 million was prepared and submitted to the Congress. In 1955 and 1956 the Congress granted additional funds, primarily to mount the earth satellite program, for a total of $39 million overall.

◀ E. *During World War II, the university grant-contract system for research and development became deeply imbedded in the federal operation. The effect of federal support on traditional university functions has since become a matter of concern to the colleges and to the government. To what extent should a university "compete" with private enterprise for research contracts? Does emphasis on contract research weaken the responsibility of the university to educate Americans in science and in all other areas of learning? What is the government's fair share of the cost of research, especially basic research? How should federal money be distributed institutionally and geographically? These and other complex problems absorbed the attention of science and university administrators between 1950 and 1957. None were solved conclusively then; they have yet to be resolved to everyone's satisfaction.*

In 1954 two committees were at work on the general policy problems of government-university relations, one sponsored by the National Science Foundation and the other assembled by the American Council on Education. The NSF committee was to look at the issues from the government's standpoint, the Council's from the colleges' American Council on Education, Sponsored Research Policy of Colleges and Universities *(Washington, 1954), 4, 11-20.*]

All accredited institutions of higher learning subscribe with varying emphases to three primary and essential aims: (a) the *extension* of the boundaries of knowledge; (b) the *conservation* of knowledge already acquired; and (c) the *diffusion* of knowledge through teaching, publication, and other accepted methods of dissemination. . . .

Suggestions and Recommendations to Colleges and Universities:

No educational institution should seek or accept funds for emergency research and development unless it has special advantages of men, experience, and facilities which make it clear that the institution can undertake the work better than some other agency. Even under these conditions, the institution might appropriately refuse the work unless it should become compellingly clear that it has a responsibility to help the government meet an emergency objective.

Except for emergency projects, sponsored research should be closely related to the normal program and recognized objectives of the institution. . . . A member of a faculty should never be assigned to contract research against his will. Normally, no project should be accepted unless it is open to qualified students.

Imposition of restrictions on publication of research results, either for secrecy or patent reasons, is incompatible with the basic concept of an educational institution as a source and distributor of knowledge and is difficult to reconcile with the other basic aims of such an institution. . . .

No institution should permit itself to become so dependent upon sponsored research that the cancellation of this research would seriously damage it.

The educational institution should carefully determine the entire cost to it of sponsored research, and if it accepts contracts or grants that do not cover both direct and indirect costs, the institution should do so with full recognition that it is itself making a contribution to the cost of the work.... The Committee recognizes that "full-cost" arrangements may be modified when appropriate by provisions regarding disposition of equipment.

Institutions should define their academic and fiscal policies and thus avoid differences and conflicts within their own organizations. To avoid disagreements about costs properly chargeable to contracts, they should follow clear accounting procedures themselves and should insist on unambiguous and equitable contracts.

Educational institutions should invite all research-sponsoring agencies, whether governmental, foundational, or industrial, to give more careful consideration to the advantages of institutional research grants over the specific project type; and in their dealings with these agencies they should exert their utmost influence toward a wider application of the principle of institutional rather than project support of research, recognizing at the same time that there are research problems that can be attacked only on a project basis....

Both the government and the institutions should be aware of and should guard against the danger that these large-scale projects may, under the exigencies of government sponsorship, take on more of the aspects of competitive business than befits an educational institution. One way to accomplish this is to insist insofar as practicable that investigations undertaken are fundamental in character....

In the event that further large-scale defense research projects become necessary, the Committee suggests that the government should give consideration to the desirability of establishing additional central laboratories involving the multiple participation of institutions. A good geographical distribution of such facilities by which the special abilities of institutions and their staffs can be utilized may provide one of the most satisfactory ways for meeting the government's needs while at the same time meeting the special requirements of colleges and universities....

No single government agency should have responsibility for managing all the government's general-purpose research

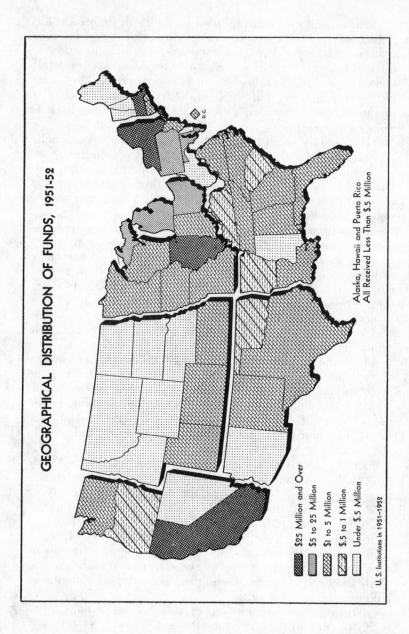

GEOGRAPHICAL DISTRIBUTION OF FUNDS, 1951-52

■ $25 Million and Over
▨ $5 to 25 Million
▧ $1 to 5 Million
▨ $.5 to 1 Million
▧ Under $.5 Million

U. S. Institutions in 1951–1952

Alaska, Hawaii and Puerto Rico
All Received Less Than $.5 Million

D.C.

220

in educational institutions. The establishment of the National Science Foundation has been welcomed by educational institutions, but occasional efforts to transfer to the foundation all general-purpose research funds in the government are viewed with apprehension. The Committee recommends that the government not concentrate its general-purpose research funds in any single government agency, since such concentration might result in creating a powerful bureaucracy, which could exert too much control of education and which might lose the great advantages in research management of diversity in method and objectives. No single government agency, however ably managed, could have all the "right" policies and methods.

Although no one agency could be expected to have enough wisdom to manage the government's entire program of general-purpose research, every effort should be made by all government agencies to achieve uniformity in contractual procedures and provisions.

❡ *F.* *Concern over the equitable distribution of federal funds for research geographically and institutionally during the period 1940 – 1960, was always more pronounced on Capitol Hill than in the granting agencies or among scientists. The merit of the project, as judged by specialists, and the location of suitable physical and manpower resources were the prime criteria; geographical location was a tertiary consideration for the last two groups. Correct as these criteria may seem, their precise application was often a matter of dispute between scientist and scientist, and especially between science administrator and politician. The map, published in the NSF series* Federal Funds for Science, *illustrated the situation too graphically. It was later omitted from the series. The fledgling NSF, in its struggle for congressional support, frequently found itself the object of criticism by politicians and from areas receiving comparatively little support. "Federal Report,"* Journal of Southern Research (*January-February 1953*), 24, 25.]

Disappointment over the administration of the National Science Foundation program is mounting rapidly as the new grant-making agency continues to favor large institutions concentrated in a few areas while generally ignoring the problem of strengthening the real weak spots in the nation's scientific activities. After more than two years of operation, observers note that the NSF is honoring a small select group with a large number of grants and with appointments to key committees and panels.

Typical of opinions in other sections of the country is the report by Clarence A. Mills, University of Cincinnati, carried in a recent issue of *Science*. Analyzing NSF grants up to the end of the last fiscal year, Mills points out that the Southern states are "faring most poorly under the NSF program" as compared with other regions. He predicts that the NSF policy will encourage students to leave the South to study in areas receiving greater support.

"Much more disturbing," according to Mills, "is the fact that 54 percent of the New England and Middle Eastern section's fellowship awards were made to students already attending five of the leading educational institutions — Harvard, Yale, Princeton, Columbia, and MIT; and 71 percent of the fellowships are to be spent at these same five institutions."

Mills also points out that on the NSF's final panels for screening fellowship applicants, the New England and Middle Eastern areas have 13 panel members (52%) to 12 for the remainder of the country. Moreover 8 of the 13 are faculty members of the area's five most favored institutions.

Going further, Mills shows that, for example, New England received $10,715 in grants for each million population, while the Southeast received only $3,774 per million population. In effect, the taxpayers of the South, where support of science is so badly needed to strengthen the nation, are footing the bill for expanded research at Harvard, Yale, and MIT.

More recently, the establishment of a special NSF panel to advise on minerals research projects offers further evidence that representation of important geographic regions is not being considered. On this new 15-man group, not one state South of Washington, D.C. and East of Oklahoma is represented. Yet this area is one of the nation's most active in minerals development.

If the NSF continues its policy, it will lose the support of many who urged its establishment. Activities conducted during 1953 will be observed with keen interest.

❡ G. *Indirect costs, according to the Bureau of the Budget's Circular A-21, September 10, 1958, are costs which, "be-*

cause of their incurrence for common or joint objectives, are not readily subject to treatment as direct costs of research agreements. ..." Indirect costs include: general administrative costs "not related solely to any special division of the institution," for example, employee benefit expenses, general operational expenses of the institution, for example, utilities; library expenses; and so forth. Indirect cost policy became the thorniest specific issue in the history of government-university relations during the middle years. Agency practice varied. The National Institutes of Health were limited by law to 15%. Other bureaus negotiated rates. Differing accounting methods employed by colleges in the conduct of their own affairs made the adoption of a single federal policy the subject of contention. A uniform system, enforced by Washington, would raise the larger issue of federal control of higher education.

The problem of imbalance in federal support for the natural sciences on the one hand, and the social sciences and humanities on the other, which came up during the debates over NSF legislation, was not resolved between 1950 and 1957. An exaggeration of the last statement in the following selection once prompted a non-scientist agency official to remark: "Very well, if support for natural science releases other monies for other disciplines, then the scientist should settle the argument once and for all, transfer his source of support to other fields, and use the 'released' funds." National Science Foundation, Government-University Relationships in Federally Sponsored Research and Development *(Washington, 1958), 19, 20.]*

It is quite clear that the natural sciences have received, since the start of World War II, outside support far greater than they received earlier or than that being received at present by the social sciences and humanities. Does this fact alone produce imbalance? Have the social sciences and humanities been deprived of funds because of the support and activities in the natural sciences? The answer generally given is "no," but with a significant number of dissents. Instances are sometimes cited of alleged favoritism to the natural sciences, e.g., building a new laboratory instead of a library.

Some university faculty members occasionally express concern about the possible imbalance or the intangible effects of the present situation. They fear that the glamour, especially of the physical sciences, with the relatively lavish support, the big machines, and larger economic rewards are creating distortions. They would not reduce the support to the natural sciences, but would urge increased funds for library facilities, for publication, and for travel for those, in other fields.

Many in the social sciences recognize the difficulties that may arise from Federal support of studies of controversial topics. Those in the humanities doubt that Federal funds could ever be made available to support the writing of an epic poem as they are for an atom smasher. But, both those in the social sciences and those in the humanities contend that their work is as important as that of the physicist.

Although the concentration of Federal funds in the natural sciences is an obvious fact, the Foundation, does not believe that the social sciences and humanities have been deprived of funds from other sources because of Federal support to the natural sciences. The social sciences and humanities have not received comparable Federal support, but reducing that given to the natural sciences would not automatically improve the lot of the former. In fact, some faculty members say that, due to outside support to the natural sciences, they now receive *university support* for research that otherwise would have gone to the natural sciences.

❡ *H. Two scientific bureaus dominated the Washington scene during the middle years: the National Institutes of Health and the Atomic Energy Commission. NIH appropriations often exceeded the President's budget allotment. Everybody was against disease and for health. Increased funds brought increased independence for the Institutes and increased problems of administration. In January of 1955, the Secretary of Health, Education, and Welfare, under prodding by the Budget Bureau, signed a letter to Director Waterman of the National Science Foundation, requesting a critical review and evaluation of the NIH research organization. The Foundation, reluctantly, appointed a committee, composed chiefly of bench scientists, to study and recommend policies and procedures for the Institutes. In December the committee reported. It recommended, among other things, no increase in the disease-oriented or "categorical" Institutes, and the establishment of a new agency in HEW to administer extramural (outside grant) support of medical research and training. Two years later a new Secretary of HEW called the NSF report obsolete, and appointed a new committee, this time one more closely representative of the science administrator's point of view.*

The Executive Office had challenged the NIH program. Both Congress and the Executive called AEC to an accounting. The awesome potentialities of atomic energy and the mystique of nuclear physics combined to make AEC a favorite scientific child in the federal family. With the liberal AEC legislation and large appropriations, the Commission, like NIH, grew fast, and became too independent for many observers. Its administrative policies were challenged by scientists in the case of J. Robert Oppenheimer. Even before that, Congress had expressed dismay at the freedom from control which the Commission enjoyed. Brien McMahon, Chairman, and Carl T. Durham, Vice Chairman, Joint Committee on Atomic Energy of the U.S. Congress, to President Truman, June 28, 1949, Truman Papers, OF 692, Harry S. Truman Library, Independence, Missouri.]

To spell out our point in greater detail, the Commission plans a reactor development program which will ultimately cost more than a half billion dollars. It so happens that the Joint Committee, after holding detailed hearings, believes this program to be highly desirable. But what if the reverse were true? What if the Committee felt that reactor construction is premature at this time? Let us even suppose the Committee had become convinced . . . that building the reactors would be a waste of resources or that the possibility of a radiation accident would endanger the lives of millions of people living near the area selected as a site. In any such case, the Commission would remain legally free—so broad is its present authorization—to proceed as it saw fit.

To be sure, Congress might decrease the Commission's annual budget by an amount equal to the sum requested for reactor development and in that way, register tangible disapproval. But appropriations to the Commission's use have been passed (with minor exceptions) on a lump-sum basis; they are not broken down into program items. Therefore, the Commission may switch funds from one program to another in its discretion. . . .

Furthermore, our fellow Congressmen are tempted to think of the Commission as a kind of specially privileged bureau whose actions are "above the law." A feeling of mistrust is engendered solely by reasons of the fact that the Commission may initiate vast new programs without the traditional and customary form of Congressional authorization. . . .

Accordingly, we feel that the need is clear for legislation limiting the sweeping authorization for the appropriation of funds which now exists.

IV. A Problem of Administration at the Top

￼ A. *Problems of efficiency and evaluation multiplied as governmental expenditures for research and development increased. Although few permanent answers were forthcoming between 1950 and 1957, hard questions were formulated about government administration and coordination at the top. Where in the political structure should the decisions be made — at the agency level, by some kind of high level adviser or committee, by a single bureau or department armed with special powers, by generalists already located in the Executive Office, by a combination of these techniques, and others? What are the limits, if any, of federal responsibility to support science? How should national resources be allocated among the scientific disciplines and projects, and between science and other governmental functions?*

Implicit in the writing of certain research administrators and scientists was an assumption that the federal government should provide public money to any scientist with an urge to investigate a problem of his own choosing, failing support from other sources, and to the exclusion of other demands of society for national resources. The assumption was unacceptable to the public's representatives because resources were not unlimited. Though definitive conclusions about the relative merit of projects and fields of science were not always possible, the need to establish priorities remained. "When" wondered an official in the Executive Office, "will the natural scientists realize that we must make hard decisions on the allocation of money without hard and conclusive evidence?" The decision-makers needed all relevant information and opinion, but they frequently found the scientific community reluctant to provide it.

Should science itself determine priorities within science, or should the public through its representatives, elected and appointed, have the final word on which scientific activities deserve support? Where does one draw the line between

*technical and public policy decisions? NSF Director Alan
Waterman thought that priorities in science should be estab-
lished by scientists. "Director's Statement,"* National Science
Foundation: Seventh Annual Report for the Fiscal Year
Ended June 30, 1957, *p. xi.*]

But, one may ask, what of the priorities of different
sciences? Are not some more important than others? To this,
science itself can make only one answer. No field of science
should be excluded from encouragement and support. The
capital discoveries in science may occur in any field. . . . The
only distinctions that can be made as to relative values are in
terms of contributions to understanding of our world, gener-
ality of findings, techniques available, current rates of progress, available skilled manpower, and occasionally neglected
or overemphasized special areas, when so identified by the
scientists themselves. This is science's own answer to the
matter of priority.

But there is, of course, another and completely different
question, namely: In what ways can science best serve the
Nation and all mankind? Here a wholly different set of criteria
apply. This question involves an appraisal of the Nation's
needs and a matching of progress in the fields of science to
national and human needs. For the service of science to the
Nation, or to mankind, is almost exclusively a practical matter
and therefore concerns the *applications* that can be made from
scientific discoveries and scientific principles.

❡ *B. James B. Conant, chemist and then president of
Harvard University, warned about the dangers of relying
uncritically upon technical advice. "Science and Politics in
the Twentieth Century,"* Foreign Affairs, *XXXVIII (January
1950), 189, 201, 202. Copyrighted by the Council on Foreign
Relations, Inc., New York.*]

By what procedures are a free people to determine the
answers to such complex questions as to whether a large
amount of the taxpayers' money is to be spent on the development of a given weapon or its auxiliary? Granted the matter
must be left to the people's elected representatives and the
President exercising through subordinates his power as Com-
mander-in-Chief, nevertheless the problem still remains, how

are politicians to resolve conflicts of opinions among scientists and engineers? Have we devised as yet even the first approximation to a satisfactory procedure for evaluating technical judgments on matters connected with the national defense, including atomic energy? ...

No one need warn those who have been immersed in the day-to-day planning of the defense of the nation that they should adopt a cautious or even skeptical mood in listening to technical experts, be they scientists or engineers. All experts are human and tend to be carried away with enthusiasm for their own ideas. ... But the existence of a conflict of technical opinion on many, many details in all manner of new developments of importance to our security requires that we take a careful look at the procedures used in arriving at decisions.

❡ *C. The committee or panel, at several levels, was a favorite device to control and direct the government's diversified research activity. In response to a recommendation in the Steelman Report, President Truman established by Executive Order 9912 of December 24, 1947, the Interdepartmental Committee on Scientific Research and Development, designed, among other things, to "study and report upon current policies and Federal administrative practices relating to Federal support for research...." The Committee, said Steelman, would "not be a coordinating group but will recommend to the President and heads of the Federal agencies concerned, how best to develop these programs." (White House Press Release, April 16, 1948.) The ICSRD never became a major instrument of policy-making. Composed of delegates from federal agencies with vested interests in their own research activities, the Committee soon agreed to stay out of substantive program content, and paid attention chiefly to administrative procedures, particularly scientific personnel matters.*

A more promising committee was formed at the beginning of the decade. Rivalry between the military services over weapon development was acrimonious in the late Forties, and signs of strain appeared between civilian scientists and the military. Congressman John W. McCormack called the situation to President Truman's attention, and at the request of the President and the Director of the Budget, William T. Golden was appointed to make a one-man study of federal science, with emphasis on the Department of Defense. In December 1950, Golden recommended a full-time Presidential science adviser and a science committee reporting to the adviser. The choice fell on Oliver Buckley of Bell Telephone Laboratories. Buckley preferred only to be chairman of a Science Advisory Committee, which was eventually placed in the Office of Defense Mobilization with an additional reporting channel to the President. The second channel was never used effectively. The next chairman of SAC-ODM, the more vigorous Lee A. DuBridge, tried without much success to re-open the channel, and to tie his Committee close to the National Security Council. When President Truman established SAC-ODM, he stated: "I have been concerned . . . that our existing arrangements do not provide adequate liaison among the agencies principally concerned with our national research and development effort, nor between them and the Office of Defense Mobilization. Such liaison is obviously essential to securing the full contribution of scientists to our defense planning." The Committee was given the following duties. President Harry S. Truman to Oliver E. Buckley, April 19, 1951, in White House Press Release, April 20, 1951.]

To provide independent advice on scientific matters especially as regards the objectives and interrelations of the several Federal agencies engaged in research of defense significance, including relevant foreign relations and intelligence matters.

To advise on progress being made in dealing with current scientific research problems of defense significance and also concerning defense research matters which need greater attention or emphasis.

To advise concerning plans and methods for the implementation of scientific effort for defense.

For transmitting the views of the scientific community of the country on research and development matters of national defense significance.

◖ *D. The National Science Foundation's broad charter authorized and directed it "to develop and encourage the pursuit of a national science policy for the promotion of basic research and education in the sciences" and "to evaluate scientific research programs undertaken by agencies of the*

Federal Government...." (Public Law 507, 81st Congress, Chapter 171, 2nd Session.) The struggle to stay alive in competition for funds during the Korean War, the necessity of establishing internal operational policies, and the philosophy of Director Waterman and his National Science Board resulted in a de-emphasis of the Foundation's policy and evaluation roles, to the disappointment of the Executive and Congress, which felt there was still too much overlapping and duplication and too little direction to the government's research programs. The Administration in 1953 worried about these debilities and, more specifically, about the alienation of scientists resulting from small NSF appropriations, atomic policy, the Astin affair and loyalty-security investigations. The White House asked the Budget Bureau for something to pacify the scientific community, and the Bureau came up with an Executive Order reaffirming NSF responsibility for basic research policy and evaluation. Consultation with other interested federal departments and with the Foundation itself resulted in additions and changes in the first draft which vitiated the Order's effectiveness. The second half of Section 4 was quoted by the Foundation to justify its laissez faire attitude toward basic research in other bureaus. SAC-ODM in 1957 still actively feared the Order's effect on the Department of Defense. Defense even quoted the second half of the Section to render the first half inoperative. The reader may decide for himself the intent of the Order. Executive Order 10521, March 17, 1954.]

... the National Science Foundation has been established by law for the purpose, among others, of developing and encouraging the pursuit of an appropriate and effective national policy for the promotion of basic research and education in the sciences:

Now, therefore, by virtue of the authority vested in me as President of the United States, it is hereby ordered as follows:

Section 1. The National Science Foundation ... shall from time to time recommend to the President policies for the Federal Government which will strengthen the national scientific effort and furnish guidance toward defining the responsibilities of the Federal Government in the conduct and support of scientific research.

Sec. 2. The Foundation shall continue to make comprehensive studies and recommendations regarding the Nation's scientific research effort and its resources for scientific activities, including facilities and scientific personnel, and its foreseeable scientific needs, with particular attention to the extent of the Federal Government's activities and the resulting effects upon trained scientific personnel. In making such studies, the Foundation shall make full use of existing sources of information and research facilities within the Federal Government.

Sec. 3. The Foundation, in concert with each Federal agency concerned, shall review the scientific research programs and activities of the Federal Government in order, among other purposes, to formulate methods for strengthening the administration of such programs and activities by the responsible agencies, and to study areas of basic research where gaps or undesirable overlapping of support may exist, and shall recommend to the heads of agencies concerning the support given to basic research.

Sec. 4. As now or hereafter authorized or permitted by law, the Foundation shall be increasingly responsible for providing support by the Federal Government for general-purpose basic research through contracts and grants. The conduct and support by other Federal agencies of basic research in areas which are closely related to their missions is recognized as important and desirable, especially in response to current national needs, and shall continue.

Sec. 5. The Foundation, in consultation with educational institutions, the heads of Federal agencies, and the Commissioner of Education of the Department of Health, Education, and Welfare, shall study the effects upon educational institutions of Federal policies and administration of contracts and grants for scientific research and development, and shall recommend policies and procedures which will promote the attainment of general national research objectives and realization of the research needs of Federal agencies while safeguarding the strength and independence of the Nation's institutions of learning.

Sec. 6. The head of each Federal agency engaged in scientific research shall make certain that effective executive, organizational, and fiscal practices exist to ensure (a) that the Foundation is consulted on policies concerning the support of basic research, (b) that approved scientific research programs conducted by the agency are reviewed continuously in order to preserve priorities in research efforts and to adjust programs to meet changing conditions without imposing unnecessary added burdens on budgetary and other resources, (c) that applied research and development shall be undertaken with sufficient consideration of the underlying basic research and such other factors as relative urgency, project costs, and availability of manpower and facilities, and (d) that, subject to considerations of security and applicable law, adequate dissemination shall be made within the Federal Government of reports on the nature and progress of research projects as an aid to efficiency and economy of the overall Federal scientific research program.

Sec. 7. Federal agencies supporting or engaging in scientific research shall, with the assistance of the Foundation, cooperate in an effort to improve the methods of classification and reporting of scientific research projects and activities, subject to the requirements of security information. . . .

◖ E.   *In the opinion of those who advocated more direction and control of the government's research, the Foundation abdicated its power and trust. To others, NSF implemented a correct philosophy of freedom from central control for science. Many doubted whether it was feasible for an operational bureau to fulfill the duties of a central scientific agency. And it was not always clear what specific policy and evaluation functions the Executive wanted the Foundation to perform. John Lear thought part of the problem was a matter of how one defined "policy."* "The Bill for Research," The New Scientist *(January 24, 1957), 23, 24.*]

I talked with Dr. Waterman through most of a Saturday recently. . . . I came away with the impression that his strength or lack of it may be entirely a matter of definition. What do we mean by direction? What do we mean by policy?

Being trained in the tradition of a free Press, I define policy to mean a course of action deliberately fixed by responsible persons and clearly understood by the people. Being trained in the equally free but more cloistered tradition of the research scientist, Dr. Waterman defines policy as something that is brought about and will, with time, become known.

"I think too much was expected of us in too short a

period," . . . [Waterman] told me. "Congress passed the law and said 'Science was a mess. But we've cleared it all up now.' Of course, it couldn't be cleared up like that. But we're making progress."

Turning a deaf ear to those who urged him to use the authority of the NSF law to knock together the heads of competing science bureaucrats, he adopted instead the consultative method of scientific decision. A dedicated follower of the scientific method himself, he acted on the principle that all other scientists are equally dedicated.

"The true research scientist is interested in only one thing: doing an original piece of work. If someone else is doing the same thing, it can't be original with both men. Duplication is professional suicide."

When confronted with the fact that scientists are first of all people, with prides and prejudices, generosities and jealousies, he conceded the obvious but insisted that most duplications in research are washed out during inter-agency bull sessions. To cut down his own sense of possessiveness, he stipulated from the beginning that NSF would never undertake to bring all basic research into its own bailiwick but would distribute the experiments wherever in the government they appeared to have the best chance of success.

This matter of not being the only fundamental research sponsor was, under the Waterman definition, a policy. Another policy under the same definition was the NSF decision to support basic rather than applied science. Still others were the determination to attack the shortage of scientists long range by improving the status of secondary school teachers and the quality of teaching, the addition of indirect costs to university grants, the rejection of classified work, and the judgment that candidates for grants be subject to no loyalty checks which do not permit an accused man to hear charges and defend himself openly.

¶ F.　*The Bureau of the Budget, in the Executive Office, as staff arm of the President with an overall view of the Executive Branch, was itself, from the late 1930s (with perhaps a break during World War II) until at least 1958, the country's central scientific organization. It was concerned with top-level coordination and national priorities, activities which it attempted conscientiously and usually*

without success to assign to other Executive organizations
and committees. Within the Bureau, generalists like William
D. Carey and Elmer Staats tried to introduce order and a
rationale into the "Balkanized" federal programs for research
and development. William Carey hatched the idea of Execu-
tive Order 10521. Carey, of all those engaged in science
administration, from the President and Congress to individual
members of research panels, came closest to being the philoso-
pher of order in the management of federal science. Carey,
"The Support of Scientific Research," Scientific Manpower-
1957: Papers of the Sixth Conference of Scientific Manpower
(Washington: NSF, 1958), 23-26.]

In recent weeks it has been fashionable to assail the
Government for missed opportunities and unenlightened
budget policies. At the risk of casting myself as a career
apologist, I will say that these criticisms greatly oversimplify
problems that are not simple; they do not do justice to the
attitude of the Government toward science; they gloss over
the powerful voice held by science in the councils of Government; and they underestimate the vexatious responsibility
resting on public management to balance divergent demands
against resources that are limited.

The point to be remembered in judging Government
policies toward the support of science is that the decisionmakers have no special insight to guide them to an absolute
value to be placed on science's aspirations. Science is "the
endless frontier," and any level of budgetary support is only
relative justice at best. Like all questions of Government
budget policy, the claims of science must be dealt with on the
basis of informed judgment, relative priorities, and open-
mindedness.

I realize that cold facts do not tell the whole story, and that
massive decisions on budgeting mask particular choices that
may, according to your lights, be wise or mistaken. Nonetheless, the facts are impressive. A hot war raised science in the
United States to the forefront of public policy. A cold war has
kept it there. In the middle of this century of desperate
decision, this is perhaps the most impressive innovation in the
American political process. . . .

As Government's role in scientific research has grown, the
problems of public management have increased in complex-

235

ity. When the budget-making authorities of your Federal Government approach decisions affecting the research and development budgets, they do so with an acute sense of responsibility. A great deal of intellectual sweat drips down over the hearing tables. The directors of research and development come before us with carefully and conscientiously arranged programs reflecting their estimate of what is worthwhile and important to do in basic research, and of what is necessary to accomplish applied research and development goals. We test the presentations with a variety of tools which are well-understood by the Government's scientific community—they concern such elements as the nature of the programing process in the given bureau or department, the quality of project evaluation as it is practiced in the daily environment of the study groups and advisory bodies, the availability of manpower and facilities, the standards of financial management and contract administration that are employed, and the outlook for sustaining support at a given level. More than this, we are of course deeply interested in decisive new departures either in research support or in developmental work. A proposal, for example, to deliberately venture into the business of underwriting the rehabilitation of obsolete privately operated research facilities, or to seed small colleges with computer or reactor equipment, invites a full-scale interrogation and a demand for a showing of the relevance of such departure to the national interest. By the same token, the entire range of major developmental undertakings in the national security-oriented agencies comes under scrutiny to ascertain the state of the art, the reasonableness of the costs, the time schedule, obsolescence rates, and the prognosis for success. In this area we must concern ourselves with the priority of the need for the end product in the light of competing demands for resources. In the case of long-range missiles, the President himself has given us our guidance, namely, the highest national priority.

All budgeting is difficult, and the results seldom bring applause, but the particular difficulty in budgeting for research is the necessity for effective translation of scientific objectives into lay terms. This is an art that the scientist-administrator has still to develop into proficiency.

But over and above the techniques of review, we are genuinely concerned about the soundness of this vast research and development structure that has come into being. We think that, important as it all appears to be in its own right, our common statecraft has still to recognize and deal with profound issues generated by Government-in-science on a large scale.... Since World War II, the Government has needed science, and has demanded much of it. But when science and education, together, find themselves so unqualifiedly dependent upon the Government to sustain them, then a basic political and cultural equation has been so altered that we cannot shrink from assessing its implications....

We must realize that when science and education become instruments of public policy, pledging their fortunes to it, an unstable equilibrium is established. Public policy is, almost by definition, the most transient of phenomena, subject from beginning to end to the vagaries of political dynamism. The budget of a government, under the democratic process, is an expression of the objectives, aspirations, and social values of a people in a given web of circumstances. To claim stability for such a product is to claim too much. In such a setting, science and education become soldiers of fortune. Today, their fortunes happily are in the ascendant. My advice is to let us together so construct this union of scientific invention and political action that each party does not lose sight of its right of self-determination; in the words of the philosopher, "Let them stand together, yet not too near together, for the pillars of the temple stand apart, and the oak tree and the cypress grow not in each other's shadow."

In fairness, I think it must be conceded that the art of public administration has not kept pace with the rise of scientific research as a public responsibility. Research and development on the grand scale resulted from wartime necessities and the psychology of the "crash" approach. There has been a tendency to attempt to manage research and development with the homespun techniques of a less complex age that antedates World War II. Progress is being made, to be sure, in recognizing the claims for flexibility that long have been asserted by the scientific community. Even so, we have still to develop within Government a comprehensive view of research and development roughly similar to what we long ago devised in such areas of public policy as agriculture, land and resource conservation, labor, and national defense. Science in Government continues in this critical age to prosper as a sideline of separate and unrelated departmental missions; it is not seen as a unity either in the executive or the legislative process. This certainly does not call for a compression of research services in a single-purpose department, which could create wholly different problems. We must, however, reorient our management philosophy toward a serious search for a national science policy based on the mobilization of human and material resources guided toward the attainment of some goals.... I return to the proposition that it would be worthwhile to experiment with long-range research goals expressed in annual increments of applied resources—men, money, materials, and laboratory hardware. Call this a "research model," if you will. Constructed in a cooperative effort by consultation between the Government agencies and the scientific community, this "model" would comprise objectives to be sought over a longer period than a single year, and would be subject to revision in accordance with the dynamics of science. Public management would be better able to make decisions for a stated period in a proper policy setting, taking into account goals, magnitudes, balance, resources, and the interrelationships among the chief support groups—industry, education, and Government. From the standpoint of the orderly formulation of public policy, this process could be an improvement over the tools now at hand and could lead to greater financial security for publicly supported research.

I suppose this proposition is vulnerable to the criticism that it lends itself to bureaucratic interference and an undesirable concentration of science through a species of packaging. To this, I can say only that if the scientific community expects Government to deal in a more understanding way with its problems and aspirations, and reform its processes accordingly, then science and its spokesmen will have to come halfway in satisfying the needs of Government. As long as science in Government continues to be "Balkanized"—and efforts are in progress to remedy this—just so long will decisions of public policy remain fragmented and outmoded for the century of crisis and opportunity in which we live.

V. A PROBLEM OF ORGANIZATION AT THE DEPARTMENTAL LEVEL: MILITARY RESEARCH AND DEVELOPMENT

◖ A. *When the Korean war began in June 1950, unification within the Department of Defense was chiefly a paper reality. Each military service still retained a large degree of individuality. Nowhere was rivalry between the services more acute than in the area of weapon development. Periodically, the public observed bitter controversies over the relative worth of one device or weapon and another—the aircraft carrier versus the long-range bomber, the pilotless aircraft versus the rocket, one type of missile versus another. Yet it was in the organization of research in the Department that pioneering efforts were made to affect unification. The Research and Development Board was one such attempt. To almost everyone concerned, it was a tragic failure. It tried to be too specific in a frequently hostile setting. It reduced to the absurd the committee-panel approach. A new charter for the Board, promulgated in 1952, gave more authority to RDB, but it still was not an operating agency letting contracts and directly administering research programs. Next year the Board was replaced by two Assistant Secretaries of Defense, one for Research and Development and one for Applications Engineering.*

Congress took a special interest in all this shuffling of functions and duties in the Department. R. Walter Riehlman's subcommittee of the House Committee on Government Operations focused on the problem of civilian-military relations in the conduct of research and development. U.S. Congress, House, Committee on Government Operations, Subcommittee on Military Operations, Hearings, "Organization and Administration of Military Research and Development," 83 Cong., 2 sess. (1954), 2, 3,]

MR. RIEHLMAN: During the course of the subcommittee's investigation of several specific military research and development centers, it appeared that the program was plagued with several problems. The subcommittee has formed no conclusions at this time concerning the validity of these reported problems. It does have some evidence that these problems have some factual basis in certain military research operations, and it intends to hear testimony from selected witnesses. The subcommittee sincerely presents the reported problems as a series of working hypotheses, and we hope that the presentation by top officials from the Department of Defense can aid the subcommittee in evaluating these hypotheses and formulating informed, constructive conclusions....

Reported Problems in Military Research and Development Programs.

I. Civilian scientists in military research and development centers are reported to be generally dissatisfied with military domination and administration.

II. Civilian scientists are leaving military research and development centers.

III. When a military organization is imposed on a research and development program there is a tendency for the military to expand its control over technical decisions and operations in the research laboratories.

IV. With a few notable exceptions, military research and development officers are not scientists who command the respect of the civilian scientists.

V. The policy of rotating assignments for military officers militates against the retention of officers who in some cases have the training, talents, and disposition to guide scientific research centers.

VI. Research centers often are organized and administered as military organizations with the attendant restrictive forms, procedures, regulations, and military discipline which do not provide the optimum climate for research work by civilian scientists.

VII. The lack of either a definite or consistent policy for organizing and administering research and development centers leaves each center at the mercy of each change in commanding officer and Executive. This creates an instability with no assurance that even the well-run research and development center will not become, with a change of officers, an unbearable situation.

VIII. Several outstanding civilian scientists who have

been associated with military research and development programs are reported to be in favor of changes in the governmental organization and administration of these programs.

IX. The funding of research and development is confused when handled with military budgets. Direct research and development costs are justified to and appropriated by the Congress as such. However, this does not give a true picture of the actual total cost of military research and development programs inasmuch as there are substantial indirect costs arising from military support functions in the form of pay for uniformed officers, provision of capital facilities, and certain maintenance and operation expenditures.

In this connection, it is reported that it is often felt necessary to build up a research and development center with such support functions in order to make it "respectable" in terms of size and complexity as a command for a colonel or general. This, in turn, sets off a vicious cycle in that the existence of military support elements becomes a further excuse for military domination, more officers, regulations, etc.

❡ B.   *Vannevar Bush cited the Korean conflict as a failure for American military weapons development. Riehlman Committee, Hearings, 452, 453.*]

DR. BUSH: Let me say first of all that the development of weapons is very closely interlinked with their use; and it is impossible to separate the discussion of their development completely from the way in which they are used in practice.

I think there are two serious weaknesses today that impede our program of research and development.

First, the security clearance system as now practiced is, in my opinion, doing great damage to the relations between science and Government, and particularly to the relations between scientists and weapons development.

Second, it seems to me that we have lost our effectiveness in getting new weapons tested, tried out, produced on an experimental basis, and finally introduced in use.

Now, let me take the second one first, if I may. About a year ago when I appeared before a committee that was examining into the organization of the Department of the Army, I was asked whether I felt there was anything wrong with the organizational situation in regard to new weapons.

I told the committee that we had just fought a war in Korea in which we had used no new weapons—no new improvements over World War II except the helicopter—and that was evidence of something wrong. Either the Army had spent a very large amount of money on development and produced nothing, or possibly it had thought that everything that had been produced was too important for use in a minor war where it would become known to the enemy, or there was something wrong in the organizational system that prevented the new things from really getting into use.

I am still of the same opinion, and I believe that the difficulty lies in our planning at the very top echelons. Unless our planning there is modern, forward-looking, alert, particularly on the matter of weapons, the whole system bogs down and things fail to move.

Now, I have felt for many years quite strongly that we are not organized at the present time for good vigorous planning at the top levels.

When unification was brought about the primary objective was to produce unitary war plans—to produce a unity in planning so we would have a single war plan with everything fitting into it. All other objectives of unification were more or less secondary to that one. Modern war so interrelates Army, Navy, and Air efforts that it is quite artificial to plan separately, and the Joint Chiefs organization was set up for the purpose of joint planning. But the Joint Chiefs are themselves the commanding officers of their services. They can give only part of their time to Joint Chiefs operations and planning. They are the primary group that is advisory to the Secretary of Defense and the President on war planning. And I have felt that they do not handle their affairs so that we have objective and vigorous planning at the top level. I have said so many times— even in speeches.

Now, I am still discouraged on this point. A year ago the Rockefeller Board met and was charged with the job of recommending reorganization in the Department of Defense. It was an excellent board; it made a number of excellent recommendations that have been put into effect; but, in my opinion, its most important recommendation has not been put into effect.

It recommended that there be formed at the level of the Joint Chiefs of Staff a planning committee made up of senior officers detached from responsibility to their services, men on their last assignment, properly supported by junior personnel, to be given the full-time duty of examining into the way in which modern weapons fit into warfare. This planning committee was to report to the Secretary of Defense and the President, with the provision, and the very important provision, that while the Joint Chiefs themselves might comment on the committee's findings, they could not hold them up or withhold them.

Now, that was a very radical step in organization. It did not go so far as I might have wished, but I think it would have produced some really vigorous, disinterested, objective modern planning by a competent group.

That proposal was agreed to by the full Rockefeller committee; it was approved by the military advisers to the committee, Marshall, Nimitz, and Spaatz. It was approved by Mr. Wilson and Mr. Kyes before it went into the report. The President approved the entire report. Yet that particular proposal has never been put into operation, or at least it hadn't been a few weeks ago.

❡ *C.   The testimony of John W. Marchetti, a former Technical Director of Cambridge Research Center, confirmed Riehlman's suspicion that all was not well between the civilian scientists and their military supervisors. Riehlman Committee, Hearings, 246.*]

MR. [JOHN W.] McCORMACK: Can you take men from the service, no matter how eminent they are, how good they are, how qualified they are and stick them into research?

MR. MARCHETTI: I do not believe you can. When you do you wind up with a second-and third-grade laboratory. Generally speaking, the Air Force laboratories — and I will take Wright Field as an example; it is one of the oldest of the Air Force laboratories — you will find there that they have groups on propulsion, groups on electronics, groups on antennae, and you will find the chief of these various laboratories is either a captain, a major or a colonel. In some cases these people are competent to hold their jobs, but there are very few such cases.

Down in the fine print you will find some civilian. He is the fellow that is really running the show, but he is a second-rater or a third-rater because no first-rate technical man will go into a laboratory structure where the chief of the laboratory is a titular military man and he has to carry the responsibility without having any of the authority.

This is the reason why the military laboratories with that policy are dedicated to be second- and third-rate laboratories. No competent people will go into such an organizational structure. It is the continual cry on the part of the military that they cannot entice capable technical people to work for them. But this is utter foolishness when they put captains and majors or even full colonels in there as superiors just by virtue of their military rank. That is the heart of the problem. That is the reason why Wright Field is not a good laboratory. At Cambridge this did not obtain prior to the arrival of the last commander.

I had hoped that the Air Force would see the light, would go and change gradually, because it has to be a gradual process. I had hoped that the Air Force would change the policy to fit the Cambridge pattern, where a fair amount of authority — and let me even put it this way, just plain ordinary courtesy and equality was allotted to the technical civilians. If they had changed their other laboratories to follow the Cambridge pattern, we would have a healthy condition.

I find, however, after General Maude came in and the conversion took place, Cambridge was made to follow the pattern that was established in the other laboratories where the control was fully military and the scientific people were asked to work for a continually changing, inept and sometimes pretty irresponsible military organizational structure. I think that is the very heart of the problem.

❡ D. *The rise of nonprofit civilian research corporations, sponsored by one or more federal agencies, was a common phenomenon of post World War II science in the United States. Perhaps the most famous was RAND (short for research and development). Trevor Gardner, then Special Assistant for R & D in the Office of the Secretary of the Air Force, described RAND's operation. Riehlman Committee, Hearings, 155-157.]*

MR. GARDNER: . . . There are 617 full time employees at Rand. Approximately 55 percent of these have technical degrees. As I remember, 157 have doctors degrees. Rand employs in addition to that a number of consultants. I do not necessarily mean that a Ph.D. degree means a man is bright, but it is one yardstick for measuring technical and analytical competence.

Rand is divided into six divisions that roughly correspond with the divisions of strategic air defense, tactical air, and so on. One division addresses itself to nuclear problems. They work on projects of their own initiation, with Air Force funds when approved by the Air Force, and on some other projects with their own funds. They are a nonprofit institution. This does not mean we do not pay them a fee. They receive a fee on their contract, but this fee has so far just been used to increase their working capital. At the point that working capital reaches a certain level, they begin plowing the excess part back into their own research program.

Rand operates almost as a technical assistant to our military air staff. They are all civilians, although we do have a few Air Force officers assigned there from time to time. Rand works closely with all echelons of the Air Staff and with the commands.

Since I come from southern California, I have heard about Rand in various ways for a number of years, and I went into the investigation somewhat critically where the research is principally paper and plans. After examining the Rand papers and their impact on the Air Force and the kind of things they were working on and the people running it, I feel that the Air Force is getting its money's worth from Rand. I feel they have made not one but many contributions during the past few years.

We have been a little critical that perhaps they were working on too many things and, very frankly, this is a matter of judgment and capacity. They appear to have the capacity. I personally would be happier if we could get Rand to concentrate on less projects than they have. At the present time they have 152 studies in process, some of them large and some small. Ten of these studies account for almost $2 million of the $6 million we are giving Rand each year. . . .

MR. [M. P.] BALWAN: Who heads up Rand?

MR. GARDNER: Frank Collbohm heads it up. He is the director. And there is Dr. Lee DuBridge, president of California Institute of Technology, and Rowen Gaither of the Ford Foundation, who are members of the board of trustees.

MR. BALWAN: Is this a joint venture?

MR. GARDNER: It is not. It is a private nonprofit corporation.

MR. [P. J.] COTTER: How was it conceived and how did it gain its importance in relation to the Air Force?

MR. GARDNER: At the end of World War II it was apparent that new weapons were arriving on the scene at a tremendous rate, not the least of which was the atomic bomb. The impact of these new weapons on the Air Force was not clear. What was clear was that if we did not examine the impact in an objective and realistic way we certainly would not remain superior in the air. As you will recall, at the end of World War II we were looking at the Luftwaffe, which had flown the first jet airplane; and we were looking at the Russians, with rockets as good as ours; and we were looking at the British, who had come up with the turbojet engine; and we were looking at the Swedes from whom we had to borrow the Oerlikon gun. We were looking at wind tunnels the Germans had conceived and had in warehouses when we were not even thinking of wind tunnels. . . . General Arnold and General Doolittle and others appreciated this and set up an inquiry as to what might be done about it, to which I refer later, the so-called Ridenour report. They did a number of other things, such as the determination that we should have, must have, a large wind tunnel; we must have a guided missile test range; we must have a scientific advisory board to the Chief of Staff, and some sort of entity which could, on a continuing basis, feed the Air Force with analyses of promising ideas. This entity could not be found in the Air Force but was found in a group located at the Douglas Aircraft Co. The group began their work there, but when it appeared they would be a technical servant of our Air Force, it was appreciated if they remained at Douglas they might certainly be accused of having a bias, so in order to give this group as unbiased a flavor as possible, in a world filled with bias, the Rand Corp. was formed. . . .

MR. COTTER: Is the Air Force the sole source of their income?

MR. GARDNER: Not completely. This is a very controversial point and one on which you can get several answers. I will have to be very frank about it. There is not an agreement, but there is an accepted practice that Rand will tend to concentrate on our Air Staff problems. They have taken jobs for the Army and they have taken contracts with the Air Defense Command directly. So they do things other than the $6 million contract.

MR. COTTER: But not for private industry?

MR. GARDNER: They have not done anything for private industry to the best of my knowledge.

◀ E. A Task Force Subcommittee on Research and Development of the second Hoover Commission examined the achievements and failures of Defense research organization, and recommended an Assistant Secretary for R & D in each of the services. U.S. Commission on Organization of the Executive Branch of the Government, Research and Development in the Government (Washington, May 1955), 1, 2, 8-16.]

The budget proposals for expenditure on Research and Development in the defense services for the fiscal year 1956 are estimated at $1,648,335,000, with an additional $214,600,000 for improved facilities, or a total of about $1,862,935,000. To this must be added roughly $190,000,000 for personnel budgeted to other agencies, or a grand total of about $2,050,000,000. . . .

These operations are performed in the installations of the military, industrial, academic, and nonprofit organizations. In 1954, more than 120 installations of the military were involved, and at these installations approximately 39,000 military and 63,000 civilian personnel participated in the programs. A few thousand installations of the civilian economy were active in the programs. More than 8,000 separate projects were active. Some 40 percent of the appropriated funds that year were expended in the installations of the military departments, 50 percent in installations of industry, and 10 percent in those of academic and nonprofit institutions.

The Research and Development programs for military strength extend across the entire forefront of basic research in the physical sciences and the technologies of their application. . . .

The Task Force Subcommittee states:

(a) There has been much concern about waste and excess expenditure through duplication in the Research and development programs of the Army, Navy, and Air Force. The Subcommittee finds some basis for this concern.

(b) That the deficiencies primarily reside in the "self-sufficiency complex" of each of the services. There are areas of "warranted duplication" as well as those that are "unwarranted." In many of the forefront areas of weaponry, multiple approach through parallel developments are essential and should be continued. The "warranted" can be planned for and controlled, and the "unwarranted" prevented by the present patterns of organization and relationships between the Secretary of Defense level and the level of the three Services. . . .

Criticisms have been expressed in various quarters that the Armed Services are not sufficiently daring and imaginative in their approach to radically new weapons and weapons systems. . . . The present organization, with its procedures, is inadequate for the initiation of such projects. It [the Subcommittee] states that the three Military Services have not distinguished themselves in the initiation of radically new approaches to weapons systems. . . .

[Recommendation No. 7]

That an Office of Assistant Secretary for Research and Development be established in each of the three Military Departments. . . .

That the Assistant Secretary be trained in science and technology and experienced in the operations and administration of research and development. . . .

Research and development and design operations are, in general, best performed by civilian agencies. Since the close of World War II, the Military Departments have greatly expanded their facilities and personnel for the operations of research and development. The operations performed there are generally at a lower level of effectiveness than could be realized if suitably placed in the civilian economy. The Task Force Subcommittee estimates that in 1954 there was a $125,000,000 volume of such work that was susceptible to shift into the civilian economy.

❡ F. *The highly publicized race with Russia for an effective intercontinental ballistic missile initiated an intense controversy over the comparative worth of Army and Air Force missile efforts. The Nickerson case was just one incident in the missile imbroglio. Hanson W. Baldwin, "The Nickerson*

Case," New York Times, *July 16, 1957; reprinted by permission.*]

A comparatively light sentence, but one of the stiffest reprimands an officer could receive, has ended, it is to be hoped, the unfortunate case of Col. John C. Nickerson Jr.

Colonel Nickerson is the Army officer who pleaded guilty to using documents marked secret to proselytize writers and manufacturers in behalf of the Army's intermediate range ballistic missile, the Jupiter. The facts reported from the court-martial—many of them based on Colonel Nickerson's own testimony, appear to justify the harsh language of the reprimand. In and out of court Colonel Nickerson talked too much; in the words of the official reprimand he "presumed" himself to "be above law and regulations." There was bound to be punishment, as Colonel Nickerson himself agreed.

Yet a consequence considerably more important than a ruined career is the possible effect of the Nickerson case upon the development of the intermediate range ballistic missile. Colonel Nickerson not only showed an excess of zeal and a deficiency of judgment, but the means he selected to achieve his ends, and particularly the things he said before and during his court-martial, tended, unintentionally on his part, to defeat the purpose he wished to attain.

Colonel Nickerson was carrying the torch for Jupiter, the Army's version of the intermediate range ballistic missile, which has been under development at Redstone Arsenal, Huntsville, Ala. in competition with the Air Force Thor. The ruling last year by Charles E. Wilson, the Secretary of Defense, that the Air Force would operate any intermediate range ballistic missile led to Colonel Nickerson's unwise acts.

Yet Mr. Wilson's decision did not by any means exclude the Army from the use of ballistic missiles or from the development of long-range missiles. The Jupiter, fortunately, has continued under development.

Yet the Nickerson court-martial might well tend to prejudice judgments and imperil continued development of the Jupiter.

By Secretary Wilson's ruling, the Air Force, which will operate the 1,500 mile missile when it is ready for use, is now the Army's sole customer for the Jupiter. The Air Force, through private contractors, has been developing the Thor, another version of the intermediate range ballistic missile.

To date, the Jupiter appears to have been more successful than the Thor; it may well be, as Redstone Arsenal claims, a much superior missile. But the Army has to convince the Air Force and the Department of Defense of the truth of these claims.

In mid-June shortly before the Nickerson court-martial, Redstone Arsenal, headquarters of the Army Ballistic Missile Agency, played host to Maj. Gen. Bernard A. Schriever of the Air Force and his staff. General Schriever and the Air Force ballistic missile experts were thoroughly briefed on Jupiter, on the Army's ballistic missile team and on the great capabilities—in missile development—of Redstone Arsenal. They came away impressed.

Then came the court-martial and Colonel Nickerson's testimony in and out of court, which was certainly not calculated to win friends and influence people in the Air Force. The testimony seemed to hint that Secretary Wilson's verdict giving operational control of the 1,500-mile missile to the Air Force was influenced in part by vested interests of aviation companies. It cast aspersions not only at Thor but at the Air Force.

It defended Jupiter but the defense was an attack upon the Air Force, which is the potential user of Jupiter. It showed, what was already known, that the Jupiter was potentially an excellent missile, whose development should be continued. But its attacks upon the Air Force, and particularly the unproved and implied inferences in the testimony, were bound to react against Redstone Arsenal and the Jupiter missile.

One cannot but conclude that Colonel Nickerson talked too much. The sooner the wounds left by the Nickerson case are healed the better for the nation. We are engaged in what could be a life-and-death missile development race with Soviet Russia.

Already budgetary pressures appear to be curtailing United States missile developments. The promising Navaho long-range missile, for instance, has just been abandoned. A technical evaluation of the potential capabilities of other more promising missiles and of new chemical-powered piloted jet bombers may offer some justification for this cancellation. But there is no doubt that the defense dollar squeeze was a major factor.

There are several timely lessons, therefore, to be drawn from the Nickerson case. The first is that there must be only one criterion in the selection of weapons and in development plannings; the criterion must be what is best for the country, not merely for the individual service.

The second is that the Administration will make a major mistake if it adopts in military budgetary matters a penny-wise – pound-foolish policy in research and development. Parallel and competitive, but different, approaches to the same end — for instance, the Jupiter and the Thor — are absolutely essential to the best product.

And government research teams, laboratories and arsenals like Redstone are an important part of the whole development effort, and should serve as a kind of guide and yardstick for private industry in the development of the new technology of the missile age.

❡ *G. Navy was given the job of launching America's civilian IGY satellite, a program in which there was also an element of Soviet competition. The American program had lower priorities than missile weapon development, at least until June 18, 1957. Embassy of the Union of Soviet Socialist Republics, Washington, D.C., Press Release, June 26, 1957.*]

A whole series of artificial satellites will be launched in the USSR during International Geophysical Year. Differing in weight and size, they will be fitted with scientific equipment for all kinds of observations.

The satellites will be launched to heights of from 125 to 300 miles, and the findings will be reported to all countries, Yevgeny Fedorov, famous polar explorer and Corresponding Member of the USSR Academy of Sciences, told a press conference for foreign journalists held on June 18 by the State Committee for Cultural Relations with Foreign Countries. . . .

The journalists were shown three dogs that had made rocket flights to heights of more than 60 miles.

PART FIVE

THE YEARS OF RESPONSE 1957–1965

The closer the story moves to the present, the less dependable becomes the one faculty essential to every historian— judgment. And yet the historian least of all can afford to draw a temporal line beyond which conclusions cannot be drawn. The study of the past is an endless flow in which the present is merely the process by which the future becomes the past. So it is in a mood of undaunted trepidation that the following selections are presented. The years and months just behind us were years and months of response: to Sputnik and the threat from abroad, and to problems of organization and control stemming from twenty years of intemperate growth.

I. Organization

❧ A. *A year before Sputnik, in a book called* Soviet Professional Manpower, *Nicholas DeWitt had demonstrated that the Soviet Union was training scientists and technical personnel at a pace considerably faster than that of the United States. Congress was sufficiently shocked to increase substantially the appropriation of the National Science Foundation, which in the five years past had grown steadily but unremarkably. Nevertheless, Americans, even those who should have known better, were shocked by the Russian achievement. Myths do not topple easily, and Americans had long believed that the Russians were essentially a backward people, dependent for what science they could boast upon captured German scientists and espionage. President Dwight D. Eisenhower, whose popularity had always been based in part on his possessing the glands of the sociologists' average man, registered the shock of the nation in a press conference on October 9, 1957, a part of which is quoted below. Notice the symptom of shock: profound ambivalence. On the one hand, the Russians succeeded because our own superior scientific machinery was never in competition; on the other hand, the Russian scientists had the advantage of living in a dictatorial society.* Dwight D. Eisenhower, Public Papers of the Presidents of the United States *(Washington, 1958), 719-724.]*

Q. MERRIMAN SMITH, United Press: Mr. President, Russia has launched an earth satellite. They also claim to have had a successful firing of an intercontinental ballistics missile, none of which this country has done. I ask you, sir, what are we going to do about it?

THE PRESIDENT: Well, let's take, first, the earth satellite, as opposed to the missile, because they are related only indirectly in the physical sense, and in our case not at all.

The first mention that was made of an earth satellite that I know of, was about the spring of 1955—I mean the first mention to me—following upon a conference in Rome where plans were being laid for the working out of the things to be done in the International Geophysical Year.

Our people came back, studying a recommendation of that conference that we now undertake, the world undertake, the launching of a small earth satellite; and somewhere in I think May or June of 1955 it was recommended to me, by the Committee for the International Geophysical Year and through the National Science Foundation, that we undertake this project with a satellite to be launched somewhere during the Geophysical Year, which was from June 1957 until December 1958.

The sum asked for to launch a missile was $22 million and it was approved.

For the Government, the National Science Foundation was made the monitor of the work, for the simple reason that from the beginning the whole American purpose and design in this effort has been to produce the maximum in scientific information. The project was sold to me on this basis.

My question was: What does mankind hope to learn? And the answer of the scientists was, "We don't exactly know, and that is the reason we want to do it; but we do hope to learn lots of things about outer space that will be valuable to the scientific world."

They did mention such things as temperatures, radiation, ionization, pressures, I believe residual pressures, from such air as would be at the altitude where successful orbiting was possible.

That is the kind of information the scientists were looking for, and which they hoped to obtain from this project.

Now, in the first instance they thought they would merely put up a satellite, and very quickly they found they thought they could put up a satellite with a considerable instrumentation to get, even during the Geophysical Year, the kind of information to which I have just referred. So they came back, said they needed some more money. This time they went up to $66 million, and we said, "All right; that is—in view of the fact we are conducting this basic research, this seems logical." So we did that.

Then they came back, and I forget which one of the steps it came along, and they realized when you put this machine in the air, you had to have some very specially equipped observation stations. So the money, the sum of money, again went up to provide for these observation stations. And so the final sum approved, I think about a year ago, something of that kind, was $110,000,000, with notice that that might have to go up even still more.

There never has been one nickel asked for accelerating the program. Never has it been considered as a race; merely an engagement on our part to put up a vehicle of this kind during the period that I have already mentioned.

Again emphasizing the nonmilitary character of the effort, we have kept the Geophysical Year Committees of other nations fully informed all the time as, for example, the frequencies we would use when we put this in the air so that everybody, all nations, could from the beginning track it exactly, know exactly where it was—I believe it was 108 megacycles we were to use, and that was agreed throughout the world.

We are still going ahead on this program to make certain that before the end of the calendar year 1958 we have put a We are still going ahead on this program to make certain that before the end of the calendar year 1958 we have put a vehicle in the air with the maximum ability that we can devise for obtaining the kind of scientific information that I have stated.

Now, every scientist that I have talked to since this occurred—I recalled some of them and asked them—every one of them has spoken in most congratulatory terms about the capabilities of the Russian scientists in putting this in the air.

They expressed themselves as pleased rather than chagrined because at least the Soviets have proved the first part of it, that this thing will successfully orbit. But there are a lot of other things in the scientific inquiry that are not yet answered, and which we are pushing ahead to answer...

As to their firing of an intercontinental missile, we have not been told anything about the details of that firing. They have proved again and, indeed, this launching of the satellite proves, that they can hurl an object a considerable distance. They also said, as I recall that announcement, that it landed in the target area, which could be anywhere, because you can make target areas the size you please; and they also said it was a successful re-entry into the atmosphere, and landing at or near the target.

Now, that is a great accomplishment, if done. I have

talked to you in the past about our own development in this regard as far as security considerations permit, and I can say this: the ICBM, the IRBM, we call them, are still going ahead —those projects—on the top priority within the Government, incidentally a priority which was never accorded to the satellite program.

The satellite program, having an entirely different purpose, even the scientists did not even think of it as a security instrument; and the only way that the Defense Department is in it at all is because one of them, the Navy, was called upon as the agency to have the sites and the mechanisms for putting it into the air. . . .

Q. MRS. MAY CRAIG, Portland (Maine) Press Herald: Mr. President, you have spoken of the scientific aspects of the satellite. Do you not think that it has immense significance, the satellite, immense significance in surveillance of other countries, and leading to space platforms which could be used for rockets?

THE PRESIDENT: Not at this time, no. There is no— suddenly all America seems to become scientists, and I am hearing many, many ideas. [Laughter] And I think that, given time, satellites will be able to transmit to the earth some kind of information with respect to what they see on the earth or what they find on the earth.

But I think that that period is a long ways off when you stop to consider that even now the Russians, under a dictatorial society where they had some of the finest scientists in the world who have for many years been working on this, apparently from what they say they have put one small ball in the air.

❡ B. In the selection below, Arthur S. Flemming, Secretary of Health, Education and Welfare under President Eisenhower, explained "the philosophy and objectives of the National Defense Education Act," passed by Congress in the wake of Sputnik. The Annals of the American Academy of Political and Social Science, Vol. 327 (January, 1960), 132-138.]

The objectives of the National Defense Education Act have their source in a political philosophy that has consistently characterized federal aid to education from the beginning of our nation's history. This philosophy or, rather, this traditional principle, is based on two empirically derived premises. The first confines federal aid to specific programs devised to help the states solve those problems that bear upon national needs and that surpass the states' capabilities to resolve them unaided. The second asserts the sovereign right of the states to administer educational policies, devise curricula, select textbooks, educate and license teachers, supervise methods of instruction, and in general to maintain, manage, and direct the forms, substance, and tempo of their own systems of public education.

These premises have been constant factors in determining the objectives and scope of every act of Congress in aid of education from the Northwest Ordinance of 1787 to the National Defense Education Act of 1958.

In our country's formative years, total reliance on local autonomy in the management of schools was a practical necessity. Out of the self-contained and socially isolated nature of American communities in those early years, a unique and powerful sense of local responsibility for the schooling of children developed. Nevertheless, despite this strongly held conviction and the fear of the tyranny believed to be inherent in centralized government, the states accepted numerous grants of federal aid with no consequent loss of autonomy nor diminution of their control.

From the Revolution to the Civil War, the federal government encouraged and financially aided education in the states. It endowed higher and common schools with lands and granted funds to supplement these endowments. On no occasion did the federal government seek to control public education in the states.

In 1862, under the Morrill Act, the federal government provided an eventual grant of eleven million acres of land for the endowment of at least one college in each state and territory that would provide much needed instruction in agriculture and the mechanic arts. The recipients of the Morrill Act's benefits, the so-called "land-grant colleges," have not experienced any difficulty in maintaining control of their academic programs. Moreover, the extensive public services rendered by these institutions are proof of the enduring value of federal-state co-operation.

This pattern of federal stimulation without federal domination characterized such subsequent legislation as the Smith-Hughes Act and the George-Barden Act, both of which helped the states to strengthen and extend vocational education. It determined the numerous legislative provisions for education during the depression years, the post-World War II provision of tuitional and maintenance assistance to veterans under the "GI Bills," and programs in aid of federally affected areas. These were all manifestations not only of the national concern for education, but also of the federal government's recognition of the supremacy of state responsibility.

To guarantee the continuing separation of federal and state functions, the national government must constantly be on the alert to avoid jeopardizing the vital role of pluralism and thus of freedom and experimentation in education. Indeed, if it is to remain true to its proper purposes, the federal government must clearly define and delimit the scope of its educational role through unremitting scrutiny of the letter and spirit of proposed legislation lest it be interpreted as permitting trespass on state and local jurisdictional supremacies.

Present times and immediate circumstances have heightened the national concern for education. In the last half century our society has become an intricate network of diverse but related interests, each dependent on all others for effective functioning.

The obligations of world leadership, the increasing demands of industry and the armed forces for highly trained personnel, the requirements of foreign trade and international diplomacy for personnel having mastery of languages other than their own, and the increasing complexity of our economic and social arrangements have imposed on every school district and on every institution of higher learning insistent demands for a greater quantity and improved quality of educational opportunities and facilities to create an adequate national resource of well trained and intellectually enlightened young men and women.

To help solve these problems and to ease the fiscal burden carried by the states are prime purposes of federal aid to education. Accumulated experience over more than 170 years enables us to perceive that, properly utilized with due regard to state responsibility, federal funds can be useful in many ways to both the states and the nation. The National Defense Education Act of 1958 is an excellent illustration of this fact.

Marion B. Folsom, then Secretary of Health, Education, and Welfare, appointed a committee to review the recommendations of the President's Committee on Education Beyond the High School and to draw up legislative proposals based upon them. Many of the provisions of the National Defense Education Act had their source in those proposals.

After the bill was drawn, there still was doubt that it could win Congressional approval. The reception and fate of school-construction bills in the years immediately preceding did not provide an optimistic outlook.

When Sputnik rose into orbit, it aroused more than incredulous amazement; it was a blow to American pride. Yet, its advent had positive consequences. It awakened and spurred us into rigorous self-examination of our total educational system. This in turn provided an excellent climate for the consideration of the provisions of the proposed National Defense Education Act.

The National Defense Education Act of 1958 was passed by the Senate on August 22 and by the House of Representatives on August 23. It was signed into Public Law 85-864 by President Eisenhower on September 2.

The Act authorizes a billion dollars in federal aid for a dozen separate programs as described in its ten Titles.

The Philosophy of the Act is exemplified in the Findings and Declaration of Policy of Section 101, Title I, which states in part:

The Congress hereby finds and declares that the security of the Nation requires the fullest development of the mental resources and technical skills of its young men and women. . . .

We must increase our efforts to identify and educate more of the talent of our Nation. This requires programs that will give assurance that no student of ability will be denied an opportunity for higher education because of financial need; will correct as rapidly as possible the existing imbalances in our educational programs which have led to an insufficient proportion of our population educated in science, mathematics, and modern foreign languages and trained in technology.

Title I also emphatically prohibits federal control over the curriculum, program of instruction, administration, or personnel of an educational institution or school system. . .

Although it has been in force only a year, the National Defense Education Act has had enthusiastic acceptance.

Approximately 65 per cent of the nation's 2,000 institutions of higher education, representing 80 per cent of full-time college and university enrollment, are participating in the student loan program, as authorized by Title II of the Act. The federal share, in terms of funds actually appropriated and funds requested for fiscal year 1960, amounts to $61.5 million. In addition to the federal contribution, the participating institutions provide one tenth of this amount, bringing the total to $67.6 million.

The plans of fifty states and territories have been approved under Title III which authorizes the provision of funds on a fifty-fifty matching basis to strengthen instruction in science, mathematics, and modern foreign languages. Federal funds amounting to $51.1 million have been certified for this purpose.

Title IV at present provides a maximum of 1,000 graduate fellowships. All of them were approved in fiscal year 1959. An additional 1,500 such fellowships have been requested and approved for fiscal year 1960.

Plans for the creation of state programs for guidance, counseling, and testing to identify and advise superior students, as authorized by Title V, have been approved for fifty states and territories, and $8.65 million has been certified. This Title also provides for the establishment of guidance and counseling institutes. Fifty colleges and universities were given approval to establish such institutes in the summer of 1959. Funds for fiscal year 1959 made possible 4 academic-year institutes in 1959-60. Funds for fiscal year 1960 will make possible the creation of an additional 67 summer and 26 academic-year institutes.

Under the provisions of Title VI, contracts are being negotiated for the establishment of about 20 language and area centers and 12 summer language institutes and 4 academic-year institutes. Modern foreign language fellowships, also made possible by this Title, have been awarded to 171 graduate students. In addition, 20 research projects were started with fiscal year 1959 funds.

As authorized by Title VII, a total of 68 research grants and 14 contracts for research designed to develop more effective educational media and techniques have currently been approved.

Area vocational programs are being initiated, in response

to the provisions of Title VIII, in fifty states and territories for the purpose of training students in technical skills essential to the national defense effort.

Forty-nine states have had their plans accepted under the terms of Title X for the purpose of improving the statistical services of state education agencies.

Of all the aspects of the Act, only the affidavit and loyalty oath requirements have evoked adverse reaction. Included without due consideration of the reactions they might provoke, these provisions, quite properly regarded as inadmissible by the academic community, have proved to be meaningless and discriminatory.

On May 4, 1959, the author addressed a letter to the chairman of the Senate Committee on Labor and Public Welfare urging an amendment of the National Defense Education Act that would repeal those provisions requiring affidavits of loyalty and allegiance.

The following reasons were expressed:

1. The Act's provisions make clear that, without the exaction of formal oaths, persons who belong to or support organizations dedicated to the violent overthrow of the government are not entitled to receive federal funds.

2. The formalities involved in signing affidavits and taking oaths do not deter or reveal disloyal persons. Generally, these persons are not scrupulous about the falsification of legal instruments.

3. The loyalty and allegiance requirements are discriminatory in that they single out educators and students for special treatment and in no sense ensure national security.

4. The argument that disloyal persons who sign the affidavit can be prosecuted for perjury introduces unnecessary legal skirmishing. If a person receiving assistance under this Act is identified as a violator of our internal security laws, he can be and should be prosecuted under pre-existing and current laws that are amply effective in dealing with treasonable and subsersive offenders.

The variety and scope of the National Defense Education Act's provisions make them applicable to many of the most urgent educational needs of the day. Moreover, the Act's wide acceptance by parents, educators, students, and government leaders ensures its nation-wide utilization in solving problems that the states, communities, and private institutions could not attack separately and unassisted. Such adaptability and utilization strengthen the belief that this Act will have positive effects greatly surpassing its immediate defense intentions and thus enrich and reinforce the total educational process.

❡ *C. Practically every generation in the history of the United States has witnessed the rise of an agency which predominated in the loose pluralism of federal science: the Coast Survey of Alexander Bache, the Geological Survey of John Wesley Powell, Gifford Pinchot's Forest Service, and in our own time, the Atomic Energy Commission. But fleeting is fame and power, as David Lilienthal, the first chairman of the AEC, tells us in the selection below.* International Science and Technology *(June, 1963), 98-99.*]

Everyone now knows there is no magic in uranium as a source of energy. The glamour, the excitement of the boundless possibilities of power from the peaceful atom is gone. The sooner we face up to this the better, for living in a world of unreality is as bad for technology and politics as to the peaceful atom as it is in the field of nuclear weapons.

But we have failed as a nation to recognize and give effect to this realization that the "profound changes" arising out of a revolution in atomic energy supply just aren't in the cards. And yet in 1963 we still have an organization — the AEC — that in magnitude of expenditures and personnel is geared to the objective of 1946: a revolution to bring this magic into reality, to bring on a new world.

The scale of effort today, in 1963, continues unabated. The AEC is actually pressing for a new program to cost two billion dollars over a decade. Not just improvements in existing reactors, but a whole new line of technology, the so-called breeder reactor, is now being boomed, with predictions ranging from nebulous to conservative. But the goal, the expectations that justified the earlier scale of effort, and our departure from our traditional ways of furthering technology has proved long since unattainable.

I suggest the 1963 premises should be these: (1) Energy from the atom is not now needed for civilian purposes. (2) At the time and place where it is needed it will be forthcoming without governmental prodding. If there is a real need it will be met by the utility and manufacturing industries, as it has been with the automobile, the diesel engine, the telephone and so on, in response to proved economic need. (3) There is now no urgent fuels or power crisis and no prospect of one in the forseeable future; when such a shortage looms, it will be taken care of by the atom if that is then the best alternative.

In short then, we should stop trying to force-feed atomic energy. Throw away the present time table. Don't abandon hope, of course, but deal with it realistically.

◀ D. *A new, predominantly scientific agency sprang up in the wake of Sputnik and cast its shadow over the plural community of federal science. In the selection below, T. Keith Glennan, Administrator of the National Aeronautics and Space Administration, tells us something of its origins, and incidentally, some of the problems involved in being a dominant Indian in a tribe of Chiefs. U.S. Congress, House, Committee on Science and Astronautics, Hearing, "To Amend the National Aeronautics and Space Act of 1958," 86 Cong., 2 sess., (March 8-April 4, 1960), 29-32.*]

DR. GLENNAN: Then I will proceed. I welcome this opportunity to discuss the President's proposed amendments to the National Aeronautics and Space Act of 1958 which were submitted in a special message to the Congress on January 14, 1960.

In proposing these amendments for congressional enactment, the President is taking cognizance of NASA's coming of age after a very active transitional period during which our capabilities have been developed and expanded and our goals have come more sharply into focus. The amendments are a natural evolution based upon operating experience under the present law.

Principally, the amendments would accomplish the following:

(1) Make clear NASA's unequivocal responsibility for planning and carrying out the Nation's space exploration program;

(2) Eliminate presently unnecessary organizational elements;

(3) Provide adequate safeguards against unnecessary duplication of effort by NASA and the Department of Defense, particularly in the costly field of launch vehicle development; and

(4) Provide for a clearer realization, both in this country and throughout the world, that the United States has a single space exploration program administered by NASA. Such military operations in the space environment as may be necessary for our national defense devolve from the responsibilities of the Defense Department for the defense of the Nation and clearly must be managed by the Department of Defense.

The Space Act, as you know, requires that the President supervise a so-called comprehensive program. In no other aspect of Government does the Chief Executive have such an immediate degree of responsibility for an operating program.

To assist the President in these duties, the act presently provides him with an advisory body, the National Aeronautics and Space Council, of which he is Chairman. The 1958 legislation also set up a Civilian-Military Liaison Committee to provide a channel through which NASA and the Defense Department shall—in the language of the act "advise and consult" on all matters within their respective jurisdictions as they relate to aeronautics and space.

Under the original act, and under the act as the President has recommended that it be changed, only two Government agencies have management and responsibility in the area of space activities—NASA and the Department of Defense. Numerous other agencies contribute vital elements to both NASA and Defense projects. When all the nondecision making bodies with which we deal are reduced to a chart, the resultant tangle of boxes and dotted lines gives an impression of confusion and divided authority, but such is not the case. Only NASA and the Defense Department have clear management responsibilities.

I have emphasized this last point because there has been considerable misunderstanding and criticism of the Government for having "too many fingers in the space pie."

Let me here quote the President's message of January 14, [1960]. . . .

"From now on it should be made clear that NASA, like the Department of Defense in the military field, is responsible in the first instance for the formulation and execution of its own program, subject, of course, to the authority and direction of the President."

With repeal, therefore, of the specific statutory enumeration of the President's duties, he consequently requests abolition of the National Aeronautics and Space Council which had the sole duty of advising him on those duties. He also calls for abolition of the Civilian Military Liaison Committee which has, in practice, served as only one of many channels of communication between NASA and the Pentagon. In order to coordinate activities and prevent duplication of effort and expense, it is imperative that NASA-Defense liaison be conducted at many levels. The attempt to formalize this need and center the activity in one committee has proven to be an unnecessary, cumbersome, and unworkable mechanism.

The act would retain the provision that in case of serious disagreement between NASA and Defense over roles and missions, use of launch vehicles or whatever, the NASA Administrator and the Secretary of Defense would take them to the President for his final decision.

In the single most important area requiring coordination between NASA and Defense, the President requests that the act embody a procedure whereby he assigns responsibility for development of new launch vehicles—regardless of which agency has the prime requirement for their use in space missions...

By way of summary: If enacted, the proposed amendments would make absolutely clear NASA's responsibility for the Nation's space exploration program and eliminate the present specific statutory duties of the Chief Executive in this regard. The NASA would be clearly answerable to the President and the Congress, just as the Defense Department has unquestioned responsibility for defense-related space activities and also is responsible to the President and the Congress.

NASA and Defense will continue, as at present, to cooperate closely at all levels. Undoubtedly, each program will continue to produce hardware, techniques, and scientific data useful to the other.

The President's requested amendments also include such technical changes as modification of certain provisions of the act concerning invention property rights. The modification of the patent clauses in the legislation would give NASA adequate discretionary authority concerning an equitable disposition of property rights relating to inventions produced under NASA contracts. The President has included several other proposals which will place NASA on parity with the Defense Department in dealing with contractors and in other business activities.

As you consider these amendments, I would like to review briefly with you the course of events since the evening of October 4, 1957, when the news of Sputnik I burst upon the world. More than 2 years have passed since that evening but we are still conscious of the turmoil that followed in its wake.

Sputnik arrived in the middle of an annual domestic crisis — the World Series. And while some of our citizens remained momentarily more interested in the trajectory of baseball than in the satellite's orbital flight, the Soviet accomplishment hit most thinking Americans like a dash of cold water.

The Nation began a reexamination of U.S. science, defense, education, and foreign policy that is still going strong. Out of this ferment of congressional hearings and national debate came the firm resolve of both the executive and legislative branches that a civil agency should be established to conduct the Nation's space exploration program.

The President appointed Dr. James R. Killian as his Special Assistant for Science and Technology and as Chairman of his Science Advisory Committee. This distinguished group prepared the first general outlines of a national space program and listed the following four factors involved therein:

"The first of these factors is the compelling urge of man to explore and to discover, the thrust of curiosity that leads men to try to go where no one has gone before.

"Second, there is the defense objective for the development of space technology. We wish to be sure that space is not used to endanger our security. If space is used for military purposes, we must be prepared to use space to defend ourselves.

"Third, there is the factor of national prestige. To be strong and bold in space technology will enhance the prestige of the United States among the peoples of the world and create added confidence in our scientific, technological, industrial, and military strength.

"Fourth, space technology affords new opportunities for scientific observation and experiment which will add to our knowledge and understanding of the earth, the solar system, and the universe...."

In April 1958, the President sent a special message to the Congress calling for a civilian space agency. After hearings and debate, the National Aeronautics and Space Act of 1958 was enacted in July and NASA became officially operative on October 1.

The existing act states that...

"It is the policy of the United States that activities in space should be devoted to peaceful purposes for the benefit of all mankind."

It calls upon NASA...to—

"plan, direct, and conduct aeronautical and space activities— these being defined in section 103 as—

(1) research into, and the solution of, problems of flight within and outside the earth's atmosphere;

(2) the development, construction, testing and operation for research purposes of aeronautical and space vehicles; and

(3) such other activities as may be required for the exploration of space."

Of the three objectives, only the third is unique to NASA, for the National advisory Committee for Aeronautics [NACA] and the armed services were engaged in the first two activities before the creation of NASA.

The exploration of space, then, is NASA's specific mission, and it is a mission for which it is solely and exclusively responsible under the law. This is a responsibility just as unique to NASA as the military defense of the Nation is to the armed services. It is a mission of vital importance to the security interests of the United States.

To provide the newborn agency with the capability to fulfill its mission, the act gave the President authority to transfer to NASA from Defense, projects and organizations which he deemed to be important to the fulfillment of that mission.

You are all familiar with NASA's absorption of NACA and with the transfers of other important activities immediately following establishment of NASA. With the acquisition of the Development Operations Division of the Army Ballistic Missile Agency, NASA will have developed an all-around space capability.

The consolidation of the U.S. space exploration program under NASA has greatly clarified the civilian and defense roles in space. Projects and personnel have been dropping into place like the pieces in a puzzle.

The law, as originally enacted, permitted and encouraged these actions which have had the support of the Congress. The administrative machinery to accomplish this purpose has served well the intention of its authors. Looking ahead to the heavy and continuing responsibilities which face the Nation in this highly competitive field, the President is proposing a straightforward legislative change that gives to NASA the task of meeting these responsibilities.

¶ *E. With the establishment of NASA the United States was institutionally committed to manned space flight. Shortly, we were vying with the Russians in the launching of satellites, and by the time John Kennedy entered the White House, were shooting for the moon. As the new institution grew, changes were inevitably wrought in the scientific community at large, and changes seldom occur without serious dislocation of parties in whose interest it was to keep things as they were. Many scientists agreed with Alvin Weinberg, Director of the Oak Ridge National Laboratory, who felt that "most Americans would prefer to belong to the society which first gave the world a cure for cancer than to the society which put the first astronaut on Mars." James Webb, Glennan's successor, preferred to keep the work of his organization firmly plugged into cold war circuits, and "deny the Russians further unchallenged propaganda victories or a position from which to undermine our national security." It was difficult to take either position, so obviously formulated for propaganda purposes, seriously. Beneath the growing partisanship lay the nub of the conflict: a priority decision had been made, and not only money, but prestige and power were at stake. But the scientists who suggested that a cure for cancer and reaching Mars were mutually exclusive had not yet acquired a formula for effective opposition. Certain priority decisions had been made within the government, but the popular enthusiasm for the moon race amply demonstrated that the American people themselves had made a priority decision. When that happened, leadership inevitably shifted within the scientific community. James Reston, "Kennedy and the Scientists: The Quiet War," The New York Times, May 5, 1963.]*

In some ways the most interesting conflict in Washington today is not the political war between the parties or even the cold war between the nations, but the Quiet War between the policy-makers and their expert advisers.

This takes many forms. President Kennedy versus the scientists over the allocation of the nation's money and brains; McNamara versus the Joint Chiefs of Staff over the TFX fighter plane; the Joint Chiefs versus the Pentagon civilian intellectuals over whose advice is to be taken on military strategy; the Commerce and other civilian home-front departments versus the Pentagon, the Space Agency, and the Atomic Energy Commission over research and development funds for military or civilian purposes.

"Let us explore the stars, conquer the deserts, eradicate disease, tap the ocean depths," said the President in his Inaugural. It was a noble passage, but the problem is one of priorities: which comes first—the moon or the slums, the unexplored or the unemployed, security or solvency?

The range of choice is endless and conflict over priorities is inevitable and maybe even healthy, but it is almost impossible here to find any logical pattern to the Administration's methods of deciding how science can serve the nation best.

Each department fights for the largest possible share of money and scientific and engineering brains. Each can make a good case for a larger share than it has.

For example, James E. Webb, administrator of the National Aeronautics and Space Administration, had some of his critics in for dinner this week to explain that his agency could not only justify the $5,700,000,000 budget this year but much more. He made a good case, too, but when the main question came up about whether the agency's man-on-the-moon project was as important as other worthy scientific projects here on earth, even his own space scientists disagreed.

Theoretically, the President's Assistant for Science and Technology, the Bureau of the Budget, the President's Science Advisory Committee, and the National Science Foundation, are all competent to survey the larger question of how science is to serve the nation, to answer the basic question of priorities for defense, space, foreign aid and the home front.

But if the President has put this question of priorities to those institutions, there is no public evidence of it. On the contrary, there is a great deal of evidence that men like Jerome B. Wiesner, the President's Assistant for Science and Technology; Dr. Alan T. Waterman, director of the National Science Foundation, and leading members of the Science Advisory Committees are dissatisfied with the present allocation of funds and talent.

Sir Charles Snow, the Cambridge University physicist, has pointed up the importance of this question by noting that most of the life-and-death decisions of modern political life "have to be made by a handful of men, in secret, and at least in legal form, by men who cannot have a firsthand knowledge of what those choices depend upon or what the results may be."

This was true of the decision to make and use the fission bomb, to make the fusion bomb and to produce intercontinental missiles. But it is also true of an increasing number of other scientific questions, beginning with the first: how are the immense forces of sciences to be used?

Since this question of priorities has not been resolved by the President, it is not surprising that there is constant conflict between the policy-makers and the experts.

This is not to suggest that the scientists and engineers should take over the policy decisions of how their skills are to be applied. These decisions have to remain with the elected officials of the Government, even if, as Snow says, they lack firsthand knowledge of "what these choices depend upon or what their results may be."

But this is all the more reason for confidence that the President has at least an orderly method of deciding the question of scientific priorities, and there is no such confidence in Washington today. The Quiet War merely goes on and it is getting noisier every year.

❧ *F. The predominant agency has always provided cohesion and focus for a pluralistic system. But in American history a countervailing theme to the demands of the pluralism has always been found in the demands of the center. This contrast has its counterpart in the history of American science in the quest for a central scientific organization which would provide coherence for all science, in and out of the government. The national university envisaged by Thomas Jefferson, the National Academy of Science, the National Research Council, the Office of Scientific Research and Development, these were the great landmarks of that quest. Even as the NASA arose as the predominant agency of the post-Sputnik era, the ancient dream of a central scientific organization hovered about in the form of plans for a cabinet level Department of Science and Technology. In the selection below, a University of California historian, A. Hunter Dupree, relates the origin of the dream to a subcommittee chaired by Senator Hubert Humphrey of Minnesota, the author and sponsor of a*

*bill designed to create a cabinet level post for science. U.S.
Congress, Senate, Subcommittee on Reorganization and International Organizations of the Committee on Government
Operations, "Create a Department of Science and Technology," 86 Cong., 1 sess., (April 16, 17, 1959), 84-88.]*

(1) The very names of Department of Science and Technology, and Secretary of Science and Technology suggest a
central organization speaking for and acting on science as a
whole, not simply on the scientific agencies within the Government and certainly not for a small fraction of them.

(2) The recognition of a need for some sort of central
scientific organization has occurred in every generation of our
history. Thoughtful men have felt that science, even while
organizing everything else, cannot organize itself effectively.

(3) The recurrent attempts to create a central scientific
organization have by their very failures gradually delineated
two major characteristics which such an organization must
have: (a) an ability to represent science as a whole and to have
sufficient grasp of the complex interrelations of the various
parts of the research enterprise to make intelligent choices
among the issues raised by science; and (b) a clear relation to
the chain of responsibility within the Government so that the
organization can make policy and give it the same force as
other political decisions.

(4) As a policy area in the Government, science must be
compared not with agriculture or commerce but with economics or security. It is a pervasive thing, which had, even by the
1880's penetrated so many different areas of Government
activity that a joint congressional committee found it impossible to define a separate area for a Department of Science.

(5) Science is now administered by a complex array of
agencies — in the Government, in the universities, in industry,
and in the private foundations. Since World War II these
agencies have been welded into a single interdependent unit
by a network of grants and contracts. In many of the individual
units of this system the administration is given direction by
the fact that science is in close conjunction to the problems to
be solved. Agriculture research has been effective historically
because it has brought to bear science of every sort on its
particular problems. Thus the problem implied by a bill to
create a central scientific organization has to do not with the

administration of individual agencies but with the setting of a general policy for the whole unit.

(6) It is increasingly difficult to leave a general science policy to the chance adjustment of the many administrative units involved. Science is a national resource, and a scarce one. It consists of men and equipment as well as money. Choices as to the use of scarce resources are the policy decisions which most urgently need to be made, and made by those who owe responsibility to none of the individual competing units. At the same time the decisions are rightly and essentially political and should be made by officials responsible under the Constitution to the people as a whole.

In my opinion the Department of Science and Technology proposed in S. 676 would not adequately fulfill the need of the Government and the Nation for a central scientific organization.

(1) The Secretary of Science and Technology would not speak for science as a whole, but only for a few areas—atomic energy, space, basic science as represented by the National Science Foundation, standards [i.e., the Bureau of Standards], and part of the present Smithsonian functions. He would indeed be competing for appropriations and the use of scarce research manpower with power agencies which would merit the name of science as richly as he. He would have direct administrative responsibility for his own area and hence would be bound by his responsibility to speak in the Cabinet and before the country for his own particular areas primarily.

(2) The question must arise as to whether the agencies listed in the bill represent the ultimate boundaries of the department or whether this group is only a core to which other agencies will be transferred later. It is always possible to pick out a few scientific agencies which have either a tradition of independence or a tradition of instability in their administrative arrangements. But beyond this rather short list one finds agencies equally scientific in their orientation which are deeply enmeshed in the solution of problems in the operating units of the Government. Not only are their places well established by the history of the agency, but their scientific effectiveness depends on their close conjunction with the problems on which they work. No one seems hardy enough to suggest that military research be removed entirely from proximity to the using arms, and few would suggest the transfer of

the Agricultural Research Service or the National Institutes of Health. Yet the very existence of the possibility that such transfers might come in the future would throw scientific agencies into conflict. The effort in the 1930's to organize a comprehensive Department of Conservation raised just such a specter for the Forest Service in the Department of Agriculture and led to a clash.

(3) Major reorganizations of the scientific establishment do become advisable from time to time, and a central scientific organization should have as a major responsibility the identification of such areas. But if the Department of Science and Technology were an active competitor for scarce resources it would not perform any coordinating function among the competing units.

(4) The bill itself in section 11(a)(5) reveals the difficulty of making distinctions as to what is properly in the realm of science and what is not. It can be argued that the research programs in the National Museum are just as properly called science as is astrophysics, and that a museum is a tool of research only incidentally different from a telescope. But the crucial thing in the section is that the bill itself shows the need of a decision made on a level above what are essentially two competing units — the old Smithsonian Institution and the new Department of Science and Technology. Significantly, the official chosen by the bill to make this highly technical decision is the Director of the Bureau of the Budget. Not only is he in the Office of the President, but he is in possession of the one tool for the overall allocation of scarce scientific resources which now exists, the budget.

(5) In the absence of any provision in the bill for the continuing development of an overall science policy, those organs already created in the Office of the President would still be required to attempt to grapple with the problems of overall policy.

(6) The proposed Department of Science would include agencies of very different aims. The Atomic Energy Commission and the National Aeronautics and Space Administration have large research programs at several different levels on the scale which runs from basic to applied science. The thing which gives them unity is their concern with a particular set of research problems. The National Science Foundation, on the other hand, is primarily concerned with the support of basic

research. Its task is made necessary by the fact that the urgency of applied research in the military and in the Atomic Energy Commission has claimed a very large share of the scarce scientific resources of the country since World War II. Hence for the Secretary of Science to speak for both types of agency would precipitate serious questions of policy within the Department itself. It also would make the adjustments between the programs of the Foundation and those scientific agencies not included in the Department more difficult.

Unlike some critics of the creation of a department, I feel that the concern implied in the Congress' interest in the problem of overall science policy is justified. The shape of a science policy cannot safely be left to the blind clash of competing agencies both in and out of the Government. My preference for the Office of the President stems not from any overwhelming belief in the benevolence of this particular form of organization. Rather it comes from the fact that science pervades the whole of the governmental structure. Hence coordination can be achieved only at the highest level of authority. The implementation of such a coordination must emanate not from some irresponsible science czar but from officials with constitutional responsibilities to the people of the United States. The President is the only officer in the administrative branch of the Government with the breadth of authority to cope with the problem. I feel that this is also true in such broad fields as shaping a continuing economic policy to fight a depression. And the presence in the Government structure of the Department of Defense has in no way relieved the necessity for a National Security Council.

Since last summer, when I submitted a statement to this committee, much has been done to fill the need of an overall science policy. The creation of the Federal Council for Science and Technology looks in such a direction. There is a history of difficulty in the principle of agency representation as the base for a council, witness the Division of Government Relations in the National Research Council after the First World War. But the implied permanence of the post of Special Assistant to the President for Science and the continued presence of the Science Advisory Committee offer at least a hope that these three elements will together fuse into something like the central scientific organization which I consider desirable...

Of all the missteps that could be taken in forming a central scientific organization, either in the Office of the President or in a new executive department, the one which would most surely render its comprehensive view of the whole policy field impossible would be to give it direct administrative responsibility for some particular scientific activity. I am thinking here not only of my objections to S. 676, but also of proposals to use the framework of a Department of Science to exploit some area of research not now adequately provided for in the Federal structure. The changing picture of research does indeed require the periodic development of new clusters of agencies around new leading ideas. But in no case is such a necessary readjustment properly deserving of the name of science as a whole. A Department of Science and Technology centered around meteorology or geophysics would not provide central scientific organization for more than a very small sector of the Government's scientific front.

Finally, the role of the Congress in making science policy deserves consideration. In the early part of the 19th century Congress was a distinct deterrent to the development of the Federal research establishment. Late in that century indirect methods of legislating scientific agencies into existence made possible the creation of the basic agencies which today still carry an important part of the Federal responsibility for science. In the 20th century the support which the Congress has given science and the understanding with which it has designed legislation in this field has become increasingly evident. Yet the Congress has been hampered in developing an overall policy by the fact that it has normally considered the needs of science in connection with the particular areas of policy in which the research is serving. Since science must continue to intertwine itself with the problems it seeks to enlighten, this pattern must inevitably continue. But in the area of the dynamics of research as a whole, the Congress as well as the executive must attempt to achieve an overall view. For this reason I feel that standing committees on science and technology would aid immensely in adjusting the total pattern of legislation which affects science. It is as important here as in the executive that the committees be free of immediate concern with particular programs, such as astronautics.

In conclusion, I wish to emphasize the distinction between the administration of science and the setting of overall policy for science...

◀ G. *With NASA the predominant agency, with the proposal for a department of science sidetracked in a bill to create a commission to study the need for such a department, a bill which rested demurely but securely in the arms of the House Committee on Science and Astronautics four years after it was first proposed, there still remained another sensitive area to watch for those interested in the quest for a central scientific organization. The National Science Foundation had abdicated all authority delegated to it by law to coordinate federal science, but, as Dupree noted, within the office of the President himself a new "agency" was developing which conceivably had behind it all the tremendous prestige of the world's most powerful elective office. Message from the President of the United States Transmitting Reorganization Plan No. 2 ... in U.S. Congress, House, Subcommittee of the Committee on Government Operations, Hearing, "Reorganization Plan No. 2 of 1962," 87 Cong., 2 sess., (April 17, 1962), 2-3.*]

Part I of the reorganization plan establishes the Office of Science and Technology as a new unit within the Executive Office of the President; places at the head thereof a Director appointed by the President by and with the advice and consent of the Senate and makes provision for a Deputy Director similarly appointed; and transfers to the Director certain functions of the National Science Foundation under sections 3(a)(1) and 3(a)(6) of the National Science Foundation Act of 1950.

The new arrangements incorporated in part I of the reorganization plan will constitute an important development in executive branch organization for science and technology. Under those arrangements the President will have permanent staff resources capable of advising and assisting him on matters of national policy affected by or pertaining to science and technology. Considering the rapid growth and far-reaching scope of Federal activities in science and technology, it is imperative that the President have adequate staff support in developing policies and evaluating programs in order to assure that science and technology are used most effectively in the interests of national security and general welfare.

To this end it is contemplated that the Director will assist the President in discharging the responsibility of the President for the proper coordination of Federal science and technology functions. More particularly, it is expected that he will advise and assist the President as the President may request with respect to —

(1) Major policies, plans, and programs of science and technology of the various agencies of the Federal Government, giving appropriate emphasis to the relationship of science and technology to national security and foreign policy, and measures for furthering science and technology in the Nation.

(2) Assessment of selected scientific and technical developments and programs in relation to their impact on national policies.

(3) Review, integration, and coordination of major Federal activities in science and technology, giving due consideration to the effects of such activities on non-Federal resources and institutions.

(4) Assuring that good and close relations exist with the Nation's scientific and engineering communities so as to further in every appropriate way their participation in strengthening science and technology in the United States and the free world.

(5) Such other matters consonant with law as may be assigned by the President to the Office.

The ever-growing significance and complexity of Federal programs in science and technology have in recent years necessitated the taking of several steps for improving the organizational arrangements of the executive branch in relation to science and technology:

(1) The National Science Foundation was established in 1950. The Foundation was created to meet a widely recognized need for an organization to develop and encourage a national policy for the promotion of basic research and education in the sciences, to support basic research, to evaluate research programs undertaken by Federal agencies, and to perform related functions.

(2) The Office of the Special Assistant to the President for Science and Technology was established in 1957. The Special Assistant serves as Chairman of both the President's Science Advisory Committee and the Federal Council for Science and Technology, mentioned below.

(3) At the same time, the Science Advisory Committee,

composed of eminent non-Government scientists and engineers, and located within the Office of Defense Mobilization, was reconstituted in the White House Office as the President's Science Advisory Committee.

(4) The Federal Council for Science and Technology, composed of policy officials of the principal agencies engaged in scientific and technical activities, was established in 1959.

The National Science Foundation has proved to be an effective instrument for administering sizable programs in support of basic research and education in the sciences and has set an example for other agencies through the administration of its own programs. However, the Foundation, being at the same organizational level as other agencies, cannot satisfactorily coordinate Federal science policies or evaluate programs of other agencies. Science policies, transcending agency lines, need to be coordinated and shaped at the level of the Executive Office of the President drawing upon many resources both within and outside of Government. Similarly, staff efforts at that higher level are required for the evaluation of Government programs in science and technology.

Thus, the further steps contained in part I of the reorganization plan are now needed in order to meet most effectively new and expanding requirements brought about by the rapid and far-reaching growth of the Government's research and development programs. These requirements call for the further strengthening of science organization at the Presidential level and for the adjustment of the Foundation's role to reflect changed conditions. The Foundation will continue to originate policy proposals and recommendations concerning the support of basic research and education in the sciences, and the new Office will look to the Foundation to provide studies and information on which sound national policies in science and technology can be based.

Part I of the reorganization plan will permit some strengthening of the staff and consultant resources now available to the President in respect of scientific and technical factors affecting executive branch policies and will also facilitate communication with the Congress.

Part II of the reorganization plan provides for certain reorganizations within the National Science Foundation which will strengthen the capability of the Director of the

Foundation to exert leadership and otherwise further the effectiveness of administration of the Foundation. Specifically:

(1) There is established a new office of Director of the National Science Foundation and that Director, ex officio, is made a member of the National Science Board on a basis coordinate with that of other Board members.

(2) There is substituted for the now existing Executive Committee of the National Science Board a new Executive Committee composed of the Director of the National Science Foundation, ex officio, as a voting member and Chairman of the Committee, and of four other members elected by the National Science Board from among its appointive members.

(3) Committees advisory to each of the divisions of the Foundation will make their recommendations to the Director only rather than to both the Director and the National Science Board. . . .

II. Control

⁋ A. In April 1962 the Bureau of the Budget compiled a report for the President, the full ramifications of which are yet to be felt. A portion of the letter forwarding the Bell report, as it was called, is reproduced below. The letter was signed by Robert McNamara, Secretary of Defense, James E. Webb, Administrator of NASA, John W. Macy, Jr., Chairman of the Civil Service Commission, the Chairman of the Atomic Energy Commission, Glenn T. Seaborg, Alan T. Waterman, Director of the NSF, Jerome B. Wiesner, the Special Assistant to the President for Science and Technology, and David E. Bell, Director of the Bureau of the Budget. Only the President himself was influential enough to lead the captains of so many diverse constituencies to present a facade of evident unanimity to a skeptical world. U.S. Bureau of the Budget, Report to the President on Government Contracting for Research and Development, (30 April 1962).]

...we have reviewed the experience of the Government in using contracts with private institutions and enterprises to obtain research and development work needed for public purposes...

1. Federally-financed research and development work has been increasing at a phenomenal rate—from 100 million dollars per year in the late 1930's to over 10 billion dollars per year at present, with the bulk of the increase coming since 1950. Over 80 percent of such work is conducted today through non-Federal institutions rather than through direct Federal operations. The growth and size of this work, and the heavy reliance on non-Federal organizations to carry it out, have had a striking impact on the Nation's universities and its industries, and have given rise to the establishment of new kinds of professional and technical organizations. At present the system for conducting Federal research and development work can best be described as a highly complex partnership

among various kinds of public and private agencies, related in large part by contractual arrangements.

While many improvements are needed in the conduct of research and development work, and in the contracting systems used, it is our fundamental conclusion that it is in the national interest for the Government to continue to rely heavily on contracts with non-Federal institutions to accomplish scientific and technical work needed for public purposes. A partnership among public and private agencies is the best way in our society to enlist the Nation's resources and achieve the most rapid progress.

2. The basic purposes to be served by Federal research and development programs are public purposes, considered by the President and the Congress to be of sufficient national importance to warrant the expenditure of public funds. The management and control of such programs must be firmly in the hands of full-time Government officials clearly responsible to the President and the Congress. With programs of the size and complexity now common, this requires that the Government have on its staff exceptionally strong and able executives, scientists, and engineers, fully qualified to weigh the views and advice of technical specialists, to make policy decisions concerning the types of work to be undertaken, when, by whom, and at what cost, to supervise the execution of work undertaken, and to evaluate the results.

At the present time we consider that one of the most serious obstacles to the recruitment and retention of first-class scientists, administrators, and engineers in the Government service is the serious disparity between governmental and private compensation for comparable work. We cannot stress too strongly the importance of rectifying this situation, through Congressional enactment of civilian pay reform legislation as you have recommended.

3. Given proper arrangements to maintain management control in the hands of Government officials, federally-financed research and development work can be accomplished through several different means: direct governmental operations of laboratories and other installations; operation of Government-owned facilities by contractors; grants and contracts with universities; contracts with not-for-profit corporations or with profit corporations. Choices among these means should be made on the basis of relative efficiency and

effectiveness in accomplishing the desired work, with due regard to the need to maintain and enlarge the long-term strength of the Nation's scientific resources, both public and private.

In addition, the rapid expansion of the use of Government contracts, in a field where twenty-five years ago they were relatively rare, has brought to the fore a number of different types of possible conflicts of interests, and these should be avoided in assigning research and development work. Clear-cut standards exist with respect to some of these potential conflict-of-interest situations—as is the case with respect to persons in private life acting as advisers and consultants to Government . . . Some other standards are now widely accepted—for example, the undesirability of permitting a firm which holds a contract for technical advisory services to seek a contract to develop or to supply any major item with respect to which the firm has advised the Government. Still other standards are needed, and we recommend that you request the head of each department and agency which does a significant amount of contracting for research and development to develop, in consultation with the Attorney General, clear-cut codes of conduct, to provide standards and criteria to guide the public officials and private persons and organizations engaged in research and development activities. . . .

4. We have carefully considered the question whether standards should be applied to salaries and related benefits paid by research and development contractors doing work for the Government. We believe it is desirable to do so in those cases in which the system of letting contracts does not result in cost control through competition. We believe the basic standard to be applied should be essentially the same as the standard you recently recommended to the Congress with respect to Federal employees—namely, comparability with salaries and related benefits paid to persons doing similar work in the private economy. Insofar as a comparability standard cannot be applied—as would be the case with respect to the very top jobs in an organization, for example—we would make it the personal responsibility of the head of the contracting agency to make sure that reasonable limits are applied.

5. Finally, we consider that in recent years there has been a serious trend toward eroding the competence of the Govern-

ment's research and development establishments—in part owing to the keen competition for scarce talent which has come from Government contractors. We believe it to be highly important to improve this situation—not by setting artificial or arbitrary limits on Government contractors but by sharply improving the working environment within the Government in order to attract and hold first-class scientists and technicians. . . .

◀ B. *The Department of Agriculture with lines out to land-grant colleges, the state experiment stations, and the extension service, is a vast research structure built around the needs of the farmer. Nothing comparable exists for industry, but since the nineteen-twenties when Herbert Hoover was Commerce Secretary the thought has been there, sometimes emerging in Congress as a distinct anti-big-business bias. There were overtones of this bias in the late Senator Harley Kilgore, with whom the reader is already familiar. Something of the same spirit has been afoot in the Department of Commerce itself under Luther Hodges of North Carolina. In the selection that follows, note the direct comparison to Agriculture, and the emphasis on providing research facilities for companies presently unable to support research alone. Many of the larger concerns were less than warm to the latter proposal. Few Washington observers were surprised when the House slashed the department's Civilian Industrial Technology Program (CIT) from a requested $7.4 million to a totally inadequate $1 million. Although one might safely predict that the spirit behind the program will live to fight again, future warriors could profit from a close study of the vagaries of CIT. As a reporter of the Washington scene said of J. Herbert Holloman, the Assistant Secretary of Commerce and brains behind the Hodges program, "What gaineth a man if he speaketh the truth and loseth his program?" Luther H. Hodges, "Growth through Technology," Address Prepared for Delivery to Association Public Affairs Conference, Chamber of Commerce of the United States, (Department of Commerce Press Release, January 23, 1963).*]

I am happy to have this chance to talk to you about a matter that bears importantly on business progress and prosperity: what we are putting into science and technology today and what we are getting out of it for the consumer.

With all that has happened since World War II, most Americans, I daresay, are aware of how much our scientific and engineering capability has to do with our world position, our military effectiveness, and, certainly, our hopes for leading man's conquest of space.

I think, too, there is general recognition of how much research and development means to our economy — invention, new techniques of production, along with improved skills, are the lever of rising living standards and economic growth.

We now know, for instance, that less than half the rise in this country's output since 1900 can be accounted for by increased amounts of labor and capital. The rest, it appears, has come largely from improved skills and education of the labor force and from advances in management and technology.

Because we have had a great surge of research and development activity in the past decade, we have also seen accepted a third "truth," one that, unfortunately, is as faulted as it is well-rounded. This is the assumption that all the money we're spending for research and development will not only give us military security and space supremacy, but will automatically provide improvements in productivity and a cornucopia of new products and processes to invigorate and expand the economy.

As anyone can see, research and development has become big business. The total of a century and a half of R & D spending — that is $18 billion — has been matched in just five years, from 1950 to 1955. And it was almost equalled in one year, fiscal 1962, when we spent an estimated $15 billion, or about 3 percent of our gross national product, on research and development.

Today about three-fourths of all research and development in the United States is being done by corporations. If government now finances some 60 percent of this work — versus 40 percent in 1953 — it is nonetheless true that business has doubled its aggregate outlays for R and D in the last eight years and has largely validated the prophecy of "a new industry of discovery."

The trouble is that relatively few people have bothered to see exactly what sort of discovery industry this is.

By wrongly assuming in the first place that research and development for any purpose — space, military, or whatever — automatically fosters economic growth, they have completely missed the point that this is a highly concentrated industry, restricted by purpose, by geography, by company. Of the total effort, overwhelmingly oriented to defense, relatively little is directed to the creation of new consumer products, or to improved machines to make the products, or to improved processes to use in the machines. In short, the national R and D effort is not the incubator of demand and productivity increases that people think it is, or that the country needs for a growing, healthy economy.

Actually, only about a quarter of our huge R and D expenditures — or an estimated $4 billion — is being spent by industry for civilian purposes. And only about $1.5 billion of this is aimed at work that is likely to increase productivity.

In many companies and industries that are important contributors to gross national product — textiles and construction, for example — there is relatively little research and development. Nor is there much being done on the needs and conditions of our urbanized society. Transportation, air pollution, water resources — all require research and interested technical people, but they are attracting relatively little of either.

What makes this situation doubly disturbing is that our competitors in the world are not caught in this net.

Other industrialized nations, free from a burden of large military and space commitments, are able to devote almost their entire scientific and technical effort to developing the civilian economy and their social welfare. West Germany, for instance, spends a far larger portion of its total resources on civilian needs and product development than we do. The speed with which other nations adapt scientific advance to practical use often exceeds ours, which explains, in part, why they are able to compete against us today in both price and quality.

Given the fact that good ideas won't keep — that all nations today share each other's discoveries and that it's mainly a matter of which one applies them first — it seems to me that if we don't want to spend the next decade just talking about competition and inadequate economic growth, we are going to have to do something to strengthen civilian technology and correct the imbalance in our scientific and engineering effort.

Now what are we up against in doing this?

The crux of the matter is people — technically educated people. Even if we were prepared to double our outlays for civilian research and development next year, we could not double our effort. There just would not be enough technical people available to do the job. And, unfortunately, we can't increase the supply of brains on an assembly-line basis.

Consider what's been happening to technical manpower in the past few years:

Since 1954, the number of scientists and engineers doing research and development in industry has risen by 160,000. But all but 30,000 of these have been absorbed by projects for government. The demands for personnel doing R and D for government purposes jumped more than 300 percent, ten times the increase for industry-oriented R and D.

In 1963, the supply of scientists and engineers for R and D is expected to enlarge by about 30,000. But the increase in space R and D alone this year will require almost the entire new supply.

With engineering enrollments dropping — and engineers, remember, are the people we count on to apply technology — the manpower problem in civilian research and development is, obviously, beyond short-run solution. This fact makes it all the more urgent, that we take steps now to conserve and husband our scientific resources, while at the same time working toward improving the supply of personnel for improving industrial technology in the future.

What steps, specifically?

At the direction of the President, the Department of Commerce has initiated a Civilian Industrial Technology Program to be guided by the new Assistant Secretary of Commerce for Science and Technology. Initially, it will rely on Federal funds. But its continuation and expansion, as well as its areas of concentration, will depend directly on the extent to which Federal funds are matched by state and local governments, and by industry associations.

Let me emphasize that this program will be to stimulate and invigorate, not to control industrial or university work.

We have asked the Congress to provide funds for:

1) Attracting personnel at universities to work in industrial research and development. Through the award of research contracts, we hope to provide incentives and training for research workers and educators in specific industrial fields

and, at the same time, develop new knowledge on which to base industrial innovations.

2) Stimulating research in industry institutions. The idea here is to generate technical work, necessary to progress advance, but not normally undertaken through simple profit incentives. We want also to provide additional research services and facilities for those firms that lack a broad enough line of products and services to support an efficient R and D program. Federal funds through contract awards, will be used primarily to stimulate industry and local initiative. And the selection of particular industries for contracts will be guided by the advice of industrial leaders, educators, and others.

3) Developing an industry-university extension service. This service, I think, can be extremely important in increasing the rate and extent of diffusion of technology throughout industry.

Just 100 years ago, we took a giant step in this country by establishing land-grant colleges to provide broad education . . . and research activities where, under local control, agricultural technology was developed and made available to the American farmer. The resources thus open to agriculture have been immeasurable and have contributed mightily to the rise of U.S. farm productivity.

Through an industry extension service, we hope to provide similar root-feeders for civilian technology.

Working with the business community, the universities, and local governments, we hope to define technical problems affecting local industries and seek solutions for them. In some cases extension research teams may initiate the studies. Or industrial groups, or government, may bring problems, bearing on an industry or the local economy, to the centers.

Here, as elsewhere, the key element will be the encouragement of local, grass-roots initiative and specialized attention to the problem of developing technology to fit specific local needs.

Fourth, and finally, we have asked for funds to support technical information services that meet industry's specific needs for knowledge about technological activities and developments. These information services would collect, abstract, review, and disseminate pertinent information from government, universities and foreign laboratories, in forms that industry can use. The information would also enable workers at universities and in industry to remain up-to-date on the state-of-the-art of their respective fields. In addition, these services would alert technical people to existing developments and thereby reduce duplication of effort.

The initial effort of the Civilian Industrial Technology Program will be applied to industries that are major contributors to our gross national product and our export trade, and that also currently have limited or dispersed technological resources. Among them, we envisage, will be textiles, construction, machine tools, and metal fabrication, lumber, foundries, and castings.

But even with a more far-reaching program, which may evolve, our main hope for improving civilian technology is business itself. In large matters, as in small, there is much that government can do to help scale down the barriers that stand between us and a higher rate of technical development. But unless industry itself recognizes the basic problem—that we must find ways to make engineering education possible for everyone capable of it and desiring it, and that we must put more of science to practical use—we shall not achieve the productivity rises or the new products that can lead us to faster growth.

Let me make it perfectly clear, too, that how much we increase productivity will have great bearing on our effort to expand American exports and to ease our still-critical balance of payments problem.

If American goods are to remain competitive in world markets, we have no choice but to accelerate the productivity rise. Nor is this simply a matter of productivity—and costs—in export commodities and services. It goes, rather, to the whole of the domestic cost structure, and therefore, to productivity in fields such as energy, construction, and transport, all of which affect substantially the cost of the goods we sell abroad.

World War II and our postwar commitments taught us that we must be economically strong to repel threats to freedom and help strengthen the other democracies of the world. Our ability to defend ourselves, to assist underdeveloped areas, to lead the way in space, depends on science and technology.

If public and private policymakers can bear down on the problems of investment in plant and equipment and in education; if we can accelerate the rate of technological progress in the nonspace, nonmilitary parts of this economy; if we can raise disposable incomes of consumers; we will be able to achieve our target of an economy of maximum employment, maximum production and maximum purchasing power. It's a big order, but this is not the first time that this country has faced, and met, a challenge of this magnitude.

⟨ *C. The Executive Office of the President prepared to pick up the reins of control for a sprawling scientific establishment which no other agency could safely grasp. The leaders of a department which had declined in prestige sought and (at least temporarily) failed to recoup their fortunes by building a research establishment for their own constituency. In the search for control marking recent years, still a third type of activity has prevailed. The Research and Development program of the Department of Defense, referred to affectionately as "R and D", comprehending all of the estates of science — government, industry, the universities, and foundations — has long been recognized as a jungle of duplication and cut-throat competition among the various services. Secretary of Defense Robert S. McNamara tells in the selection below of his attempts to tame this jungle. There are wags in the city of Washington who refer to McNamara as "the first Secretary of Defense." Robert S. McNamara, Statement before the Subcommittee on Defense Procurement of the Joint Economic Committee, March 28, 1963 (Department of Defense Press Release).*]

As the members of this Committee well know, it is extremely difficult to change the traditional way of doing things in the Defense establishment. Many of the actions we have taken during the last two years to improve the management of our procurement and logistics operations were recommended by this and other committees of the Congress and by various non-governmental committees and commissions, ten and even fifteen years ago. For example, the reorganization of the Army technical services, which we put into effect last year, had been recommended to the President by Secretary of Defense Lovett in 1952 with the comment that "A reorganization of the technical services would be no more painful than backing into a buzz saw, but I believe that it is long overdue.". . .

The term "logistics", in its broadest application, encompasses the entire spectrum of activity beginning with research and development and extending through procurement, production, construction of facilities . . . etc. and ending with the disposal of surplus materiel and facilities. In this sense, our logistics operations account for about three-quarters of the total Defense budget. . . .

Truly important savings in defense expenditures can be achieved only by attacking this entire spectrum of logistics activities, and that is precisely what we are trying to do. Decisions in the development phase of a weapons system will affect not only the cost of development but also the cost of production and operation of the system throughout its life. As this Subcommittee noted in one of its recent reports, "It is apparent that two identical items can be procured, stored, inventoried, issued and maintained in a common way much more economically and efficiently than can two different items." Yet, each new weapon or piece of equipment that enters the inventory brings with it thousands of new and different items of spares and supporting equipment. That is why any serious attempt to reduce the number of different items in our logistics system and thereby reduce costs, must begin in the research and development phase.

The research and development phase itself can be broken down into a number of significant sequential steps:

1. Research (basic and applied)—the effort directed toward the expansion of knowledge in such fields as the physical and environmental sciences, i.e., mathematics, physics, psychology, biology and the medical sciences.

2. Exploratory Developments—work directed toward the solution of specific military problems, but stopping short of the actual development of experimental hardware for technical or operational testing.

3. Advanced Developments—projects which have advanced to a point where the development of experimental hardware for technical or operational testing is required, prior to the determination of whether the item should be designed or engineered for eventual Service use.

4. Engineering Developments—developments which are being engineered for Service use, but which have not as yet been approved for production and deployment.

5. Operational Systems Development—continued development, test, evaluation, and design improvement of projects

which have already entered the production-deployment stage.

It is from the first three categories — Research, Exploratory and Advanced Developments — that we acquire the "technical building blocks", i.e., the new technologies and critical components, that we need for major systems development. We cannot do a proper job of engineering development, least of all operational systems development, unless these building blocks are available. Lack of attention to this principle in the past has been one of the major causes of waste and inefficiency in the research and development program. All too often large-scale weapon system developments, and even production programs, have been undertaken before we had clearly defined what was wanted and before we had clearly determined that there existed a suitable technological base on which to draw in developing a system. And, all too often insufficient attention has been paid to how a proposed weapon system would be used; what it would cost; and, finally, whether the contribution the weapon could make to our military capability would be worth the cost. . .

Perhaps the most important single action we have taken thus far to reduce the number of different weapon systems in our inventory is the TFX, which has been so prominent in the news of late. This aircraft development is designed to provide a replacement for the F-4. Instead of developing and producing two separate aircraft, one for the Navy and another for the Air Force, as was done in the case of the F-105 and the F4H, we decided to develop and produce one aircraft which would meet the requirements of both Services. Admittedly, this is not a simple undertaking. The development of a major weapon system to meet the requirements of more than one Service is something of a precedent in the Department of Defense. It took more than a year and a half and tens of thousands of man-hours of intensive study by both the Defense Department and industry to perfect this plan.

Yet it should be clear to all who are interested in economy and efficiency in the Defense establishment that we can no longer afford to undertake major development projects to meet unilateral Service requirements where a single project can meet the requirements of more than one Service. The additional costs involved are much too great. From here on out, we must seek to develop weapon systems to perform a military task, and if it so happens that more than one Service has the same task then they will be required, as a general rule, to use the same weapon system wherever this can be accomplished without compromising essential military requirements. Where operational conditions vary, as for example, in attack carrier operations, the minimum number of changes in the common system will be made to accomodate these differences.

This is the principle involved and I think everyone will agree it is an entirely sound one. While one might argue as to precisely how much one system would save as compared with two, I believe everyone would agree that the saving in logistics costs, as I am using the term here today, cannot help but be very substantial. In the case of TFX we believe these savings will amount to at least a billion dollars in development, production, and operating costs over the life cycle of this aircraft. . . .

◀ *D. In the search for control, whether of the whole or within the various parts of the federal scientific establishment, administrator-politicians generally found themselves engaged in a struggle for balance of the constituencies whose relative power in relation to one another provided the dynamics of federal scientific activity. All too often beleaguered officials have been encouraged to think of the Congress itself as just another of these hungry constituencies to be manipulated and controlled and pacified. But Congressional committees with their staffs of experts capable of providing continuous administration and supervision have grown into a congeries of bureaucracies coordinate with the executive arm that are potentially controlling agents. In recent years this development has been brought most sharply to the attention of a scientific agency long the darling of Congress. Throughout the nineteen-fifties the National Institutes of Health were consistently voted more money than the agency itself requested. The Director of NIH was a powerful science-administrator presiding over an informal constituency of lay organizations, the American Cancer Society, the National Heart Association, the Arthritis and Rheumatism Foundation, etc., each with its own connections on Capitol Hill. Few were the congressmen in either house who wished to register a vote against cancer research. And yet in a brief two year period the NIH developed into an object of Congres-*

sional concern, and a long love affair began to show signs of wear and tear. Science, Vol. 140 (June 7, 1963), 1076-78. Reprinted by permission.]

In the strained relationship that has developed between Congress and the National Institutes of Health, the principal figure on the congressional side is Representative L. H. Fountain, a reserved, religiously devout North Carolinian, little known outside of Capitol Hill and his home district but generally admired in both places as an industrious and conscientious public servant.

As a man who is clearly satisfied to be a lineman on a field crowded with flamboyant, aspiring quarterbacks, Fountain could probably disappear tomorrow without causing a political ripple. His departure, however, would probably be applauded within the medical research community, for it has now become a fairly popular pastime to vilify Fountain as the man who forced NIH into adopting increasingly restrictive administrative practices. He is, indeed, the man, but if medical research finds some satisfaction, as it does in asserting that Fountain doesn't know what research is all about, it should also be willing to acknowledge that it doesn't know what Fountain is about; this is unfortunate, for in looking over the cast of congressional characters, it is plain that medical research could do far worse than fall under the jurisdiction of L. H. Fountain.

Politically safe in a district where he no longer encounters even primary opposition, Fountain is a five term Democrat who came up the very hard way. His father died when he was five, and thereafter it was a life of penny-scraping to get through college and law school and finally into Congress by unseating an incumbent with 29 years' service. Along the way, he came to accept the not-unreasonable view that money is a valuable commodity and that, when the government doles it out for a stated purpose, it's not asking too much to ask for assurance that the money is going for that purpose. If NIH finds it hard to accept this view for the research process, Fountain finds it hard to accept NIH's view that the ethical standards of the scientific community are a sufficient safeguard of public funds.

If his views are hard for NIH to swallow, NIH's manner of dealing with him is equally hard to swallow, for it is

marked by a series of ineptitudes that are difficult to comprehend. The result is that Fountain and NIH are now involved
in long-running hostilities, which wouldn't matter very much,
except for the fact that tremors from their row are producing
disturbing effects in laboratories across the country. Un-
happily, whatever can be said about the conflict, neither side
can be accused of statesmanship or any serious effort to
comprehend the responsibilities of the other, and, in this
situation, probably the only safe conclusion is that medical
research and Congress have fallen into a deplorable state of
misunderstanding.

Fountain, a 50-year-old political middle-of-the-roader, is
chairman of the House Intergovernmental Relations Subcommittee, a standing investigatory body that includes NIH in its
broad jurisdiction. The task of the subcommittee is to promote
the efficient and economical use of federal funds, and in 1959,
attracted by that traditional catnip for congressional attention,
rapid budgetary growth, the subcommittee began to look into
NIH. The result was a mildly worded report issued in 1961,
containing a series of recommendations for administrative
changes, aimed principally at obtaining assurances that NIH
grantees were using government funds for the purpose for
which they were granted. This, of course, is easy to recommend but difficult to achieve when the guiding assumption of
NIH is that the grantee should be as unhampered as possible
by paper work and inquisitive bookkeepers from Washington.
Nevertheless, NIH director James A. Shannon, with some
reservations, wrote Fountain that he considered the report
"excellent." Meanwhile, Shannon's superior, Surgeon
General Luther L. Terry, wrote, "may I compliment you upon
a searching and constructive inquiry into the growing and
complex set of activities administered by the National Institutes of Health. I am confident that many of the committee
recommendations will be adopted more easily by reason of
your independent recognition of their significance."

Fountain then withdrew from the field and waited, only to
find, as NIH officials later conceded, that virtually nothing was
being done to comply with the recommendations. The publicly stated reason was that NIH found it difficult to hire the
type of administrative personnel who could perform the delicate task of checking without intruding. Persons with this
capability are unquestionably in short supply, and NIH can be

excused for not having assembled such a staff overnight. However, according to one high NIH official, the problem ran deeper than the difficulties of recruiting.

"Fountain is right that nothing was done after the first report. At that time, we had no comprehension of the seriousness of the matter. We had differences among ourselves as to what should be done, and as a result, we did nothing. Some people felt that no changes were needed, and there was a feeling that time would pass and the whole thing would be forgotten."

If this approach had worked, it wouldn't have been the first time that a government agency had sidestepped congressional recommendations, but the decision to do nothing was accompanied by a policy, formally or informally arrived at, of making believe that Fountain wasn't there. Instead of looking upon the Fountain committee as a permanent fixture in NIH's political environment, one to be courted and educated in the problems of administering a massive, nationwide research effort, NIH chose to regard it as a nuisance that was best forgotten. NIH officials, for example, never made an effort to get acquainted with Fountain. He has been to NIH to visit constituents working there, but outside of one invitation from the NIH administration, which he was unable to accept, he has not been invited to tour NIH's impressive facilities. There is nothing to suggest, of course, that his views would be altered by a walk through a laboratory, but the lack of personal contact between Fountain and the officials who feel afflicted by him does not contribute to better understanding. (Fountain himself, it might be added, has not gone out of his way to become acquainted with NIH or its grantees, but since NIH needs him more than he needs NIH, it would seem that the burden is on NIH.) Nor has understanding been furthered by relations between NIH and Fountain's chief aide in the investigation, Delphis C. Goldberg, a studious, persistent worker who joined the committee staff in 1956 after receiving a Ph.D. from Harvard in political economy and government.

Goldberg, after innumerable frustrations and delays in trying to obtain information from NIH, feels that NIH is going to budge only as far as the committee pushes it and he has no high hopes about NIH's good faith in its dealings with the committee. While stressing that he agrees with NIH that the desirable goal is to achieve accountability without interfering with the research process, he adds that "they [NIH] have a tendency to romanticize research, to try to convince you that it cannot be subjected to any sort of accountability. Before we came along, they were operating in a never-never land. They were not operating according to the rules of the government. They clothe themselves in a mystique, and they constantly act as if nothing is important unless they decide it's important. When we point out undesirable practices to them, they answer that they didn't know they were going on. It's an ostrich approach. They see only what they want to see. They talk of achieving excellence, but by excellence, they mean passability."

Last year, after Fountain found that his initial recommendations had been largely unheeded, the committee called NIH in for a second hearing. The result was a sharply worded, highly critical report that dissolved NIH's complacency about ignoring Fountain. A direct outgrowth of this report was the issuance, at the beginning of this year, of the *Public Health Service Grants Manual,* which put into effect many of the accountability recommendations that are now causing cries of distress among NIH grantees.

Fountain and Goldberg tend to discount these cries as further examples of NIH's attempt to exaggerate the difficulties of responding to their demands for accountability.

"There are many complaints about the requirement for estimating time spent on' grant projects," Goldberg said. "They tell us that you can't possibly figure out how much time a man spends on research, that you can't figure in the time that he uses for meditation and so forth. But that's a lot of nonsense, part of the effort to romanticize research and create the impression that it is beyond accountability." Goldberg, who circulates among scientists at NIH and elsewhere in quest of material for the committee, added, "it just isn't that hard to come up with a reasonable estimate of how much time a man is giving the government in return for a grant."

In response to the charge that NIH has been forced into precipitately adopting regulations to satisfy the committee, Fountain says he doesn't think this is a likely possibility. "I don't think NIH has overreacted to us," he said. "When you look into the history of their response to us, you see that there's no danger that they'll go too far. And if they do, we'll be the first to call them on it. Our aim is not to interfere with research. We simply feel that it is possible to support research and still have some reasonable accountability for public funds."

To this Goldberg adds, "NIH is so tied up with its grant recipients that we don't see how they can possibly do anything that runs against the interest of their people."

NIH officials, who are aware of these sentiments, comment, "We have an unhappy relationship with Fountain," but they don't have any proposals ready at hand for improving that relationship. "We were aware of many of these problems before Fountain was," they explain, "but there is no doubt that he precipitated events. Still, we can't get a sense of his constructive intent. Fountain and Goldberg are interested in what's happening with grant X and what's going on at institution Y, but they don't seem to comprehend that the problem at this point is not to pick on examples here and there, but to carefully evolve policies that will provide accountability without interference."

The best way to do this, they contend, is to make the grantee's institution responsible for protecting the use of public funds. "But many institutions are not equipped for this task, and it is a long and difficult process to bring them to meet this responsibility," one NIH official explained. "We would have preferred to move slowly in this process, but with Fountain pressuring us, we have been forced into some steps that, frankly, we would not have taken, at least at this time. We were concerned about the use of grant funds for salaries, but I don't think we would have adopted the time-estimating rules without Fountain. We would have preferred to see the time rules evolve slowly."

NIH officials agree that they are reluctant to give information to Fountain, and that complaints about poor cooperation on their part are, to some extent, well based. "We have appointed one man to serve as our liaison with the committee and to supply them with the information that they request, but it's true that we're reluctant to give them information. We just don't know how it's going to be used."

The chilliness of the relationship is partially explained by the fact that Fountain's committee is an investigatory one, and that it wasn't established to pile up reports saying everything is okay. The function of an investigatory committee is to find things that are amiss, and it is customary for federal agencies

to have as little as possible to do with investigatory committees that have them under surveillance. Nevertheless, this
principle can be followed out the window, which is what
seems to have happened in the case of NIH. It might as well
be realized that L. H. Fountain is now a permanent fixture in
the politics of medical research and that no good can come of
maintaining only distant relations with him.

Fountain has made it clear that his interest in NIH is
neither short-range nor casual. "My feeling is," he said, "that
the committee will have to keep surveillance over NIH
indefinitely, particularly because of the wide range of discretion that they have in using funds."

At the moment, no date has been set for further hearings,
but material is being collected, some of it not particularly
flattering to NIH (disappointed grant applicants are the source
of some of it), and before the session is out it is probable that
Congressman Fountain and NIH will meet again in the hearing room. In the meantime, would it be too impertinent to
suggest that since Fountain and Shannon are in the same
business — promoting the public welfare — they might find
something useful to discuss over lunch?

III. Prospects for the Future

‹ A. *The most dramatic changes wrought by the staggering growth of the federal scientific estabishment since 1939 were experienced by the nation's colleges and universities. These changes have been touched upon from time to time in the course of these readings. The two selections which follow were chosen because they attempt to assess the university situation from a perspective of over twenty years and to project from that assessment the shape of things to come.*

Harvard and the Federal Government: A Report to the Faculties and Governing Boards of Harvard University (Sept., 1961), 3-27]

Harvard is by no means unique in its new relationship with Government. At least 80% of the institutions of higher education in the United States now receive Federal funds, and Harvard is one of those heavily involved in Federal programs. It is difficult to obtain precise totals but a sampling of seventeen institutions with large Federal programs showed Harvard in ninth place both in the amount received and in the relation Federal money bore to the total university budget.

Government funds tend to concentrate in the relatively few institutions with strong graduate and professional programs in the natural sciences because of the heavy national emphasis on research. A recent study of Federal expenditures for research in 287 institutions showed that 5 institutions received 57% of the total, while 20 institutions received 79% and 66 received 92%. In Harvard's sampling of seventeen institutions there were three administering Federal laboratories as a public service where Federal funds comprise more than two thirds of the annual university income budget and there were three others where the proportion was greater than a half of the total, based on 1960-61 figures.

Federal programs . . . involve various parts of Harvard University in different degrees. Whereas Federal funds in

1959-60 supplied one quarter of the budget of the University as a whole, they supplied 55% in the School of Public Health, 57% in the Medical School and 30% in the Arts and Sciences (of which almost half, however, went to the Cambridge Electron Accelerator, operated jointly with M.I.T.).

This new relationship with the Federal Government began only with the Second World War, the Office of Scientific Research and Development contracts, and the "GI bill of rights". Since then, in the country as a whole, science and defense have brought Government and the educational community together to such an extent that 20% of the total expenditures in higher education in the United States now comes from Federal sources.

While the use of Federal funds at Harvard has, up to the present, served the interests of both public policy and the advancement of knowledge, there are enough potential difficulties in the relationship to warrant taking a careful look at where we are and where we seem to be going.

With the First Morrill Act of 1862, the Congress turned from the idea of a national university that had intrigued a number of the Founding Fathers and adopted two policies that have persisted as the basis of Federal programs in higher education. It decided to give land grants to both private and state institutions, and to this day Federal grant programs do not discriminate between them. At the same time it decided to give support not to the general purposes of education, but to the improvement of the "agricultural and mechanic arts," and Federal support is still granted not for "education" but rather to further the specific purposes of particular Federal departments and agencies. But this leads inevitably into a complicated situation. For example, the national programs in which universities are now involved are not confined to the field of defense; they are also growing wherever the advancement of knowledge may make a contribution to the solution of social problems or the advancement of human welfare. For instance, Congress has multiplied by ten times in eight years the resources of the National Institutes of Health whose grants have done so much to support research, and provide research facilities, at Harvard.

Federal support is most conspicuous in the research portions of the University's budget. For example, the Division of Engineering and Applied Physics supported 95% of its research, but only 44% of its total expenditures, with Federal funds. Federal funds similarly supported 67% of the research and 48% of the total expenditure of the Chemistry Department; and in the Physics Department 90% of the research and 63% of the total. Even though some parts of the University have a larger proportion of private money in their research funds than do the departments noted above, none could carry on anything like the present level of scientific investigation without Federal aid.

During 1959-60, Harvard received more than $18 million from the Government of which $11,860,000 was solely for research purposes. This total included $6,512,000 from the Department of Health, Education and Welfare, of which $5,495,000 came from the various National Institutes of Health for research toward the cure of specific deseases, $826,000 from the Division of General Medical Science, and $132,000 from The Office of Education. The other major sources were The National Science Foundation, established to foster basic research, which provided $1,155,000, and the Office of Naval Research which provided $1,704,500.

The several Faculties of the University obviously did not share equally in Federal support for research. The principal benefactors . . . were the three schools in the Medical area and the Faculty of Arts and Sciences. Moreover there are variations among the departments within the Faculty of Arts and Sciences, with the chief research support going to departments in the Natural Sciences, including the Division of Engineering and Applied Physics, and to the museums. But small amounts do come to the Russiam Research Center and the Laboratory of Social Relations, and programs in mental health are beginning to bring some support to the social sciences.

The Federal Government has been even more generous, in certain specialized fields, in the construction and operation of research facilities. The Cambridge Electron Accelerator will be completed in 1962 at an estimated cost of $11,630,000. This sum will have come from the Atomic Energy Commission. While the Commission will retain title to this facility for 25 years, Harvard and M.I.T. will operate it jointly so as to provide new research opportunities not only for their own Faculties, but for an additional research staff. The work made possible by this new facility is of such importance that the

Atomic Energy Commission will support additional research staff and the entire operating costs, which are expected to total approximately $5 million annually by 1963-64.

Here clearly is a wholly new dimension in higher education. Advance in nuclear physics requires expenditures beyond the capacity of private donors. In the main, Federal backing does not in this case involve financial cost to the Universty nor does it impose limitations on freedom of inquiry or the right to publish. The scientific community in Harvard, in M.I.T., and in the Government agreed that a facility of this sort should be built. Its presence near the Harvard Yard is eloquent testimony to the joint concern of the university world and the Federal Government for the advancement of nuclear physics.

Other research facilities have been made possible by generous sums made available by the National Institutes of Health through its Division of Research Grants. In the Faculty of Arts and Sciences, the Chemistry and Biology Departments have acquired new facilities, notably the new James Bryant Conant Laboratory for Chemistry, a portion of the cost of which was paid by the U.S. Public Health Service. In the Medical School the Departments of Anatomy and Pharmacology have been rehabilitated, and animal research facilities provided. Similarly the National Institutes of Health has contributed to the cost of constructing the new University Health Center. In every instance more than matching funds from non-public sources was required.

By 1962 it is estimated that the Federal Government will have contributed nearly $14 million to the construction, modernization, and remodeling of research facilities which will be owned and operated by the University. Of this total the National Institutes of Health will provide nearly $12,883,000 and the National Science Foundation something over $1 million.

To complete the account it should be mentioned that, in addition to the construction and modernization of these research facilities, Harvard received from the U.S. Public Health Service (including the National Institutes of Health), the Atomic Energy Commission, and the National Science Foundation roughly $35,800 worth of research equipment and material during the same academic year; and substantial grants were received, soon after the fiscal year we are considering, from the Advanced Research Projects Agency.

While many colleges and universities have benefited from the Federal housing and loan program which has aided in the construction of dormitories and non-instructional and non-research facilities, Harvard has not yet done so. On the other hand, Harvard from its own resources is contributing indirectly to the Federal Urban Renewal program by participation in, and contributions to, the Citizens Advisory Committee of Cambridge. Harvard has expended $800,000 in land acquisition since 1955 in Federally approved urban renewal areas. This sum and other sums to be expended, according to Section 112 of the National Housing Act of 1959, become a non-cash urban renewal credit to the City of Cambridge in the amount of $1,000,000. Harvard's share will thus materially reduce the City's cash expenditures for urban renewal. Similar urban renewal credits are in prospect for Boston in the Medical area.

While it might seem the Federal Government makes an arbitrary distinction in favor of research and against instruction, there are exceptions. The School of Public Health received from the Public Health Service in 1959-60 almost $154,000 to support its general instructional programs. Furthermore, support for instructional programs in certain foreign languages was provided by the Office of Education. Under the National Defense Education Act, that office paid out over $80,000 for instruction in Far Eastern and Middle Eastern languages, on condition that this be matched in equal amounts by the University. The three Armed Services contributed nearly $130,000 toward the ROTC program. The School of Public Health participated in a program, aided by a $23,000 grant from the International Cooperation Administration, for teachers of preventive medicine and public health. The Atomic Energy Commission and the National Science Foundation sought to promote the training of science teachers by furnishing the School of Education and the Faculty of Arts and Sciences something over $283,000.

In addition the Federal Government has turned to universities for specific advice on important issues. In the summer of 1960, for example, the Senate Foreign Relations Committee asked the Harvard Center for International Affairs to prepare studies on certain problems in American foreign policy at a cost of approximately $20,000 to the Government.

Far more often, however, the Government turns to individual Faculty members, through consulting arrangements which may benefit both the Government and the University. So long as a Faculty member is able to carry out his academic responsibilities, he is free to consult as much as he wishes. Practice varies from Faculty to Faculty. The Business School alone chooses to place the consulting activity of its Faculty members on a formally organized basis and places a limit on the amount of consulting done by the faculty during the academic year. When Departments are considered as a whole, the average number of days of off-campus consulting per month per Faculty member is surprisingly small. In the Faculty of Arts and Sciences, it was exceptional to find that the average number of days per member spent on Government business exceeded a day a month. It is true that the University continues to pay fringe benefits and salaries to Faculty members while they are consulting in Washington or elsewhere. Unreimbursed costs of this kind were estimated to amount to $211,310 for the academic year 1959-60. Such an amount, however, cannot properly be considered an unreimbursed cost in the sense that reimbursement should be expected or desired. Nor is such Faculty consulting without benefit to the University or to the faculty member. The figure is simply a measure of the University's involvement with the Federal Government through consultation by Faculty members on an individual basis.

In any year a number of Faculty members are likely to be on leaves of absence working for Federal agencies. The year 1959-60 was no exception, and twelve permanent members of the Faculty were so engaged. In addition, twenty-one Faculty members received travel grants from Federal agencies. The University continued to make the necessary contributory payments toward the retirement of these Faculty members, even if they were on leave without pay to accept Federal salaries. Here again, such unreimbursed costs are simply an index of the extent to which the University renders a public service. Such leaves of course also provide new knowledge for instruction in the University as well.

Particular mention should be made of other programs that are intended to contribute to student and professional advancement. For example, the Department of Health, Education and Welfare provided in 1959-60 nearly $1,753,000 for Training Grants to the three schools in the Medical area (Medicine, Dental Medicine and Public Health) and the Faculty of Arts and Sciences. About 300 individuals, of whom about three-quarters already had doctoral degrees, were supported while studying at Harvard by this important program. Most of these trainees were being prepared for careers in research rather than for the practice of medicine. This large effort, moreover, was undertaken at considerable expense to the University in terms of Faculty supervision and facilities — amounting to a total of $310,390 in unreimbursed costs, a figure that fails to take into account such problems as crowding, staffing, and possible impingement on the training of medical students.

In addition to those who received Training Grants through the University, hundreds of graduate and post-doctoral students came to Harvard either on Federal fellowships, or under some Federal program for the advanced training of its Military, Foreign, or Civil Service, notably in the Graduate School of Public Administration. The University, of course, retains the right to accept or reject these students. The list of agencies awarding fellowships is a long one. The natural science departments in the Faculty of Arts and Sciences have had a considerable share of the total available National Science Foundation Fellowships. A number of National Defense Foreign Language Fellowships encourage study of Far Eastern and Near Eastern languages. By bringing able professional men and women, including government officials, to many parts of the University, these programs have contributed heavily to our academic life.

There is very little Federal assistance for undergraduates. A National Science Foundation program a year ago did permit twenty undergraduates to participate in research in biochemistry and biology during the summer months. But this is about the extent of it. It seems to us at Harvard that the country needs and would welcome a Federal undergraduate scholarship program based on both need and ability.

Harvard has found it impossible to participate in the loan program of the National Defense Education Act (Title 2) on account of the objectionable disclaimer affidavit requirement. It is a source of concern to us that the Congress has completely failed to understand the position of Harvard and the Association of American Universities in the matter. There is a danger signal here.

By intervention of one kind or another, the Federal Government has enabled the University to play a considerable role in world affairs. During 1959-60, for example, there was an exchange of a few Soviet and American students involving the Faculty of Arts and Sciences. A Fine Arts professor and a member of the Faculty of the School of Education also participated in an international exchange of faculty with the Soviet Union. A considerable number of foreign faculty members taught at Harvard, and hundreds of foreign students received instruction. The Graduate School of Design, the Business School, and the Law School entered into cooperative programs with foreign universities, while the Graduate Schools of Education, Public Health, and Public Administration provided technical assistance to foreign governments. It should not be hard to demonstrate that long range purposes of our Government are clearly served by these exchanges.

By 1960 Harvard was participating in at least thirty-four categories of programs managed by two score Federal agencies, under the general oversight of a dozen Congressional Committees. Since all the Faculties were involved, though in widely varying degrees, Harvard's relationship with Washington was clearly managed on a highly decentralized basis.

While this decentralized pattern, with its heavy emphasis on particular fields and specific activities, has brought about a great many difficult problems, it has probably made it easier to maintain the essential academic freedom of the University. The Federal Government has clearly not interfered in the direction of Harvard's research projects. It has certainly sought to encourage, in fields colored by a national interest, research which our Faculty members wished to undertake. The variety of sources of support helps make it possible for a distinguished scientist in a respected institution to obtain backing for his research on terms acceptable to him and his university. The image of a coercive government dictating what shall and shall not be done in university laboratories and libraries simply does not fit Harvard's experience with Washington.

The nature of the relationship becomes clearer if we examine the ways in which support for research is obtained. The University's basic purposes have been well served by Federal programs because the University is encouraged to assist in defining the terms of participation. Typically, a Faculty member develops his own project and then seeks funds for its execution. A key role in the awarding of funds is played by various advisory boards and panels, established by the various agencies, which permit men from institutions of higher learning to advise in managing Government programs. In deciding on the scope of a research project, Faculty members deal with professionally trained personnel in the agencies themselves and with professional colleagues from the university world who serve on these boards. As a consequence, communication and understanding between the University and the Government regarding the conduct of the research are generally satisfactory, and the impact of Federal funds on a particular research project does not seem to differ basically from the impact of money in similar amounts from private sources.

The procedure of the National Institutes of Health affords an example of the satisfactory University-Government relations in fostering basic research. Although established to combat specific diseases, the National Institutes have administered their funds so as to encourage basic research in such disciplines as Chemistry and Biology. The goal of independent uninhibited research is served by a combination of specific disease institutes and advisory panels of scientists. The Institutes secure public funds, which the panel allocates to best advantage. Similar procedures link the defense interests of the nation with the University in mutually beneficial ways.

This degree of decentralization and of initiative by individual Faculty members is desirable as long as we follow clear policies to maintain the basic purposes and principles of the University as a whole. Such policy with respect to acceptance of Federal funds is established in broad outline by the President and Fellows of Harvard College, with the advice of the Faculties and Deans concerned, and is applied uniformly throughout the University. Harvard's practice of not undertaking classified research except in times of grave national emergency affords one example. While such projects were undertaken during the Second World War and would undoubtedly be undertaken again under similar circumstances, research that cannot be published immediately seems incompatible with the University's basic purpose to seek and disseminate knowledge. This policy, however, does not preclude the participation of Faculty members as individual consultants in classified work.

The University will apply for a Federal grant or contract

only after careful consideration. An individual research project must be selected for professional reasons by the individual investigator, who must be free to decide whether to publish or not and must have the right to do so. Such investigators are free to receive Government or other support for their research projects provided there is no interference with Harvard's role as an educational institution.

It has been necessary to provide some measure of direction and coordination in such matters, in order to preserve the basic character of the University as a whole, without infringing on Faculty responsibility and individual initiative. Among the coordinating instruments are the Committee of Deans and the Committee on Research and Development, with the President of the University serving as chairman of each. The Administrative Vice President has special responsibility for all Federal programs in any department of the University, although his responsibility in the Medical School is shared in some measure with the Associate Dean. When it was decided, after World War II, to continue to accept Federal funds for research under contract with the government, a single office, the Office for Research Contracts, was established to administer the details of research contracts formerly handled by the Treasurer's office. The present Office has been of immense value to the University in maintaining a uniform policy, protecting it against improper commitments, assuring its reimbursement of proper costs, and providing assistance to Faculty members in the negotiations that lead to a contract. Every contract must have the approval of the Department Chairman concerned and of the Dean of the appropriate Faculty, and must be drawn so as to be compatible with University policy, before being presented to the President and Fellows for approval.

The Office for Research Contracts deals with all Federal grants and contracts for research and development, with the exception of grants from the U.S. Public Health Service. For these the Administrative Vice President or, as appropriate, the Associate Dean of the Medical School signs grant applications. Although there are a number of reasons, historically speaking, why grants from the United States Public Health Service should be handled separately, an argument can be made that all grants and contracts should be administered in a single office in the University.

The decentralized nature of Federal research programs

may help the university protect itself against deliberate encroachment, but it makes it all the more difficult to preserve the proper balance either among various schools and departments, or within each of them between research and teaching. The availability of Federal grants for project research tends in any university to divide the responsibility of the faculty, and to weaken the influence of the president and the deans, in planning the content, emphasis, and direction of research and teaching. Individual faculty members tend to be influenced less by their colleagues and the needs of their faculty or department as a whole than by the interests they discover can be implemented through their channels of communication with Government agencies. Is it possible to get the tremendous advantages of Federal support and at the same time to maintain a proper balance among the several interests of the University?

Harvard seems to have done so, but it may nevertheless be useful to review our problems as well as our opportunities.

One of the most serious of questions in Federal programs is that of unreimbursed indirect costs on grants. Most spectacular in 1959-60 were the unreimbursed costs arising from research grants, which made satisfactory allowance for direct, but not for indirect costs. While spending $11,860,836 of Federal funds for project research, the University incurred $687,500 in unreimbursed indirect costs.

What a university thinks about the issue of indirect costs depends a great deal on the size of the grants. If a faculty looks to Washington for little of its support, indirect costs are negligible and may in fact be difficult to identify. In sufficient magnitudes, however, Federal grants can make a university poorer rather than richer by building up unreimbursed costs. More than one Faculty at Harvard has found it necessary to limit its participation in desirable programs lest their indirect costs drain away its unrestricted income.

Government agencies differ in their attitudes toward this problem. For the year in question, Harvard, on the basis of the formula of the U.S. Bureau of the Budget, determined that 28.5% of the total direct costs was an allowable charge for indirect costs. Some Federal agencies were willing to pay this figure. Congressional appropriations for the Department of Health, Education and Welfare, however, limited by a legislative rider payment of indirect costs to an arbitrary 15% of direct costs. Some agencies have not felt obliged to pay the full institutional rate for indirect costs, either because they believed that the university ought to share in the expenses or because their scientists wished to have as large a share of the limited funds as possible go to direct research costs in their special fields.

The Federal policy of encouraging construction and modernization of research facilities by a "matching fund" formula, with the University and the Government sharing costs on a dollar for dollar basis, also presents a complex of opportunities and difficulties. A lack of space in some areas of the University has forced the postponement of important research and instruction. Meanwhile, unreimbursed costs of Government-sponsored research have delayed the accumulation of funds that could be used to match the Federal contributions for construction.

The matching fund formula has, of course, long been used by private donors. Whether used by them or the Government, the formula tends to channel funds to the stronger institutions with adequate financial and research resources for facilities which they are fully equipped to support. The matching requirement also helps to prevent universities from becoming dependent on any one source of financial support, thus protecting their freedom of scientific investigation. At present, the matching requirement seems most feasible in construction grants for research facilities, in which private corporations and foundations seem also to be primarily interested. Matching funds for teaching facilities from private sources are manifestly more difficult to obtain. The School of Public Health, for example, has found private foundations, industries, and individuals extremely reluctant to finance the kind of teaching facilities required to train individuals for careers in the public health field. As a result of similar experience, the Association of Schools of Public Health has suggested a Federal share of 85% for teaching facilities construction. It should also be noted that the Association of American Medical Colleges proposed a Federal share of 75%.

Even with respect to research facilities, there is a real question whether the need in all institutions of higher learning can be met in the next ten years by a rigid application of the fifty-fifty matching formula. Estimates have been made that more than one billion dollars will have to be invested in graduate research facilities in the next five years in order to provide space for graduate students who are already in school and college. The matching formula would require that some $500 million, or $100 million a year, be forthcoming from non-Federal sources to meet this need; but it seems doubtful whether this can be realistically expected.

Federal grants for research and for construction have brought great benefits to Harvard yet there is a danger that the total program of the University could be affected by the extent that the unreimbursed costs and matching funds involved in such grants use up the precious unrestricted funds that would be available for other purposes. The three greatest threats posed by Federal aid are likely to be in the balance among the several fields of learning; in the balance between teaching and research; and in the balance within the Faculty between those with and those without tenure appointments.

On the first point, the problem is obvious. An overwhelming proportion of Federal support goes to the sciences. To maintain a balance, a university must make a special effort to provide support from private sources for other fields of knowledge. Harvard has been relatively successful in this effort. The growth of the humanities and social sciences has been maintained at a respectable rate with the support of private funds. . .

The second and third points, while no more important, are more complicated and difficult to assess, in part because the problems of the balance between research and teaching, and between tenure and non-tenure personnel, are interwoven. Moreover, the relationships in each case have varied considerably from one part of the University to the other. In some Faculties, Federal funds have brought about a marked increase in the total teaching and research staff. While our tenure ranks have not been increased directly by Federal support, some indirect increase, impossible to measure, may have occurred as a result of the capitalization of funds made possible by Federal support of various activities in the University. There has however been a marked upward trend in the number of non-tenure appointments since Departments and Faculties have employed Faculty members who are paid from Federal funds for the portion of their time spent on federally supported research, and from University funds for the time spent on instruction.

The Medical School and the School of Dental Medicine have estimated that 60% of their teaching and research staff are available owing to Federal funds. In these two Schools, the staff has increased over a twenty-year period at a faster rate than the size of the student body, and as a consequence the teaching load has decreased. However, Federal policy distinguishes between medical teaching and research and devotes most of its support to the latter. The experience of the School of Public Health, however, has been more satisfactory because the teaching of public health, unlike medical instruction, is supported by Federal programs. In this School during the past twenty years, the Faculty and the student body have each doubled in size, while the amount of teaching time per man has also increased substantially.

The most obvious increase in staff has been in the number of post-doctoral fellows. The Chemistry Department in Arts and Sciences, to take a notable example, had one hundred such fellows, most of them employed specifically to work on Federal programs. Their availability has encouraged that Department to institute undergraduate tutorials, although it must obtain special funds to reimburse the post-doctoral fellows for time spent in instruction.

It would be a great mistake to assume that because large amounts of Federal money are available for research, instruction is bound to be neglected. Project directors are normally Faculty members, and the results of their research contribute toward lively instruction for both graduates and undergraduates. There are hopeful signs, moreover, that the Federal Government is recognizing that the distinction between research and teaching is arbitrary and dangerous. Certain post-doctoral fellowships and project training grants of the National Institutes of Health, for example, permit those funds to support teaching as well as research. In a number of instances scholars who have been employed in part for research supported by Government grants and contracts have also offered stimulating new courses available to both graduate and undergraduate students. On balance, however, instruction is in danger of neglect unless a Faculty is sound enough financially to avoid committing its unrestricted money to underwrite research inadequately financed by the Government.

The availability of research funds does not appear to have caused any major reduction in the teaching loads of Faculty members in science in the period since 1940. The availability of Federal support has not led Harvard to set up separate faculties for research and teaching. No one is expected to teach without time for research. In the Faculty of Arts and Sciences, a single staff teaches both graduate and undergraduate students, and every Department, with occasional exceptions to meet special circumstances, has a strong tradition that senior members teach undergraduates as well as graduate students.

It seems clear, however, that there has been a slight reduction in the teaching load of most Faculty members in science over a twenty-year period. While more time is now probably spent by Faculty members in research, particularly in those departments where research has been financed by the Government, it is also true that formal teaching loads seem to run somewhat higher in the social sciences and the humanities than they do in the natural sciences.

These facts by themselves, however, do not tell the whole story. The Faculty spends a great deal of time, which is difficult to measure, in directing doctoral dissertations or other individual graduate instruction. This point is of special importance in all science departments of the University, where the number of graduate students and post-doctoral students has enormously increased. What is more, the altered structure of the student body has been accompanied by changes in teaching methods so that there is now more individual instruction than used to be the case twenty years ago, particularly in the medical area and in some parts of the Faculty of Arts and Sciences.

As a result of the emphasis on research in the sciences, graduate and postgraduate students benefit far more than undergraduates from the various Federal programs. They have apparently been restricted very little, if any, by the conditions of Federal grants in their free choice of subjects. Like the grants for research projects, the Government fellowship programs in science, such as the National Science Foundation Fellowships and the National Institutes of Health Fellowships, are neutral with respect to the special fields of investigation within a major branch of science.

The so-called "regular" National Science Foundation Fellowships have until very recently imposed a handicap on undergraduate teaching by requiring that a student holding such a Fellowship may not receive additional pay from the University for assisting in instruction. These Fellowships have therefore diminished the attractiveness of Teaching Fellowships, so that in some Departments graduate students of the very first rank have not always been available to serve as course assistants. The Government's concern is to enable a student to complete his doctorate in short order, for which, it must be said in fairness, Harvard does not count performance in teaching. Even so, there is a real question whether the able graduate student should not be encouraged to obtain teaching experience in order to meet the Government's objective of raising the general level of scientific achievement in the country at large. It should be noted in this connection that some National Science Foundation Fellows have chosen to serve as course assistants without pay, and this fall new administrative rulings now permit National Science Foundation Fellows to earn up to $600 annually by teaching.

Many graduate students are supported, especially during their third and fourth years, by employment as Research Assistants on projects financed by Federal funds. (In some Departments, a minority of these appointments go on a part-time basis to graduate students who also serve as Teaching Fellows; University funds are of course used to pay for the share of time devoted to instruction.) It has been estimated, for example, that half of all research in the Division of Engineering and Applied Physics is used in the preparation of doctoral dissertations. An appointment as Research Assistant can thus serve the purpose of a fellowship as well. This arrangement is wholly satisfactory to the Federal agencies, and most important for scientific achievement at Harvard.

Some Departments have been reluctant, however, to allow any graduate students to be supported with funds from research projects, lest senior Faculty members be put in the position of "buying" their students. This point of view doubtless originated at a time when fewer Faculty members had research funds at their disposal, and to most Faculty members it seems less valid today.

Undergraduate students, in contrast, however, as stated earlier, receive little direct benefit from Federal programs. The point that should be made here is that the Federal government, by distinguishing between teaching and research, often handicaps the effort to bring the knowledge gained from research into the undergraduate classroom. For example, the "facilities program" of the National Science Foundation and the National Institutes of Health cannot be used to aid undergraduate instruction; consequently, the Government was recently unwilling to match part of the money Harvard was prepared to make available to the Biology Department, because the proposed facilities were to be used in part for undergraduate instruction. This policy seems particularly unwise to Harvard since we draw upon the same instructors for graduate and undergraduate instruction, believing that the combination makes for better research and better teaching.

There is a suspicion that the increased emphasis on research, post-doctoral scholars, and graduate students in our science Departments has contributed to a remoteness between Faculty and undergraduates. Whether this stems from Federal research support, or from the general characteristics of modern science, or from other factors is hard to say. Science seems to play less of a role than other fields in the undergraduate Houses, and some of the Departments not involved in Government programs, such as the English Department, actually offer more undergraduate tutorial instruction. It is perhaps inevitable that a scientist eager to concentrate on his research will be reluctant to take on the hard work of teaching a large introductory or General Education course. Nevertheless, undergraduate work in a laboratory is analogous in many respects to an individual or group tutorial in the humanities or social sciences, and much Faculty time is devoted in the scientific Departments to supervising such work. And against distractions of Federal programs must be balanced the enormous interest students of all ranks take in a teacher who is known to have made a significant discovery, or to have played an influential role in public affairs.

While all Harvard professors are expected to engage in research, the University community, as a result of Federal funds, now includes a large and growing proportion of research workers who are not members of the teaching Faculty. In view of the type of work they do, Harvard may now have to adjust some of the rules that were designed to maintain the proper balance between those Faculty members with, and those without, permanent tenure.

The problem arises especially in connection with the growing numbers, in many Departments, of Research Assistants, Research Associates, and Research Fellows. These staff members, most of whom are scientists, are recognized as important members of the University community. Most of them (with the exception of the Research Assistants who are primarily students) have corporation appointments, and receive the same fringe benefits as regular Faculty members. The quantity of Federal funds for research has greatly increased the numbers of such staff members, and thus intensified the perennial problem that a great many more able scholars are attracted to Harvard by temporary positions than can possibly be given tenure appointments. The temptation is very great to use the short-term Federal funds to keep at Harvard scientists for whom there is no prospect of a permanent position being available, to an age when their opportunities elsewhere diminish.

To protect against this danger, we have a general rule that non-tenure appointments for Faculty or research personnel shall not be extended beyond a total of eight years (eleven in the Medical area) or beyond a total of three years for those 35 years of age or older. A facility such as the Cambridge Electron Accelerator, however, will require the continued presence of skilled personnel. At least some of the scientists who are being attracted to this facility are doubtless the equal of scientific colleagues who hold Faculty appointments. Although both groups will be working together on research projects, only one will have Faculty status. It may well be necessary, therefore, to introduce some flexibility into our personnel practices so as to retain key research personnel beyond the usual limit of annual appointments whenever it is necessary in order to make the most effective use of research facilities. Harvard has for some time been prepared to make exceptions to normal procedure so that a few highly-qualified individuals may be given appointments without limit of time without being tenure members of the Faculty. It should be possible to continue these appointments so long as contract funds are available. Science has become increasingly complicated, expensive and dynamic, and new fields and subjects appear on the scene with astonishing rapidity. As a result scientific instruction today doubtless requires more hours of preparation and research than formerly. A first-class Faculty is dependent on moderate teaching loads and on ample opportunity for research. In the scientific areas, in particular, such a Faculty also needs the carefully planned growth that avoids proliferation of highly specialized courses to the detriment of scientific education of appropriate depth and breadth. In order to encourage the closest relations between research staff and regular Faculty, and to take maximum advantage of research programs for instructional purposes, Harvard is planning to make a few teaching appointments by means of one-year lectureships, granted strictly on individual merit, to staff members employed and nominated by a research facility, with the endorsement of the Faculty concerned.

But the most difficult problem is that of the relation of the massive research programs to the permanent Faculty. The traditional policy at Harvard has been to pay no permanent Faculty member from short-term research funds. If Federal funds were to be cut off tomorrow, Harvard would be able to honor its commitments to all its permanent Faculty members. Whether this rule now needs to be so rigidly followed, in order to protect the essential values of academic freedom and intellectual independence, may be open to question. There is clearly a serious shortage of tenure members in some Departments and Faculties, notably those in the Medical area, even though those very Faculties have received their research funds largely because of the quality of their tenure Faculty members. All the evidence suggests that Federal funds for these fields will be forthcoming for the foreseeable future and on increasingly acceptable terms, provided, of course, that the quality of the Faculty is maintained.

That quality, however, cannot be maintained by endowment funds alone, since a first-rate scientist is not attracted mainly by his salary, but by all the facilities and resources that make for a desirable scientific environment. The research facilities, training grants, graduate and postgraduate fellowships, and the international exchanges of students and Faculty which are so important in attracting able scholars to Harvard are now heavily dependent on Federal funds. While no Faculty member likes the necessity of spending valuable time and energy in making appeals for the renewal of such support, it is generally conceded that to get comparable aid from private sources would involve equal or greater difficulties.

In order to maintain the essential quality on which all the rest of our scientific and medical activities depend—the quality of our tenure Professors—it may be necessary for us to experiment cautiously to achieve greater flexibility by paying tenure salaries from Federal funds in certain Departments, for whose fields of interest steady and continuous Federal support may be most confidently predicted for the future.

University and Government people alike have been slow to realize the significance of their new relationship. The Government now calls on the universities for achievements that depend on the highest qualities of creativity, but sometimes through purchasing procedures that could destroy the environment in which such qualities flourish. This is not from any wrong intentions on the part of individual agencies; in general, they have bent over backward in favor of academic freedom, and have done a great deal to adapt Government methods to the requirements of a university. Indeed, in the process of asking Congress for funds, they sometimes exaggerate the potential practical achievements of the basic research they propose to support. But a relationship based on a short-term grant for specific purposes, which was perfectly sensible when such grants were only a tiny increment to an academic budget, may be self-defeating when the grants have become a major reliance of the university. At that stage, the donor would do well to consider the general health of the institution which he is building up, if only in order to protect his investment.

This first becomes apparent in such practical details as the payment for overhead expenses, or the requirement of matching funds. But it is true in a more profound sense. For research can be carried on effectively in the long run only if a university maintains its overhead in an intellectual and academic, as well as an administrative, sense. This is the case for asking the Government to support basic as well as applied science, and teaching as well as research. It is not a question of asking the Government for more money, but, rather, of asking it to give its funds with a proper regard for the total function of the university.

As universities recognize that there is no substitute today for Federal support in many fields of science, they must ask the Government to recognize, in the way it makes its grants, that the university is a creative force because it is concerned with all fields of knowledge, and because it offers scholars the intellectual independence that goes with permanent status. If they are to make this clear, universities themselves need to understand their relationships with Government, and to set up proper channels through which to inform Government of their point of view on the issues which may well affect their basic character in the future. This is the real point of the affidavit controversy.

A half-dozen major organizations represent institutions of higher education in Washington, including the American Council on Education and associations of urban, state, land-grant, and church-related institutions. In particular fields, the Association of American Medical Colleges and the Association of Schools of Public Health have presented their views to the Executive agencies and the Congress, and a committee of the Federation of College and University Business Officers Associations have served as a useful "listening post" in Washington. Most suitable to represent Harvard's point of view, potentially speaking, are the Association of American Universities and its sub-group, the Association of Graduate Schools.

Harvard does not favor the establishment of separate organizations to present the particular views of private, as distinguished from public, institutions in Washington or elsewhere. This University has as much in common with the major state universities as it has with independent universities. On the familiar issues in our relations with the Federal Government—overhead, flexibility of contract terms, long-term support, the construction of facilities—there is scarcely any important difference between what Harvard thinks and what is thought in the major public universities. Differences in point of view arise not so much between public and private institutions as between strong and weak ones. While public and private institutions obviously differ on significant points, these differences seem much less important than their common ground. The Association of American Universities has already provided a platform from which testimony was presented to a Congressional Committee on the NDEA disclaimer affidavit. It goes without saying, of course, that the academic side of a university must be represented as carefully as the financial side.

The close relationships between universities and Federal Executive agencies have already been discussed. To an unfortunate degree, however, there is too little communication in important matters between the universities and Congress. If this had not been true, for example, the objectionable affidavit provision of the NDEA would never have been enacted without more thorough consideration. University spokesmen must understand Congressional politics and policy-making and be prepared to discuss with Congressmen and Senators the basic issues confronting higher education. Unfortunately, university spokesmen often disagree among themselves on points of fundamental importance. We must, therefore, try to reach a consensus on important issues within our own family and with like-minded institutions, if we are to develop satisfactory relationships with Congressional Committees as well as Executive agencies. It is in Congress that the crucial decisions are made on Federal-university relationships, and Executive agencies cannot be expected to represent the universities' interests on every point.

If universities are prepared, individually and cooperatively, to affirm and defend their central educational purposes, and to resist the temptation to expand particular functions at the expense of their primary obligations, they will then be in a position to urge the Federal Government to show some concern for higher education as a general element in the national interest. Representatives of the Government might well be able, then, to agree with universities in a general approach to their future relationship, along lines which might guide the programs of the Federal departments and agencies. . . .

A great deal could be done to reduce the dependence of universities on project grants, which always tend to make the strong Departments stronger, and weaken the university's ability to develop with a proper balance. One way would be to develop a system of institutional grants for unrestricted purposes in particular areas of learning, such as — to take random examples — mathematics or language study. Such a system, supplementing project grants, would enable universities themselves to make the basic decisions on their academic programs within very much broader limits than they can today. It would be only a reasonable extension of a course of action already marked out by the Institutional Grants Programs of the National Science Foundation and the National Institutes of Health, which provide general grants to a university in some proportion to the amount of money received through research grants and contracts. . . .

◄ B. Homer D. Babbidge, Jr., "Scientist Affluent,

Humanist Militant," The Graduate Journal, V (1962, Supplement), 153-162.]

My foremost concern here ... is to shed light on some defects that appear to emerge in graduate education itself. For it seems evident to me that our brief experience with federal programs has destroyed the illusion that graduate education is a seamless whole; it has, in fact, raised the question whether or not some of the seams may not be about to part.

Two grand deficiencies of federal programs stand out against a background of myriad annoyances, mechanical flaws, petty confusions, and other lesser complaints. Stated briefly, these are that federal programs in the aggregate do not provide sufficiently broad support for all those disciplines that enjoy academic respect; and that they do not contribute sufficently to a vital broadening of the base of institutional excellence throughout the nation. . . .

The manner in which these deficiencies might be repaired and the chances, in fact, of doing so, depend in part upon the dynamics of the current situation. The answer to what might happen in the future largely lies imbedded in a maze of current attitudes, organization, and inertia. One must consider, for example, the mood and tenor of our Congress, the bureaucratic jealousies of the executive branch of government, and a variety of other dynamic factors that bear upon the prospects for the future. So-called extraneous issues of federal control, separation of church and state, and racial segregation, and their implications for the future, cannot be overlooked.

But I should like to look at another set of factors—a set that I think has largely been overlooked in discussions of the future; what is the posture of higher education— and graduate education in particular—as it regards the future of federal involvement? How is it mustering its forces for an attack upon the deficiencies of federal programs?

I am principally interested in the fact that we are witnessing the emergence, within the general field of higher education, of distinct interest groups. And the phenomenon is evident within graduate education, too. Now it may be that graduate education once was a seamless whole, and that federal programs have, indeed, rent the fabric; or it may be that we are only being made conscious again of ancient imperfections in the weave.

One recalls, certainly, that the departments and fields of study now bountifully supported by federal largesse were once the ugly ducklings of the academic family; and that the now starved humanities were loathe to share either their relative abundance or their station with science and engineering a century ago. To President MacLean of Princeton in 1854, such meddling with the proven curriculum was a "chimerical experiment." Any lessening of emphasis on ancient languages was, in the words of the Yale Report of 1828, "a scheme calculated ... fatally to affect the prosperity of the college."

So it may well be that the seams have been there all along, and that the dramatic growth of federal programs has served only to reveal them. But the fact of the matter is that factions are appearing in the educational world. That they are developing largely in higher education hints that federal involvement may be a causative factor.

Let me try to suggest a few of the interest groups that are beginning to emerge, symptomatic, I think, of anxiety over the deficiencies of federal programs, and significant, I am sure, for the future prospects of remedying those deficiencies. In the first instance, we have the *humanist militant.* Understandably disappointed in the failure of federal policy to acknowledge fully the importance of the humanities to the maintenance of national vigor and irked by some fairly obvious Congressional rebuffs, the nation's humanists show signs of becoming an aggressive interest group. Their recent proposal for the creation of a National Humanities Foundation is an evidence of this aggressive spirit, just as it is also a reflection of a deep sense of frustration with existing arrangements. I happen myself to think that Congressional disinterest in the humanities at this point in history is such that there is no real prospect for the creation of such an agency of government; but what is of greater interest is the desire on the part of humanists to have such an agency. The clear implication is that they feel sufficiently bound together by unhappiness and neglect that they seek a political weapon with which to fight back in the arena of federal policies. There is a suggestion that they no longer seek to be heard in existing agencies of government; they desire to possess their own. Their objective, of course, is to redress the disciplinary imbalance of federal programs.

As have-nots, the humanists are bound to encounter another interest group, in the form of the haves. Scientists and engineers, it seems evident, must be regarded as having a vested interest in existing programs. They have been impressively consistent in paying tribute to the need for support of the social sciences and the humanities, but their spirit of *noblesse oblige* does not extend to the point of surrendering any part of their federal programs. Indeed, they are aggressive in seeking additional federal support for their areas of concern and interest. This is not to suggest that scientists are a uniform lot, working in harness toward common objectives. In fact, they are a weak federation, the parts of which are hardly satisfied to have a National Foundation named in their honor. Medical scientists have not even been satisfied to have their own National Institute of Health, but have succeeded in having National Institutes designated for each major category of disease. Their history suggests that fractionation is a continuing process within educational interest groups, as well as among them. . . .

The injection of educational institutions into the discussion prompts me to identify another class of interest groups, not according to academic disciplines but by institutional type and size. While the militant humanist and the insatiable scientist counterpose themselves in the tug-of-war of academic balance, educational institutions divide themselves along analogous have and have-not lines.

The have-nots are most readily identifiable as an interest group, largely because their methods are more obvious. Small colleges, junior colleges, former teachers colleges, and growing but still small universities have all given evidence in recent years of their desire to find support at the federal font. They form national organizations because the existing ones do not seem to be getting far enough fast enough to satisfy their youthful appetites. They advocate specialized legislation because they fear that generalized legislation will only contribute further to the enhancement of prestigious, mature institutions, at their expense. In their eagerness to win their place in the federal complex, they are not above "knocking" the haves —just as some humanists openly express their resentment of the affluent scientists. A fellowship proposal that would allow the winner to choose his own graduate school is contemptuously called a "Harvard Bill," and the implication is left that the only reason anyone would choose to go to Harvard is its prestige—with no suggestion that there is any foundation for that prestige. Reason and valid arguments for broader federal support are discarded as too subtle and cumbersome, and the political barb is substituted.

The exasperation of the have-not institutions is made more understandable by the identification of the growing vestedness of the "haves" in the *status quo*. We are ... breeding up a category of "economic royalists" in higher education who make themselves, it must be admitted, an attractive target. They like things as they are. They thrive on the deficiencies of federal programs, for they have demonstrated their ability to win in a competition under the present rules. Listen to the following words of the president of a university that receives a large share of its current income from federal sources:

> ... It is often said that a central government agency should be created to "coordinate" existing programs of federal participation in education. But one of the best features of the present system is that it is not co-ordinated. It contains the same diversity that our institutions themselves cherish. One federal policy for higher education is what we should avoid—for then comes uniformity and regimentation.
>
> I know that without federal subsidy many institutions will have a difficult time surviving. But to support the weak at the expense of weakening the strong is not in the American tradition—and would not lead to a finer educational system. ...

The use of the specter of federal control, the use of quotes around the word "co-ordinate," the use of strong words like "forcing" and "regimentation," and the unreasonable implication that strengthening the weak means weakening the strong; these are the devices worthy of the creator of Daddy War-bucks.

We are experiencing a polarization of the haves and the have-nots of higher education. Humanists and smaller institutions seek by political action to improve their lot; scientists and large universities seem better satisfied with the *status quo*.

I hope I have made my point: that as a consequence of rapid growth in federal programs and the appearance of at least two major deficiencies in the aggregate federal policy, we are witnessing the emergence of factions in higher education; that these have a tendency to proliferate; and that our future prospects for the development of sound federal policies toward graduate education are going to be largely affected by this current tendency. I have already suggested that there are powerful currents and undercurrents at play at the Washington end of this relationship, and it is increasingly evident that higher education itself is a churning pool of complexities as well.

In what framework – other than confusion – can we consider the possible courses for the future?

Herman Melville has suggested one approach. It was, you may recall, the practice of whalers to hoist up the head of a sperm whale on the ship's side to let it hang until time permitted it to be worked on. Ahab was persuaded to kill a right whale and hoist its head up on the opposite side, on the advice of Fedallah that this would keep the Pequod from capsizing. Melville goes on to observe:

> As before, the Pequod steeply leaned over towards the sperm whale's head, now, by the counterpoise of both heads, she regained her even keel; though sorely strained, you may well believe. So, when on one side you hoist in Locke's head, you go over that way; but now, on the other side, hoist in Kant's and you come back again; but in very poor plight. Thus, some minds for ever keep trimming boat. Oh, ye foolish! Throw all these thunderheads overboard, and then you will float light and right.

So when you hoist up science on the one side, it is argued that the humanities should be hoisted up on the other, to keep the vessel from capsizing. . . .

The federal government has hoisted up the head of science, in the form of the National Science Foundation, and a group of eminent educators has described this as "a perfect formula for a legislated imbalance in higher education." and now the suggestion is made that the federal government hoist up the National Humanities Foundation. . . .

Some caution is in order for fear the vessel may, in all its balance and symmetry, sink. . . .

The question for government organization is . . . whether it should continue to rely upon solution by proliferation. And the question that confronts American higher education is essentially the same. The organization of higher education into growing numbers of hard-driving interest groups seems to suggest that the way to correct the institutional imbalances of today is to have additional, specialized programs of support—that are themselves unbalanced—for currently neglected institutions. In the other major dimension of imbalance, it seems to suggest that more categorical support programs are the answer to the evils of categorical support. Is there no more fundamental and essentially logical approach to these problems? . . .

Is there no place in all this for the development of policies for higher education that have their foundations in more than the welter of particular interests within higher education? Is it not possible to allot federal support to institutions on some basis other than the present shortsighted one or its principal alternative of a trough for every pig? Is it not possible to develop a rationale for support of disciplines that goes beyond the present lopsided one but stops short of gimme-too? To answer in the negative is to say that there is no foundation for federal support of higher education beyond what can be resolved in rough-and-tumble political competition between the haves and the have-nots.

I am very much afraid that American higher education—and graduate education insofar as it suffers from the same tendencies—is in danger of dissipating its energies and losing control of its future, as a consequence of fragmentation; of becoming an assemblage of particular interests rather than a cohesive force for the development of sound national policies. To what extent this tendency can be blamed on federal involvement itself, is hard to say. More probably, it is the unsought harvest of years of categorical, piecemeal approaches to the federal government. Many educators have conscientiously sought to Balkanize educational responsibility within the government, for example, with the result that we now have no strong agency of government concerned with the whole breadth and range of the national interest in education. As I have suggested, this has resulted in large part from dissatisfaction and impatience with the agency that might most logically have assumed such responsibility [The U.S. Office of Education].

Similarly, outside the government, educators have often

tended to by-pass those agencies that might be able to lend some coherence to national educational policy. And on individual campuses, it has become increasingly common for parts of the university to disregard the interests of the whole. We must pause, it seems to me, to consider whether or not the concept of the organized educational institution is valid. And if it is, we must make some effort to get it under control, to see to it that the activities of the institution get into some reasoned concept of its purposes and functions. Similarly, we must consider whether or not these institutions in the aggregate cannot similarly regain control of their common destiny in the realm of national policy.

I am not so naive as to believe that we can turn back the clock. Much of the fate of organized education is now in the hands of scattered agencies strongly buttressed by counterpart factions within education itself. These are legitimate and important arrangements, but if all we can look forward to is the further extension and expansion of such piecemeal, categorical relationships between the federal government and higher education, the future is not bright. It is well worth the effort, I think — and the effort involved is considerable — to work on developing a rational, comprehensive set of priorities for higher education that can be put before the nation as a basis for the formulation of a national policy.

But it will be necessary for higher education to show considerable restraint and to subject itself to some self-examination and self-discipline that have not been notably evident in the recent past. The *ad hoc*, opportunistic coloration of higher education's posture must be modified in the direction of longer-term and more rational policies. The qualities of restraint and self-discipline that we are so fond of encouraging in our students must increasingly characterize institutional relationships with the government. We must somehow re-enlist the leaderless troops who are storming Capitol Hill, and give them purpose and cohesion. If we fail to do so, I am afraid that the evident deficiencies of federal programs in education will only be compounded.

James Madison wrote in 1787 that "the most common and durable source of factions has been the various and unequal distribution of property. Those who hold and those who are without property have ever formed distinct interests in society... The *causes* of faction," he concluded, "cannot be removed, and that relief is only to be sought in the means of controlling its effects."

Factionalism in higher education cannot be removed. It is probably a normal, even inevitable, if not entirely attractive stage in our development. But responsible leadership in higher education will seek, as Madison did, "a well constructed union" to "break and control the violence of faction."

PART SIX

A SYSTEM IN DECAY 1965–1970

At the annual meeting of the American Association for the Advancement of Science in Chicago, during December, 1970, many of the oldest and most distinguished statesmen of American science joined to celebrate a quarter century of close partnership between the scientific community and the federal government. The mood was nostalgic and self-congratulatory. The system (some called it plural, but it had no name) that linked professional to national purpose had borne proud fruit: a military establishment that was universally feared if not uniformly successful, an industrial plant productive beyond dream or reason, and an academic science that acknowledged foreign peers in but few fields. The few imperfections were annoying enough, but quite familiar and, it was hoped, temporary: a slowing growth rate of the R&D budget, a handful of Luddites on campuses who sought to stop progress and the free exchange of knowledge, and a few backward congressmen who had yet to understand the virtues of basic research.

But there were others in attendance also at what they called the "meeting of the AAA$." An address by the President of the National Academy of Sciences, on the subject of "Obligations of the Scientific Community," was interrupted by an unscheduled call for scientists to "work constructively with the movement for revolutionary change." When the physicist Edward Teller arrived to take part in a program on the question "Is There a Generation Gap?" he was presented with the "Dr. Strangelove Award" for his role in helping to place science "in the service of warmakers." The election of Glenn Seaborg, chairman of the Atomic Energy Commission, as new president of the AAAS brought *charges that such interlocking directorates compromised the independence of the private scientific organization.*

Probably few scientists felt entirely comfortable with such theatrical gestures, but there was ample evidence that the serious purpose behind them found wide support. The structure of science built up over a quarter century of cold war and economic expansion had accomplished some things very well and had left other things not only undone but unrecognized. It was a special case of the general rediscovery of basic problems in American society after a generation of resting on the laurels of the Roosevelt era. Rachel Carson had shown that the conservation movement had not solved all environmental problems. Michael Harrington had reintroduced the public to The Other America *and helped inspire a War on Poverty. The 1954 Supreme Court decision in Brown v. Board of Education had triggered the realization that the problem of racism in America had not yet been solved. Caesar Chavez's grape strike dramatized the fact that too many of the country's workingmen still exercised little or no control over the conditions under which they lived and worked. Ralph Nader sparked a new consumerism with his revelations of corporate irresponsibility in the automobile industry. The nightmarish war in Vietnam called into question the dogma that "collective security" was the final and proper foreign policy for the nation.*

The consensus of the 1950's had been based in part upon the presumed reforms of the 1930's and 1940's. When these reforms proved something less than complete, eternal, and totally effective, a massive reappraisal was inevitable and bound to be painful. Science, which had benefited so markedly from the consensus, could hardly hope to remain aloof from the reappraisal. The outlines of the new science policy which must result from this reappraisal will depend to no little extent upon the direction taken by American society as a whole. Both issues are still in doubt.

I. The Military and American Science

◖ A. *In his autobiography the late Hungarian émigré scientist Theodore von Karman, of the California Institute of Technology and the Jet Propulsion Laboratory, wrote characteristically: "some scientists worry a great deal about associations with the military.... I have never regarded my union with the military as anything but natural. For me as a scientist the military has been the most comfortable group to deal with, and at present I have found it to be the one organization in this imperfect world that has the funds and spirit to advance science rapidly and successfully."*

On two of his points, at least, all observers would have to agree — the world is indeed imperfect, and the military has an unusual amount of funds and spirit. One example was provided not long after President Lyndon B. Johnson undertook to put his brand on the configuration of American science. After the shock of President Kennedy's assassination, one of the first problems faced by the new president was a growing political battle over the location of a new linear accelerator for which midwestern scientists had schemed for years. With perhaps some exaggeration, he later declared that he had "devoted more personal time to this problem than to any nondefense question that came up during the budget process."

The basic conflict arose from the desire of midwestern physicists to break the monopoly on high-energy physics held by the East and West coasts. Aided by such midwestern congressmen as Senators Hubert Humphrey of Minnesota and William Proxmire of Wisconsin, they demanded a larger share of the research pie that had for twenty years been divided in favor of a small number of eastern and western schools. The older policy of geographical distribution held a certain appeal to the President from Texas. In the following message to his Cabinet, he announced a new emphasis in federal research support. Lyndon B. Johnson, "Statement of the President to the Cabinet on Strengthening the Academic Capability for Science Throughout the Nation," from the Office of the White House Press Secretary, September 14, 1965.]

Throughout the postwar years, it has been my abiding and actively supported conviction that the policies of this nation in support of the advance of science would have a decisive role in determining the extent to which we fulfill our potential as a nation — and a free society.

On occasion, during these years, there have appeared attitudes almost medieval in their myopia toward the meaning and promise of the growth of human knowledge. Happily, these attitudes have not prevailed and our national policies have been guided by reason, light, and faith in the future of man. As a result, American science today leads the world — free, unfettered, and devoted to the ends of bettering the condition of man in every land.

I say this, by way of preface, because I am proud of the part I have been privileged to play — in the Congress and as Vice President — in opening the doors through which we have moved to some of our most significant scientific gains. Now, in this office, I am determined that we shall marshal our resources and our wisdom to the fullest to assure the continuing strength and leadership of American science and to apply the information yielded by its inquiry to the problems which confront our society and our purposes in the world.

Our policies and attitudes in regard to science cannot satisfactorily be related solely to achievement of goals and ends we set for our research. Our vision in this regard is limited at best. We must, I believe, devote ourselves purposefully to developing and diffusing — throughout the nation — a strong and solid scientific capability, especially in our many centers of advanced education. Our future must rest upon diversity of inquiry as well as the universality of capability.

This is very much a concern and a responsibility of the Federal Government and all the Departments and Agencies of the Executive Branch.

Today the Federal Government is spending $15 billion annually on research and development activities. Nine percent of this — $1.3 billion — is being spent in our universities on research grants and contracts. Additional sums are spent for educational purposes such as fellowship or training grants and the programs provided by the Higher Education Facilities Act or the National Defense Education Act.

The impact of these Federal funds is significant. They account for about two-thirds of the total research expenditures of colleges and universities. The manner in which such funds are spent clearly has a most important effect upon advanced education in this country and upon the future of our nation's universities.

Almost all of the Federal research money is provided to produce results that are needed now and in the future to achieve our many national goals in health, in defense, in space, in agriculture and so on. Of the total provided to universities, 34 percent comes from the National Institutes of Health, 23 percent from the Department of Defense, 9 percent from NASA, 6 percent from the AEC, and 4 percent from Agriculture. Only 13 percent is provided by the National Science Foundation — the only agency which supports science and science education as such.

The purpose of the new policy statement I am issuing today is to insure that our programs for Federal support of research in colleges and universities contribute more to the long run strengthening of the universities and colleges so that these institutions can best serve the nation in the years ahead.

At present, one-half of the Federal expenditures for research go to 20 major institutions, most of which were strong before the advent of Federal research funds. During the period of increasing Federal support since World War II, the number of institutions carrying out research and providing advanced education has grown impressively. Strong centers have developed in areas which were previously not well served. It is a particular purpose of this policy to accelerate this beneficial trend since the funds are still concentrated in too few institutions in too few areas of the country. We want to find excellence and build it up wherever it is found so that creative centers of excellence may grow in every part of the nation.

Under this policy more support will be provided under terms which give the university and the investigator wider scope for inquiry, as contrasted with highly specific, narrowly defined projects. These and many more actions will increase the capacity of our universities to produce well-trained scientists and to serve as a source of the ideas on which our national welfare depends.

By adopting this policy, I am asking each agency and department with major research responsibilities to reexamine its practices in the financing of research. I want to be sure that, consistent with agency missions and objectives, all practical measures are taken to strengthen the institutions where research now goes on, and to help additional institutions to become more effective centers for teaching and research.

◀ *B. President Johnson's statement to his Cabinet on "Strengthening the Academic Capability for Science Throughout the Nation" had been preceded by one day by a similar "Memorandum to the Heads of Departments and Agencies" in which he spelled out their responsibilities for the new policy. With responsibility, of course, went opportunity, and the Department of Defense was not laggard about implementing the presidential directive. Called Project THEMIS, the new DOD program sought to extend military funding to campuses not yet receiving large amounts of Pentagon funds. The following description of Project THEMIS is taken from* Department of Defense, Project THEMIS *(Washington: Office of the Director of Defense Research and Engineering, November 1967), pp. iii–iv, 1–3.]*

Through Project THEMIS, the Department of Defense intends to meet part of its long-term research needs, strengthen more of the nation's universities, increase the number of institutions performing research of high quality and achieve a wider geographic distribution of research funds, and thus enhance the United States' academic capability in science and technology. This project was established in response to President Johnson's request that each Federal agency help to develop new centers of excellence in areas relevant to its goals....

The Department of Defense has compelling reasons to achieve these objectives. Clearly, the history of the last 30 years demonstrates that our national security depends upon the quality and exploitation of our research. Equally important, many notable scientific and technological achievements have emerged in the past from university research sponsored by the Department of Defense.

The Department is both a producer and a consumer of research results in many fields of science and technology. Accordingly, we have a vital stake in the nation's resources of scientific talent and ideas. We believe that opportunities to participate in research should be available on a still broader geographic basis.

Project THEMIS is intended to provide new opportunities for defense-related research programs at universities that are not now heavily engaged in research for the Federal Government. The step-funding plan permits universities to make commitments up to 3 years in advance. Each new university program should present a stimulating challenge to faculty and students and, at the same time, contribute to basic knowledge needed for solving problems in national defense.

We believe Project THEMIS will become part of a growing national program of research that will further strengthen and mature the capabilities of our academic institutions. . . .

The general objective of Project THEMIS is to further strengthen the scientific and engineering capabilities of selected academic institutions throughout the country, enabling a larger' number to carry out high-quality research in areas related to national defense problems.

Because of the increasing need for knowledge in a great number of scientific disciplines and technological areas, the Department of Defense will:

(1) Establish university-administered programs in specialized areas relevant to the Defense mission. These programs should develop the potential of groups and individuals, including young faculty members, for research of high quality leading to results of significant value to Defense agencies and departments.

(2) Encourage cooperative programs in which universities may use Government research facilities, when available; and facilitate the two-way flow of scientific information in fields of mutual interest between participants in the university programs and personnel of the in-house Defense laboratories.

(3) Continue to utilize the universities' technical management as the means of improving organizational cohesiveness by bringing together, at the level of a local program manager, the authority and responsibility for local management of the research program.

Project THEMIS is designed to stimulate and provide initial support for a research effort. It is anticipated that, as a THEMIS research activity gains a higher degree of competence, it will become increasingly active in the regular research programs of the DOD and other agencies.

It is intended that all THEMIS research be unclassified so that the results may be published openly....

   ❡ *C. The growing dependence of academic researchers upon Pentagon subsidy — as represented by such programs as Project THEMIS — caused concern within both the government and the scientific community. While accepting the need of the Department of Defense for a large amount of mission-oriented research and development, Senator Mike Mansfield (D-Mont.) took the lead in attempting to cut the military's assumption of responsibility for supporting basic research and higher education. Author of the controversial Mansfield Amendment, the Senator here calls for "Rechanneling the Public Resources for Basic Science Through the Civilian Agencies: A New Goal for National Science Policy,"* National Science Policy: H. Con. Res. 666. *Hearings before the Subcommittee on Science, Research, and Development of the Committee on Science and Astronautics, U.S. House of Representatives, 91st Cong., 2 sess., 1970, pp. 604–609.*]

I have been asked to comment on the government's role regarding the support of research. I appreciate this invitation by the Chairman of the Subcommittee on Science, Research, and Development. Specifically, I suppose the question really is whether adequate government support of science can be carried on if there is a permanent shift away from the role of the military in the conduct of research. What must be considered is the relationship of the Department of Defense and other mission agencies to the matter of research; what part research plays in their overall functions and as a related matter, whether strong ties should be continued between the Pentagon and our universities. The answer to these questions by and large will determine this nation's entire science policy for the years ahead.

At the outset I should say that the quality of life on earth tomorrow will be determined in large part by the measure of the scientific research undertaken today. There is thus a significant public responsibility to sponsor research in the various scientific disciplines and to keep the way clear to follow up on new discoveries. Determining the emphasis, however, is a most delicate responsibility. To a greater extent the emphasis is determined by the size of the resource devoted to the various disciplines.

Since the end of World War II, the government's contribution to research, development, and the supporting facilities has reached nearly $200 billion. Where and by whom that money was spent has determined not only the science policy of this nation but the entire emphasis in science education and training. During this time well over half of the government's contribution to science has been channeled through the Department of Defense. It must be clearly understood that most of this money purchased research of the highest quality. However, not nearly so clear is the rationale that dictated that the Department of Defense should be the principal sponsoring agency for much of this vital research.

For the past 25 years the Pentagon has sponsored research in almost every scientific discipline imaginable. From the most esoteric examinations of ornithology to the study of broad social movements in foreign countries, the Pentagon has run the gamut in its research endeavors. By necessity, therefore, the Pentagon assumed a significant role in determining the nation's science policy. The desirability of such a large role for this mission agency is the basic issue confronting us.

It is not difficult to understand how we got where we are today. The phenomenon of channeling so much of our research money through the Defense Department developed over the years not only from normal bureaucratic urges to grow but because the science community and the Congress acquiesced in that growth. So the question is not how we got here. It is why. To put it simply: Why should the Defense Department be the principal government agency through which is funded the federal research that has no apparent relationship to the security needs of this nation?

To reply by saying that the research community has found that funds simply were more readily available at the Defense Department rather than at other civilian agencies states a fact. But it is not an answer. Nor is it sufficient to say that Pentagon requests for funds receive less Congressional scrutiny than those requested by nonmilitary agencies. Too often in the past the prevailing attitude has been expressed by the question: Are we giving you enough? Perhaps it should have been: Why do you need so much? In part the historical answer lies in the fact that the cloak of national security lined with the international threat of communism simply prevented a close scrutiny of Defense requests including requests for research and development. In part, the answer is that Defense spending requests became so large that even billions for research and development seemed dwarfed. As a result the scientific community came to rely upon the immunity of Defense funding from close scrutiny and occasional budgeting squeezes. For years Defense funding provided a very stable source of research money. It was the easiest path for the research community to follow.

It wasn't long before many of the most able members of the science community gravitated to this source of funds. It became apparent, too, that although only a relatively small fraction of the federal research dollar was spent on university campuses, that money was very important to those universities in maintaining their status. The salaries paid by the research grant paid in effect the salary of the faculty member and a good share of the institution's overhead as well. The universities were not prepared to accept direct subsidies for fear of losing their autonomy — but they were apparently prepared to accept such a dependence indirectly with no questions asked.

Two years ago during Senate debate on the Defense appropriations bill for fiscal year 1969, I offered an amendment which would have limited the payment of indirect costs for a research grant or project to 25 percent of the direct costs. From my preparation for this measure and subsequent debate, I saw the grave financial difficulties faced by our universities today and noted the disturbingly heavy dependence of virtually all of our leading universities upon subsidy via indirect costs. A total of 620 academic institutions in fiscal year 1968 received federal support for research and development totalling $1.4 billion. Of this the Department of Defense accounted for $243 million and the National Science Foundation, $212 million. This money largely benefited only a few institutions. The top 100 accounted for 87 percent, or $1.2 billion.

Even under the limitation of my amendment, these top 100 would have received $300 million for indirect costs; money that the individual scientists would never see but which would go into general university funds. Of this, in turn, 20 percent would have come from the military appropriations. And since overhead charges by many institutions were higher than the 25 percent limit I proposed, the Defense Department in 1968 was supplying more than $60 million to the indirect cost accounts of leading universities. Under these circumstances, I concluded that the situation was most unhealthy. To better gauge the ramifications of the federal subsidy to universities through overhead payments, I wrote to Philip Handler, then Chairman of the National Science Board and now President of the National Academy of Sciences. In a frank reply, he pointed out that of $1,671 million of federal funds for research at universities for fiscal year 1967, only about $426 million were utilized to support research in the most immediate sense. The remainder found its way into institutional funds and departmental funds.

Subsequently the National Science Board proposed to the President that this situation of a hidden and unhealthy subsidy be corrected through grants to the universities so that future proposals for research would need cover only the direct and out-of-pocket costs of the work. I hope that the silence which greeted this recommendation within the Executive Branch will not be permanent and that Congress will assess its practicability as a way to establish more honest relations between the universities and the agencies of the federal government that fund on-campus research and higher education.

A contributing reason for the expansion of defense interests into almost each imaginable field of research in my opinion is the past and present inadequate information about what kind of research is being done by whom and where.

It has often occurred to me, and to other Members of Congress, that because many federal departments and agencies fund so many research projects, there is a real possibility of overlap and duplication simply because "the word" does not pass between federal research administrators. Note that I am not speaking of research that one scientist deliberately carries out to confirm or refute the discovery of another, for this is an essential part of the scientific process. Rather, I have been and am still concerned with the probability that needless and unwitting duplication of work occurs which could be minimized if scientists and administrators had a current, reliable, and complete source of information about who is doing what research with federal funds. So I asked the agencies to supply me with a list of current research projects. Having little success with the direct request, I arranged for the Bureau of the Budget to ask the agencies to comply.

When all of the replies finally trickled in, it was evident that whatever the agency project information systems may be, they are simply incapable of readily providing summary information on research. Eight departments and agencies finally responded. Five separate replies were sent by Defense and six by the Department of Health, Education, and Welfare, bringing the total number of project information readouts to 17. Eight replies appeared to be printouts of computer systems, with the rest manually prepared. Two defense agencies submitted computer products and three manual ones. Later it was reported to me informally that project information had been taken from the computer-based systems, edited, and put back in before being printed out for transmittal. Three of the agencies of HEW and four other agencies used the science classification system specified by the Bureau of the Budget in its Circular A-46. The remainder employed their own systems for identifying fields of science. The system used by the National Science Foundation, presumably the lead agency for federal information on science and technology, was different from that specified by the Bureau of the Budget.

Parenthetically, considering the many computers and elaborate information systems of government agencies, this simple request should not have produced the administrative convulsions that it did. The administrative entanglement indicated to me that each department goes its own way in research with little attention to that funded by others. There simply does not exist a system capable of quickly and easily informing research administrators in one department of what research of potential interest or use to them is currently funded by another federal agency. While coffee-break exchanges among scientists have their value, they are not an adequate substitute. It is well over a year since I inquired into this matter. Yet the Office of Science and Technology has not decided what current information about research projects should be collected, who should do the collecting, how it should be collected, and who can have access to it. Perhaps we need someone to tackle this issue with the vigor of past efforts when the related question of cataloging and making available the results of research already done was exhaustively considered. Perhaps the reorganized Office of Management and Budget can give this a priority among its management functions.

My experience in trying to get current information on research confirmed yet again my observation that bureaucracies must often be kept after to obtain improvements in the administration of government-funded research. These improvements are all the more necessary in a time when the dominant question has changed from: "What can we spend our increasing research appropriations on?" to "How can we best spend the available appropriations for research?"

In this connection, to overcome the inertia, to get out of comfortable, well-worn ruts sometimes require heroic measures.

It was during the Senate's appropriation hearings in 1968 that I asked Dr. Foster of the Defense Department about duplication of research and about the relation of Defense-sponsored research, particularly its basic research, to that of other agencies. It was abundantly clear in his response that the Pentagon then believed all fields of science and technology were open to it, that it saw no inconsistency in funding basic research in fields already funded by civil agencies, and that all research projects it sponsored were somehow relevant to Defense needs. The Defense Department was adamant in its position that it must continue the full spectrum of research then being undertaken, even though by definition the outcome of much such research can neither be predicted nor its possible relevance to military science known. This testimony reinforced the conviction that research funded by the military appropriations had built up an enormous momentum, and that only the most forceful efforts by Congress could effect change in the direction of rechanneling federal responsibility for the funding of basic research. At the time, it seemed clear that there was not a national policy that viewed the nation's long-term interests. What to do about it was another question.

During the floor debate on the military authorization bill (PL 91-121) for fiscal year 1970, I added a rider which appeared as Section 203. It reads as follows: "None of the funds authorized to be appropriated by this Act may be used to carry out any research project or study unless such project or study has a direct or apparent relationship to a specific military function or operations."

That provision became law and the same provision now appears as Section 204 of the military authorization bill reported to the Senate for fiscal year 1971, but does not appear in the bill reported in the House.

I believe Section 203 is a necessary and practicable step towards the goal of reducing the heavy dependence of American science that has built up since the early 1950's. Properly and imaginatively administered, it can also lead to a strenthening and a rebuilding of the foundation for the future of much of American science.

343

The intent of the provision is clear. It is a mandate to reduce the research community's dependence on the Defense Department when it appears that the investigation under consideration could be sponsored more reasonably by a civilian agency. After all, the National Science Foundation was created by Congress back in 1950 specifically to channel federal funds into basic research. Since its creation, it has been the orphan child of the federal government's science policy. Since 1955 NSF has been given $2 billion to sponsor basic research. During this same period, Pentagon spending has been $3 billion on this same type of research; it has spent 50 percent more for the fundamental investigations — in addition to the many billions on advanced research and development of specific military needs — than has the agency set up for this sole purpose.

The addition of Section 203 to the military authorization law thus sought to set in motion a realignment. The language was intentionally imprecise in an effort to afford the Executive Branch an opportunity to start a process that would lead to the transfer of resources from the Defense Department to the civilian agencies — primarily to the National Science Foundation.

Clearly, Congress does not exist to operate the daily workings of the Executive. By law, however, Congress does have a responsibility, together with the President, to establish broad policies. Congress has a right to assume that policies so established will be followed. Much progress has already been made since Section 203 became law in the face of the resistance that has lingered in some quarters. The authorization for NSF funding for this coming fiscal year has been increased by about $75 million over last year. By comparison, this year the Defense Department's share of basic research funds will be $50 million less than that of the National Science Foundation.

By no means, however, does Section 203 intend to cut off the Defense Department from research that it needs. It is neither anti-military nor anti-research. Whether the language chosen is interpreted strictly or loosely, it is hoped that the ultimate result of this whole endeavor will be a continued high level of basic research funding by the federal government. Hopefully, we will see in the near future that the civilian agencies under the leadership of the National Science Foundation will develop as the primary source for these research funds. The responsibility of the civilian agencies to fund an appropriate share of basic research is in no way diminished by Section 203.

The Pentagon will continue to have a responsibility for research — even basic research, one that allows those entrusted with military defense to maintain a full and necessary exchange with the researchers at the frontiers of science. The role of the Defense Department in sponsoring basic research, however, is intended to be incidental rather than predominant.

Turning now to the DOD response to Section 203, I believe that the review of research by DOD could have benefited from guidance and criteria issued by its top management. That did not happen. Instead, all that the Defense Department did was to send a memorandum to its constituent agencies informing them of Section 203 and telling them to comply.

When I inquired of DOD about their follow-through on this provision, Deputy Secretary of Defense Packard replied in part that the Department had contacted the National Academy of Sciences and invited them to consider carrying out an examination of all projects which might be affected. I thought this a constructive idea and wrote to Dr. Handler on December 5, 1969, to support this participation by the Academy. To my disappointment, Dr. Handler replied on December 12 that he must decline to involve the National Academy of Sciences directly in the review. He did volunteer to offer the Academy for any followup review. More important, he agreed it would be useful for the Academy to do two things. First, to formulate principles which might guide the administration of Section 203. Second, to undertake a projection of the implications and consequences of Section 203 with respect to the future of federal research policy and the national welfare. While I did not ask the Academy to do so then, experience with Section 203 indicates that it should do so now.

To date, there have been differences in application within the Department of Defense. On the one hand, for example, the Advanced Research Projects Agency asserts that none of its projects fail the test of Section 203, even though the General Accounting Office has singled out some as questionable in terms of this legislation and as more properly supportable by the State Department than by military appropriations. On the other hand, the Department of the Air Force has seized upon Section 203 to terminate research funded from appropriations prior to fiscal year 1970, with the excuse that they were carrying out the "Mansfield" philosophy.

Of the 6,600 research projects that were reviewed, 220 were

found affected by Section 203 which involved fiscal year 1970 funds totalling $8.8 million. This is about 4 percent of the $223 million that DOD obligated during this fiscal year for research at colleges and universities, and less than 1 percent of the $1,295 million of federal funds for university research and development estimated by the Bureau of the Budget for fiscal year 1970.

By comparison, the general tightening of the Defense research budget for fiscal year 1970 caused a reduction of $64 million, notwithstanding Section 203.

Recently, the Secretary of the Air Force testified that approximately 7 percent of the research projects, representing 3 percent of the Air Force research program, failed to pass Section 203. In comparison, tightening funds required a cut of over 10 percent.

Of course, Section 203 goes beyond the 220 projects immediately affected. Research projects funded from prior years' funds that do not meet the test of this legislation will be affected as they come up for renewal. The Comptroller General was unable to provide us with an estimate of the number of projects in this category or their total funding. Nonetheless, in my judgment, such projects should continue to their normal expiration, which will provide time for coordinated review by the Department of Defense with the civil agencies and for leadership and initiatives from the Office of Science and Technology. Despite its limited reaction to date, I still look to the Office of Science and Technology to provide the leadership necessary so that research affected by Section 203 which should be continued in the national interest will have a fair chance at the available basic research funds.

All that is required under Section 203 is relevance, which is not a dirty word as some critics of the Section sometimes seem to suggest. Relevance does not preclude agencies from funding basic research. Section 203 does not forbid the Defense Department from funding any and all research at colleges and universities. Had that been our purpose, we would have so written this legislation. What Section 203 does is to begin to close out a second and a backdoor National Science Foundation which has grown up in the Department of Defense.

It seems to me that the Defense Department can readily identify and justify many fields of fundamental research about which enough is known to judge their relevance to defense needs now and in the foreseeable future. Research funded in such fields as a result of announcement and publication of such DOD interests should produce proposals for research that would permit scientists to explore aspects of science which add to understanding in fields reasonably related to Defense needs.

The idea of relevance is not new. I should think that the Science Advisor to the President would be well acquainted with the following statements that support the principle of relevance.

First. "The Foundation shall be increasingly responsible for providing support by the federal government for general-purpose research through contracts and grants. The conduct and support by other federal agencies of basic research *in areas which are closely related to their missions* is recognizable as important and desirable, especially in response to current national needs, and shall continue."

Second. "Mission-oriented governmental agencies do and should support much long-range basic research, information from which is calculated *to have a direct bearing on some aspect* of their mission. . . . All mission-oriented agencies need to be in close contact with the best and most advanced research which can apply to their problems."

The first is from President Eisenhower's Executive Order No. 10521 of March 15, 1954, on scientific research. This order still stands. It was not rescinded by President Kennedy, by President Johnson, or by President Nixon. The second comes from the recent advice to the President by his Task Force on Science Policy.

Section 203 opened to the Administration a unique opportunity to set in motion a rebalancing of the responsibilities of federal agencies for the funding of basic research. The section became law on November 19, 1969. Yet the budget for fiscal year 1971 does not indicate that this opportunity has been taken. There is no indication of a shift of basic research unrelated to defense needs to the National Science Foundation or other agencies and, at the same time, a corresponding reduction in Defense funding.

In short, timely arrangements have not been made for orderly decisions pursuant to Section 203. I wrote last fall to the Director of the Budget Bureau and to the Cabinet officers of Departments and other agencies concerned on that point. The letters have had no appreciable effect. The Research Management Advisory Panel to your Subcommittee recommended that the Section be administered so as to produce an orderly shift in sources of research support. What has happened to that recommendation? In the meantime, where is the contribution of the interdepartmental system for coordination in research to which reference is always made when Congress starts to talk about improving the administration of federal appropriations for research? What has it done?

All that is heard are requests for the abolition of Section 203. Indeed, there seems to be almost a willingness to risk the wreck of the whole DOD basic research program rather than take an innovative and imaginative response to the law. Again, however, what may be involved is the built-in inertia of bureaucracy.

To carry out the intent of Section 203 will require new ventures in interagency coordination. That is the responsibility of the reorganized Bureau of the Budget and the Office of Science and Technology under the President. Thus far, unfortunately, the White House science office apparently sustains the rigid opposition of the agencies to Section 203. That is most unfortunate because if there are to be improvements in coordination and a shift in the emphasis of federal policy with regard to support of basic research, it is going to take a joint effort by the President and the Congress.

To sum it up: We are in dire need of a new national policy on the federal role in science. Whether technological progress depends upon basic research is no longer an issue. That was agreed upon years ago; and I am sure it is the conviction of Congress that maintenance and hopefully growth in scientific activities are essential to the public welfare and the nation's future. But the policies of the 1950's and 1960's are not suitable for the already perplexing 1970's. Too much is at stake to depend upon fortune, upon luck, upon happenstance. Our policies must be soundly and thoughtfully conceived and guided.

If the Executive Branch is thinking about policy in these terms, no evidence of it has yet appeared in the public press despite recent inputs from the President's Task Force on Science Policy and the National Goals research staff.

I hope we can look to the scientific community for advice. Yet I recall that this community speaking through the National Academy of Sciences in 1965 was unable to answer the questions on how much money should be spent for research and how it should be divided up.

Recognizing the risk of oversimplifying, it would be my

judgment that we can no longer rely for guidance upon an un-coordinated, unplanned collection of laws, orders, statements, understandings, and traditions. These all have their place. But we must now bring them together, which is what the inquiry of the Subcommittee is all about. I would hope that the Sub-committee on Science, Research, and Development will continue its role of Congressional leadership and stimulate enough in-terest so that our leaders of government and science will sit down together and work out the principal outline and content of the kind of policy that is needed. It is up to Congress to assert its long-neglected responsibility and set forth a national policy for science. It is long overdue.

⟨ *D. In the face of mounting criticism of its research policies, the Department of Defense has chosen to emphasize our international competition with the Soviet Union and to see attacks upon Pentagon science as only a special example of a general disenchantment with science and technology. The following testimony was given by Dr. John S. Foster, Jr., Director of Defense Research and Engineering.* National Science Policy. H. Con. Res. 666. *Hearings before the Subcommittee on Science, Research, and Development of the Committee on Science and Astronautics, U.S. House of Representatives, 91st Cong., 2 sess., 1970, pp. 553–559.*⟩

Today science and technology are under heavy attack, yet our national welfare is strongly dependent on our scientific and technological capabilities. In essence:

First-rate science and technology are vital ingredients to our national security. The United States simply cannot risk a condi-tion of military technological inferiority in today's world.

Maintenance of economic growth, provision of increased per capita income, and alleviation of personal and social ills will require a large measure of contribution from science and tech-nology.

Science and technology will be a necessary part of our efforts to improve the quality of our environment.

The competitive position of the United States in world trade is equally dependent on U.S. science and technology.

Despite these clear needs, we are reducing our national support of research and development. . . .

In the past 4 years our Federal funding of research has remained constant in absolute dollars, which represents an actual decline in effort of 20 to 25 percent. The estimated national expenditure for research and development in 1970 is almost $1 billion less than it was in 1968 — a decline in effort of at least 15 percent, if one accounts for inflation.

While it is important to understand these trends, it is equally instructive to see what other nations are doing. The nation closest to the United States in industrial and technological capability is the U.S.S.R. The comparative investment in R&D of the two countries for the past 15 years is shown below.

Now, the numbers given in this table are the total national investments, as we understand them, in each country. So it would include Federal support, industrial support, and so on.

NATIONAL R&D INVESTMENT
[in billions of 1966 dollars]

	1955	1960	1965	1968	1970 (estimate)
United States	5.1	13.7	20.6	25.4	24.6
U.S.S.R.	3.5	7.8	13.9	17.7	21.3

Projection of these trends shows that the U.S.S.R. will surpass the United States in research and development effort within the next few years.

In the area of R&D related to defense, the Soviets have already gone ahead. They are expected to spend some $16 to $17 billion this year, compared to our $13 to $14 billion including the DOD, AEC, and NASA budgets.

The U.S.S.R., however, is not the only nation challenging our technological and industrial leadership. Both West Germany and Japan have shown remarkable growth and have attained economies with gross national products of $150 and $200 billion, respectively, passing both the United Kingdom and France.

Japan may well become the next superpower. It has already attained first place in shipbuilding, radio sets, cameras, transistorized TV's, and commercial motor vehicles, and ranks second or third in at least 10 other industrial sectors.

Over the past 5 years its economy has grown at an annual rate of 12 to 14 percent, and governmental policies toward R&D, education, and business seem intelligently directed toward facilitating such growth. The Japanese expect to reach a GNP of $1.5

trillion by the end of the century, and some observers believe it may reach a figure two or three times that size.

Mr. Chairman, I have taken some time to outline the competition that the United States faces in both military and industrial sectors because I believe it to be a central issue in the deliberations of all who consider our policies on science and education.

Our national security and our industrial leadership are at stake. Both demand very great scientific and technological capability, and this capability is directly dependent on the wisdom of the policies we establish to guide our educational and scientific endeavors and the financial support we give them.

Let me turn now to the important and perceptive questions you posed in your letter asking me to appear before this subcommittee.

There are three questions that are related and can best be discussed together. You have asked:

Can we make a determination as to whether and how government science support can be carried on if there is a broad shift away from traditional military research?

To what extent can NSF shoulder the additional burden for basic research as military support lessens, as the rise of social sciences increases, as environmental problems become greater and the needs for multidisciplinary research increase?

How do we fulfill DOD's continuing need for research which bears on its critical mission?

In answer to these questions, Mr. Chairman, my first point is that military research and development is determined by the activities of potential adversaries and opportunities in science and technology. We must do that R&D which needs to be done. We must be led by the requirements of national security, and this is a dynamic, changing situation. It cannot be met by a static and rigid structure of organization and policy.

The second point is that we must do the necessary R&D as efficiently and effectively as possible. To this end, we turn to four classes of performers, each having unique capabilities for certain types of problems. They are the universities, the Federal contract research centers, the DOD in-house laboratories, and industry.

The FCRC's provide a group of highly skilled and knowledgeable analysts who are impartial because they have no ties to industrial or military organizations, who examine the many facets of particular problems, especially in areas where continuity of effort is desirable.

The DOD laboratories are used to turn concepts into prototypes, to test the worth of an idea. Being part of the military system, they also play an important role in coupling technological opportunities to military needs. The special capability of industry is to bring a wide array of talent to bear on the design, development, and production of complex equipment.

These three groups are capable and important, but they do not fulfill the role of university research in national defense. The DOD must continually push at the frontiers of science and technology in order to prevent technological surprise. The problems encountered are very tough, and they can be solved only by the most capable, creative, and highly trained scientists. These people are most often found in universities, and it is only by supporting university research that we can promptly obtain the contributions from scientists working in areas relevant to national security.

Because they become informed and knowledgeable about national defense problems, these university scientists form a reservoir of consultants that is invaluable to the DOD in providing advice on especially important defense problems and in times of national crises.

The Nation benefits additionally because this group of informed scientists is available to comment on important policy questions. Over the years, our public discussions and debates on topics such as nuclear weapons, missiles, ABM's, and others have been greatly facilitated by the information contributed by knowledgeable academic scientists.

These advantages would be lost and our national security seriously weakened if DOD support of university research were significantly curtailed. It has been suggested that this be done and that defense research be transferred to the National Science Foundation. I believe that such an attempt would make the situation worse. The reason is that one of the most difficult tasks in research management is to couple research to applied research and development, but it is essential that this be done. The introduction of a third party into the coupling process would lead to great inefficiency and confusion.

You have also asked: "How can support for basic research

be integrated with applied research and made an integral part of policy decisionmaking?"

To answer this question, I would first recall that there are two reasons for doing research. The first is to widen the frontiers of our knowledge. Our society supports research as well as education because it believes that knowledge is better than ignorance. For example, the knowledge of the true source of infectious diseases has relieved us from the superstition that disease was caused by demons and ill spirits.

The second reason for doing research is to gain knowledge in order to accomplish a specific mission such as the protection of health. Knowledge of the process of infectious disease has enabled us to develop vaccines for their prevention and antibiotics for their cure. Both basic and applied research are necessary if our scientific efforts are to flourish and yield dividends for our society.

The integration of basic and applied research is the coupling problem to which I referred earlier. It is a difficult problem, but not impossible to solve. If one has a precise goal, the coupling can be immediate. If one is doing research to advance knowledge, the detailed coupling may come at a later time when some newly felt need puts the previous research in a new perspective.

Coupling can be fostered by arranging easy and frequent communication between the basic and applied groups, by placing them in the same overall organization so that they operate with the same general set of goals and priorities, and by imbuing them with a sense of urgency. This urgency is most particularly felt in mission agencies faced with a particular challenge.

For example, when drug-resistant malaria became a problem for our forces in Vietnam, the Army Medical Department initiated an intensive program to develop a new therapeutic drug. This program was multidisciplinary, ranged from the most basic aspects of cellular biology to applied clinical programs, and was performed by universities, in-house laboratories, and industry.

There was never any problem of coupling — all groups engaged in the work fully understood both the goal and the urgent need to attain it, and results from one group were quickly used by others. In 3 years this program reduced the malarial attack rate from 80 in 1,000 to 30 in 1,000, and shortened the average hospital stay from 30 to 17 days. It prevented some

20,000 cases of malaria and saved almost 1,500 man-years of time and $30 million.

Mr. Chairman, from this example, and there are many others, you see that we do integrate basic research and applied research, and such integration is part of our decisionmaking process.

Another inquiry you made was: "How can we synthesize knowledge gained from the space program with the contemporary social needs?"

This is being done, but the full impact is yet to be felt. Research and technology have always been attracted to areas of low productivity. They have generally been able to increase productivity and raise efficiency. The DOD has for many years been part of this process. For example:

The DOD is performing research on construction of family housing because we can save substantial sums of money if we can build and maintain military housing at less cost.

The DOD contributes significantly to the national meteorological capability.

Almost every commercial airplane flying today had a military predecessor.

Radar techniques developed by the DOD are the basis for commercial air traffic control.

We are trying to apply technology to reduce the spiraling costs of providing health care for military personnel. And there are other examples, involving lasers, microminiaturization, and the use of large computers, and so on.

You also asked: "How far should the government support the joining of research with higher education?"

Some have said that Federal support of research in universities should be stopped because it takes the faculty away from the students. This misinterprets the process of graduate education in science, for in this area research and education are inseparable.

For several decades the excellence of our science and technology has stemmed from the close association of individual faculty members and very small groups of graduate students, creatively working as on-campus research teams. The many hours outside the classroom spent on research serve as an intensive apprenticeship for those who wish to make research their career. This is not just an American educational method — it is the method used throughout the world for graduate education in science.

It has more than merely traditional value. It supplies funds not only for the support of individual graduate students but also for adequate laboratories and instruments. Most important, it introduces the graduate student to tough, real-world problems, which he can perceive as worthy of the highest effort. It is through this process that we educate future scientists and engineers in the background and problems of our Nation, and thus assure a supply of knowledgeable people to tackle future problems.

Mr. Chairman, I have described the process of research and graduate education, and I believe that the Government should not take steps that might divide that process.

You also posed a particularly difficult question: "Should there be new organization and administration of the Federal science activities in the Executive Branch?"

There have been suggestions that we create a large science department at cabinet level. Proponents of such a plan point out that science would be better served by representation in the cabinet, that better integration of science activities could be achieved and duplication avoided, and that the various sciences could be supported more in accord with their needs than is true under our present system.

It seems to me that these proposed benefits all relate to the welfare of science. Perhaps it would be best for us to follow this course, but I believe our judgment should be based on a higher criterion — the welfare of our Nation and its people. I believe that support of research by mission agencies is essential if they are to carry out their respective responsibilities and provide the expected benefits to the citizens whose taxes they spend.

It seems to me that, in the long run, science can attract and justify continued Federal funding only when the representatives of the people believe that there is good cause for this investment in preference to other pressing needs for funds.

The coupling of most science support with mission agencies produces a public understanding that is preciously necessary in a democratic system. It establishes a reason for the expenditure and an expectation of future benefits. I believe there is a continuing need for such demonstration of the relevance of research to the needs of society in the years ahead— particularly now that science and technology have become large consumers of the tax dollar.

It seems to me that the centralization of science could increase the difficulty of coupling and make the transfer of knowledge from basic research to the solution of societal problems more difficult.

If this country did not have a large and capable effort in science and technology, then, in order to galvanize ourselves into action, it might be appropriate to establish a Cabinet-level office. A similar process was followed to initiate our space program, and NASA was established. It does not seem to me, however, that today there is a need to do this for our whole science and technology effort. We already have the best in the world. We need only to value it and maintain our position.

You also asked: "How can we supply proper mechanisms for technology assessment?"

Of course, we must do that which is necessary and within our capabilities to determine and assess hazards, and preclude them or reduce their impact. However, my experience warns me that there is clear need for caution. Today science is being stifled by ever-increasing efforts to control and regulate it.

We have an example in the Department of Defense. In our efforts to reduce costs and improve the reliability of hardware, we instituted programs in such areas as value engineering, reliability engineering, cost consciousness, and so on. The costs to run these programs absorbed funds; the additional reviews and demands for data and reports took scientists and engineers away from productive work; and, on balance, the way we implemented these programs did more harm than good. We are attempting to redress this situation. Good scientists and engineers will constantly seek to design and build improved, more reliable and less costly products whether or not such programs as value engineering exist.

Consequently, I fear that programs of technological assessment would result in another large staff of reviewers, not engaged in productive effort, but hampering the work of those who are.

These points are made as a general caution, Mr. Chairman. Nothing I have said is intended to be critical of your attempts to provide the legislative branch with a source of independent scientific advice and information. In particular, I do not want you to think I have any objection to your bill, H.R. 18469, for I have none.

Finally, you raised the question: "Must there be a redefinition of the mission of universities during the 1970's?"

Let me briefly summarize the DOD's position with respect to the university community.

First, our Nation needs excellence in research, and it is frequently found at universities. This resource should be preserved.

Second, freedom of choice is a cardinal principle of our democracy, and must be guaranteed — in research and education — for both individuals and institutions.

Third, Federal agencies should support research based on the Nation's needs, on the one hand, and technical opportunities, on the other.

Fourth, the research that supports our Federal missions is a primary form of public service open to universities and is vital to our national welfare.

It is my own belief that there is no need to redefine the missions of our universities. They educate our young, advance the state of man's knowledge, and provide a source of criticism and advice for the benefit of mankind. I hope they continue these efforts. But, in consonance with the second point I just made, if a university's mission is to be redefined, then that institution should do it.

In summary, the pluralistic form of research support that we now employ deserves our advocacy. There has never been a time when the Federal Government was expected to act on so many different fronts on behalf of its citizens. As a nation, we have decided that, in addition to maintaining our security and fighting disease, we must fight against poverty, pollution, poor housing, inadequate transportation, and a host of other problems. These newer areas of Federal responsibility involve difficult problems; we appear to have relatively few options for attaining notable and rapid progress in any one of them. These are problem areas in which most of our universities are anxious to become involved — in the same sense that they have become involved in defense, health, and other areas, contributing solutions and training needed manpower. This should be encouraged, and that can be done best by those who know the problems and have an urgent sense of responsibility for solving them — the mission agencies.

Finally, let me take this opportunity to urge that we do

everything possible that will enable us to revitalize our Nation for the strenuous era of competition that lies ahead. There are divisive forces in our society today that limit our capabilities. We must recognize these problems, for they lead many to question the worth of our democracy, foment unrest on the campus and in our cities, and cause sincere and able people to make the serious error of questioning the value of technology in helping redress the wrongs they see about them.

Our problems cannot be solved by irrational and emotional response. A retreat to the days of our forefathers, when thousands of children died of diphtheria and other diseases now virtually eradicated by technology, is no solution. The solution lies in the intelligent and dedicated use of all available tools – technological, economic, political, sociological – whatever their nature may be, to achieve those goals that we desire. We will have shirked our responsibilities and failed in our leadership if we do less.

II. Toward New Priorities

⊂ A. *In an address delivered March 4, 1969, George Wald,
Professor of Biology at Harvard University and Nobel Prize
winner, charged that "the only point of government is to safeguard and foster life. Our government has become preoccupied
with death, with the business of killing and being killed." The
occasion was a day of concern (some called it a strike) called by
the Union of Concerned Scientists at the Massachusetts Institute
of Technology. Scientists and nonscientists, students and faculty
members addressed themselves to the fact that universities, and
the people in them, had for a quarter of a century lent themselves willingly to "the business of killing." Like Senator Mansfield, not all were convinced that science should avoid all contact
with war. But most of those who spoke underwrote the need for
a reorientation of priorities — between the military and civilian
needs of the nation, between what is trivial and what important,
between killing and life.*

*One scientist who has helped to dramatize the call for new
priorities is Jonathan R. Beckwith, professor of bacteriology and
immunology at the Harvard Medical School. Beckwith was head
of a team of researchers who successfully isolated a gene, a
breakthrough for which he was given the Eli Lilly Award. The
research had been funded by the National Science Foundation,
the National Institutes of Health, the American Cancer Society,
and the Jane Coffin Childs Memorial Fund for Medical Research;
the award was provided by one of the giants of the pharmaceuti-
cal world. After accepting the award and describing his research
before the American Society for Microbiology, Beckwith added
some thoughts on the social responsibilities of science in modern
America. Jonathan R. Beckwith, "Gene Expression in Bacteria
and Some Concerns About the Misuse of Science,"* Bacteriologi-
cal Reviews, 34 (1970), 224–227.]

It is probably clear from the work I have described that we
derive a great deal of pleasure from the type of work we do. The
manipulations of genes, practically at will, has been a lot of fun.

359

It is a constant temptation for me to spend all my waking hours thinking and working in this area. However, I believe that this is a temptation that I and other scientists must avoid. We must avoid it, for we have a special responsibility in this society because of the way we and our work are used.

Now I wish to discuss some of our concerns about the role of scientists in this society. Before I do, I would like to explain why I am using the award in the way I am and why I feel that it's my responsibility to discuss the political issues.

When I first learned that I was the recipient of the Eli Lilly Award for this year, I was obviously very pleased. However, since that time and as these meetings approached, I became more concerned about the meaning of this award and of awards in general in this country. First of all, these is the obvious concern about the awarding of a prize to an individual for work to which many people have been important contributors. It helps to maintain an inaccurate image of the way science is done.

In addition, I worried about getting the award, particularly the money, when there are so many more worthy causes which are in desperate need of funds.

Finally, and most importantly, I have questioned the political significance of awards in general. Since last November, when a group of us made a rather awkward attempt to issue a political statement surrounding our isolation of pure *lac* operon DNA, my concern about the misuse of science in this country has increased, and my feeling of the necessity for scientists to take clear positions has increased. During this period, I have given some talks and participated in discussions with various groups in which I, along with others, tried to point out the misuses of science by our government and by industries in this country. One of the examples I have consistently used is the role of the drug companies. Oddly enough, it wasn't until very · recently that I saw any contradiction in accepting an award donated by a drug company and speaking on these issues on other occasions. Therefore, I recently confronted myself with the choice of turning down the prize on these principles or using the opportunity of the award to discuss some aspects of the relationship between science and society. I obviously have decided that it might be a valuable contribution on my part (1) to use the financial part of the award in helping an organization which I believe is making some important contributions to changing this society so that it serves people and (2) to express my concerns about the problems of scientists in an effective way. It remains to be seen whether I am doing that. At any rate, I have decided that what I am doing has the greater possibility of contributing to the movement of people in this country who believe that a radical change in the way we operate is the only way in which the benefits of science can be spread among all people.

My concern about awards is that a society gives its awards to those who serve it. Unfortunately in this country, those who make the decisions about awards equate serving society with serving the interests of that small number of people who run our government and our industries. In a just society, those who received the awards should be those who are contributing in a meaningful way to the welfare of all people.

In that light, I consider that the Black Panther Party is an organization which is so contributing. They are not only helping their own people to lose their feeling of powerlessness, but are also setting up free health clinics and free breakfast programs in their communities, which could be models for the type of society we would like to see. They also recognize that it is the system of capitalist exploitation which is an essential component of the way in which our society oppresses people. Our society has rewarded them with the worst example of repression seen in this country in recent years. Therefore, after consultation with my colleagues, who have contributed to the work for which I am receiving the prize, we have decided to donate one-half of the prize money to the Boston Panther Free Health Movement and the other half to the Defense Fund for the Panther 21 in New York.

It is almost trite now to go over the ways in which science has contributed to many of the ills that we and nations all over the world are facing. It's enough to pick up the newspaper almost any morning and think about how many of the problems being discussed derive more or less directly from work that we scientists are doing or have done. One of the most frightening events in recent history has been the use of basic scientific knowledge to develop the horrible atomic weapons of destruction. The present use of overwhelming technology to try to eliminate a people in Southeast Asia should in itself wake up scientists to this problem. I don't think that any scientist can safely say today that his work is immune from such misuse. I am familiar with examples of work in the same field as mine in which developments in basic bacterial genetics have ultimately been used to develop repulsive weapons of biological warfare. Although we recently expressed our fears about the eventuality of progress in genetics leading to the misuse of techniques of eugenics and genetic engineering, we are also aware that there is always the possibility that a negative use of work in genetics may be realized in some quite different and quite unexpected way.

What I am trying to say is that science in the hands of the people who rule this country and who run our industries is being used to exploit and oppress people all over the world and in this country. And it is not only the natural sciences which are being used. There is a tremendous investment by the military in this country in developing social scientific methods to the point where it will be possible to use computer technology to give answers on such problems as "conditions under which peasants are strongly patriotic as in Turkey and the conditions under which they are purely local in orientation as in Vietnam," or "[which] Vietnamese civilians [are] Vietcong sympathizers," or provide analysis on contemporary radical movements. It has been related to me that in some instances these techniques have already been used in Southeast Asia with some success. An article appeared last year in the London *Sunday Times* describing how computers are used to pick out targets for bombing in Vietnam.

The tremendous distortions in the budget of our government come not only from expenditures for, among other things, scientific weapons in Vietnam but also from our "great" scientific achievements in space. Do we scientists really want to be responsible for the one-third of a billion dollars wasted on the recent moon trip when people are starving and receiving grossly inadequate health care in this country? I'll repeat in different words what I'm trying to say — scientists by playing the passive role assigned to them are just as much accomplices as those scientists who directly do research for this country which benefits the war makers.

It is clearly not only our government which uses science in this way, but also industries use our science to benefit those who lead them, by maximizing their profits. The solution to the problem of pollution will not come until the leaders of industry decide that profits are not important. I'm afraid they're going to need a little help on that problem.

One of the most obvious examples of the way in which

science is misused is the case of the drug companies. I don't think that the drug industry in this country is behaving in any different way than the rest of the industrial establishment. However, to many it is a more disturbing instance because these companies are dealing directly with people's health. The drug industry makes much higher profits than most of the industries in this country. The case is always made that a good deal of their profit is used for research and development. But this research is directed to what? A drug company to effectively extend its patent rights will do "research" to modify in some small way an already existing drug. In this way, they are able to keep their exclusive hold over the sale of the drug and thus continue to make enormous profits. The same is done by marketing combinations of drugs which turn out to have no enhanced effectiveness. Further, they plow back their profits into a campaign of public relations which hits medical students from the moment they enter medical school and is unceasing until they have finished their medical careers. Presents for medical students, lavish dinners for interns, presents and constant pressure on doctors help the drug industry to maintain its exploitation of people. We are responsible for that, too.

I think that we must recognize that these problems are not aberrations of any specific government we have had in this country or of specific industries, but are in fact an inevitable result of a system which is based on maximum profit. If you agree that we have a responsibility because of the misuse of our work, then, I believe, it must be recognized that there must be a radical change in society before we will have an opportunity to be absolved of our responsibility. I do not believe that scientists working in isolation from the rest of the people can hope to make any significant changes. It is possible that scientists who attempt to influence the scientific policy of our government will have some incremental effects on policy — that probably is even debatable. I know that the change in policy on chemical and biological warfare came in part from the intensive efforts of a small number of scientists. But, no matter how much I am pleased at any change in that policy, I wonder first of all how significant it is and, second, whether that decision was actually not made as sound defense policy. At any rate, those instances are few and far between.

While I do not believe that scientists working as a group alone to change policy will be effective, I object to this approach

363

much more strongly because of the elitist attitudes that it indicates exist in the scientific community. Not only do scientists
not have the power to change things, but also they have no
special political expertise. I do not think scientists have a superior
ability to judge what the problems are in our society and how
they can be solved. Instead, scientists, recognizing their responsibility, must ally with other workers, the poor people, and other
oppressed groups to work together for meaningful radical political
change. I know the term "radical political change" is vague. I
am not going to offer any blueprint for change because I believe
that I and all of us have a lot to learn about the world going on
around us. I think the form of that change will emerge as we
continue what I believe will be a long struggle.

What should scientists do? These are my suggestions.

(1) We can work first to organize other scientists to recognize their responsibilities as I have discussed them.

(2) Scientists should not do research which directly benefits
the ability of this country to make war or benefits those industries
which are exploiting the people for profit. We should even consider the implications of that research which might be related
to these potentials in less obvious ways.

Obviously, we will not stop progress in these fields by such
actions. However, the taking of such a stand can serve to raise
the level of consciousness among scientists about these problems.

(3) Wherever possible, scientists should contribute their
knowledge and abilities to the benefit of groups which are working toward fulfilling the needs of working people and poor
people. I feel that the groups most likely to be doing this are
those working within a context that recognizes that it is the
exploitation of the capitalist system which is at the root of
society's ills.

(4) Scientists should operate within their own institutions,
their places of work, to help in the struggles of working people
there and to affect the way in which these institutions interact
with the surrounding community. Such activities can help to
build the ties necessary for important change.

Finally, I want to reemphasize that scientists should not
consider themselves a special elite. Before we can make real
contributions we must recognize our own feelings of elitism
which have been bred into us by our class, our educational
institutions, and our present places of work. We have a lot to
learn. We must recognize how in many ways our interests are

common to those of other working people and that before effective change can take place, we must ally with these people — and not from a position of superiority.

⁋ *B. By the end of the 1960's it had become obvious that environmental problems had been among those neglected in our concentration on national security. Ever since the days of John Wesley Powell and Gifford Pinchot science and technology had been intimately involved with national resource problems and policy, serving both exploitation and conservation. When scientists and government officials looked for an example of how research and development could enhance rather than threaten life, environmental problems offered an attractive moral equivalent to war. To the extent that researchers like Beckwith coupled industry with the Pentagon as illegitimate exploiters of science, however, the liberating role of environmental concern was flawed by a more than casual deference to corporate needs and capabilities.* Environmental Pollution: A Challenge to Science and Technology. *Report of the Subcommittee on Science, Research, and Development to the Committee on Science and Astronautics, U.S. House of Representatives, 89th Cong., 2 sess., 1966, pp. 3–8.*]

Environmental quality, pollution abatement, waste management — these are concepts closer to everyday life than some other highly technical programs such as military weapons or space projects. The intricacies of pollution are of keen interest (which leads to public awareness and consensus for action) because each one of us is immersed in the environment. We are the polluters and the polluted, and our own senses tell us that the surroundings are not right. There is no need for detailed instrumental measurement or for emotional appeals of naturalists, we freely admit that we have a problem. Further definition of the problem, however, becomes a very difficult project involving natural and social sciences, economics, and governmental and private institutions. Making appropriate choices as we proceed will depend on much more knowledge than we now have.

Since man is very much a part of the biosphere, the living environment, he has always been changing and using the natural resources for his own benefit. Mistakes have been made and consequences have not always been foreseen, but civilization has advanced by taking risks which were largely overshadowed by obvious benefits. Furthermore, man is an adaptive creature, a product of evolutionary processes through which he could cope with these slow environmental changes.

The hearings illuminated the distinctive changes today in man's relationship to the environment – differences which have occurred within only the past few decades, and which make the preservation of natural resource quality so imperative. First, almost all the desirable areas of the earth are populated. There is no longer the possibility of choosing convenient dumping grounds or streams or air currents without infringing on the rights or property of others.

Second, our power to disturb or alter the ponderous forces and rhythms of nature by man-induced manipulations has increased to the point where mistakes or unknown effects may be profound and irreversible. Some examples are familiar to everyone. Persistent, mobile, and biocidal chemicals can disrupt the "web of life." Nuclear energy by-products and wastes are a recognized threat to normal genetic processes. The aging of lakes and estuaries is speeded up by contaminants from entering waters. Carbon dioxide accumulations from the burning of gas, petroleum, and coal change the nature of the atmosphere. Weather patterns can be altered purposefully or accidentally by human activity. These powerful forces have only come about recently and are not well understood. As a consequence, in many risk-benefit questions, the magnitude of the risk is relatively unknown.

Third, none of our natural resources is in so great a supply that it can any longer be considered inexhaustible or truly consumable. A highly industrialized society in a heavily populated world suggests that (apart from energy) all resources must be perpetually reused, renewed, and recycled. When a resource is contaminated or dispersed after use, the costs of recycling increase, as well as the possibility for damaging pollution. Pollution abatement and resource conservation go hand in hand. The resource conservation problem is essentially worldwide and no one geographical or political area is independent of others.

Fourth, the processes of adaptation through the selection processes of genetics have taken generations, whereas some environmental effects of a large magnitude now take place within a few years. This compression of time may overwhelm the ability of human beings to accommodate to the changes, even if we wish to accept all of them. So our very nature may define the limits on both the amounts and rates by which the environment can be modified.

Finally, the hearings indicated that environmental quality, with its deep roots in the natural sciences, has not yet attracted sufficient attention from the scientific and engineering community. This is a problem worthy of the very best thinking we can muster. It should receive a more generous allocation of the scientific resources at our disposal. Corrective activities involve long-term commitments and high costs which provide clear motivation for additional research, development, and demonstration projects. Technology is available to accomplish some urgent objectives and should be used without delay. In many other instances, the knowledge is lacking to define objectives and to deal with pollution on a cost-effective basis.

In addition to imaginative and competent science and engineering, the problem demands a research strategy including the systems analysis and management approach which has proved useful in other large, complex technological programs.

It cannot be said that any technology is, or is not, adequate without a stated goal. For example, technology available today is capable of meeting any technical goal for purifying water. What technology cannot do is simultaneously provide extreme purities at a cost that fits the value judgments of the society to be served. It is important to recognize that available technology can meet technical and cost goals to a far greater extent than it has been called upon to provide. When this point is made, it can then be reasonably argued that much work will be required to extend the ability toward higher purity at lower costs.

Pollution is often well understood until a definition is requested. Some simple terms are very useful — such as "too much." More elaborate expositions have resulted from two major recent studies:

> Environmental pollution is the unfavorable alteration of our surroundings, wholly or largely as a by-product of man's actions, through direct or indirect effects of changes in energy patterns, radiation levels, chemical and physical constitution, and abundances of organisms.
>
> Pollution is the undesirable change in the physical, chemical or biological characteristics of our air, land, and water that may or will harmfully affect human life or that of other desirable species, our industrial processes, living conditions, and cultural assets; or that may or will waste or deteriorate our raw material resources.

The subcommittee believes that an important concept may be conveyed if environmental pollution is regarded as waste management gone wrong. Wastes will be with us always and the key to satisfactory quality of our surroundings is to control the location of wastes at all times until they are recycled for further use or safely transferred to long-term storage. It is when we do not know where wastes are, or do not take the trouble to confine and control them, that unwanted contamination occurs. Pollution abatement thus is a function of the technical ability to understand what we are doing and the will to control our activities.

1. The pollution problem is composed of two related concepts: the kind of natural surroundings we want and need; and the cost and means of obtaining these qualities. The first concept is exemplified in the title of the PSAC report, "Restoring the Quality of Our Environment." The second concept is the subject of the NAS study, "Waste Management and Control." The hearings testimony demonstrates that there are inadequacies of knowledge in both areas that are frustrating the further definition of the problem and that are barriers to abatement progress.

2. Considering the powerful forces for ecological change which are at man's disposal, admitting the impossibility of complete foreknowledge of the consequences of many activities, and granting that a highly technical, overpopulated world must continue to take risks with natural resources, an "early warning system" for unwanted consequences is extremely important. We do not have such a system at present.

3. Other than in the case of gross and obvious pollution, there is insufficient information to set ultimate objectives, criteria, and standards. The directions of improvement are usually clear enough so that near term objectives can be set in terms of percent reduction. But short of the unrealistic zero point, few limiting conditions or ultimately allowable concentrations can be specified on a scientific basis. Nothing about the testimony suggested that present legislation had gone beyond the existing technological basis. But the urgent and insistent nature of the Clean Air Act and the Water Quality Act is a strong stimulus to R&D to provide more knowledge and better techniques.

4. Firmly established criteria and standards for environmental quality are necessary to give industry a basis for planning and action.

Only then will the science and the engineering resources

in the private sector be fully motivated. These skills and facilities are needed to solve internal corporate problems and to meet the market demand for abatement processes and techniques which enforcible standards will generate.

5. Therefore, the immediate research needs are in (a) improved abatement methods for gross and obvious pollution, and (b) ecological and human health data for criteria and standards setting.

Any large and rapid expansion of research and development will have to be performed to a great extent in the private sector (with contracts and grants if necessary) because Federal laboratories and personnel cannot expand fast enough. However, some considerable capabilities, which could be applied to pollution, exist in Federal research centers established for other primary missions.

6. Federal Government scientific activities are not yet channeled to support announced goals in pollution abatement. There is no organization or coordinating group capable of systems analysis and broad management of Federal projects. Insufficient funding has made support of research spotty and disproportionate among problem areas. Agency missions may inhibit long-term and comprehensive ecological studies. "Pollution" can cover an enormous variety of Federal agency programs ranging from water resources research to agricultural engineering. Limitations of definition will be necessary for effective program coordination.

7. Technical manpower will be a limiting factor in abatement progress unless additional effort is organized into retraining, graduate education, and transfer of skills from other technology programs.

8. Ecology, as an organized profession, is not in good condition to become the umbrella for increased research. As a scientific discipline it is the logical focal point. As a point of view it is already effective in coordinating other sciences, and this may be the most important function in the long run.

9. Complete solution of pollution problems may not be possible, but two trends are discernible. More recycling of materials is a way of managing and eliminating wastes as well as a sound conservation policy. The impact of recycling on the economy can be lessened by imaginative product and process design. The other trend is the controlled transport of unusable wastes to some sort of perpetual safe storage. The use of ocean depths, deep wells, salt domes, burial and caves needs careful study to

assure that there are no undesirable effects on the biosphere from such disposal.

10. Large-scale demonstration of new and improved abatement methods will be necessary to establish efficiency and costs. Massive city-sized experiments, freed from the inhibitions of present institutional practices and investments, are the nature of research in urban ecology. Government funding in an underwriting or risk-sharing role is justified to move technology from the development stage, through demonstration, to wide application.

11. The interactions of Federal science funding with industrial research resources is quite different in pollution from those relationships in the military space programs. The Federal Government is not the major customer for the products and processes resulting from R&D in pollution. Industry may be alert to its responsibilities, but Federal research support will be needed to stimulate development of abatement methods to show when standards can be met and to bring improvements in a timely manner. Beyond these points, abatement technology should be in the control of normal commercial enterprise.

RECOMMENDATIONS

It is clear from the testimony that the goals in environmental quality can be reached only by minimizing wastes at their sources. The concept of using the "natural assimilative capacity" of the environment is not yet feasible, because it cannot be defined. Where contamination cannot be completely eliminated, precise knowledge of its effects must be obtained. Therefore:

1. To improve our knowledge of what we are about, scientific activity in ecology and related fields should be immediately expanded to provide

    a. Baseline measurements in plant and animal communities and the environment — an ecological survey.
    b. Continued monitoring of changes in the biosphere.
    c. Abilities to predict the consequences of man-made changes.
    d. Early detection of such consequences.
    e. Knowledge of the environmental determinants of disease.

2. Ecological surveys and research should be centralized as to management in some one science-based Federal agency. The

scientific activity should be performed (whether in Government laboratories or under contract by local universities and research institutes) in geographical regions which correspond generally to natural environmental boundaries.

3. To place pollution abatement on a comparable basis with other national technology programs, systems analysis and management capability should be established within the Federal Government. This approach should be used along with the "planning, programing, budgeting" technique to organize both near and long-term Federal research and operational efforts in pollution abatement. More attention should be paid to interfaces between agency missions which make the management of environmental problems difficult.

4. To improve and enhance waste treatment practice, an abatement extension service should be established by Federal funds to provide information and technical advice to local governments, regional compacts, and industry. A continuing survey of operating practices and successful industrial abatement methods should be undertaken to identify new and better technology as quickly as possible. The service could contract locally for the performance of its functions and become at least partially self-supporting through fees.

5. To stimulate the acquisition and development of new technology, Federal contracts for research, development, and demonstration should employ a cost recovery principle where commercial success occurs. Return of the ownership of the technology to the private sector for exploitation should be a part of contracting policy.

6. The Federal Government should undertake an analysis to identify and separate those abatement action programs which are well supported by facts and for which practical answers are available, from those problem areas where more R&D is needed. A public information program should make these differences clear to the Nation so that installation, enforcement, and research can each proceed on a logical timetable. Actions to decrease pollution should continue even though the ultimate criteria cannot be set at this time.

7. The Congress should endeavor to review its broad authorizations and appropriations for water, reclamation, transportation, and conservation in the context of environmental quality goals. The diversity of executive agency missions places an

added responsibility on the legislative branch to avoid conflicts in large-scale engineering projects.

8. The scientific and engineering community should respond to the challenge of the pollution problem as a major opportunity to serve a public need. Work in this field should be recognized as interesting, rewarding, and important. Proposals for organization, funding, and schedules which will assure the participation of excellent technical personnel in adequate numbers should be the joint responsibility of Government and private sector research and development leaders.

9. The subcommittee believes that the hearings testimony supports a significant increase in Federal funding for science and engineering related to environmental quality. The field is extremely broad, and certain specific problems should receive greater effort as well as a general advance of the state of the art. Although many projects in biology, chemistry, etc., in several agencies may be related to waste management, the missions within the Departments of Interior and Health, Education, and Welfare are the heart of the Federal program. The present level of research, development, and demonstration funding ($30 million per year) should be expanded about 10 times within the next 5 years in order to bring waste management properly under control.

❡ C. *The flurry of activity and publicity that surrounded Earth Day on the nation's campuses in April of 1970 was anticipated by a report that reached back to the research patterns of the Department of Agriculture for inspiration and guidance.* The Universities and Environmental Quality − Commitment to Problem Focused Education. *A Report to the President's Environmental Quality Council by John S. Steinhart and Stacie Cherniack (Washington, D.C.: Office of Science and Technology, Executive Office of the President, September, 1969), pp. 1–5, 7–12.*]

INTRODUCTION

We, as individual people, are immersed in our environment. We can change it but we can never escape it. We perceive it most often as physical and biological surroundings and, somewhat less well, as cultural and social surroundings. The growing public concern about the degradation of our physical environment and the hazards to our biological environment is obvious and will not be detailed further. Prophets of environmental disaster on every hand are quite ready to conduct us collectively or individually through a house of horrors of possibilities for the immediate or not very distant future. Many of the outcries of the young and of the minority groups relate to the environment and the quality of life as compared with what these groups intuitively feel are the possibilities for this country at this time. That the concern is much more widespread can be ascertained from the response of the stable middle part of society to such issues as the Santa Barbara oil spill, transportation of dangerous materials, or the use of pesticides.

A very serious risk is that we may follow some few of the traditionally minded engineers and equate environmental quality with pollution abatement. If pollution were brought under control and clean air and clean water became a reality it is doubtful that the malaise about the quality of life would disappear. In any case, a program based only upon taboos — a program stating that "thou shalt not pollute" — has very limited appeal among all the alternative futures that may possibly await us. We have intervened in the environment whether we wished to or not and our only real hopes lie in deciding how it is we wish to live and inquiring whether we can achieve it or not.

The case is summarized by Hans Gaffron, one of America's leading biologists, in a recent statement.

This restless urge to mold a world according to his, unfortunately quite limited, imagination — this force has pushed man himself into a corner from which he must now try to liberate himself. At the moment it looks as if stupidity and meanness, combined with the forces of technology, are going to win the race towards cultural extermination before reason has had a good chance to discover the best way to reverse the trend.

To end and reverse the degradation of our physical and biological environment, to identify the alternative future options open to our society, and to define the common elements of the kind of life to which our society aspires will require strenuous efforts by all the people and institutions of the American society. This report is a brief but intensive study of the contributions that can be made by one of these institutions — the colleges and universities of the United States.

Education has always played a central role in the American

dream, and the many and varied uses we have made of our universities illustrate society's faith in education. Of all subjects, it is easiest to get firm and solid opinions concerning the education of the young from all members of society. It should be noted that within the next few years more than 50 percent of the nation's young people will attend colleges and universities at some time. If we are truly concerned about the quality of environment and quality of life this concern must be illustrated and participated in by our educational system.

It is patently obvious, but bears repeating, that the problems and opportunities related to our environment in a growing and increasingly technological society are multidisciplinary as viewed from the traditional dissection of knowledge, engineering, and action into academic disciplines. Many of our most serious problems have arisen because narrowly conceived technological improvements have failed to take account of side effects, deleterious or otherwise, which inevitably accompany a widespread technological change in society. The question then, for universities, is how to pursue multidisciplinary education, multidisciplinary research, and a wide ranging discussion of our human problems irrespective of disciplinary boundaries or professional descriptions. In a way, the use of the word "multidisciplinary" betrays the history of the problem. We are talking about the approach to and the solution for problems and not about the scientific disciplines which can bring to the problem some important knowledge or evidence.

PROBLEM-FOCUSED ACTIVITY AT UNIVERSITIES

In popular discussion of how to solve our environmental problems the space program or, less frequently, the success of our efforts to solve technical problems during World War II are cited as models. For the universities neither of these examples is particularly relevant; the World War II efforts were conducted under a suspension of the university "rules" in which everything was put aside in favor of this consuming effort with the idea that normalcy would return when the war was finished, as indeed it did for the most part. The space program has been primarily an effort of the Federal Government and industry with important, although modest, contributions from the universities. More appropriate examples of ways that universities may contribute to the solution of society's problems may be found in the areas of agriculture and public health. Although these problems are somewhat simpler than the complex problems surrounding the environment and the quality of life, these efforts, persisting for fifty to one hundred years, are more nearly comparable to the kinds of problems we face in environmental quality. The schools of agriculture, established under the Land-Grant College Act of 1862, have been successful in terms of their original purpose beyond anyone's wildest dreams. The schools of agriculture together with the agricultural experiment stations and the county agricultural agent program have increased agricultural productivity to the point where it, too, is a problem. The gains in public health to which the university schools of public health and medicine made important contributions are too well known to require recapitulation. What is perhaps most impressive is that these units of universities have always had reputations of being second rate intellectual efforts and, like all prophecies, repetition of such statements is self-fulfilling. That they succeeded in spite of this is a remarkable accomplishment. The common feature of both of these efforts is that they are problem focused.

It will not be easy to begin new problem focused programs at universities, despite the need for trained professionals and the seriousness of the problems. . . .

THE DESIGN OF THE STUDY

What Has Been Tried? It is not the function of the Federal Government to order the universities to undertake specific programs. It is idle to pretend, however, that Federal funding policies do not play a very large role in what happens and, equally important, what does not happen at universities. The response to various funding programs of the government in defense, space, and a variety of other areas have caused universities to erect a wide variety of institutes, centers, and programs to respond to the available funds. In most cases these institutes have been largely paper structures and their impact on the universities and, especially, on the students and the public discussion of the issues surrounding the work has been negligible. Curriculum, faculty rewards, and most of the research has been controlled within the departments representing the narrow academic disciplines. These departments grow narrower and more numerous year by year as the advance of modern science results in increasing specialization. These institutes and centers contrast strongly with the history of agriculture and public health in which curriculum, faculty, and research were centered in schools that were nearly autonomous.

This study set out to examine the range of institutional arrangements that have been tried in dealing with environmental problems and to determine, as nearly as possible, which kinds of arrangements have proven to be successful. We return at the end of the report to inquire how the government funding policies effect university work in the environmental area. It is important that funds made available to work on environment quality problems be supportive of those efforts likely to result in success, and equally important that they are not wasted on the kinds of efforts that have already proven to be unsuccessful. The urgent and long-term needs to examine the quality of our environment and identify what alternative futures may be open to us suggest that a vigorous program comparable in vision to the Land-Grant College Act would be extremely important if there were any chance whatever of success.

Society, through its government, does not deal in academic disciplines. It deals in problems and opportunities. Society has a right to expect, as a part of the educational process, discussion of the prominent issues, problems and opportunities of the day, and training of professionals who can deal with these problems on a professional level. A second function of the universities is a prominent role in the long range public discussion of alternative futures. Many of our government policies, now commonplace, have originated in academic discussions of an earlier generation. Yet, except for the doomsayers, discussion of possible future environments among the world's academic community is surprisingly muted. We do not have offered to us the variety of alternatives that may be possible, and from which society and its elected representatives can select pieces to become part of our policy and national goals. The recent establishment of the President's Committee on National Goals is, in part, a recognition of this shortcoming. The increasing concern of the younger generation for the future quality of life in America suggests that the universities could play a very important, perhaps even a crucial part in such a wide ranging public discussion. Thus we certainly ought to inquire as to whether Federal funding policies could encourage this discussion forward and as a minimum ask that Federal funding policies do not discourage such discussion.

Criteria for Evaluation. What is it we expect of universities?

Can education be all things to all people? How can one maintain rigorous standards? The universities can never respond to a crisis! An interdisciplinary education will sacrifice rigor! These questions and statements, whether from faculty, students, or ordinary citizens, commonly occur. Rather than try to answer them on intuitive grounds we set out to examine some institutions with ongoing programs related to the environment and of multidisciplinary content to inquire how well they have worked.

It became obvious early in the study that *two criteria* were of significant interest when examining the ongoing programs related to the environment:

1. The degree to which the program, center or other structure participated in the faculty reward structure — including appointment of faculty, promotion, salary, tenure, and other benefits afforded faculty members.
2. The degree to which the program, center, or whatever participated in the generation of curricula, degree requirements, and new or innovative approaches to education for these multidisciplinary problems.

If a program had no influence over either of these areas we found it to be ineffective and powerless within the university. Its contribution to education and public discussion was very limited even though significant research might have been done by faculty members. We also examined the relationship of such programs to real world problems (through work-study programs or other mechanisms) and the degree of participation by students educationally, in research, and in the formulation of policy for the program.

One further word about students is in order. Unrest on the campus has been forcefully brought home to us by the newspapers and television, yet those of us beyond student age still have some difficulty in understanding exactly what is happening on the university campuses. The problem is a complex one, but the following comment by the twenty-two Republican Congressmen who visited fifty campuses during the spring of 1969 briefly summarizes the nature of the problem:

We came away from our campus tour both alarmed and encouraged. We were alarmed to discover that this problem is far deeper and far more urgent than most realize, and that it goes far beyond the efforts of organized revolutionaries. . . . Too often, however we saw their idealism and concern vented in aimless or destructive ways.

No reasonable man countenances violence. Nevertheless, direct attempts to suppress violence are dealing with symptoms, not causes. Society must respond to the searching questions students are asking. Prominent among these are the concern about the environment and the quality of life. A concrete way that the government can express its agreement about the seriousness of environmental problems is to do what it can to encourage students to work on these problems. We certainly desperately need qualified professional people who can help us solve the serious problems besetting our physical environment. The Republican Congressmen again state: "We found an encouraging desire on the part of many students to do something to help overcome the problems of our society. This dedication or commitment to help others is a hopeful, important area which should be encouraged."

In the discussion and recommendations that follow we have tried, by talking directly to students in environmental programs, to determine their reaction to these programs and to obtain some idea whether, in addition to being effective, these programs answer the deep and justifiable wish of the students to help in the solution of our problems.

Finally, we tried to examine the present participation of the government through its agencies or individuals in the interchange with the universities — faculty and students — in consideration of these environmental problems. The leavening effect of students and others participating in the government has been aptly demonstrated by the Executive Intern and White House Fellow programs. The contribution federal officials could make to the educational process of faculty and students at universities through brief participation there should not be overlooked, and the rejuvenation of a man from an operating agency worn down by long work on persistent and difficult problems should stimulate the agencies involved.

◖ D. *Despite the fact that it had become a cliché during the 1930's that the natural sciences had outstripped the social sciences (and therefore our command of means had developed faster than our understanding of ends), the establishment of the National Science Foundation in 1950 had left the support and use of the social sciences in doubt. Like other more fortunate fields, it had received military support (Project Camelot was one of the scandals of the 1960's), but it remained one of the over-looked opportunities of American science. The following selection is taken from* Knowledge Into Action: Improving the Nation's Use of the Social Sciences. *Report of the Special Commission on the Social Sciences of the National Science Board (Washington, D.C.: National Science Foundation, 1969), pp. xi–xxi.*]

The Special Commission on the Social Sciences, established by the National Science Board in 1968, was charged with making recommendations for increasing the useful application of the social sciences in the solution of contemporary social problems. The Commission believes the nation is missing crucial opportunities to utilize fully the best of social science knowledge and skills in the formation, evaluation, and execution of policies for achieving desired social goals.

The Commission's recommendations are focused on: (1) the revitalization of existing organizations, (2) the establishment of new social institutions, and (3) the development of better channels for the flow of social science resources into American life. To implement certain of the recommendations requires little or no increase in expenditures at the community or federal level, but implementation of other recommendations will require substantial additional funds.

Our survey of the present state of utilization of the social sciences demonstrates that they have developed acceptable scientific procedures for collection of valid information on the problems they confront. They have substantially increased their scientific body of knowledge over the past decades. They have also developed excellent methods of analysis and evaluation for testing theoretical and practical propositions. Even where great gaps of knowledge remain, as they undoubtedly do, the social scientists' experience can offer valuable intuitive understanding and special insight.

Because of these gaps, and because of the complexity of the social world, social scientists are not always prepared to formulate appropriate hypotheses for testing. But this does not imply that the social sciences cannot help the nation solve its social problems. We are convinced, indeed, that they can contribute to solving the nation's problems if full advantage is taken of their strengths.

Social scientists manifestly must be consulted in the collection of relevant information, and in evaluating social policies already in existence; their knowledge and informed intelligence should also be sought out before new social programs are instituted. Even where they may not know how to design substantially better programs than those presently responsible for such programs, their professional knowledge enables them to detect and avoid pitfalls in social program design — particularly those pitfalls into which nontrained planners are enticed by the charms of conventional wisdom.

There are several major obstacles to the utilization of social science knowledge. (1) There is frequently no institution or agency to note such knowledge and act upon it. (2) In many instances the social sciences provide accurate descriptions or predictions of events, but no solution to the problem. It is too easy to reject such relevant knowledge out of hand, in the belief that it is simply troublesome when it provides no answers. (3) Some reject social science knowledge because it is threatening to their own views, or to the security of their personal situations during periods of social change. (4) Some reject social science knowledge even when they agree with it, when the resources needed to attain the indicated solutions are too demanding. Even in a nation as wealthy as ours, resources are limited, and policies based on social science findings must compete in the political arena for implementation. Whether or not the nation will use the social sciences in a given instance depends upon the outcome of this political competition.

Although our concern is to increase the use of existing knowledge, the Commission fully recognizes the importance to the nation of public and private support for objective social research to provide a knowledge base from which applied insights and policy formation can proceed. Even the present utilization of the knowledge and insights of the social sciences is possible only because of the preceding half-century of such basic research. Accordingly, we urge that implementation of the Commission's proposals and recommendations in no way deter the growth of the indispensable companion support for basic research in these sciences.

The major recommendations below, then, are designed to increase and improve the nation's utilization of the strengths of the social sciences. The specific plans and suggestions to implement these general recommendations of the Commission are presented in the body of the report.

THE SOCIAL SCIENCES AND THE PROFESSIONS

The professions are among the main institutions through which social science knowledge can be translated into day-to-day practice. During the past several decades the contribution of the social sciences to professional practice has been increasing. Education has been most notable in this respect; but medicine and public health, social work, and (more recently) law have also made effective use of such knowledge.

Still, the expressed demand by the professions for social science contributions is infrequent and generally unsystematic. The Commission reviewed the utilization of the social sciences by seven professions: education, engineering, journalism, law, medicine and public health, mental health, and social work. Those sections of the report dealing with each profession contain many specific recommendations for action in accord with the Commission's general conclusions, which are the following:

• *Professional schools should include in their curricula more of the social science knowledge relevant to the particular profession.* With professional schools supplying the leadership, resources for staffing schools with social scientists should be provided from federal, state, foundation, and university funds. Three fundamentals must be observed in this staffing process. (a) The object is not to make social scientists of the professionals, but to assure their exposure to the methodology, capabilities, and knowledge of the social sciences relevant to that profession; (b) the social scientists must retain association with their particular discipline to insure continued competence in that discipline; and (c) there must be institutional recognition of such collaboration, in the form of salary, promotion, and status.

• *Provision must be made for increasing collaborative social science-professional research efforts — not only on basic scientific questions of common interest, but also in joint attacks on social problems within the compass of the specific profession.* The Commission views the funding of such collaborative studies both as a responsibility of the federal government, and as an opportunity for private organizations. The social problem research

381

institutes, to be described below, should provide a valuable institutional base for this type of attack.

THE SOCIAL SCIENCES AND THE FEDERAL GOVERNMENT

The Social Sciences at the White House and Departmental Level. At those levels in the federal government where major policy is made, the social sciences should be deeply involved. Policies for handling the nation's most pressing issues and problems — whether they relate to the cities, pollution, inflation, or supersonic transport — must rest not only on knowledge drawn from the physical and biological sciences, but also on the best available knowledge about human individual and social behavior. Many of our most urgent domestic policy issues, indeed, are more closely related to the social sciences than to the other sciences. Social sciences must be treated, not in isolation, but in their proper position as a part of the entire national pool of scientific and technological knowledge and skill.

• *The new policy of appointing social scientists to membership on the President's Science Advisory Committee should be continued, and the social science members increased, to assure identification of the social science knowledge that should be available to the Committee.*

• *Professional social scientists with backgrounds in relevant areas should be added to, and become an important part of, the Office of Science and Technology staff.* While able staff members drawn from the other sciences have given vigorous and intelligent assistance to panels dealing with such topics as the development of the social sciences, and educational research and development, there have as yet been no appointments of social scientists to the OST.

The Commission recognizes the current interest in establishing a Council of Social Advisors in the White House Office to serve an advisory role parallel to that of the Council of Economic Advisors. While we strongly agree that social science data should be fully and effectively transmitted to the Administration, we are not prepared to recommend the establishment of such a Council. The Commission has become convinced that this goal can be achieved more efficiently by the inclusion of appropriate social scientists in such key advisory groups as PSAC and OST, and through action by the Council of Economic Advisors.

• *We urge the CEA to give explicit attention to the need for including in its professional staff and consultants: (1) persons drawn from the relevant social sciences outside economics, and (2) persons drawn from the physical sciences and engineering who can bring to bear relevant knowledge about scientific and technological trends and developments.*

Effective Employment of Social Sciences in Government Agencies. Social scientists properly belong at all staff levels and in all functions in federal agencies where they can contribute importantly to performance of their agencies' mission.

• *The Commission recommends strengthening and extension of present practices of employment of social scientists in the federal government, and specifically recommends that an extensive program of periodic leaves of one academic term at full salary (comparable to academic sabbatical leaves) be instituted to enable professional employees to bring themselves up-to-date with the very rapid developments of their own and related disciplines — either by means of specially designed refresher course, or by working on research of their own choosing.* Even research not directly related to their employment can contribute effectively to the currency of their knowledge. Eligibility for such leave should be based upon continuous employment with the federal government as a whole rather than with any individual agency.

Because the federal government employs a great number of professional people throughout the country — only 10 percent of all employees are based in Washington — it should consider multiple programs through which updating can be offered. The federal agencies and the Civil Service Commission as well as the colleges and universities must cooperate in this endeavor. Federal agencies have authority to carry out such programs under the Federal Government Training Act of 1958; and several agencies, such as the National Institutes of Health, have already adopted such a program.

Providing Better Social Science Data. Regularly collected statistical data describing the people in American society and their major institutions have been valuable in the development of successful policy formation and execution. Growing reliance on statistical data for policy decisions has led to an increased demand for data that can be used for projection and prediction. Over the years the social sciences have developed an ever greater capacity for measuring, evaluating, and predicting social change; at the same time the federal government has developed an increasing commitment to serve as a positive force in bringing about such change.

Although there are still large areas of uncertainty in the social sciences, although there are limits to the programs government can effectively manage, and although there are constitutional and political limits to the extension of federal authority, these two trends have converged to produce a strong interest in the further development of statistical time-series data (i.e., social statistics).

• *To improve the quality, range, and utilization of social statistics, the federal government should provide for increased linkages between the bodies of data now routinely collected.* This must, of course, go hand in hand with both federal and private efforts to develop the means for protection of privacy. (Such data linkages and access to data centers should not be allowed, indeed, unless individual and institutional privacy can be protected.)

• *The federal government, universities, and private funding groups should provide the resources necessary for both government and private research organizations to develop new, more frequent, and better social statistics to record the important aspects of American life as yet relatively unstudied.*

THE SOCIAL SCIENCES AND BUSINESS AND LABOR

Business leaders and social scientists have increasingly found areas where they have mutual interests. Executives have been alerted to the complexities of knowledge required for effective decisionmaking, and social scientists have found that large business organizations provide living laboratories for observation and analysis. Business schools now provide technical training in economics, and in principles of organization and decisionmaking processes that employ mathematical and statistical techniques. They are also making efforts to expand their social science staffs. Corporations have recruited social research in such sensitive areas as the introduction and management of change, and have extended these lessons to programs recently developed for recruiting and training hardcore unemployed.

Organized labor and collective bargaining present additional opportunities for the application of the social sciences. Statistical information has been used to relate economic and social characteristics of the collective bargaining environment to the multifaceted decisions that must be made. Labor unions have turned to the social sciences for assistance in adapting their structures and activities to rapidly changing structures in corporation, markets, the economy, and society generally. Social scientists have found living laboratories in labor union organizations that are as vital and dynamic as the business enterprise.

Business firms and labor unions have turned to the social sciences whenever they have seen prospects of gains to the organization. Recognition of the advantages of interchanges between the social sciences on one hand, and business and labor on the other, has been instrumental in establishing important relationships. The past, however, has reaped only a small portion of the potential benefits.

• *The Commission urges the officials in business and labor organizations to strengthen and broaden their existing associations with the social sciences.*

THE SOCIAL SCIENCES AND COMMUNITY ORGANIZATIONS

It is the Commission's view that efforts should be made to appraise the opportunities for direct social science application to the work of community organizations. A primary need is a comprehensive inventory, on a national basis, of the social science work going on in community organizations. This should identify the notable successes, in order to isolate the common elements in such successful collaboration. Identification of successful programs, however, is not possible until better evaluative research studies are carried out on community-organization programs.

• *Accordingly, careful evaluation studies of the effectiveness of community organizations should be greatly expanded.*

A systematic appraisal is required of the opportunities for social science to be brought to bear in community organizations. Without such an appraisal, there can be no basis for sound planning to develop further collaboration between the social sciences and community organizations.

• *Accordingly, such an appraisal should be undertaken — either by appropriate federal agencies, or through a task force or commission sponsored from the private sector.*

Since successful demonstrations of social science contributions already exist in some number, the Commission wishes, at the same time, to encourage the support of existing channels for the dissemination of such knowledge. Most typically, the transfer of useful information takes place through social scientists in various relationships to community organizations — consulting, for example — and through the employment of social scientists in a staff or research capacity for a short- or long-term period. Information is also transferred through workshops, institutes, and conferences between organization representatives and social scientists.

After these recommendations concerning social scientists and community organizations have been implemented, it is desirable that there should be available to such organizations — perhaps through an appropriate government organization —opportunity to gain an assessment of how they might benefit from social science knowledge and techniques. Funds should then be made available to the community organizations themselves in order to implement well-planned requests. We believe that community organizations, both public and private, are definite frontiers of possible social science utilization and, as such, deserve systematic exploration.

THE SOCIAL SCIENCES AND THE PUBLIC

Improved dissemination of social science knowledge to the public is desirable. (1) The knowledge and insights of the social sciences are directly applicable by each individual to his own life — particularly in such areas as career planning, childrearing, and voluntary community activities. (2) A more receptive attitude and increased knowledge among the general public will raise the public expectations as to the value of social science in dealing with public problems.

To improve the direct utilization of social science knowledge by the public through elementary and secondary school education and continuing education for adults, the following are recommended:

• *The National Science Foundation should increase its support of efforts to improve social science curricula, and it should encourage the professional social science associations to take responsibility for developing curriculum materials.*

• *Social science associations and funding organizations should encourage the efforts of scholars studying how children develop over time an understanding of basic social science concepts;*

special attention should be given to the implications of this research for redesigning the elementary and secondary school social science curriculum.

To improve the direct utilization of social science knowledge by the public through continuing education for adults, the following is recommended:

• *Consideration should be given to launching new federal efforts to develop and increase the social science component of continuing education programs. More funds should be assigned to the appropriate divisions of the Office of Education so that it can add professional and technical staff for this purpose, and additional effort should be made through other appropriate agencies, perhaps the National Science Foundation or the National Endowment for the Humanities. Grants to continuing education organizations, primarily university-based but not solely so, should be made to enable these organizations to further develop their work in the social sciences.*

The mass media provide an effective means of educating the public about the social sciences. Television programming presents a large and unrealized opportunity for social science education, and the Commission believes that much more can be done in the other media also — through magazine articles, newspaper reporting, and books. A number of specific recommendations have been developed by the Commission to increase and improve the mass media reporting of social science knowledge, and these are stated in detail in the body of the report.

SOCIAL PROBLEM RESEARCH INSTITUTES

Engaging the best of our social science resources to meet contemporary social problems requires the establishment of a new kind of institute with the clearly defined purpose of conducting applied social science research on problems of public significance. The Commission proposes the formation of special social problem research institutes where social problems will be analyzed by teams of specialists from the social sciences and other sciences and professions. Engineers and other professionals must join with social scientists in these efforts. Their technical knowledge is indispensable to any analysis of causes of and solutions to various social problems. Furthermore, each institute must establish close relationships with the agencies or organizations faced with the problem and responsible for its solution at the policy and action level, so that the implication of the institute's studies can be carried forward to the development of policy alternatives and action programs.

In proposing the formation of social problem research institutes, the Commission seeks to bring change to the management of applied social science. The present organization of social science research is not well oriented to attacks on national social issues. The Commission believes that the proposed institutes offer a reasonable hope for more rapid progress in the utilization of social science knowledge. New social problem research institutes will provide a means for implementing many of the recommendations made previously in the report, namely, increased collaboration between the social sciences and the professions, provision of social science knowledge to community organizations, liaisons with business and labor, and more effective transmission of social science information to government.

There have been a number of important attempts to develop this type of institute, and these have had an important influence on social science research and have led the way for the social problem research institutes recommended by the Commission. One can mention specifically the problem-oriented centers established by the Department of Health, Education, and Welfare, and by the Office of Education; and certain nongovernment centers focusing on violence and on manpower problems. Nevertheless, mobilization of social science for solutions to social problems customarily has been ineffective because the problems themselves do not fall solely within the traditional areas of a given social science. Instead, they require for their solution the collaborative focused efforts of the several social sciences, the professions, and other resource groups. Research conducted separately by members of one or another social science rarely provides the necessary broad insights into the nature and resolution of a major social problem. With a few notable exceptions, social research institutes have not been able to broaden their research programs to perform the duties the Commission assigns to the proposed social problem research institutes. The objectives of existing research centers frequently are the development of basic research in a discipline; that is, they are guided by the theoretical interests of the developing science rather than by the need for a solution of current social problems. Even those research centers with an applied social problem orientation usually emphasize a single scientific discipline; or, their research clientele is business and the subject matter fundamentally related to a specific firm's concerns; or, when governmental, they tend to be either short-range in outlook or focused closely upon a specific agency's mission. Such research is valuable to its clients, and there is undoubtedly a genuine need to increase it, but it does not possess the interdisciplinary scope needed for the study of complex social problems. The proposed social problem research institutes will provide an essential missing element in the process of bringing social science research to fuller utilization at the policymaking and action level.

The Commission believes that several problem research institutes are needed so that each then can deal with a specific social problem and be organized more effectively than would be the case if a single institute were spread thinly over a wide variety of social concerns. Moreover, such pluralism gives the opportunity for having several institutes whose subject matters and research projects overlap and thus provide the benefits of diversity and competition that are not likely to emerge from a very large but single national institute. And, a larger number of sharply focused institutes means they can be established throughout the country at universities and in urban centers, which will add to the diversity of analyses, perspectives, and insights.

The Commission therefore recommends the following:

• *$10 million should be appropriated in fiscal year 1970 to the National Science Foundation for the establishment of social problem research institutes; this budget should increase in subsequent years . . . with an objective of about twenty-five institutes.*

Firm commitments should be made to underwrite the full costs of the social problem research institutes during the first years of each institute's life; commitments for funds should be reduced to 20 or 25 percent of probable expenses as soon as the institutes can compete for research support.

In establishing these institutes by competition among interested universities and other organizations, the following criteria should be operative:

1. a capable interdisciplinary professional staff that will concentrate its efforts on the chosen subject;
2. the identification of appropriate client-sponsors, either within or without the federal government, and a proposed

way to communicate with and respond to the client-
sponsor;

3. the establishment of appropriate mechanisms to insure a
flow of qualified and experienced people through the
institute into the user agencies.

If it is apparent from the quality of the proposals for attack
on a given social problem that effective resources cannot yet be
mobilized in an institute form, the National Science Foundation
should not feel constrained to establish an untimely institute. It
should, however, explore each such field to learn the difficulties
and obstacles, in the expectation that these may be removed.

❡ *E.   It did not escape observation that the comparative
undernourishment and serious use of the social sciences might
have something to do with the fact that national priorities,
though nowhere set down, were under increasing criticism. In
1966 President Johnson directed the Secretary of Health, Education, and Welfare to "search for ways to improve the Nation's
ability to chart its social progress." Secretary John W. Gardner
thereupon appointed a Panel on Social Indicators, chaired by
Daniel Bell of Columbia University and Alice M. Rivlin, Assistant Secretary of HEW. The following selection is taken from
their report submitted by Gardner.* Toward a Social Report
(Washington, D.C., 1969), pp. xi–xxii.]

The Nation has no comprehensive set of statistics reflecting
social progress or retrogression. There is no Government procedure for periodic stocktaking of the social health of the Nation. The Government makes no Social Report.

We do have an Economic Report, required by statute, in
which the President and his Council of Economic Advisors report to the Nation on its economic health. We also have a comprehensive set of economic indicators widely thought to be
sensitive and reliable. Statistics on the National Income and its
component parts, on employment and unemployment, on retail
and wholesale prices, and on the balance of payments are collected annually, quarterly, monthly, sometimes even weekly.
These economic indicators are watched by Government officials
and private citizens alike as closely as a surgeon watches a fever
chart for indications of a change in the patient's condition.

Although nations got along without economic indicators for

centuries, it is hard to imagine doing without them now. It is hard to imagine governments and businesses operating without answers to questions which seem as ordinary as: What is happening to retail prices? Is National Income rising? Is unemployment higher in Chicago than in Detroit? Is our balance of payments improving?

Indeed, economic indicators have become so much a part of our thinking that we have tended to equate a rising National Income with national well-being. Many are surprised to find unrest and discontent growing at a time when National Income is rising so rapidly. It seems paradoxical that the economic indicators are generally registering continued progress — rising income, low unemployment — while the streets and the newspapers are full of evidence of growing discontent — burning and looting in the ghetto, strife on the campus, crime in the street, alienation and defiance among the young.

Why have income and disaffection increased at the same time? One reason is that the recent improvement in standards of living, along with new social legislation, have generated new expectations — expectations that have risen faster than reality could improve. The result has been disappointment and disaffection among a sizable number of Americans.

It is not misery, but advance, that fosters hope and raises expectations. It has been wisely said that the conservatism of the destitute is as profound as that of the privileged. If the Negro American did not protest as much in earlier periods of history as today, it was not for lack of cause, but for lack of hope. If in earlier periods of history we had few programs to help the poor, it was not for lack of poverty, but because society did not care and was not under pressure to help the poor. If the college students of the fifties did not protest as often as those of today, it was not for lack of evils to condemn, but probably because hope and idealism were weaker then.

The correlation between improvement and disaffection is not new. Alexis de Tocqueville observed such a relationship in eighteenth-century France: "The evil which was suffered patiently as inevitable, seems unendurable as soon as the idea of escaping from it crosses men's minds. All the abuses then removed call attention to those that remain, and they now appear more galling. The evil, it is true, has become less, but sensibility to it has become more acute."

Another part of the explanation of the paradox of prosperity and rising discontent is clearly that "money isn't everything." Prosperity itself brings its own problems. Congestion, noise, and pollution are by-products of economic growth that make the world less livable. The large organizations that are necessary to harness modern technology make the individual feel small and impotent. The concentration on production and profit necessary to economic growth breeds tension, venality, and neglect of "the finer things."

WHY A SOCIAL REPORT OR SET OF SOCIAL INDICATORS?

Curiosity about our social condition would by itself justify an attempt to assess the social health of the Nation. Many people want answers to questions like these: Are we getting healthier? Is pollution increasing? Do children learn more than they used to? Do people have more satisfying jobs than they used to? Is crime increasing? How many people are really alienated? Is the American dream of rags to riches a reality? We are interested in the answers to such questions partly because they would tell us a good deal about our individual and social well-being. Just as we need to measure our incomes, so we need "social indicators," or measures of other dimensions of our welfare, to get an idea of how well off we really are.

A social report with a set of social indicators could not only satisfy our curiosity about how well we are doing, but it could also improve public policymaking in at least two ways. First, it could give social problems more visibility and thus make possible more informed judgments about national priorities. Second, by providing insight into how different measures of national well-being are changing, it might ultimately make possible a better evaluation of what public programs are accomplishing.

The existing situation in areas with which public policy must deal is often unclear, not only to the citizenry in general, but to officialdom as well. The normal processes of journalism and the observations of daily life do not allow a complete or balanced view of the condition of the society. Different problems have different degrees of visibility.

The visibility of a social problem can depend, for example, upon its "news value" or potential drama. The Nation's progress in the space race and the need for space research get a lot of publicity because of the adventure inherent in manned space exploration. Television and tabloid remind us almost daily of the problems of crime, drugs, riots, and sexual misadventure.

The rate of infant mortality may be a good measure of the condition of a society, but this rate is rarely mentioned in the public press, or even perceived as a public problem. The experience of parents (or infants) does not ensure that the problem of infant mortality is perceived as a social problem; only when we know that more than a dozen nations have lower rates of infant mortality than the United States can we begin to make a valid judgment about the condition of this aspect of American society.

Moreover, some groups in our society are well organized, but others are not. This means that the problems of some groups are articulated and advertised, whereas the problems of others are not. Public problems also differ in the extent to which they are immediately evident to the "naked eye." A natural disaster or overcrowding of the highways will be immediately obvious. But ineffectiveness of an educational system or the alienation of youth and minority groups is often evident only when it is too late.

Besides developing measures of the social conditions we care about we also need to see how these measures are changing in response to public programs. If we mount a major program to provide prenatal and maternity care for mothers, does infant mortality go down? If we channel new resources into special programs for educating poor children, does their performance in school eventually increase? If we mount a "war on poverty," what happens to the number of poor people? If we enact new regulations against the emission of pollutants, does pollution diminish?

These are not easy questions, since all major social problems are influenced by many things besides governmental action, and it is hard to disentangle the different effects of different causal factors. But at least in the long run evaluation of the effectiveness of public programs will be improved if we have social indicators to tell us how social conditions are changing.

THE CONTENTS OF THE REPORT

The present volume is not a social report. It is a step in the direction of a social report and the development of a comprehensive set of social indicators.

The report represents an attempt, on the part of social scientists, to look at several important areas and digest what is known about progress toward generally accepted goals. The areas treated in this way are health, social mobility, the condition of the physical environment, income and poverty, public order and safety, and learning, science, and art.

There is also a chapter on participation in social institutions, but because of the lack of measures of improvement or retrogression in this area, it aspires to do no more than pose important questions.

Even the chapters included leave many — perhaps most — questions unanswered. We have measures of death and illness, but no measures of physical vigor or mental health. We have measures of the level and distribution of income, but no measures of the satisfaction that income brings. We have measures of air and water pollution, but no way to tell whether our environment is, on balance, becoming uglier or more beautiful. We have some clues about the test performance of children, but no information about their creativity or attitude toward intellectual endeavor. We have often spoken of the condition of Negro Americans, but have not had the data needed to report on Hispanic Americans, American Indians, or other ethnic minorities.

If the nation is to be able to do better social reporting in the future, and do justice to all of the problems that have not been treated here, it will need a wide variety of information that is not available now. It will need not only statistics on additional aspects of the condition of the Nation as a whole, but also information on different groups of Americans. It will need more data on the aged, on youth, and on women, as well as on ethnic minorities. It will need information not only on objective conditions, but also on how different groups of Americans perceive the conditions in which they find themselves.

We shall now summarize each of the chapters in turn.

HEALTH AND ILLNESS

There have been dramatic increases in health and life expectancy in the twentieth century, but they have been mainly the result of developments whose immediate effect has been on the younger age groups. The expectancy of life at birth in the United States has increased from 47.3 years at the turn of the century to 70.5 years in 1967, or by well over 20 years. The number of expected years of life remaining at age 5 has increased by about 12 years, and that at age 25 about 9 years, but that at age 65 not even 3 years. Modern medicine and standards of living have evidently been able to do a great deal for the young, and especially the very young, but not so much for the old.

This dramatic improvement had slowed down by the early fifties. Since then it has been difficult to say whether our health and life status have been improving or not. Some diseases are becoming less common and others are becoming more common, and life expectancy has changed rather little. We can get some idea whether or not there has been improvement on balance by calculating the "expectancy of *healthy* life" (i.e., life expectancy free of bed-disability and institutionalization). The expectancy of healthy life at birth seems to have improved a trifle since 1957, the first year for which the needed data are available, but certainly not as much as the improvements in medical knowledge and standards of living might have led us to hope.

The American people have almost certainly not exploited all of the potential for better health inherent in existing medical knowledge and standards of living. This is suggested by the fact that Negro Americans have on the average about seven years less expectancy of healthy life than whites, and the fact that at least 15 nations have longer life expectancy at birth than we do.

Why are we not as healthy as we could be? Though our style of life (lack of exercise, smoking, stress, etc.) is partly responsible, there is evidence which strongly suggests that social and economic deprivation and the uneven distribution of medical care are a large part of the problem.

Though the passage of Medicare legislation has assured many older Americans that they can afford the medical care they need, the steps to improve the access to medical care for the young have been much less extensive.

The Nation's system of financing medical care also provides an incentive for the relative underuse of preventive, as opposed to curative and ameliorative, care. Medical insurance may reimburse a patient for the hospital care he gets, but rarely for the checkup that might have kept him well. Our system of relief for the medically indigent, and the fee-for-service method of physician payment, similarly provide no inducements for adequate preventive care.

The emphasis on curative care means that hospitals are sometimes used when some less intensive form of care would do as well. This overuse of hospitals is one of the factors responsible for the extraordinary increases in the price of hospital care.

Between June 1967 and June 1968, hospital daily service

charges increased by 12 percent, and in the previous 12 months they increased by almost 22 percent. Physicians' fees have not increased as much — they rose by 5½ percent between June 1967 and June 1968 — but they still rose more than the general price level. Medical care prices in the aggregate rose at an annual rate of 6.5 percent during 1965–67.

SOCIAL MOBILITY

The belief that no individual should be denied the opportunity to better his condition because of the circumstances of his birth continues to be one of the foundation stones in the structure of American values. But is the actual degree of opportunity and social mobility as great now as it has been?

It was possible to get a partial answer to this question from a survey which asked a sample of American men about their fathers' usual occupations as well as about their own job characteristics. Estimates based on these data suggest that opportunity to rise to an occupation with a higher relative status has not been declining in recent years, and might even have increased slightly. They also show that by far the largest part of the variation in occupational status was explained by factors other than the occupation of the father.

These encouraging findings, in the face of many factors that everyday observation suggest must limit opportunity, are probably due in part to the expansion of educational opportunities. There is some tendency for the sons of those of high education and status to obtain more education than others (an extra year of schooling for the father means on the average an extra 0.3 or 0.4 of a year of education for the son), and this additional education brings somewhat higher occupational status on the average. However, the variations in education that are not explained by the socioeconomic status of the father, and the effects that these variations have on occupational status, are much larger. Thus, on balance, increased education seems to have increased opportunity and upward mobility.

There is one dramatic exception to the finding that opportunity is generally available. The opportunity of Negroes appears to be restricted to a very great extent by current race discrimination and other factors specifically related to race. Though it is true that the average adult Negro comes from a family with a lower socioeconomic status than the average white, and has had fewer years of schooling, and that these and other "background" factors reduce his income, it does not appear to be possible to explain anything like all of the difference in income between blacks and whites in terms of such background factors. After a variety of background factors that impair the qualifications of the average Negro are taken into account, there remains a difference in income of over $1,400 that is difficult to explain without reference to current discrimination. So is the fact that a high status Negro is less likely to be able to pass his status on to his son than is a high status white. A number of other studies tend to add to the evidence that there is continuing discrimination in employment, as does the relationship between Federal employment and contracts (with their equal opportunity provisions) and the above-average proportion of Negroes in high status jobs.

The implication of all this is that the American commitment to opportunity is within sight of being honored in the case of whites, but that it is very far indeed from being honored for the Negro. In addition to the handicaps that arise out of history and past discrimination, the Negro also continues to obtain less reward for his qualifications than he would if he were white.

THE PHYSICAL ENVIRONMENT

This chapter deals with the pollution of the natural environment, and with the manmade, physical environment provided by our housing and the structure of our cities.

Pollution seems to be many problems in many places — air pollution in some communities, water pollution in others, automobile junk yards and other solid wastes in still other places. These seemingly disparate problems can be tied together by one basic fact: The total weight of materials taken into the economy from nature must equal the total weight of materials ultimately discharged as wastes plus any materials recycled.

This means that, given the level and composition of the resources used by the economy, and the degree of recycling, any reduction in one form of waste discharge must be ultimately accompanied by an increase in the discharge of some other kind of waste. For example, some air pollution can be prevented by washing out the particles — but this can mean water pollution, or alternatively solid wastes.

Since the economy does not destroy the matter it absorbs

there will be a tendency for the pollution problem to increase with the growth of population and economic activity. In 1965 the transportation system in the United States produced 76 million tons of five major pollutants. If the transportation technology used does not greatly change, the problem of air pollution may be expected to rise with the growth in the number of automobiles, airplanes, and so on. Similarly, the industrial sector of the economy has been growing at about 4½ percent per year. This suggests that, if this rate of growth were to continue, industrial production would have increased tenfold by the year 2020, and that in the absence of new methods and policies, industrial wastes would have risen by a like proportion.

The chapter presents some measures of air and water pollution indicating that unsatisfactorily high levels of pollution exist in many places. There can be little doubt that pollution is a significant problem already, and that this is an area in which, at least in the absence of timely reporting and intelligent policy, the condition of society can all too easily deteriorate.

As we shift perspective from the natural environment to the housing that shelters us from it, we see a more encouraging trend. The physical quality of the housing in the country is improving steadily, in city center and suburb alike. In 1960, 84 percent of the dwelling units in the country were described as "structurally sound"; in 1966, this percentage had risen to 90 percent. In center cities the percentage had risen from 80 percent in 1960 to 93 percent in 1966. In 1950, 16 percent of the nation's housing was "overcrowded" in the sense that it contained 1.01 or more persons per room. But by 1960, only 12 percent of the nation's housing supply was overcrowded by this standard.

The principal reason for this improvement was the increased per capita income and demand for housing. About 11½ million new housing units were started in the United States between 1960 and 1967, and the figures on the declining proportions of structurally unsound and overcrowded dwellings, even in central cities, suggest that this new construction increased the supply of housing available to people at all income levels.

Even though the housing stock is improving, racial segregation and other barriers keep many Americans from moving into the housing that is being built or vacated and deny them a full share in the benefits of the improvement in the Nation's housing supply.

INCOME AND POVERTY

The Gross National Product in the United States is about $1,000 higher per person than that of Sweden, the second highest nation. In 1969 our GNP should exceed $900 billion. Personal income has quadrupled in this century, even after allowing for changes in population and the value of money.

Generally speaking, however, the distribution of income in the United States has remained practically unchanged over the last 20 years. Although the distribution of income has been relatively stable, the rise in income levels has meant that the number of persons below the poverty line has declined. The poor numbered 40 million in 1960 and 26 million in 1967.

A continuation of present trends, however, would by no means eliminate poverty. The principal cause of the decline has been an increase in earnings. But some of the poor are unable to work because they are too young, too old, disabled, or otherwise prevented from doing so. They would not, therefore, be directly helped by increased levels of wages and earnings in the economy as a whole. Moreover, even the working poor will continue to account for a substantial number of persons by 1974: about 5 million by most recent estimates. This latter group is not now generally eligible for income supplementation.

The Nation's present system of income maintenance is badly in need of reform. It is inadequate to the needs of those who do receive aid and millions of persons are omitted altogether.

This chapter concludes with an analysis of existing programs and a discussion of new proposals which have been put forward in recent years as solutions to the welfare crisis.

PUBLIC ORDER AND SAFETY

The concern about public order and safety in the United States is greater now than it has been in some time.

The compilations of the Federal Bureau of Investigation show an increase in major crimes of 13 percent in 1964, 6 percent in 1965, 11 percent in 1966, and 17 percent in 1967. And studies undertaken for the President's Crime Commission in 1965 indicate that several times as many crimes occur as are reported.

Crime is concentrated among the poor. Both its perpetrators and its victims are more likely to be residents of the poverty areas of central cities than of suburbs and rural areas. Many of

399

those residents in the urban ghettoes are Negroes. Negroes have much higher arrest rates than whites, but it is less widely known that Negroes also have higher rates of victimization than whites of any income group.

Young people commit a disproportionate share of crimes. Part of the recent increase in crime rates can be attributed to the growing proportion of young people in the population. At the same time, the propensity of youth to commit crime appears to be increasing.

Fear of apprehension and punishment undoubtedly deters some crime. The crime rate in a neighborhood drops with much more intensive policing. But crime and disorder tend to center among young people in ghetto areas, where the prospects for legitimate and socially useful activity are poorest. It seems unlikely that harsher punishment, a strengthening of public prosecutors, or more police can, by themselves, prevent either individual crime or civil disorder. The objective opportunities for the poor, and their attitudes toward the police and the law, must also change before the problems can be solved.

LEARNING, SCIENCE, AND ART

The state of the Nation depends to a great degree on how much our children learn, and on what our scientists and artists create. Learning, discovery, and creativity are not only valued in themselves, but are also resources that are important for the Nation's future.

In view of the importance of education, it might be supposed that there would be many assessments of what or how much American children learn. But this is not in fact the case. The standard sources of educational statistics give us hundreds of pages on the resources used for schooling, but almost no information at all on the extent to which these resources have achieved their purpose.

It is possible to get some insight into whether American children are learning more than children of the same age did earlier from a variety of achievement tests that are given throughout the country, mainly to judge individual students and classes. These tests suggest that there may have been a significant improvement in test score performance of children since the 1950's.

When the chapter turns to the learning and education of the poor and the disadvantaged, the results are less encouraging.

Groups that suffer social and economic deprivation systematically learn less than those who have more comfortable backgrounds.

Even when they do as well on achievement tests, they are much less likely to go on to college. Of those high school seniors who are in the top one-fifth in terms of academic ability, 95 percent will ultimately go on to college if their parents are in the top socioeconomic quartile, but only half of the equally able students from the bottom socioeconomic quartile will attend college. Students from the top socioeconomic quartile are five times as likely to go to graduate school as comparably able students from the bottom socioeconomic quartile.

It is more difficult to assess the state of science and art than the learning of American youth. But two factors nonetheless emerge rather clearly. One is that American science is advancing at a most rapid rate and appears to be doing very well in relation to other countries. The Nation's "technological balance of payments," for example, suggests that we have a considerable lead over other countries in technological know-how.

The other point that emerges with reasonable clarity is that, however vibrant the cultural life of the Nation may be, many of the live or performing arts are in financial difficulty. Since there is essentially no increase in productivity in live performances (it will always take four musicians for a quartet), and increasing productivity in the rest of the economy continually makes earnings in the society rise, the relative cost of live performances tends to go up steadily. This can be a significant public problem, at least in those cases where a large number of live performances is needed to insure that promising artists get the training and opportunity they need to realize their full potential.

PARTICIPATION AND ALIENATION: WHAT WE NEED TO LEARN

Americans are concerned, not only about progress along the dimensions that have so far been described, but also about the special functions that our political and social institutions perform. It matters whether goals have been achieved in a democratic or a totalitarian way, and whether the group relationships in our society are harmonious and satisfying.

Unfortunately, the data on the performance of our political and social institutions are uniquely scanty. The chapter on "Participation and Alienation" cannot even hope to do much more than ask the right questions. But such questioning is also of use, for it can remind us of the range of considerations we should keep in mind when setting public policy, and encourage the collection of the needed data in the future.

Perhaps the most obvious function that we expect our institutions to perform is that of protecting our individual freedom. Individual liberty is not only important in itself, but also necessary to the viability of a democratic political system. Freedom can be abridged not only by government action, but also by the social and economic ostracism and discrimination that results from popular intolerance. There is accordingly a need for survey data that can discern any major changes in the degree of tolerance and in the willingness to state unpopular points of view, as well as information about the legal enforcement of constitutional guarantees.

Though liberty gives us the scope we need to achieve our individual purposes, it does not by itself satisfy the need for congenial social relationships and a sense of belonging. The chapter presents evidence that suggests (but does not prove) that at least many people not only enjoy, but also need, a clear sense of belonging, a feeling of attachment to some social group.

There is evidence for this conjecture in the relationship between family status, health, and death rates. In general, married people have lower age-adjusted death rates, lower rates of usage of facilities for the mentally ill, lower suicide rates, and probably also lower rates of alcoholism than those who have been widowed, divorced, or remained single. It is, of course, possible that those who are physically or mentally ill are less likely to find marriage partners, and that this explains part of the correlation. But the pattern of results, and especially the particularly high rates of those who are widowed, strongly suggest that this could not be the whole story.

There are also fragments of evidence which suggest that those who do not normally belong to voluntary organizations, cohesive neighborhoods, families, or other social groupings probably tend to have somewhat higher levels of "alienation" than other Americans.

Some surveys suggest that Negroes, and whites with high degrees of racial prejudice, are more likely to be alienated than other Americans. This, in turn, suggests that alienation has some importance for the cohesion of American society, and that the extent of group participation and the sense of community are important aspects of the condition of the Nation. If this is true, it follows that we need much more information about these aspects of the life of our society.

It is a basic precept of a democratic society that citizens should have equal rights in the political and organizational life of the society. Thus there is also a need for more and better information about the extent to which all Americans enjoy equality before the law, equal franchise, and fair access to public services and utilities. The growth of large scale, bureaucratic organizations, the difficulties many Americans (especially those with the least education and confidence) have in dealing with such organizations, and the resulting demands for democratic participation make the need for better information on this problem particularly urgent.

•   •   •

Though almost all Americans want progress along each of the dimensions of well being discussed in this Report, the Nation cannot make rapid progress along all of them at once. That would take more resources than we have. The Nation must decide which objectives should have the higher priorities, and choose the most efficient programs for attaining these objectives. Social reporting cannot make the hard choices the Nation must make any easier, but ultimately it can help to insure that they are not made in ignorance of the Nation's needs.

❡ F. *Despite the ancient precedents for cooperation between American science and the federal government, and despite the flourishing liaison between science and the Pentagon in particular, proper relations were neither always obvious nor easy. At the behest of the Congress, a study was made in 1969 of fourteen occasions on which the legislative branch had been called upon to legislate in scientific or technical areas. These case studies led to the following "General Observations on Science and Government,"* Technical Information for Congress. Report to the Subcommittee on Science, Research, and Development of the Committee on Science and Astronautics, U.S. House of Representatives, 91st Cong., 1 sess., prepared by the Science Policy Research Division, Legislative Reference Service, Library of Congress, April 25, 1969, pp. 5–13.]

THE SEARCH FOR A COMMON GROUND

The interaction of science and politics has often proved rewarding to mankind. Great periods of science have had direct bearing on political innovation and advance. For example, the scientific achievements of Isaac Newton, early in the 18th century, were the primary motivating force in the "age of reason," a period in which, perhaps for the first time, man perceived the possibility of scientifically designing his government to fit his needs on a practical basis. This rational, analytical approach to the political order was one of the main intellectual ingredients of the Constitutional Convention that met in Philadelphia in 1787.

One of the great accomplishments of science in the 20th century was the development and confirmation of the theory of equivalence of matter and energy. Up to this time, these two physical quantities had been regarded as separate and unrelated. The theory of the equivalence of matter and energy merged two great sets of information, linked up two worlds, and generated countless new opportunities for further scientific discovery and practical human benefits.

The stimulus given to science by this latter event has been matched by the stimulus given to the effort to make effective political use of the skills and methods of science. However, as this effort proceeds, mankind encounters the extremely difficult task of reconciling scientific values with human values. For there is no theory of the equivalence of the physical world and the normative world. The values of science remain distinct from the values of politics.

Even between the scientist and the politician, in a pure sense, there are differences in habits of thought and language. These differences can easily be exaggerated, and are rarely as pure as the following enumeration might be taken to imply. However, for purposes of simplicity, the important differences in tendency between these two groups can be stated in absolute terms, as follows:

The vocabulary of science is elaborate and specialized, but objective and factual; that of politics is more everyday, and is centered on value judgments.

The rules of science data differ from the rules of legal evidence: scientific truth is established by objective demonstration and confirmed by replication; political truth is established by consensual agreement, usually after an "adversary" contest.

Science deals with its subject matter in mainly quantitative terms, politics in mainly qualitative terms.

The subject matter of scientific issues is foreign to the experience of political decisionmakers; few scientists join the ranks of the political decisionmakers, and few political decisionmakers can accept the product of scientific analysis as unqualified guidance in making political decisions.

Basic science is insulated from personal desires, expectations, or motivations as to what is discovered; applied science is concerned with meeting a social goal, but the scientific tests of effectiveness of any particular project of applied science are objective rather than subjective. Conversely, the thrust of politics focuses on human desires, expectations, and motivations; the political test of effectiveness is mainly whether or not the social response to a project is (or is likely to be) favorable.

Given these two differing groups, with differing habits of thought, sets of values, and rules of evidence, how does communication flow from the scientific world to the political world? How are "spokesmen for science" selected to give evidence on scientific aspects of pending legislation? Is it important that they be regarded by political leadership as "eminent scientists" or that they are accepted by the scientific community as its authentic spokesmen and interpreters? How is scientific information converted from data into evidence useful to political decisionmakers? To what extent is there a tendency for scientific witnesses to volunteer information or respond to questions beyond the limits of their competence? To what extent do political decisionmakers accept the unquestioned eminence of chosen scientists in particular disciplines as a general certification of their wisdom respecting matters external to their discipline? Do the personal biases and motivations of scientists impair the objectivity of their testimony or render it suspect to the political decisionmaker?

In a broader sense, how do political decisionmakers weigh the relative merits of scientific and social values? Do scientists have a legitimate role in assessing the relative importance or merit that society should attach to scientific truth and political value? Are normative judgments outside the scope of competence of the scientists? How far should a scientist go in interpreting his data in support of an issue in which both scientific and political factors are involved? These questions underlie the quandary of the political leaders of society in attempting to harness science to the achievement of social goals.

A practical illustration of the interaction between science and politics, and between the scientific goal of achieving the best combination of measurable quantities, and the political goal of expanding human freedom, can be drawn from the system of personal transportation by automobile. In this case, human freedom is defined as the absence of regulation of the behavior of the individual. Extreme assertion of individual freedom in the use of this means of transportation, experience suggests, would take such forms as competitive behavior, discourtesy, flouting of commonsense precautions, the right to drive unsafe vehicles, etc. Untrammeled freedom on the highway would almost certainly have intolerably dangerous consequences: practically speaking, motorists would be denied freedom to drive in reasonable safety. Even with present highway regulations and enforcement levels, some 50,000 persons are killed and millions are injured annually in the operation of the system. With less control, these numbers could be expected to be higher. On the other hand, it would be technically feasible to reduce this carnage virtually to zero by the development of a comprehensive and disciplined system of highway transportation designed to do the best possible job of moving people about as they wish, but giving an absolute, overriding priority to the total elimination of all causes of unsafety. It is possible to do this. But the inconvenience to the individual highway user would be intolerable.

The costs of such a system would almost certainly include decreased personal freedom of all highway users under close regulation. Up to now, society has rejected such an extreme solution, and has accepted the compromise between complete (unregulated) freedom on the highway and complete (closely regulated) safety on the highway. The practical question facing society is whether the compromise is at a satisfactory balance point between freedom from regulation and freedom from risk of accident; any political action respecting this balance point might logically be subjected to scientific analysis to determine such questions as: What are the costs and benefits of the proposed change? What reduction in the probability of accident and what reduced freedom will result from some new control or technological innovation? At the same time, political analysis might consider such issues as: Does society find the cost acceptable in terms of the benefit? Have the scientific potentials been fully exploited within the limits of tolerable levels of regulation?

For practical purposes, accident victims are not merely those self-selected by their own carelessness. Everybody is exposed to some average level of risk, and the total amount of risk per individual depends on how much time he spends on the road. Risk is thus a factor of use, and in this sense it is "equitable." If society at large were to pay all direct and indirect costs of highway unsafety, each reduction in personal freedom caused by safety regulations could be related to actual dollar savings achieved by the reduction of accidents. The gain could be measured and indicated in dollar terms. But the cost — in human freedom — cannot be measured or expressed in dollars. It would be impossible to say — scientifically — that any given reduction in freedom in order to achieve a given increase in highway safety is warranted by the dollar savings. In the language of the systems analyst, science cannot "optimize" for freedom but only for system performance. As long as society continues to aspire to the political goal of freedom, there will remain an inherent disparity between social goals and scientific goals.

The role of the political system is to mediate this conflict, to resolve these two sets of goals and standards in a practical way. Somehow the political system has to decide how much freedom ought to be sacrificed, in the interest of achieving some generally satisfactory or tolerable level of safety. The scientist measures quantities, defines alternatives, and states the physical costs and rewards of the alternatives. But it is up to the politician, not the scientist, to choose the preferred alternative. Can a scientist advocate a policy decision without either (1) discounting as inconsequential such political values as freedom, happiness, and the like; or (2) accepting responsibility for making unscientific comparisons of scientific values with intangible normative values?

In general terms, the problem of the Congress in dealing with scientific issues of politics appears to be fourfold: first, to identify and delimit the scientific content of political issues; second, to devise intellectual bridges to enable the scientific world to communicate effectively with the political world; third, to establish practical political techniques for assessing and validating scientific evidence; and fourth, to formalize the process by which the quantitative cost/effectiveness concepts of science and technology are weighed along with, or balanced against, the qualitative values of politics and society. In the projected series of case histories of recent political decisions involving science and technology, attention will be given to ways in which the Congress came to grips with this fourfold problem. Specifically, answers will be sought to the following questions:

1. How are scientific issues brought to the Congress and how does the manner of their presentation influence the outcome?
2. What information from what sources, bearing on the issue, was received by the congressional decisionmakers, and how did it influence the outcome?
3. What institutional decisionmaking method was employed in the Congress for each issue, and how did the method of decision influence the outcome?
4. What was the outcome of each issue, both in terms of the values expressed at the time of decisionmaking, and in retrospect — as judged by the values of the present day?

THE POLITICAL FRAMEWORK

It would seem to be a basic proposition that any assessment of the social function of science, or of political decisionmaking as to the social uses of science, must be relative to the goals of the society. The primary goal that has historically been shared by all political factions in the United States is personal liberty or human freedom. All functions of government in the United States can surely be regarded as contributing to this unifying goal. Freedom, in this context, is a very broad and comprehensive term. It may generally be taken to mean the protection of man against undesired compulsions of the environment, both physical and human, and protection against undesired compulsions of the body and mind of the individual. Science undoubtedly contributes in many important ways to the means by which freedom is sought and attained. But the determination of which program to carry out, or which aspect of freedom to emphasize, is essentially a political task.

Because freedom is elusive, political means to achieve and expand it in the United States have taken many directions and raised many issues. Its achievement has been sought according to different political and economic concepts, logically developed and pragmatically tested. Emphasis has been placed successively on centralized government, with strongly enforced legal responsibility, economic mercantilism, and expanding credit resources (up to 1800); then on local initiative, local police power, and local monetary management (up to 1860); then on national resource and facility development, large corporate organizations, and concentrated investment (up to 1930); then on welfare capitalism, Federal paternalism, and minimum standards of economic well-being (after 1930). During these successive evolutionary periods of U.S. growth, until after World War II, science was largely peripheral. Except for the encouragement of scientific agriculture after 1863, science remained largely a private matter. Technological support for economic growth rested on domestic technological innovation, drawing largely on basic research conducted in Western Europe, and exploited by private citizens and companies for their own profit.

An accelerating tendency has been evident in the United States since about 1915 for the problems and tasks of society to be recognized as national in scope and amenable to solution in primarily national terms. These have included the great depression, war, education, civil rights, environmental pollution, health and medical science, the exploration of space and the oceans. The trend toward a national approach in problem solving has been reinforced by such factors as

1. The sheer magnitude and scope of the problems and tasks.
2. The appearance of an increasing array of major tasks essential to society but offering no evident opportunity for direct profit in their execution.
3. The superior financial resources of the National Government.
4. The growing technical sophistication of Federal administrative staffs in tackling large assignments.
5. The growing skills of the political decisionmakers in defining problems and assigning responsibility for solving them.
6. The expanding scope of the scientific method, and concurrent political acceptance of the method, in dealing systematically and objectively with an ever-larger fraction of public concerns.

Perhaps the most significant — certainly the most dramatic — event evidencing this centralizing trend was the successful scientific and technological effort in World War II to develop the atomic bomb. The mounting of a large technological effort under Federal sponsorship was not inconsistent with the historical growth of the American Nation. Great national programs had been undertaken in the recent past to dig the Panama Canal, to harness the Tennessee and western rivers, to restore the Dust Bowl. These were in the tradition of a pragmatic Nation that had tied political power of the States to a national head count, that located its county seats for 1-day access by local populations, that built post roads and railroads as national enterprises. But the idea of a national effort toward a big goal achieved a higher level of refinement in the atomic bomb project. It required the marshaling of a large team of scientists, backed by the financial resources and authority of the National Government, coordinated in the quest for a defined objective; its outcome was the achievement of a scientific goal long thought impossible. By the Congress and the public, the conclusion was plausibly drawn in 1945 that the creativity of science could be harnessed similarly to achieve other specific goals of society as these were defined and adopted through the political process.

It is relevant to ask whether the attitude of Congress toward science has been influenced by partisan considerations — whether, for example, it has been closely involved with the contest between liberal and conservative. The details of method, procedure, and scope of the political uses of science are indeed exposed at times to the stresses of political controversy, but there appears to be general agreement that science as an institution ought to be vigorously supported. Both major political parties have accepted the initiative in encouraging expanded Federal sponsorship of scientific research and education. Political activists have recognized in the scientific method a powerful instrument for achieving social objectives while conservatives have seen in science a means by which the products of many independent researchers can stimulate economic and cultural growth with a minimum of Federal contribution or intervention.

The pragmatic character of the American Nation was reinforced by the dramatic lesson of the atomic bomb project. But other less dramatic forces were at work that also encouraged public belief in the efficacy of science for public purposes, such as

1. A rising level of public education, with increasing emphasis on scientific materialism;
2. A great increase in the population of trained scientists; and

3. A proliferation of demonstrations of scientific success, such as in military hardware and systems, space projects, achievements in biomedicine, and the bewildering proliferation of computer technology.

Science has apparently been enlisted in the national effort to achieve the political goal of freedom. As with each previous period of U.S. history, the means used has tended to shape the objectives and the methodology by which the objectives are sought. Since science is inherently materialistic and systematic, the application of science to the preservation and expansion of human freedom have led to the extensive use for this purpose of the computer, systems analysis, cost/effectiveness calculations, and quantitative standards of measurement. Political leaders apparently look to the skills and techniques of science to wipe out disease, guarantee military security, extend man's life, control his numbers of progeny, eliminate the hazards of accident and environmental degradation, ensure economic growth and stability, erase pockets of poverty, expand the utility of leisure time, achieve the exploration of space and the oceans, and perpetuate the resource base needed to feed, clothe, house, and equip man for safety, comfort, and happiness.

More specifically, science is to be the means by which the political system is to achieve a long list of concrete national projects such as an anticancer campaign, a communications satellite, a rapid transit system, improved technical standards of highway and automotive safety, a desalting plant, and so on.

In the political world, science has become a foremost national resource whose exploitation is regarded as contributing to the enlargement or preservation of human freedom. Basic research is judged to contribute by enlarging human understanding, applied research by enlarging human options, and technology by putting selected options to work to create beneficial structures and systems.

However, as the automotive safety illustration demonstrated, science is not in complete harmony with the political objective of the United States. The achievements of science can sometimes extend freedom, but they also act at times to constrain it. Science is based on the exercise of human discipline to establish a rigorous characterization of cause and effect relationships. Applied research exploits these relationships by being obedient to them. Engineering materializes these relationships into coherent structures and systems. In these contexts, man emerges as a human component of systems, subservient to the same natural laws of cause and effect as are the inanimate elements of systems.

If the Congress is confronted by the opportunity to exploit science to expand human freedoms, the Congress would also seem to be confronted by the obligation to constrain or resist the encroachment of science on human freedoms. Science does not create ideal relationships of man and nature; it identifies and applies the laws of nature. Man can achieve a wider range of goals by the use of science than without. But the application of science defines limits as well as opportunities, and sometimes both together. Science has become the art of the possible; politics is evolving into an institution for reconciling the force of inexorable cause-and-effect natural law with the perversities of human desires and preferences. It must answer the question: How much science does society want?

THE SCIENTIFIC FRAMEWORK

The concept followed in this study is that basic scientific research has as its goal the discovery of facts about nature. It is structured into such disciplines as physics, chemistry, biology, astronomy, etc.; into such subdisciplines as solid state physics, inorganic chemistry, solar astronomy etc.; and into such integrating disciplines as physical chemistry, astrophysics, ecology, etc.

Applied research is the use of information about nature, derived from basic research, and employed to make feasible some social goal. It is structured in two ways: (1) Into loose categories of like fields or disciplines, such as meteorology, metallurgy, electronics, agronomy, etc.; these overlap with (2) subject categories suggesting purpose, such as transportation, communications, materials, and standards, etc. All goals of applied research aim at a single overriding objective, which is to improve the compatibility between man and his environment.

For purposes of social analysis, it is convenient to classify applied scientific research into four types of activities by broad social purpose, as follows:

1. Physical modification of man: An improvement in the feasibility of man's capability to adapt himself to his environment by physical changes of his own structure.
2. Application of natural resources: An improvement in the

feasibility of man's exploitation of the resources of nature to change the physical environment to render it more compatible with man.

3. Environmental restoration: An improvement in the feasibility of corrective actions to restore the physical environment by reversing impairments wrought by man or by natural forces.

4. The social environment: An improvement in the feasibility of actions by man to enhance his compatibility as an element of the changing social/human environment.

The relationship between science and politics is epitomized by a comparison of their respective goals: environmental compatibility versus human freedom. Human freedom is evidently diminished by man's incompatibility with his environment. It is also diminished by the imposition of regulation and control to improve his compatibility with his environment. In assessing each issue involving scientific matters, Congress appears to need advice that will help to answer three fundamental questions:

1. What is the potential contribution of the action to improved compatibility of man with his environment?
2. What are the costs and benefits of the action, in terms of human freedom?
3. In the particular issue, how much freedom is equal to how much compatibility?

The formal limits of the scientific method are that it can describe relationships and outcomes of given conditions, but cannot make value judgments about these relationships and outcomes. The trained scientist can collect and examine the scientific data in his field, and can draw conclusions as to their validity and meaning. In basic research, he can conclude that further research in some particular area has some degree of probability of disclosing information of significance relative to many elements of nature — contributing new knowledge to fill many gaps or open up many new possibilities of understanding. In applied research, he can identify possible scientific solutions affording alternative means of achieving some social goal; he can estimate what order of magnitude of effort would be required by each alternative and what probability each has of succeeding. The trained technologist can calculate the relative cost/effectiveness of carrying out alternative engineering approaches to the achievement of social goals (or of not doing so). But the scientist or technologist transcends his discipline when he advises on whether society should exploit some technical opportunity, should embark upon some applied project, or should apply some particular set of performance criteria.

Full compliance with this disciplinary constraint on science advice is rarely observed. In the purest philosophic sense, even the invariable appeal of the scientist that more money be invested in research in his area of interest is a technical violation. Evidently there is a quandary here. Basic research, applied research, and technological engineering are peopled by motivated specialists with personal hopes and professional ambitions. For them to live within the philosophic constraint of nonadvocacy is to deny themselves the opportunity to increase the probability of achieving their ambitions. For them not to practice this self-denial is to contravene their own discipline.

The opportunities in all three areas of technical endeavor are limitless, while the availability of supporting resources is not. Since society cannot support all worthy projects, on what basis can it choose, other than by consultation with those who seek to carry out the endeavors, who are the most knowledgeable about the possible rewards of doing so?

On the other hand, several pitfalls lie in the way of communication from the scientist to the politician relative to public issues with a scientific content. Some of these have already been enumerated in Chapter One, such as differences in vocabulary, rules of validation, quantification, subject matter, etc. However, a general characterization of these pitfalls is illustrated by a social phenomenon classically known as the "Egyptian priesthood." Under the Pharaohs, the Egyptian priests had special knowledge of geometry, which enabled them to control the distribution of lands. They had special knowledge of the mysteries of nature, and special vocabularies in which to express their findings. By this exclusive knowledge they were able to control and influence the administration of the government. Their judgments were unchallenged because only their associates in the temples knew the language; the loyalty of the cult preserved their solid front. In a sense, the Pharaohs had the same problem as the Congress of today; how to achieve credible communication with a knowledgeable cult of specialists whose social contribution was undeniable, but whose ways were obscure and whose findings were not subject to proof test outside of the priestly cartel.

Under these conditions the scientist is — or may be thought to be — subject to the temptation of advising not only on *what* but as to *whether*. Even when a survey of a field of science concludes that more money should be spent on research, it is in effect making a value judgment on social priorities. Another danger is that in the interpretation of data to the politician the scientist will incline, or permit himself to be encouraged, toward a finding in response to the situation rather than strictly limited to the data. Scientific data are rarely absolute and are more usually approximations or probabilities. Informed judgment plays an important part in scientific decisions. Here the politician may be at the mercy of the scientist, but at the same time the politician — by structuring the situation — may influence the interpretation of the data.

The difficulty is compounded by the difference in symbols of the scientific and the political subcultures. Communicating among themselves, scientists express technical issues in confidence levels, figures of merit, uncertainties, and probabilities, all in quantitative terms. But in communicating with politicians, they encounter the obstacle that the accustomed quantitative indicators lack significance and need to be translated into words. For example, the difference between a purity of aluminum of "four nines" and "six nines" is understandable to a scientist, but not necessarily to a politician. (These are 99.99 percent pure and 99.9999 percent pure.) Both forms of aluminum are very pure, but one is more so than the other. The communication could be improved by giving relative costs per pound of material at each level of purity (say, 40 cents and $800). Or by indicating how much of each is normally produced (say, several tons versus a few pounds). Or it might be helpful to indicate the kinds of uses each level of purity has. The purpose of scientific language is to concentrate meaning. The necessity to explain and clarify his terms leads the scientist to virtually endless explanation, and it is sometimes easer to accept shortcuts in which the truth is somehow lost.

❡ *G. In October of 1969 President Richard Nixon announced the formation of another of his Task Forces, this one to "review the Federal Government's present science policy and make recommendations as to its future scope and direction."*

Headed by Ruben F. Mettler, Executive Vice President (and later President) of TRW, Inc., the aerospace giant, the Task Force charted a course for the new Administration. The following selection is from Science and Technology: Tools for Progress. Report of the President's Task Force on Science Policy *(Washington, April 1970), pp. 4–13.*]

SCIENCE, TECHNOLOGY, AND NATIONAL GOALS

The Task Force recommends that the President explicitly enunciate, as a national policy, the need for vigorous, high-quality science and technology, focusing on our national goals and purposes, and recognizing the cultural and inspirational values in man's scientific progress.

The Task Force also recommends that the President call for — as one national goal — continuing leadership in science and in the technology relevant to our other national goals and purposes.

Finally, it is recommended that the President direct that increasing emphasis be given to using our scientific and technological capabilities to *quantitatively* develop and project long-range requirements in support of our national goals.

EXPANDING APPLICATIONS FOR SCIENCE AND TECHNOLOGY

The Task Force recommends that the President direct the appropriate Departments and Agencies to strengthen their capability to utilize science and technology effectively in a broad-scale attack on social, urban, and environmental problems. More specifically, the Task Force recommends that:

1. Each Executive Department and Agency responsible for a significant portion of the total national social, urban, and environmental programs be directed to develop (on a periodically updated basis, tied to the budget cycle) a ten- to fifteen-year projection of specific steps toward achievements of their principal goals. These projections should include sufficient quantitative detail, including costs and schedules of results to be achieved by particular points in time, to permit integrated review for adequacy and consistency by the Council on Urban Affairs and the Council on Environmental Quality. These reviews should ultimately lead to Presidential approval, and where needed, Congressional authorization. It is recommended that these Councils be supported by sufficient staff, on an ad hoc basis if necessary,

to help define the initial task and to monitor its implementation.

2. In preparing these proposed long-range programs (which, the Task Force recognizes, have already been initiated by some Agencies), particular attention be given to identifying long-range requirements for basic and applied research and the institutional machinery for its achievement. This should include identification of opportunities for the utilization of existing but underexploited technology, and for the identification of technical and economic issues which must be analyzed and resolved to permit timely downstream decisionmaking. Additionally, attention should be given to the development of statements of requirements that will, when approved, permit universities, business, labor, professional, and other institutions to gain understanding of long-range national needs and planning factors pertinent to their separate functions.

3. As part of this general effort, the Office of Science and Technology should strengthen its own resources in the social and behavioral sciences, and should work jointly with the appropriate mission agencies and with the National Science Foundation to develop specific programs for enlarged support and increased utilization of the social and behavioral sciences.

4. The Office of Science and Technology should be directed by Executive Order to develop a Federal structure for technology assessment, in general accord with the recent National Academy of Sciences and National Academy of Engineering reports to the Congress on this subject. Such development should be carried out in close coordination with the Congress and the National Science Foundation, and in consultation with the NAS and the NAE.

MANAGEMENT OF DIRECT FEDERAL SUPPORT
FOR BASIC AND APPLIED RESEARCH

The Task Force recommends that the President direct the Office of Science and Technology, in coordination with the Bureau of the Budget, and with the advice and cooperation of the Executive Departments and the National Science Foundation, to develop improved machinery for the integrated management of direct Federal support of basic and applied research. This effort should be related properly to long-range projections of total national interests and requirements, and should include Congressional approval as needed. To accomplish this general intent, the Task Force recommends that:

1. The level of support provided to the National Science Foundation and other basic research agencies (e.g., the National Institutes of Health) be increased as rapidly as feasible. A level of support of approximately 0.1 percent of the gross national product (GNP) is suggested as a reasonable level for support of the National Science Foundation, to be achieved as soon as possible. The level of support should permit the NSF to be responsible for approximately one-third of all Federally supported basic and academic research. A transition phase extending over several years may be necessary to insure continuing support (without reductions in total levels) of projects and facilities which should be supported nationally and phased out of mission agencies. Great care must be exercised to maintain close connection between each mission agency and basic research in areas which can reasonably be expected to bear strongly on that agency's problems. This would mean continuing support of considerable basic research by mission oriented agencies and avoiding too narrow an interpretation of the relevance of such research.

2. A specific program be developed and proposed to the Congress in general accord with the National Science Board Report NSB 69–1 on Federal support of graduate scientific education. Key steps in implementing this program should receive legislative authorization and initial appropriations not later than fiscal year 1972.

3. A review be made of the role and future plans of all Federal laboratories be carried out by a commission made up primarily of persons outside the sponsoring agencies, and possibly organized through the coorperative efforts of the President and the Congress.

4. The Office of Science and Technology be designated by Executive Order as the principal organization within the Executive Branch for establishing the priorities among the various competing scientific research programs and major projects that will be considered in developing the Federal budget to be recommended to the Congress, beginning in fiscal year 1972. In accomplishing this task, the OST, in close coordination with the Bureau of the Budget, should receive the advice and cooperation of the Executive Departments and the National Science Foundation, and should seek advice from outside the Government, including the National Academy of Sciences and the National Academy of Engineering.

STIMULATING TECHNOLOGICAL INNOVATION
BY PRIVATE INSTITUTIONS

The Task Force recommends that the President enunciate a national policy of increasing long-term participation by private institutions — particularly business — in social, urban, and environmental programs.

It is also recommended that the President direct the appropriate Departments and Agencies of Government to establish broadly based efforts systematically to identify the deterrents to private investment of capital and technology in social, urban, and environmental programs, and to suggest specific incentives for action and remedies for each such deterrent.

SCIENCE POLICY AS RELATED TO NATIONAL SECURITY

The Task Force recommends that the President enunciate a national policy of increased emphasis on research and development for national security purposes — even at the expense of current military hardware procurement, if necessary.

INTERNATIONAL INITIATIVES UTILIZING SCIENCE
AND TECHNOLOGY

The Task Force recommends that the President continue to encourage the major Departments and Agencies of Government to suggest specific new science-based foreign policy initiatives and opportunities for international cooperation.

It is also recommended that the Administration make clear a policy of technical assistance, with increased emphasis on providing assistance to underdeveloped nations, which will help them build their own institutions of scientific research, education, and technical training.

CONTINUING DEVELOPMENT OF SCIENCE POLICY

The Task Force recommends that the President direct his Science Adviser to develop, for the President's approval, a broadly based program for the continuing development of national science policy. This program should provide for full participation by individuals from both within the Government and from outside the Government, experienced in politics, economics, management, labor, and engneering, as well as practicing scientists and science administrators. . . .

THE NATIONAL NEED FOR SCIENCE AND TECHNOLOGY

Our national progress will become ever more critically dependent upon the excellence of our science and technology. A vigorous, high-quality program aimed at advancing our scientific and technological capabilities (including the social, economic, and behavioral components) is vital to all national goals and purposes. Such a program is especially vital to our national defense and security and to our international posture generally; to our ability to negotiate properly safeguarded arms limitations; to our continued economic growth and development and to our international trade balance; to the health of business, labor, and the professions; to the quality of our environment; to the personal health and welfare of all; to the scope and quality of our educational processes; and to the culture, spirit, and inspiration of our people generally. The effectiveness of essentially all our social institutions, including particularly Government itself, is deeply influenced by the quality of our science and technology.

The Nation, therefore, has a fundamental need for excellence in science and technology. Accordingly, it also needs to insure that the effectiveness of our science and technology is not downgraded or destroyed by the unthinking or the uninformed. That is not to say that the limitations of science and technology should not be recognized. We do not suggest complacent acceptance of the unwanted side effects of narrowly motivated or incompletely understood applications of science. Nor do we suggest that technology should dictate social purpose. On the contrary, we wish to emphasize the importance of seeking to optimize utilization of science and technology in the service of social, political, and economic goals.

Anti-Science Attitudes. The rapid rise of attitudes disdainful of science and technology and the disillusionment of many young people with science and technology is of grave concern. The sources of these attitudes include deficiencies in the application of science and technology that should in fact be criticized and should be corrected. Inanimate technology is not of itself the problem; rather the primary need is "to conceive ways to discover and repair the deficiencies in the processes and institutions by which society puts the tools of science and technology to work." The sources of the shift in attitudes toward science and technology also include widespread lack of perspective and understanding of their nature and role in past and future improvement in the human condition. The public and its elected representative must have a better grasp of both the limitations and the promise of science and technology. Priority should be given to presenting this complex matter to the public in a balanced and understandable fashion. The responsibility for achieving this understanding starts with the Executive and Legislative branches of the Federal government and spreads to include state and local government, universities, business and professional organizations, and other private institutions in positions of leadership.

Scientific Leadership. The scientific and technological resources of this Nation are among its most powerful tools for the achievement of our social, political, and economic purposes. The management, strength, and proper allocation of these vital resources are political responsibilities of the highest significance, with not only short-term but also very long-term implications both nationally and internationally. The leadership of today must provide the legacy for tomorrow.

The Task Force believes that one of the important national goals for which this Nation should strive is leadership and excellence in science itself — as a long-range investment in achieving the Nation's other goals, as a precursor to more directly applicable and controllable technology, and as a contribution to the culture, spirit, and inspiration of our people.

DEFINING LONG-RANGE NATIONAL GOALS AND ISSUES
IN QUANTITATIVE TERMS

National policy governing science and technology should in principle be a mirror image of our national goals and purposes. Science policy should in part be a statement about the priorities of the future. While these generalized statements have wide acceptance, many of the mechanisms and concepts implicit in them are difficult to define in detail and complex to administer.

Regional goals. The machinery of Federal, state, and local government is vast. Each major problem, such as environmental pollution, is pervasive and interdependent with others. Hundreds of separate institutions, both private and public, must function as a part of a team if the problems are to be solved. Proper distinctions must be made between the responsibilities and opportunities of Federal, state, and local government, as well as between those of universities, business enterprise, and other private institutions. National goals and purposes have distributed (e.g., geographical) as well as central components. The "points of principal action" — and hence the foci of primary responsibility and opportunity for solution — of some of our most urgent national concerns are central (e.g., national defense). Others are regional (e.g., air and water pollution, interurban transportation), while still others can best be managed at the state or city level.

Definition of Goals. The central crisis is one of management, of leadership, of inspiration, with an eye to the future as well as the present. Generalized goals must be broken down into specific subelements and specific realistic milestones established; specific responsibilities must be assigned with clear-cut processes of review, specific attainable criteria and standards with quantitative as well as qualitative substance must be promulgated; and all of these should be projected over suitable periods of time (e.g., ten to twenty years), with specific machinery for review and projection.

Such long-range national programs should, of course, have the benefit of searching Congressional debate and formal legislative approval as appropriate. Frequently heard reasons why ten- or fifteen-year national programs cannot be established (e.g., the yearly budget cycle, the short-term nature of legislative and executive terms, the unwillingness to commit future administrations) are not convincing.

The Contribution of Science and Technology. We have been discussing one of the central responsibilities of government. The more restricted question here is: What special contribution can science and technology make to the definition and achievement of long-range national goals? Of course, basic and applied research can contribute to understanding — the vital basis for all other parts of the process — if focused properly on these problems. In addition, "technology has a direct impact on values by virtue of its capacity for creating new opportunities. By making possible what was not possible before, it offers individuals and society new options to choose from." (2) Finally, a great majority of our current urban and environmental problems have important technological or scientific components. That is not to say that science and technology alone can solve these problems or even that the technological component is normally the dominant one — in most cases, it is not.

Because of the technological components inherent in many current problems, however, and because of the nature of the tools of science and technology, they can make a special and vitally needed contribution to the definition of long-range goals, and to the central *management* problems inherent in broad long-range national programs. Detailed quantitative development of qualitative goals — which engineers and scientists are especially equipped to do — can aid in choosing wisely among alternatives. It can also help define the subelements of a particular program with sufficient clarity to permit each of the widely dispersed elements in our society to grasp its part, and to assist in reviewing and reprojecting the program as needed.

It is the view of the Task Force that a special effort is needed to make fuller use of the tools of science and technology in *quantitatively* projecting long-range requirements associated with our many pressing social, urban, and environmental problems: air and water pollution, waste disposal, educational services, health care, mass transportation, housing and urban development, crime prevention, and energy requirements, for example. The magnitude of concern and awareness for such problems, and increasing realization of the urgent need to mobilize our resources to combat them, is clearly reflected in such recent actions as the establishment by the President of the Council on Urban Affairs and the Council on Environmental Quality.

We can no longer afford to approach the longer-range future haphazardly. As the pace of change accelerates, the process of change becomes more complex. . . . Our need now is to seize on the future as the key dimension in our decisions, and to chart that future as consciously as we are accustomed to charting the past.

Richard M. Nixon, *July 12, 1969.*

THE IMPORTANCE OF SCIENCE AND TECHNOLOGY
TO ECONOMIC GROWTH

Economic growth will, over a long period of time, define the total level of resources within which our national goals must be achieved. Because of the central significance of economic growth to all other national goals, it is especially important to point out its dependence on science and technology.

It is generally recognized that the economic growth of highly industrialized countries in the western world has been heavily dependent on the technological developments which have been incorporated into their societies. In the past half century the economic growth of the United States has been as much determined by new technology as it has by the continuous investment of capital. If a major national goal is increasing the quality of life for the mass of our population, it becomes essential that continued technological development also be a high priority national goal. A stagnant technology will mean a stagnant economy. In this regard, it is of interest to note the statement of Mr. Kosygin to the XXIII Party Congress in March 1966: "... The course of the economic competition between the two world systems depends on the rate of development of our science, and on the scale on which we use the results of research in production. ..."

The growth and diffusion of technology have expanded the goods and services available to the people by improving the inputs used for production, by improving the outputs flowing from the production line, and by reducing the volume of inputs needed per unit of output. Scientific and technological advances have led to the invention or discovery of new and improved materials, or materials that can substitute for limited or vanishing natural supplies. The quality of machines, plant, and rolling stock has been improved and their ability to deliver output at less cost greatly enhanced. New or better final products have been turned out. Better production processes and better organization of the flow of materials and of production have cut costs. Better control has made for economies in the use of inventories. People have been encouraged to improve their productive capacity and to engage in economically productive work by the attraction of the new products made available for consumption by technological advance.

However, technological change also leads to regional shifts in the distribution of resources, the obsolescence of skills, etc., which require movement, retraining, and other adjustments by people. Such change puts a high premium on those who are current in scientific and technical skills, and on continued education of personnel already in responsible jobs. The costs entailed in all of these adjustments should, of course, be deducted in assessing the contribution of science and technology to the growth of output. Although difficult to measure, some place these costs very high, even to the point of questioning the social value of any significant degree of technological change. Most economists believe, however, that a reasonable allowance for such costs does, on the whole, leave a substantial net gain.

Continued study of the role and potential of science and

technology in promoting and enhancing economic growth — both nationally and regionally — is important to the setting of realistic long-range quantitative national goals.

RECOMMENDATIONS

The Task Force recommends that the President explicitly enunciate, as a national policy, the need for vigorous, high-quality science and technology, focusing on our national goals and purposes, and recognizing the cultural and inspirational values in man's scientific progress.

The Task Force also recommends that the President call for — as one national goal — continuing leadership in science and in the technology relevant to our other national goals and purposes.

Finally, it is recommended that the President direct that increasing emphasis be given to using our scientific and technological capabilities quantitatively to develop and project long-range requirements in support of our national goals.

❡ H. *The members of President Nixon's 1969 Task Force represented some of the most powerful centers of American scientific activity: TRW, Inc., Du Pont, RCA, the National Academy of Sciences, the University of California, the Oak Ridge National Laboratory, and even included Mr. Oscar Ruebhausen, a veteran counselor of Vannevar Bush in the days of the OSRD. Increasingly, however, there are numbers of scientists for whom these men do not speak. Charles Schwartz is a nuclear physicist who has been a leader in the new generation of dissenting scientists who are demanding not only a reordering of priorities, but a new method of establishing them. Charles Schwartz, "The Movement vs. the Establishment," originally appeared in the* Nation, *June 22, 1970, and was reprinted in* National Science Policy. H. Con. Res. 666. *Hearings before the Subcommittee on Science, Research, and Development of the Committee on Science and Astronautics, U.S. House of Representatives, 91st Cong., 2 sess., 1970, pp. 924–928.*]

Science means knowledge, a thing pure and noble in itself. Or is it? The question being asked more and more frequently today is whether our great increase in scientific knowledge and skill is helping mankind or threatening it. The enterprise of science is made up of men and money; it is a big and powerful business, a vital part of the national and world scenes, and it is governed by a set of institutions. The radical movement in science is a body of people who see the need for drastic change in the institutions that control science and are willing to work toward this end. Their number is small, their organizations are young and scattered, and they do not enjoy the outspoken support of prestigious big names — yet, I believe their mission is essential and I hope to see the movement grow.

I do not regard myself as an expert on the complex, interlocking structures of the institutions of science, but rather as an interested and concerned observer. Perhaps, being removed from the tangle of the trees, I can see the outlines of the forest.

Men of science are mostly to be found congregated at the universities (as teachers and students) and at research laboratories run by universities, private industries, and various branches of the government. The money for science comes mostly from the federal government (two-thirds of the $26 billion spent annually in this country for research and development comes directly from the federal government; about half of this is from the Department of Defense). Thus while it is obvious that the operation of science is thoroughly enmeshed in politics, most individual scientists like to pretend that politics and science are disjoint — which means that they abdicate any personal responsibility for the development of science as an activity which affects the lives of the people at large. All such worries are left to a small number of experts: a few self-appointed moralists, whom nobody listens to seriously; and a corps of big-time operators, who are relied upon to bring in the funds.

A remarkable system of scientific advisers to government has evolved since World War II. Over these years a large and friendly structure of committees, advising many branches of the government, has had the services of most of the best scientific minds. This apparatus, based in Washington but connected by the jetways to the major scientific centers, has established the myth that the government is getting the best expert independent advice in shaping its science policy. It is of primary importance that this myth be exposed. (A second myth is that the government would follow good advice if it received such, but that one is already pretty much discredited.) I don't question the technical competence of these government science advisers; the myth I speak of concerns their *independence* (as, for example, one assumes that a court judge is independent of political control).

At the pinnacle of the science adviser scheme is the President's Science Advisory Committee (PSAC). This group of eighteen men, deriving prestige from their own knowledge and the considerable resources open to them, can fairly be described as the nation's "high court of science." The members of PSAC come closer to the seats of power than any other formal group of scientists; and, although its members disclaim that they in any way represent the scientific community, it is inescapable that laymen (both in and out of government) will look to PSAC as the best authority on scientific matters of public concern.

The most difficult part of understanding PSAC is simply to find out what it is doing: all its work is secret. Recently I invited an old friend, now on PSAC, to speak to a small group of graduate students about the workings of this committee. The meeting was more instructive for its frustrations than for any open communications. Sample: "What advice did PSAC give to Nixon on the ABM issue?" "That is confidential, I can't tell you." "Did PSAC ever consider the Safeguard ABM an issue?" "I can't tell you that either."

It should be clear that in complaining about this governmental secrecy I am not even raising the traditional problem of specific technical data which might be thought of military advantage to a potential enemy. What I am concerned with is the fundamental need in a democracy for the basic inputs and processes of governmental decisionmaking to be exposed, so that every citizen and every component of the government may consider the available alternatives. Particularly in the realm of complex technical matters, such as nuclear weaponry, the Congress and the public very much need expert advice that they can rely on. Thus when the President announced (in March 1969) his decision to proceed with the Safeguard ABM system it was naturally *assumed* that this decision had the support of the scientists who stand ready to advise the President. However, the fact that PSAC members observe total silence allows their endorsement to be stated by implication and means that we may be victims of a "scientific lie." (The best rumors on this issue are that PSAC had for years consistently advised against an ABM system; and that it was not consulted about Nixon's Safeguard proposal until after that decision had been announced.)

The argument given in defense of the present arrangement is that the President is entitled to the best scientific advice available, and that any advice given to him is a personal service which must remain confidential. This might be persuasive if the President were a king. However, in our society there is a higher priority: it is that the *citizen* must have the best scientific advice. At present there is no institutional arrangement with prestige and resources equivalent to those of PSAC to provide open technical advice to the Congress and to the public. The best experts have been pre-empted by the Pentagon and the White House. Thus the *inside* experts are muffled (in cases where the political forces wish to ignore their opinions) and the *outside* experts can be denounced as fuzzy-headed know-nothings.

A few individuals have dropped out of the government-advising business because they were unhappy about some aspect of policy, but I am aware of no man of stature who has publicly complained of the way in which science is manipulated by the government. Some of the scientists who personally espouse liberal views rationalize their complicity on the basis of "win a few, lose a few." I shudder to think that there may be others, like one distinguished colleague with whom I spoke recently, who think that they are members of a select "gentlemen's club." This man was justifying his participation in the Jason division of IDA (the Institute of Defense Analysis) by saying that he greatly enjoyed working on these fascinating problems of national defense in the company of many of the brightest theoretical physicists in the country. I said that I would rather think of their work as representing "public trust" rather than a "private club," since the work they did and the recommendations they forwarded would have very important consequences not only for him but also for me, my children, and every other man in the street. His reply was, "You don't know the half of it!"

The manipulation of scientific data is not limited to PSAC and the ABM. I have heard of IDA reports being suppressed because their conclusions disagreed with the preconceived position of a politically powerful person; and I have heard that this happened with civilian issues (the SST) as well as with military projects [Rep. Henry S. Reuss has in fact turned up four or five "secret" reports on the SST.] The Pentagon has made the "selective declassification" of technical information a familiar game.

To complete the picture of the institutions that control science one more category must be mentioned: the professional societies — AAAS, APS, ACA, IEEE, *ad infinitum*; and also the honorary National Academy of Sciences. Most of these associations were formed many years ago for the purpose of advancing knowledge in particular areas of science and engineering; and as the professions have grown in numbers and importance, societies have remained the primary framework within which to conduct the basic commerce of science. Aside from publishing journals and arranging meetings, the assumed mission of these organizations has been the self-aggrandizement of the members of the profession. A few now seem to be trying to develop a social conscience and to relate their work to the woes and needs of the general society. Much of this is only gloss. The professional societies all strive to remain "apolitical," but what this really means is that they wish to avoid public controversy, particularly the kind that might put them at odds with the Establishment. For whether it is acknowledged or not, the current first "responsibility" of the profession is to maintain the influx of money that has allowed it to flourish.

The science establishment consists of that set of men who have sat on the several important science advisory committees in Washington, have held office in the leading professional societies, have served as deans and similar potentates at the major universities, and have done other good deeds as consultants and directors of corporations heavily committed to modern technology. It would be a revealing task to collect the names of these men and the posts they have held over the past twenty years. Many of the most successful have naturally moved among several of these chairs; the overall picture is one of interlocking solidarity.

This science establishment has very real power inside the national political Establishment, a power that was most openly demonstrated several months ago in the case of the appointment of Dr. Franklin Long to the directorship of the NSF. When President Nixon vetoed Dr. Long's appointment (because of his stated opposition to the ABM program) there was a sharp outcry about "political meddling in purely scientific areas," and the President was forced to recant. Mr. Nixon fought the U.S. Senate all the way on the Haynsworth nomination, as he did on the ABM issue; but he quickly bowed to the collected leaders of science on the Long case, as he bowed to the wishes of another powerful professional lobby — the AMA — in blocking the Knowles appointment.

Despite many protestations to the contrary, self-interest comes first in the thinking of the science establishment. Eminent scientists help the Department of Defense on its military problems, and the DOD has been a continuing source of generous grants for the abstract research that these men pursue at their universities. (As for the big accelerator laboratories, the AEC is a convenient cover-up source of funds. It is nominally a civilian agency of the government; but the Congressmen who approve these expenditures understand that the AEC serves our military program.) If the scientists and the military seem to have such a mutually beneficial arrangement, one should not jump to the conclusion of some improper liaison. The science advisers say that they are really good liberals, working hard to keep the military in check; and the military people say that they are really concerned with the long-range technological development of the country and are happy to divert a small fraction of their huge budget for basic research, since the Congress is not wise enough to do so directly. It sounds like a nice plan to those inside the machine; but on the outside one can see that the military power grows and grows, and the public welfare encounters only greater burdens.

I would like to bring a general indictment against the structure and operation of the whole science adviser system in the government, and wish I could present more concrete evidence than the few rumors and generalizations cited above. To do this properly would probably require the full power of a Congressional investigation. However, the items I have cited and the picture I have painted are really not new; they are matters of common knowledge among a great many established scientists. At the least, one can say that once the *potential* for political misuses of scientific information and advice is made clear, the situation is already dangerous. As matters involving more and more complicated technology occupy the stage center of national debates, it becomes imperative that we maintain public confidence and trust in the soundness of our scientific competence. This burden falls not only upon the federal government but, even more separately, upon the whole scientific community.

Science as a whole is being abused by the powerful political, industrial and military interests, and we are all losers. The distinguished statesmen or the traditional organizations that one might have hoped would step forward to set this trouble aright cannot be found. So, in response to this specific corruption of science (which some see as an inevitable part of the general corruption of America today), a radical movement has sprung up. The general style and tactics of this movement follow the larger student radical movement that has arisen on the campuses in the last five years; but the radical movement specific to the scientists is only about one year old. It is vigorous, but polite; and it is not encumbered by any great amount of political ideology.

The March 4, 1969 research stoppage is its single most enterprising activity to date. Invented by a few graduate students at M.I.T., taken over by a sincere group of faculty members at that venerable institution, and replicated at thirty or so other research centers throughout the country, this event was billed as the scientific community's own protest against the grave misuses of science and technology. After the one day of fervid breast-beating, most scientists went back to their laboratories. Some, such as the Union of Concerned Scientists (UCS) at M.I.T. and elsewhere, formed study groups to advance scholarly solutions of the many technical problems they had just complained about. A few groups, such as the Science Action Coordinating Committee (SACC), became the gathering points for the younger scientific protesters, dedicated to action and eager for some results.

Beginning at about the same time, but independent of the M.I.T. movement and growing out from the San Francisco Bay Area, a radical caucus of scientists took the name of Scientists and Engineers for Social and Political Action (SESPA). The announcement of its formation said in part:

An essential task is one of self-identification. We reject the old credo that "research means progress and progress is good." Reliance on such simplistic ethical codes has led to mistaken or even perverted uses of our scientific talents. As an antidote we shall establish a forum where all concerned scientists — and especially students and younger members of the profession — may explore the questions: Why are we scientists? For whose benefit do we work? What is the full measure of our moral and social responsibility?

This group held its inaugural meeting at the annual convention of the American Physical Society in New York in February 1969, and stimulated the formation of numerous small groups across the country. Communication is maintained through a regular newsletter, but the emphasis is on local initiative and action rather than on centralized policy. The group generated considerable fanfare and official discomfort at the APS meeting

431

and, as a radical caucus, continues to play two roles: Its members will try from within to broaden the scope of the parent body's activities; and as independent concerned scientists, they will take public positions on controversial issues of their own choosing.

The country-wide debate over the Safeguard ABM proposal was an unavoidable issue, and scientists right across the political spectrum took part. It was of course the leading topic at the March 4th symposia. The UCS published a good booklet for laymen on the facts of ABM (and later another on the MIRV); SACC and SESPA in Boston leafletted at shopping centers; SESPA organized a scientists' march on the White House; men with distinguished records of government service testified before Congressional committees. Even the standoffish APS became involved. Some activists requested that the society hold a session on the "technical aspects of the ABM system" at SESPA's Washington meeting; and faced with repeated emphasis on the word "technical," the conservative council of this society could find no honorable way to withhold its consent. It was clear to most people before this meeting — and to everyone after it — that it was impossible to talk about technical aspects without getting involved in political aspects. SESPA distributed a simple questionnaire to the assembled physicists and was able to announce to the press the next day that the sample of 2,000 informed professionals had expressed more than a 3-to-1 opposition to the Safeguard ABM proposal. That is public service.

Physicists have not been alone in their emergent science activism. Perhaps the most dedicated group is the Medical Committee for Human Rights, a group of mostly young doctors engaged in a David vs. Goliath struggle to eradicate the inadequacies and corruptions entrenched in the profit-oriented medical profession. Some members of the biological sciences have been actively opposing chemical and biological warfare research. An interesting situation arose in connection with a proposal to conduct a scientific investigation of the efforts of military defoliation operations in Vietnam. Early in 1968 the AAAS said that it could not and would not get involved. Then at its annual meeting later that year it agreed to set up a committee to investigate the question. When the officials delayed taking action, an ad hoc Scientists' Committee got together and paid for a preliminary fact-finding visit to Vietnam by two university biologists.

While big national issues, such as ABM and CBW, draw much attention, it is recognized that the problems facing members of the radical movement are deep-rooted, and that the best place to concentrate is close to home. The most prominent events of the last year have been the forceful protests against war-related research on university campuses — principally at Stanford and M.I.T. Most of the student demonstrations involved a body larger than the scientists and engineers themselves, and were probably inspired by a general revulsion to anything that is related to war. Yet the activist scientists have played an important role by trying to give these protests a meaningful objective. If objectionable war research is simply separated from the campus, it will undoubtedly continue elsewhere. The aim must be to reduce the amount of this weapons work and in particular to stop the more dangerous projects. Many scientists would prefer that the university maintain a strong influence in the weapons laboratories, thus exerting some humanizing pressures. Others think that prospect is hopeless and they talk of "destroying" the weapons research programs.

The radical movement in science is real and alive, though still in its infant years. Most people who sit in "positions of leadership and responsibility" have managed thus far to ignore it. Those of us involved see it primarily as an informative program, aimed as much at our silent professional colleagues as at the bewildered public. How long this specific movement will last, whether it will grow or dwindle, I cannot guess; but there is certainly plenty of work to be done.

Beyond the squabbling between "the Establishment" and "the movement," beyond the occasional campus confrontation, there is a deep, inescapable question for all of us who work as scientists and teachers of science. The idea of the social responsibility of the scientists has been widely accepted — at least in the abstract. We must now ask: How shall this doctrine be implemented? How can we set about to reach the ideal of science as a servant and not the master of a humane society?

First, it is a matter for individual understanding and self-dedication. Each scientist and engineer must analyze as best he can the consequences of his work and then decide whether he is helping or harming the well-being of all people.

Second, it is a matter for collective understanding. It is difficult for an individual to make moral choices in a void; some community norm must emerge. Here the professional societies should become involved, and we scientists should work out something along the line of a professional code of ethics.

Third, it is a matter for us to teach in the schools. Here, I think, is a glaring deficiency which we, the teachers of science and engineering, could readily repair. When we teach about science to nonscience students we mostly brag of our achievements in understanding the physical universe, but fail to point out the dangers inherent in man's ability to exploit nature. When we train young men and women who will become tomorrow's scientists and engineers we teach them *how* to do great things with modern theory and technology, but we do not teach them *why* they should do these things — or when they should not. We are thoughtful to provide a "liberal education," so that every scientist and engineer is exposed to the noble literature about man's heritage — but those courses are conducted on the "other" side of the campus; "here" is where they get their technical training, their real education. Like oil and water, the two cultures are not brought to mix with each other. When we have finished training them, most of our science students work as part of the war machine (because that is where the jobs and money are).

We professors of science and technology are given to wringing our hands about the carelessness with which "someone else" has allowed these things to happen. I think that we, perhaps more than anyone else, are to blame for the mindlessness of a runaway technology. A few attempts have been made to teach regular college courses on the social responsibility of scientists. I found conducting such a course both difficult and exciting. It was not like any (science) course I had ever taught, because there were many more problems than solutions. The students, however, seemed famished for the type of discussion that developed — it is the most "relevant" subject I can imagine for the science student today. There will undoubtedly be much experimentation in this area, and I think some regular study of these problems (of and by scientists) must become a standard part of the curriculum.

Hippocrates not only set down rules of conduct for the physician but specified that each teacher should pass these precepts on to his students. I have heard that at the University of Zagreb, in Yugoslavia, it is now required that each student take an oath when he graduates. I do not know the exact wording, but it is something like: "I will use the knowledge I have gained only for the benefit of mankind, and never for any harmful purposes." The ceremony of taking such an oath by scientists and engineers (perhaps by all university graduates) is only a symbolic act, but it means that each student will have to give this problem a little thought, at least once before he leaves school.

◄ I. *Professor Hunter Dupree, of Brown University, is the leading historian of the relations between science and the federal government. Testifying before a congressional committee during the summer of 1970 he chronicled the demise of the postwar system and called for a new departure. The following statement appeared in* National Science Policy. H. Con. Res. 666. *Hearings before the Subcommittee on Science, Research, and Development of the Committee on Science and Astronautics, U.S. House of Representatives, 91st Cong., 2 sess., 1970, pp. 21–26.*]

Mr. Chairman, 85 years ago before a congressional committee John Wesley Powell said:

The learning of one man does not subtract from the learning of another, as if there were a limited quantity of unknown truth. Intellectual activity does not compete with other intellectual activity for exclusive possession of truth: scholarship breeds scholarship, wisdom breeds wisdom, discovery breeds discovery.... That which one man gains by discovery is the gain of other men.

Because knowledge cannot be traded and hoarded like other goods it has to be administered by rules of its own. Yet it is this very ability to move around and apply itself in situations never dreamed of by its creators that makes knowledge of a highly organized and systematic type the most potent force in the world today. Symbolized by the atom bomb, it has a reputation for evil. Symbolized by modern medicine, it has a reputation for good. But the inability to hoard knowledge for either good or evil prevents these moral judgments from being more than emotional hunches.

Since medicine and nuclear energy could easily change roles of good and evil if one focused on the boon of energy and the suffering of overpopulation, the only true moral judgment that can be made on science is an essential ambiguity: Science can be as good or evil as the ends to which it is put.

Between 1940 and 1947 the Government of the United States learned a lesson in the immense efficiency of investing in knowledge. The yield in power was almost unimaginable for a money investment that seemed rather breathtaking for something as intangible as knowledge, but which compared with other costs of power was vanishingly small.

At the end of the war the determination that the power of research should not be lost impelled interested people in the scientific community, the military departments, the Congress, and the institutional Presidency to join in creating the interrelated system of science support.

Because of the wartime experience the recognition of a few fields of knowledge as producers of the bulk of useful results became deeply ingrained in the consciousness of the public and in the policy of the Government.

Since nuclear physics and chemistry, electronics and medicine became almost synonymous with science because of the dramatic results of wartime applications, science policy seemed to relate to those fields alone, and the Government's support of science tended to flow in those directions.

Even when one argued for basic research as an activity removed from useful application, the unspoken addition to the argument was that basic research would pay off in the future. Hence the argument for basic research was not a recognition of the cultural value of knowledge or of the necessity for healthy universities, but an argument merely of deferred practicality.

The knowledge gained by this policy has indeed been admirable, and the research which produced it should be continued on some terms. Yet both the rationale and the relative emphasis stem from the concerns of the World War II period and not from our own.

The national science policy of the United States for the period 1946 to nearly the present had its embodiment in the whole series of relationships that made up what can be described as a plural system. The elements which made the system plural were:

1. A large number of universities and corporations outside the Government but tied to it by grants and contracts.
2. A large number of sources of support within the Government which grew up at different times. In the late 1940's almost all these sources were military, but the growth of civilian agencies for science has been a steady trend to the present, leaving military support agencies such as the

Office of Naval Research still in business. Hence no single unit in the Government below the Executive Office of the President got a look at the system as a whole.

In the short run, the Government and the scientists liked the plural system; some of the scientists even thought that the multiple sources of funds had been carefully designed to meet their needs, unmindful of the deep tides of history which had brought them into being.

The system worked, but never quite well enough to head off the demand for some sort of coordination, or at least an overview. Hence throughout the quarter-century after 1945 there have been strenuous efforts to create a central scientific organization. The National Academy of Sciences has tried to fill the role.

The National Science Board has very occasionally looked toward this function. The National Science Foundation has sometimes tried to fashion a national science policy. The Congress has provided a vehicle of discussion of the problem from Hubert Humphrey's hearings on a Department of Science down to the present hearings. Yet most efforts have focused on the Presidency as the one logical place for a central scientific organization.

Since Sputnik the elaborate structure of the President's science advisor, President's Science Advisory Committee, Office of Science and Technology, and Federal Council for Science and Technology has grown up straddling the line between the White House and the Executive Office of the President. Since it would seem the best place for a central scientific organization many people who have considered the problem have given it credit for at least a partial success through most of the years since 1957. What few of the people who built this structure contemplated was a serious change of attitude on the part of those who man the institutional Presidency itself. If the White House does not support the Government-science partnership the whole formal mechanism is useless.

To spend much time on the unpleasant details of the present disarray of the system of science support is idle because so much proof is already on the record. At the Government end of the plural system the whole of the health area has lost its bearings. Even if the departure of the Director of the National Mental Health Institute could be explained away, the damage to

437

mental health care centers at remote places where teams are being broken up and their research disrupted cannot be ignored.

Universities that have made major commitments in those fields favored in the past by the Government's science policy — physics and medicine for example — face serious problems in meeting the changed situation. The cuts in fellowship support for the formerly favored fields are not being matched by additions on those fields where an increased demand is clearly foreseen.

At the level of central scientific organization, the whole structure in the White House and Executive Office of the President has dropped right off the organization charts and major reorganizations of science agencies emerge from commissions which have not called for public discussion nor given public critics an opportunity to be heard. The emphasis on applications in the White House structure has left extremely unclear where science fits in and whether it will have a hearing on questions of its own health and survival in the administration.

In these circumstances it is too much to ask that the harried representatives of the scientific community who occupy positions in the administration can provide effective leadership in shaping a science policy for the future.

To speak of a complete demise of the Government-science partnership is much too easy. A system built in a plural and incremental way can only go to pieces in a plural and incremental way. An all too human tendency makes those scientists and university administrators who are still able to operate continue to think in the patterns of the old partnership and to depend upon the executive branch to protect their interests.

They should consider carefully, however, that the scientific community will continue to house the casualties of the present shifts. They should consider carefully too the fact that the scientific community includes a large number of people within the Government — in-house scientists, scientific administrators, and even professors serving on panels and study sections.

A possible hope for providing a new science policy is in the Congress, where the discussion of a capability in science and technology has been increasing in recent years. If the Congress could redress the imbalance with the Executive in all fields, especially foreign and military policy, the scientific community should certainly find a place in that movement and could then look toward the legislative branch for real leadership.

In spite of some imaginative moves in this direction, many of them connected with Mr. Daddario and with this subcommittee, the way is long before a broad congressional science policy can emerge.

In a scene as dismal as this one, a historian tries to get back to fundamentals by lengthening his time span. Science and Government were in an ancient and honorable partnership long before 1940. Indeed the military emphasis of the last 30 years may in the long run prove atypical. Science and the American Republic have gone together since 1787 and certain principles have emerged which form the permanent basis of the relationship.

A report of the National Academy of Sciences in 1964 listed these requirements as:

One: The need for long-term support. The scientist cannot fit his experiments or the staffing and equipping of a laboratory into short periods arbitrarily laid down by a budget tied to a calendar.

Two: The need for flexibility in objectives. Research, as an exploration of the unknown, by definition precludes rigid projection of the shape of scientific thought and experimentation very far into the future.

Three: Freedom to publish. The discovery of knowledge without its communication leaves the process of research incomplete. American scientists have insisted on this point early and late, and they have suffered when it has been breached, as when the brilliant explorations of Lewis and Clark failed to have their full effect because of the lack of machinery for publication of the results.

Four: Access to the international scientific community. Government research, like all other research in the United States, grew up under the shadow of European accomplishments. To break communication with Europe meant not only cutting off a source of knowledge of great value but also blocking the avenue for American science to add to its stature by making contributions of its own.

Five: The need to improve the position of the professional scientist in American society. The people who represented science in discussions with the government were aware that pay and conditions of work were a reflection of the value that Americans placed on science, and they worked incessantly to raise that value because of their sense of what science would contribute to the national life.

A new science policy must be based on these principles. It must not simply perpetuate the pattern of 1940 but rather do what the leaders of 1940 did according to their lights. They adapted the science of their day to the problems of their day, treating both the science and the problems with full respect.

Although both diplomatic and military policy in Indochina seem still running in the wrong direction and science has apparently dropped out of the high councils of the Nixon administration, a new science policy is a present necessity which cannot be postponed to better times.

The old Government-university partnership had already lost its basic rationale even before the events of early May, which solidified the universities of the country in a protest with the fundamental backing of administrators, faculty members, and students alike.

This unification has been widely misunderstood in the country as a whole as a straight-line extrapolation of those instances of blind vandalism and irresponsible extremism observable in the earlier unrest of the past 6 years.

The campuses are now centers of questioning of many aspects of the connection between university and Government at the same time that the administration is checking budgetary support, applying political tests to appointments for scientific positions, and dismantling the organization for science within the Government.

The two parts of the Government-university partnership are thus moving away from one another so fast that even to talk of science policy in the present circumstances is to look toward the creation of a new partnership, not a revival of the old one.

A listing of the changes now going on which will shape the new science policy might include:

1. The Department of Defense has lost its ability to justify support for basic research and also to attract the services of many scientists. Yet the problems of military research are now unprecedentedly difficult because of the serious implications of the diplomatic and military policies of the administration. If the scientists knowledgeable in military research, who provide one of the groups with the best chance to change the course of events with competent criticism, lost touch with the Department of Defense completely, an unparalleled disaster could ensue. Nevertheless a reordering of the relation of the scientific community to the Department of Defense cannot be postponed.

2. The scientific community must pay much more attention

to environmental problems. In attempting to alter priorities in favor of the environment, architects of the new science policy must bear in mind both the need for disciplines long relatively neglected and also remember the presence in the government of old and stable research traditions which have been considering the environment for more than a century.

3. The space program must find a role for itself with predominantly scientific objectives and a steady state of funding.

4. The social sciences must receive greater emphasis both because they have demonstrated increased effectiveness in the last quarter century and because the demand for their application has increased. The question must be faced of how to mesh them with sensitive social problems and also with projects heretofore considered the preserve of the natural sciences without at the same time destroying their integrity.

5. The justification of Federal support for research in the universities must emphasize the goal of building healthy institutions in the national interest. The support must extend to the humanities and to those parts of the social and natural sciences that contribute strongly to the universities and their students but whose connection with practical applications is indirect.

6. Support for education must contemplate a national research program with a radically different mix of disciplines from that recently prevailing.

A science policy that takes into account the changing realities of 1970 cannot confine itself to a single problem, a single agency, or a single mechanism for reorganization. The science agencies, the Executive Office of the President and the White House must be viewed as an interacting whole. In addition, the Congress must seriously contemplate taking responsibility for shaping the whole structure in a way that will honor both the freedom and the unique potentialities of the scientific community.

To make any suggestion as what might be done to effect a new science policy is to encounter all the obstacles well known to this subcommittee. From the subcommittee has emanated a series of important suggestions:

1. Technology assessment is a promising route because it offers the possibility of increased congressional ability to rep-

resent the public's interest in technological decisions. This subcommittee is a main force behind that movement.

2. The proposed National Institute of Research and Advanced Studies, in whose behalf I made a statement before you in the summer of 1969, has lost none of its desirability.

3. The reorganization and strengthening of the National Science Foundation now proves of great importance when the Department of Defense for whatever reason deemphasizes its support of basic research.

4. The discussion of priorities in science and their relation to national goals has prepared the Government and the scientific community to make hard choices that the years of experimental growth had spared them.

The Daddario subcommittee thus deserves the thanks of all scholars for its record of achievement and for the possibilities of its suggested changes in science policy. But if the executive branch is thinking about science policy, no evidence of it gets into the public press. If the energetic and intelligent efforts of this subcommittee over the last several years have produced good ideas, they seem still very far from realization. A single historian speaking only for himself as I do can hardly avoid gloom. The only hopeful answer lies far outside immediate practicality.

To suggest a utopian solution would be easy. I dream, for instance, of an open and adequately supported Manhattan District enlisting the universities of the country in a major surge. The effort would combine physics, chemistry, biology, and the social sciences, and the humanities in a general systems theory focused on man rather than exclusively on the external universe. Such a theory established as a comprehensive network of basic sciences, could fan out in applications to problems of the environment, population, cities, arms control. It could put an end to mindless cruelty of systems — military, social, and physical — which leave people out of their abstractions.

Such a Manhattan District would do away with the conventional divisions between the natural and social sciences and humanities, and by drawing on people from many disciplines, including those now in oversupply, would provide the enrichment and stimulation of unaccustomed patterns.

The physicists and engineers could not boss the new groups, but they could contribute their mathematical skill. Most important, the new Manhattan District would call on the abundant energies of the under-30 generation. If they found worthy goals for a broad scholarly thrust, they would eventually find the proper tools and disciplines.

I believe the internal situation in scholarship has such rich possibilities that the new Manhattan District for 1970 would actually work and be worth much more than the public funds it would cost. However, until the structure of the Government-university partnership is so thoroughly reorganized that the support of all segments of the university on one side and all branches of the Government on the other can be mobilized, the whole idea remains utopian.

We can be thankful for the pluralism that allows some fragments of the old system to survive, and we can hope for enough central scientific organization to effect glacial change.

The pace may be slowed, but if the direction is clear, the society which we have built on a rickety framework of technology can draw enough gain from the generation of new knowledge to survive. If the freedom of science and the freedom of the American democracy remain in firm alliance, the result will be, as it has been throughout the Nation's history, a practical benefit to the citizens worth many times its cost.